Parasites, Pathogens, and Progress

Parasites, Pathogens, and Progress

Diseases and Economic Development

Robert A. McGuire
Philip R. P. Coelho

The MIT Press
Cambridge, Massachusetts
London, England

For information about special quantity discounts, please email special_sales@mitpress.mit.edu

This book was set in Palatino by Toppan Best-set Premedia Limited. Printed and bound in the United States of America.

Library of Congress Cataloging-in-Publication Data

McGuire, Robert A. (Robert Allen), 1948–
Parasites, pathogens, and progress : diseases and economic development /
Robert A. McGuire and Philip R. P. Coelho.
p. cm.
Includes bibliographical references and index.
ISBN 978-0-262-01566-0 (alk. paper) 1. Parasitic diseases—History. 2. Parasitic diseases—Social aspects. 3. Parasitic diseases—United States—History. 4. Evolution (Biology)—United States—History. 5. Microbiology—United States—History. 6. United States—Economic conditions. I. Coelho, Philip R. P. II. Title.
HC105.M345 2011
330.973–dc22

2010046703

10 9 8 7 6 5 4 3 2 1

Contents

Acknowledgments

The idea in this book that the interactions between natural and human forces affect both human history and the physical environment is long in the making. The genesis is a casual luncheon comment made by Gordon Tullock in 1984 that hookworm in the American South and the Rockefeller Sanitary Commission's attempts to eradicate it warranted an economic examination. This stimulated Coelho to author an unpublished paper on the relationship between biology and economic growth in 1985. A long collaboration between the two of us began in 1986, a collaboration that has resulted in the publication of several papers on the connections among biology, parasitic diseases, and American economic development. Still the material contained herein is original to this book with the exception of what appears in two chapters. Chapter 5 on the biological consequences of economic choices in British North America is a significantly revised version of an article of ours that appeared in the *Journal of Economic History* (March 1997). Chapter 6 on the disease environment in the antebellum South is based on another article of ours that appeared in the *Journal of Bioeconomics* (1999). The chapter, though, contains substantial new material on diseases and the antebellum South as well as significant revisions of the content of the original article. Some of the findings reported in chapter 6 also are contained in two other articles of ours that have appeared in the *Journal of Economic History* (March 2000) and *Social History of Medicine* (December 2006).

Over the years, various parts of the book have been presented at many conferences, seminars, and workshops, including the Citadel Conference on the South; Pre-Conference of the XII World Economic History Congress; Third World Congress of the Cliometric Society; Economics Department, DePauw University; Research Triangle Economic History Workshop; Workshop in the Economics and Biodemography of Aging and Health, University of Chicago; and at the annual meetings of the Allied Social Science Association, Cliometric Society, Economic History Association, Public Choice Society, Social Science History Association, Southern Association for the History of Medicine and Science, and the Western Economic Association. We would like to thank the participants at each of these presentations.

As with most scholarly endeavors, we have benefited from the comments and suggestions of many individuals over the years on various parts of the work that now appear in this book. We especially thank Greg R. Alexander, Hoyt Bleakley, Janet M. Bronstein, Louis P. Cain, Lois Carr, Cheryl Elman, Stanley L. Engerman, Joseph Ferrie, Robert W. Fogel, Moheb A. Ghali, Michael T. Ghiselin, Farley Grubb, Gillian Hamilton, John Komlos, Naomi Lamoreaux, Deirdre McCloskey, James McClure, Dawn McGuire, Randy Moore, Gareth Morgan MD, Robert L. Ohsfeldt, Jonathan Pritchett, Joseph D. Reid Jr., Peter Reilly, James F. Shepherd, Tom Smith, Richard H. Steckel, Lorena Walsh, and Samuel Williamson for their assistance. We also thank Douglas McBride, Greg Madonia, Lisa Mishne, and Rui Pan for their assistance with data collection. We especially want to thank Nicholas Fritsch for his able research assistance with the mortality findings reported in chapter 7.

We also wish to thank the Rockefeller Archive Center, Sleepy Hollow, New York, for permission to access its holdings and use its materials. McGuire received support for parts of the material that appear in this book from the National Science Foundation under Grants 0003342 and 0721000, Ohio Board of Regents Individual Research Challenge Match, (1999–2001 Biennium and 2007–2009 Biennium), and a faculty research grant from the University of Akron, Akron, Ohio. Coelho received support for parts of the material that appear in this book from the National Science Foundation under Grants 0079179 and 0721070, a George A. Ball Distinguished Research Fellowship from the Ball State University Foundation, Muncie, Indiana, and a summer research grant from the Miller College of Business, Ball State University, Muncie, Indiana. Any opinions, findings, and conclusions expressed in this book are those of the authors and do not necessarily reflect the views of the National Science Foundation.

Robert A. McGuire
Akron, Ohio

Philip R. P. Coelho
Muncie, Indiana

1 Introduction: Biology, Diseases, and Migrations before the Twentieth Century

On November 29, 1847, in the Oregon Territory near present-day Walla Walla, Washington, Marcus and Narcissa Whitman were murdered. Marcus was attacked from behind by a Cayuse Indian who implanted a tomahawk deep into his skull. Later a group of Cayuse shot, beat, cut, mutilated, and, finally, decapitated and dismembered Narcissa. She died quickly; arguably her death may have been less painful than Marcus's who lingered moaning for hours before succumbing. Eleven other people died in the attack, all the survivors were women and children; many of the women were raped, all were enslaved. Within months, representatives of the Hudson Bay Company had arranged the release of the survivors. Subsequently, American settlers and soldiers sought and wreaked vengeance upon the Cayuse, guilty and innocent. By the late nineteenth century, the Cayuse had merged with other tribal groups because their numbers were too few to maintain an independent tribal society. The Whitman Massacre and the disappearance of the Cayuse society were linked, not by the retribution of avenging Americans, but by virtually invisible pathogens that were completely foreign to the Cayuse; therein lies the tragedy.

Marcus Whitman was a medical missionary who located his mission in the area east of the Cascade Mountains drained by the Columbia and Snake rivers. At the beginning of the nineteenth century, these lands were populated by an estimated 180,000 Native Americans; by the end of the century, there were less than 40,000. Whitman was sent to the Native Americans to alleviate their sickness and bring them the (Protestant) gospel. Whitman had the misfortune of being at the wrong place at the wrong time. A worldwide measles epidemic had broken out and by 1847 it had reached the Oregon Territory; it might have been introduced by the settlers who were following the Oregon Trail to the Willamette Valley. Wagon trains typically stopped and refreshed themselves at the Whitman mission, and the emigrants could have borne the virus. More ironically the measles could have come from the adoption of the horse by the plains Indians. Ironic because only after Contact with the Old World was initiated by Columbus and the European voyages to the New World did the horse come to the Americas. Horses allowed Native Americans to travel widely and rapidly; in their travels, they could have picked up the measles virus and transmitted it to the Cayuse. However it came, the effects of the measles virus were devastating; one estimate has one-half of the Cayuse in the Whitman mission area dying. If *all* the Cayuse contracted the virus, this implies a case fatality rate of 50 percent; if less than 100 percent of the Cayuse contracted it, the case fatality rate would have been even higher.[1] The death rate of whites, both resident at the mission and the pioneers who were passing through, was a small fraction of that of the Cayuse; at most 15 percent of those who contracted measles died, and those who contracted it were probably a minority of the white population.

Some of the Cayuse believed that the Whitmans were responsible for the measles and were active in spreading it. This was the genesis of the Whitman Massacre, but the massacre of Indians by measles, cholera, smallpox, and other pathogens dwarfed all forms of human violence. After centuries of continual epidemics, Native Americans today are a small minority in their ancestral territories, victims of their evolutionary heritage that made them more susceptible to pathogens that were unseen and unknown by their victims. Yet a century and half after the works of Louis Pasteur, and Charles Darwin and Alfred Russel Wallace, histories are still written as if what these men discovered had no impact on the conquest of the New World, American Manifest Destiny, worldwide military campaigns, colonialism, slavery, and the revolutionary changes in industries and economies that permeate history. In contrast, *Parasites, Pathogens, and Progress* does not ignore their discoveries; it explicitly employs them. It brings biology, parasites, and pathogens into humanity's history and the economy.

The Western Hemisphere was initially settled by nomadic Asian tribes during the last Ice Age glacial. Glaciers trapped a large amount of the Earth's water; this lowered sea levels. The Bering Sea became a Bering Land Bridge, ranging up to 1,600 kilometers (1,000 miles) wide. Northeast Asian hunter-gatherers, the ancestors of Aboriginal Americans, came to America following the animal herds that populated the Land Bridge, migrating across the Bridge or along its southern coastal waters. The end of the Ice Age glaciation led to rising sea levels and the disappearance of the Land Bridge that effectively isolated the New World from the Old. As the peoples of the Old World grew in numbers, they domesticated animals (horses, goats, sheep, cattle, fowl, pigs, and so forth) and from the diseases of animal herds pathogens jumped species and infected humans, resulting in smallpox, measles, chickenpox, mumps, and a host of other major and minor diseases. The Old World peoples gradually adapted to these diseases; humans who were most susceptible to diseases did not reproduce, those that did reproduce had, on average, more innate (genetic) resistance to the pathogens. Exposure to a specific pathogen also typically resulted in an acquired immunity that left the individual resistant to subsequent re-infection. One by one, diseases evolved from being epidemic diseases, where many are susceptible and killed, to endemic diseases whose victims are usually the previously uninfected (primarily children), leaving other groups relatively unaffected because of acquired immunities.

In his award-winning *Guns, Germs, and Steel*, Jared Diamond argues that the shape and position of the Eurasian land mass affected this process and, thereby, world history. Eurasia extends thousands of miles further in the east–west direction than it does on its north–south axis. Animals (and plants) evolve in ecologies that tend to be latitude specific, and have difficulties in adapting to the different climates that the earth's tilt imposes on its north–south axis. The east–west orientation and the vast grass lands of the Eurasian land mass allowed more animals to survive the depredations of hunter-gathers to become potential domesticates. Having more potential domesticates led to more actual ones; domesticated farm animals spread relatively easily on the east–west axis over the Eurasian land mass. Unlike Eurasia, the continents of the Western Hemisphere are much longer than wide; this contributed to the extinction of megafauna and led to a paucity of animals that could have been domesticated. In fact, the aboriginal peoples of North America had no domesticates aside from the dog (and the guinea pig in Mesoamerica). This meant that before Contact with the Old World, Native Americans were spared the ravages of the pathogens zoonoses that emerged from animal herds and flocks unlike the Old World peoples. Conversely, once intercourse started with the Old World, Aboriginal Americans were exposed to these diseases for the first time, and they died in numbers that were unfathomable to contemporaneous observers.

The disappearance of the Cayuse and the Whitman Massacre are symptomatic of the effects of pathogens on the aboriginal populations of the New World. While Diamond's *Guns, Germs, and Steel* argues that the European conquest of the New World was caused by the aboriginal populations falling victim to European guns, steel, and the diseases that Europeans brought with them, *Parasites, Pathogens, and Progress* views the European takeover of the Americas as almost solely due to the introduction of Old World diseases. European advantages in war-making technologies may have hastened the outcome, but they did not determine the ultimate Europeanization of most of the Western Hemisphere. As a thought experiment, suppose that the European voyages to the Americas in the late-fifteenth and sixteenth centuries, rather than being controlled by the Conquistadors (uncouth villains bent on looting, raping, and enslaving), were instead sponsored and controlled by people who were the moral equivalent of Mother Teresa and Albert Schweitzer (covering both the Catholic and Protestant enthusiasts). But also suppose that the voyages between the New and Old Worlds took only two weeks instead of two months. What would have happened? In our view, the Old World conquest of the New would have been even more rapid, and the decline in New World peoples more complete.

Seeking to save bodies and souls the equivalents of Mother Teresa and Albert Schweitzer would have come in droves to the New World, bringing with them a hoard of Old World diseases, and their ineffectual (at best) sixteenth-century medical knowledge and practices. With the rapid arrival, the experience of the New World peoples would have been like bacteria that are subject to multiple cocktails of antibiotics; they would have been wiped out all at once. What actually happened was that Old World diseases were gradually introduced into "virgin" populations over centuries rather than almost immediately, as would have been the case if transport times had been drastically reduced. (In demographic and epidemiological terminology, a "virgin" population is one that has had no recent exposure to a pathogen.) Death rates in virgin populations to diseases common elsewhere can be horrific. In the nineteenth century, the death rates of Polynesians first exposed to measles approached 80 percent; in the twentieth century, Amazonian tribal societies exposed to measles and influenza had population implosions similar to the Polynesian experience. The New World's distance delayed the introduction of Old World diseases; the delays meant that aboriginal populations had a chance to repair some of the damages caused by the introduction of one "new" disease before another one would devastate them. Historically, even with the introduction of Old World diseases into the New World taking centuries rather than less than a handful of years, by the eighteenth century Aboriginal populations of the New World had fallen by about 90 to 95 percent of their earlier levels. This allowed the Europeanization of much of the New World. In contrast, the European conquests and colonization of Asia and Africa were ephemeral. In these lands, Europeanization was doomed by the effects of African and Asian diseases on European peoples. So, more accurately reflecting the New World historical experience, Diamond should have titled his book *Germs, Germs, and Germs;* but then again, his publisher probably would have objected.

We tell the story of humanity's history that is an amalgam of the co-evolution of biology, the effects and efforts of humans, and economic production. Human history, much like living organisms, is an evolving entity; past, present, and future were and will be shaped and determined by the interactions among humans, the natural environment, and economic constraints. Histories that ignore the natural world, assuming that either it has little relevance for history, or if it does impact history its effects are unchanging, are, at best, incomplete. In reality, the natural world is continually changing; some changes are completely impervious to human actions, and others are a result of interactions between natural and human forces. Some of these changes materially affect both history and the physical environment. These are ongoing processes; there are no equilibria. Like life itself, history is an evolving process.

Parasites, Pathogens, and Progress integrates economic *and* biological views into an explanation of the historical development of humanity and the economy, paying particular attention to the American experience, its history and economic development. While it has much in common with the literature of medical and social historians, it still differs in several fundamental respects.[2] First, it takes a fundamentally economic approach; we are by training economists with historical bents. Second, it emphasizes the critical interactions among human choices, microorganisms, evolution, and diseases. Third, it views the environment and diseases as evolving phenomena; prior to the nineteenth century, local and regional diseases predominated. During the nineteenth century, pathogens and evolution played a different yet important role in explaining the economic development of the United States as local and regional disease pools, both within the nation and from abroad, became widespread and integrated. Fourth, it considers the establishment and growth of African slavery in the British New World as a result of colonial planters seeking the least-cost sources of labor as well as the result of the biological traits of different populations (more accurately, the frequencies of various genetic traits within different populations and subpopulations). The early importation of Africans as slaves set in motion biological forces that permanently changed disease ecologies in the New World, fixing African slavery as an economic and social institution. Fifth, it stresses that the New World disease environment was dependent on or *endogenous* to human actions, albeit the disease environment was the *unwitting* result of human choices. We do not claim that we are the first to bring parasites and pathogens into the history of humanity and the economy, but we do so with emphasis and conviction that are missing in other histories.

African Slavery in the New World

Much of our story is devoted to explaining the origins and persistence of African slavery in the United States and its colonial antecedents. Following the European voyages to the New World and the subsequent population implosion of New World peoples, European colonialists faced the problem of obtaining labor to exploit the resources of the Americas. The high cost of passage to America relative to Old World incomes inhibited the self-financed migrations by working class people; consequently, British colonialists resorted to bound servile labor for agricultural workers. People, either voluntarily or involuntarily, were obligated (bound) to provide labor services (labor servitude) to the colonist who acquired their labor.

Europeans remained the primary source of unskilled agricultural labor in the British West Indies (Caribbean) until the middle of the seventeenth century and in the southern mainland colonies until the turn of the century. African slaves began to displace Europeans as the primary source of unskilled labor in the Caribbean during the 1650s and 1660s and in the southern mainland colonies about 1700 and thereafter. European-Americans always predominated in the northern and western United States (after independence) while African-Americans were relatively concentrated in the southern United States well into the twentieth century.

What explains the concentration of African slaves in the Caribbean and the American South and why was African slavery not predominant throughout the British New World? In brief, our explanation runs like this: the migrations of Africans and Europeans and the pathogens that they (unwittingly) brought to the New World explain the evolution of regional disease ecologies in colonial America. Evolving regional ecologies along with the disparate biological reactions of Africans and Europeans to diseases explain the racial (ethnic) makeup of the regions of North America. Disparate biological reactions are an evolved response taking place over millennia to local disease ecologies. These disparate reactions to diseases explain why African slaves became concentrated in the tropics (Caribbean) and subtropics (the southern mainland). In specific local and regional disease environments, both the pathogens and the health of people of different ancestries were differentially affected. African-Americans and European-Americans reacted differently to regional disease ecologies. Differential effects persisted through the early twentieth century, impacting the health, physical development, and economic productivity of the two groups.

We write about what happened once Africans and Europeans came to British North America. Because of the heritage that their ancestral environments bequeathed to them, the eventual predominance of people of African ancestry in the tropics and subtropics of America, and the predominance of people of European ancestry in the temperate regions was predetermined. Europeans were, relative to Africans, less profitable sources of agricultural labor in the tropics and subtropics of both the New and Old Worlds; conversely, Africans were, relative to Europeans, less profitable agricultural laborers in the more temperate regions of both the New and Old Worlds. The European voyages to the New World unleashed migrations of Africans and Europeans and started an evolutionary process that changed the local and regional disease ecologies throughout the Americas. These changes had profound effects upon the course of American history and are still reverberating in the twenty-first century.

Institutions, Diseases, Development, and Diversity

Unlike recent trends in the literature on economic development and growth, our book does not emphasize the impact of institutions; we have two reasons for this omission.[3] The first is that our book is about the effects of parasites and pathogens on historical progress; because we write about this aspect of history does not mean that other aspects are unimportant. The second, and more important reason, is that institutions do not spring forth fully formed like Athena from Zeus's head. Institutions themselves are endogenous (determined within a society); disease environments, resource endowments, history, and economics all interact in forming and limiting institutional design. As mentioned earlier, bound labor was one way of bringing people to the New World. The tradition of bound labor evolved from the apprenticeship system whereby a young man bound himself to a craftsman in order to learn a trade. The contractual obligation to serve an indentureship was a solution to the problems of imperfect or nonexistent capital markets, which would have allowed the apprentice to purchase training; and moral hazard, whereby a young man who might agree to work for a craftsman could abandon his master and obligations after the acquisition of skills. The point here is that the institution of bound labor evolved from economies that had low incomes, inadequate capital and labor markets, and substantial economic returns to acquiring skills; indentureship allowed servant and master to cope with these circumstances.

Institutions are historical creations; they are like evolving organisms, changing in response to changes in their environment, replicating and spreading, subject to all matter of constraints and preconditions. Changing the metaphor, institutions are like tastes; you may assert that tastes are given and immutable (*de gustibus non est disputandum*), but that is only for analytical convenience. Both tastes and institutions are integral products of evolution: biological, historical, and economic. Analyzing the impact of an institution at a given time may yield insights, but any historical view that assumes institutions are exogenous (originating outside a society) is likely to be terribly misleading. Labor institutions, in particular, are greatly influenced by changing disease ecologies and economic conditions; changes in labor institutions have major economy-wide effects because labor is a key component of human economic activities. Again in the context of North American history, African slavery and European indentured servitude were two institutional responses to the resource endowments and costs that dominated in the early history of European involvement in the New World.

In pre-twentieth century America, blacks and whites, northerners and southerners, and various other groups faced different disease experiences. These experiences were regionally and historically different. In general, climate, urbanization, transport developments, movements of people, and increasing population densities differentially affected people of different ancestral heritages and in different areas and regions. This diversity must be recognized to understand the impact of diseases on history; one size does not fit all.

An Outline of Our Story

The next chapter (chapter 2) begins with an examination of the impact of biology and demography on the pre-history and history of humanity. It asks and answers the big question: why has the human ability to manipulate the material world been so glacially slow? Literally, "glacially" vastly overstates humanity's progress. Since *Homo sapiens* appeared on the scene (about 200,000 years ago), there have been several periods when ice blanketed much of the Northern Hemisphere, but you can count on a finger the number of technological civilizations that humanity created over this era. Chapter 2 also lays the foundations for our evolutionary approach to history and the human economy.

Chapter 3 contains the core of our argument relating progress to population and pathogens. We attribute long-run economic growth to an increasing population that led to increased markets. This induced greater specialization and a concomitant increase in productivity. Subsequent developments in transportation services and a specialized transport network reduced transport costs and time, further widening the market. This is the virtuous cycle of economic growth. Offsetting this was a vicious biological cycle of economic growth: increased market size provided resources for the pathogens that assaulted humans. With increased human densities came animals that provided humans with transportation and food. The increased waste products of the animals and humans contaminated water supplies and soils, exposing people to existing diseases and providing breeding grounds for new diseases. Infectious diseases were more rapidly transmitted and widespread; more people were sick more often.

Chapter 4 applies our disease story to the American experience with a presentation of an economic and financial analysis of the two primary sources of bound labor (European indentured servants and African slaves) available to colonialists in British North America. Using basic financial calculations, chapter 4 shows that the historical experience contradicts the belief that Europeans and Africans had identical economic productivities throughout the New World. Different productivities of indentured servants and slaves are attributed to differential resistances to diseases.

Chapter 5 provides an in depth examination of the biological consequences that accompanied the European voyages to the New World, and British North America in particular. The biological consequences and economic factors provide an explanation for colonial planters' subsequent choices of agricultural labor and the regional concentration of peoples of different ethnicities (ancestral heritages) in seventeenth-century British North America. The analysis in chapter 5 confirms the financial calculations derived in chapter 4.

Chapter 6 links the regional concentration of Africans and Europeans to the importation of African slaves into the Chesapeake Bay region and the entire American South. The chapter examines the disease environment of the antebellum American South and the linkages between infectious parasitic diseases and the productivity and physical development of peoples in the antebellum South.

Chapter 7 brings our story to the beginning of the twentieth century with empirical assessments of the impact of population growth, urbanization, increasing density, and transportation and other developments on the spread of diseases, increased morbidity and mortality, and long-run American economic growth during the nineteenth century.

The final chapter (chapter 8) emphasizes the difficulty of reconciling the time dimension over which evolutionary changes occur, and the aspects of time that surround us day to day. Small differences accumulate over centuries to become overwhelming, yet they go unremarked because they happen over time spans that human experience finds difficult to comprehend. Similarly, pathogens elude our senses because they are so minute, and human experience equates the minute with the inconsequential. Chapter 8 concludes with some comparisons and speculations.

2 Biology, Diseases, and History: The Big Picture

History is and has been an abiding concern of humanity; we want to know our past, how our ancestors lived, and how the world we live in changed. Humanity's curiosity about its past has generated an immense literature not only about the history of specific events but also about the historical evolution of humanity itself: The Big Picture. Our book tells a big picture story of history. We view the history of humanity as the product of interactions among humans, economic constraints, and the physical environment. Historians generally treat the biological environment and ecology as exogenous factors; this is incorrect in all circumstances in the long run, and more than occasionally in the short run as well. Assumptions that the natural world does not impact history, or that its effects are constant and unchanging, are also incorrect. There are continual and changing interactions or processes between natural and human forces that affect history.

The issues that concern us are not easy; we rely on the sciences, economics, history, and evolutionary processes to advance our arguments. These processes are not easily grasped. Why should a reader invest time and effort in understanding our arguments? The reason is the issues we write about delineate the possibilities and limits that humanity faces; they are extraordinarily important for understanding human history and the human condition. Explicitly incorporating economics into history yields insights that are otherwise unavailable or obscure because economics is about resources and their uses in the face of pervasive scarcity; without resources beyond those minimally required to sustain existence, humanity is, by definition, living at a subsistence level. This means that (1) there is no art, (2) culture is brutish and superstitious, and (3) physical existence is one in which people spend their waking hours looking for things to eat and warm places to sleep. Without adequate resources, we are in a Dark

Age of physical violence, unending poverty, superstition, and an environment that guaranties that most lives are short, disease-ridden, and miserable.

In present-day rich societies, it is fashionable to feign a disdain for "money-grubbing" economic activities, yet these activities provide the resources that allow humanity to rise above the slime and literally voyage to the stars. It is true that abundant resources and freedom have allowed some to dissipate their lives ignobly, yet it is also true that abundance and freedom are the hallmarks of civilization; we cannot have the good without the bad. The pursuit of wealth within the constraints of voluntary exchange and civil society has raised all boats. The increase in human well-being has done more, and continues to do more, to alleviate poverty and improve the welfare of the poor and least advantaged than all the benevolent institutions that ever existed.

The foundation of our argument may be obvious. An increase in resources available to the average family is desirable and a worthy goal.[1] We explicitly embrace the sentiment of Protogaras: "Man is the measure of all things." In judging welfare, we do not weigh nonhuman welfare against human welfare. Neither trees nor mountains speak; those who rhetorically ask "who speaks for the trees" are disingenuous. What they mean is that they have certain preferences (tastes) that involve maintaining and increasing wooded areas and forests. Similarly, those who argue for animal rights never ask the animals what they want; they just presume captivity and/or human intervention are "bad." Captivity is undesirable to most humans; domestic animals might actually prefer it to an existence that does not rely on humans. This is not as preposterous as it sounds; animal behaviorists have conducted experiments in which animals are given choices (one was for chickens between sheds and yards) to determine preferences. It seems that animals might prefer food and security more than independence and freedom (Zeltner and Hirt 2003). Moreover, activists who are self-styled advocates for their favorite animals or things make no differentiation between their desires and the "welfare" of the animals or things on whose behalf they are supposedly acting.[2]

Our anthropomorphic perspective is not without difficulties; in particular, the view of Thomas Malthus on the impact of population growth begets an internal contradiction. Malthusian economics and population theory are derived from Malthus who maintained that people will reproduce too prolifically relative to the growth of resources, and as a consequence humanity was doomed to impoverishment. Malthusian theory maintains that increasing population will reduce the level of resources per capita. Left to their own devices and in the absence of "misery" and "vice," the human population will grow until the average standard of living is at subsistence. All progress in science, technology, and the practical arts will be subsumed by population growth. Malthusians predict that all human striving is for naught because population growth will literally consume all progress. This view led to the sobriquet of the "Dismal Science" being widely accepted as an epithet for economics. The "Dismal Science" had some validity because the economic theory (as distinct from experience) conflated population growth with declining living standards; the theory and the "iron law of wages" continued apace in the economic literature throughout the nineteenth century.[3]

Malthusian doctrine has had an impact far beyond economics; the association of increased population with increased poverty and misery has a long tradition in historical studies. North and Thomas (1973) are explicitly Malthusian; they argue that population changes that lowered living standards led to the demise of the feudal system; these changes were irreversible and subsequent events led to the rise of capitalism in the Netherlands and England from whence it spread. Harris (1978, 1985) concentrates on the availability of food and protein, arguing that primitive peoples ordered their societies to protect and enhance their abilities to acquire proteins; this affected their societies in a variety of aspects from prohibitions on consuming certain animals to the frequency of conflict. Clark (2007) continues in the Malthusian tradition ascribing the lack of growth prior to the modern era to population growth that consumed all the benefits of economic growth. In his view, real growth in the average level of living took place only after cultural, societal, and (more controversially) biological changes allowed economic growth to exceed population growth.[4]

In contrast, Simon (1977, 1996, 1998) is explicitly anti-Malthusian, contending that the growth of real output is positively influenced by population, and declining populations are associated with economic retrogression. In her influential works on the transition to settled agricultural, Boserup (1966, 1981), while not explicitly anti-Malthusian, does relate increasing output per capita with increasing population; her nuanced argument is that the increase in output that accompanied population growth and settled agriculture may have been the result of an increase in the number of hours worked per day. Similarly, while not mentioning Malthus, Diamond (1997) in his prize-winning work was at least mildly anti-Malthus in arguing that the absolute size of population was positively correlated with economic growth. In a later work, Diamond (2005) espoused a much more Malthusian viewpoint. In the biological sciences, both Russel Wallace and Charles Darwin credit Malthusian doctrine as one of the inspirations that led them separately to develop theories of evolution and natural selection.

More recently and less auspiciously, Malthusian doctrine has been used to promote doctrinal belief in "sustainability." The quotation marks around sustainability are there because we do not know what the proponents of sustainability mean, nor are we convinced that the proponents know what they mean. As far as we can determine, advocates of "sustainability" believe that resources are finite and that current rates of usage are unsustainable because they will all be used up in some foreseeable future. Aside from violating the First Law of Thermodynamics that energy (matter) cannot be destroyed only transformed, to make some sense of the doctrine of sustainability, we also have to assume that the current age is a golden age; that we have attained the peak of perfection in all scientific endeavors and technical excellence, and that no further refinements can be expected that will relax resource constraints. This is palpable nonsense; barring any natural or human-made holocaust the next century will see "sustainable" standards of living that are at least threefold or greater than that of the world of 2010.

"Sustainability" advocates are neo-Malthusians in the sense that they believe that higher living standards for larger populations are both unsustainable and undesirable. Unsustainable because the physical environment is finite and undesirable because the environment is "degraded" by the usages that humanity puts it to. What is a degraded environment is an interesting question and one that raises an important series of issues regarding history and pre-history. These issues are addressed analytically and empirically. In the next chapter, we present the outlines of an analytical apparatus that incorporates a Malthusian intuition within a model of long-run economic growth that is more consistent with empirical reality than Malthusian doctrine; in chapter 7, we provide empirical evidence in support of our model.

In the remainder of this chapter, we present a synopsis of the history of the role of population growth, environmental transformation, and economic change within the limits of what we know about the history of our species. This brief history of humanity, so to speak, not only places our story in historical context but also serves as an important introduction to the issues we address in this book—the role of microbiology, evolutionary theory, and diseases in understanding human history. The synopsis is essential for understanding that the biological environment changes over time and that disease environments and ecologies are endogenous to human actions.

A Brief History of Humanity

Scholars estimate that *Homo sapiens* first appeared as separate in the hominid line from about 195,000 to 200,000 years ago. DNA analysis suggests that *H. sapiens* became a distinct species about 200,000 years ago (Cann, Stoneking, and Wilson 1987); anatomically modern human fossils are dated about 195,000 years ago (McDougall, Brown, and Fleagle 2005). The hominid line goes back much further than 200,000 years, but this does not directly concern us. What does concern us is terminology. When we refer to "humans" or "humanity" we are referring to *Homo sapiens*. We realize that this may offend some who label some other of the hominid line "human"; we truncate the human line to include only *H. sapiens* for expositional ease.

Until about 50,000 years ago, human culture and living conditions were not much changed from the first artifacts that anthropologists and archeologists have identified as human, and dated at approximately 130,000 to 100,000 years ago. Why was there almost no change for (at a minimum) 50,000 or so years? And why was change so glacial from the mid–Paleolithic Age until the eighteenth century? Starting with the Paleolithic Age, recent studies by anthropologists and other students of prehistoric humanity argue that the human populations of the Earth until about 50,000 or so years ago were too small and too scattered to maintain techniques, skills, and knowledge that increased human productivity and enhanced living standards. This explains the absence of cave paintings, obsidian blades, throwing sticks, and bows and arrows or much else before 50,000 or so years ago. These techniques could have been invented before then, but with a small population and few peaceable interactions between roaming bands of hunter-gatherers, acquired skills were easily lost.

Diamond (1997, pp. 253, 256–57) describes how and why technological regression takes place in small populations; among Diamond's examples is that of the Tasmanian Aborigines who were isolated after global warming and rising ocean levels separated Tasmania from the

Australian mainland. Another example of technological regression is that of the indigenous Polynesians of New Zealand (the Māori) who migrated to the Chatham Islands around 1500 (Diamond 1997, pp. 53–66). Because the islands could support only a small population (estimates indicate there were only 2,000 Chatham Islanders in the early nineteenth century), the Chatham Islanders did not have a large enough population to maintain the level of material culture they possessed before they migrated. Subsequently, their knowledge of the skills and technology that allowed them to manipulate the physical world regressed. The Chatham Islanders reverted from primitive agriculture to a hunting-gathering society; they lost their sea-faring skills that facilitated their migrations, and with that also lost all contact with their Polynesian compatriots in New Zealand, becoming the Moriori people in their isolation. The regression was so severe that the Chatham Islands were easily invaded and many of the Moriori were massacred and eaten by their Māori cousins in the 1830s.

The maintenance of culture (religion, taboos, beliefs, skills, technology, knowledge, etc.) in small, isolated, pre-literate populations is difficult at best because the premature demise of a few or even only one individual may result in the complete loss of valuable skills and knowledge. This means that Paleolithic peoples literally had to reinvent the wheel every few generations. Powell, Shennan, and Thomas (2009, pp. 1298–1301) present a formal model and archeological evidence to support the contention that human progress in the Paleolithic Age was hampered by a human population that was too small to maintain and enhance societal capital. They contend that simple human demography can explain cultural development without recourse to evolutionary changes in human cognition. Notice that these observations are almost the exact opposite of the predictions that simple Malthusian theory would make about the effects of population growth; in the early Paleolithic Age, the human population was too small to maintain societal capital, and when unanticipated declines occurred, living standards fell. *Contra* Malthus, no amount of misery or vice could attenuate the decrease in per capita output.

It was only after the human population was large enough to retain and improve on societal capital that a blooming in the Paleolithic culture (about 50,000 or so years ago) took place. The blossoming of culture ultimately allowed humans to acquire and preserve a technology that allowed them to harvest, and eventually hunt to extinction most of the megafauna. In other words in the late Pleistocene epoch,

Paleolithic peoples were able to harvest megafauna at an unsustainable rate because of rising cultural and technical abilities. If this scenario is correct, it means that an increasing human population was the ultimate cause of the extinction of the megafauna, but in a much more circuitous fashion than that implied in Malthusian Doctrine. The corrected sequence is that an increasing human population allowed societal capital to build up so that the harvesting of large game animals increased. The increase in food resources allowed populations to grow more rapidly thereby enhancing cultural evolution; this had a feedback effect on hunting technology and skills. When the rate of harvesting of large animals exceeded their ability to reproduce, they became extinct. The decline in easily available (low cost) animal protein forced humanity to rely on agriculture.

Now it is certainly true that the cause of the late Pleistocene megafauna extinctions has been much debated over the years and is still the subject of research among archeologists, paleontologists, and others. Nevertheless, few disagree that the scientific evidence points to a role for human influences. While the circumstances and timing of the extinctions varied depending on the continent, it is widely accepted that one or a combination of two major mechanisms (climate change and human overkill) were at play. In the Northern Hemisphere, the evidence suggests that human impacts likely interacting with climatic change determined the specific location and timing of the extinctions; in the Southern Hemisphere, the evidence is still unsettled; in Australia and most oceanic islands, the evidence indicates that humans were the likely cause of the extinctions (Barnosky, Koch, Feranec, et al. 2004). Our focus is on the North American continent where the evidence also points to the arrival of humans and human hunting. Many scientists maintain that the first Americans who migrated toward the end of the last Ice Age glacial (about 15,000 or more years ago) from eastern Siberia via the Bering Land Bridge, or along the near-shore coastal waters just south of it, harvested and eventually overhunted the North American megafauna, resulting in their permanent demise at the end of the Pleistocene (about 12,000 to 10,000 years ago).[5] Some scientists argue that climate change that followed the last North American glacial disrupted the megafauna's habitats and modes of living, leading to their ultimate extinction.[6] But given the megafauna had weathered repeated glaciations, including several major ones, before their permanent demise, the climate explanation is less convincing than a role for human impacts. An alternative human impact mechanism might appear to be consistent with our disease story of history. When humans arrived and spread into new areas, they brought with them various pathogens and disease-causing parasites; these pathogens and parasites jumped from humans (and their dogs) to the megafauna, and because these were new diseases to which the megafauna were highly susceptible it led to the megafauna extinctions (see MacPhee and Marx 1997). However, as we explain in chapter 5, since the first Americans arrived in small bands with few animals in cold weather during the last glacial they were not likely to have arrived with many parasitic diseases.

Returning to the issue of sustainability and environmental degradation; can we say that Paleolithic peoples degraded their environment? Whether we label it degradation is entirely a matter of tastes; because of changes during the Paleolithic Age, we have no mammoths or mastodons, but, conversely, we have museums. The question cannot be answered definitively because there are no agreed upon measures (metrics) for desirability, but there is one discomforting fact: if humanity had not experienced the changes it did, the human population of present-day Earth would be less than two percent of what it is now, and the humans that did exist you would not want to meet.[7]

Population growth did not cause a sudden change in the Paleolithic economy because the change in population was not sudden; the change from hunting-gathering societies to permanent agricultural settlements occurred over millennia. When there is abundant game, primitive peoples find the lifestyle of a hunter-gatherer more attractive than that of an agriculturalist. (The vestiges of this preference for hunting remain in contemporary humans; many people pay vast amounts to go hunting and fishing, sometimes not even retaining the animals for food; the same people may pay someone else to maintain their lawns and gardens. Unlike hunters, we know of nobody who pays anyone to allow him to till, plant, weed, and harvest plants.) Regardless, when game animals became scarce and too time-consuming (costly) to obtain, humanity adapted to the decreased abundance of easily harvested game by incorporating some form of agriculture into their food producing activities. The transition to agriculture was innately tied to humanity's use of fire. From early times fire was used as a hunting tool; fires set to entrap herbivores had the advantage of producing more grazing areas that served as a food for animal herds (Pyne 1991). From following migrating animals and using fire, it was only a short step to swidden (slash and burn) agriculture.

Swidden agriculture is typically one of the first steps on the agricultural ladder (Boserup 1966, 1981). A common practice in swidden agriculture is to girdle trees (rings are cut around them) in order to kill them; their death and subsequent desiccation allows the forest to be set ablaze. The fires do the hard work of clearing lands and enriching soils. Tribal peoples would then move in and establish primitive farms on a small portion of the cleared land, with the remaining portions left to grasses and shrubs. The grasses and shrubs would attract grazing animals and these would be hunted. After a few years, the land's agricultural fertility would have been depleted by cropping, and the game reduced by hunting. The tribe would then move on to another section of the woodlands whose trees had been prepared and burnt for such an eventuality. Swidden agricultural cycles were sometimes as long as twenty years (the interval between which the land was in fallow; that is, not being used for agriculture).

Were killing trees and using fire to clear the land symptomatic of environmental degradation? Again, we cannot answer that question, but if they were, they were rectified and eventually superseded by settled agricultural communities. Swidden agriculture is tenable only if the population density is low enough to subsist on a relatively low yield per acre. (In a twenty-year swidden cycle, only a small fraction of a twentieth of the land area is cropped; the remainder of the twentieth that has been burned and not used in agriculture is devoted to grass lands to attract grazing wildlife.) Paradoxically, because swidden agricultural techniques were successful in increasing food resources for the human population, the increased population made swidden agriculture untenable.

The decline in game animals was the impetus that gave early humanity reasons to find alternative ways of acquiring food. Primitive humanity knew the relationship between seeds and plants long before cultivation became a permanent form of survival. When there were sufficient numbers of easily harvested animals, the lifestyle of hunter-gatherers was more attractive than that of primitive agriculturalists. Skeletal remains from hunter-gatherer societies indicate that they were more robust, taller, and healthier than early agriculturalists (Molleson 1994). So why did they give up hunting-gathering? It was because the game animals diminished and in some cases disappeared. North and Thomas (1977) have an explanation for the transition from hunting to farming that involves increasing human populations with diminishing animal populations.

The switch to agriculture was neither sudden nor irreversible. Hunter-gatherers persisted for long periods following herds and gathering plant foods; swidden agriculture arose and long-cycle swidden agricultural periods were shortened as population grew and became more dependent on crops and domesticated animals for food. We also have noted that the increase in population positively affected the acquisition of knowledge, skills, and techniques, but there were negative consequences as well—namely the increased frequency of disease among relatively sedentary agricultural populations.[8]

Accompanying the population increase were a number of changing natural and societal circumstances that altered the disease ecology. First, even before agriculture, the increased human population and contacts between animals and humans that resulted from a change in hunting techniques allowed the transmission of infectious diseases among people, and between peoples and animals. Second, an increased reliance on agriculture reduced the quality of proteins available and caused protein deficiency diseases and skeletal deformities. The physical evidence is unambiguous; the skeletal remains of hunter-gatherers show a much healthier population than that of their agricultural successors (Molleson 1994). Third, an increased reliance on domestic animals meant that some animal diseases would have jumped from herds of domestic animals to humans; these are called zoonotic diseases. As with all "new" diseases, zoonotic diseases could have devastating effects on humans (see Cohen 1977; Diamond 1997; McNeill 1976). Some diseases that originated in animal populations and severely affected humans are measles, chicken pox, rabies, sleeping sickness, and smallpox; these diseases had immense effects on humanity. A fourth reason for increased diseases was that food storage techniques in primitive times were worse than primitive. Food-borne diseases (ergotism, botulism, *E. coli*, *Campylobacter*, *Shigella*, hepatitis A, *Giardia lamblia*, *Cryptosporidia*, among others) and diseases spread by vermin that are attracted to stored foods are much more common in sedentary populations than among hunter-gatherers. Reliance on stored food means that food-borne diseases became much more prevalent in the human community as humans made the transition from hunting-gathering to agriculture. Fifth, diseases caused by pollutants from the wastes of humans and domesticated animals increased among sedentary peoples. Hunter-gatherers left the water and soil that they fouled behind during their migrations. Sedentary agriculturists lived (and died) with the polluted water and soil they created. Water-borne diseases are extraordinarily numerous; they include infections from bacteria, viruses, protozoa, and parasites. They became rampant among primitive peoples that are sedentary; hunter-gatherers largely escaped them. Finally, the increased population allowed more contacts between peoples. This created increased chances of cultural and technological interchange; it also created a mechanism whereby epidemic diseases could be created and spread easily. The typical hunting-gathering tribal society had too few contacts among tribal groups to allow pathogens to spread. This was one of the reasons behind the relatively robust health of hunter-gatherers. With sedentary agriculture and a denser population, diseases could spread more easily to previously isolated peoples and eventually become endemic. These diseases would have had devastating effects on the human population during the transition from epidemic to endemic diseases; McNeill (1976) recounts the classic story of this transition.

It should be explicitly recognized that parasitic diseases can have a devastating impact on human development; the human brain is an immensely complex organ that requires a great many resources to grow and function. In newborns, the developing brain takes about 87 percent of an adequate metabolic budget, in five-year-olds it takes 44 percent, and its requirements level off among adults at about 25 percent.[9] Parasitic diseases reduce the quantity and quality of nutritional intake. This is particularly devastating among the young because infants and children denied adequate nutrition by being infected with parasitic diseases (or having lactating mothers infected) cannot acquire the brain development during adolescence that they missed as infants and young children. The increasing prevalence of diseases in sedentary populations would have left them stunted, physically and intellectually. So hunter-gatherers were stronger *and* smarter than primitive agriculturalists; the negative effects of diseases on human brain development would last as long as the bulk of humanity resided in a polluted and disease-ridden environment.

What we envision for the transition from hunting-gathering is an enormously long time (stretching over millennia) where the human population oscillated from one in which agriculture was very important in the human economy, to periods of population collapse where primitive agricultural societies reverted to hunting-gathering. Recall that primitive agriculture was hard work, producing few sources of high-quality protein and a continually disease-ridden community. Epidemic disease could have arisen from one of a number of sources. For example, the killer epidemics could have been derived from zoonoses that were random mutations of one of the numerous pathogens of animal herds. The diseases would, on occasions, have disastrous consequences on the population. Because these were "new" diseases (the population had not been exposed to them on a regular basis), there would be no acquired immunities and the frequency of innate immunities would be low.[10] Under these circumstances, we would expect to see occasional population implosions. A dramatic decline in the human population would have a rapid positive effect on the animal populations that humans hunted.

The generational time of early humanity was about sixteen to twenty years, while the generational time of the animals that primitive agriculturalists still hunted was much shorter, varying from months to a few years. This implies that a human population implosion would be accompanied by an animal population explosion. Surviving humans would be likely to abandon sedentary agriculture for the more leisurely protein-rich life of hunter-gatherers. Agriculturalists would have declined relative to surviving hunter-gatherer tribes. This would have made them more susceptible to attacks from foraging bands of hunter-gatherers. One of the more unpleasant aspects of primitive peoples is their more than ceremonial cannibalism (White 2001); primitive peoples might not have had good taste, but apparently they tasted good.

The transition to agriculture was not a sudden one of centuries, but one of millennia for a number of reasons. First, the large animals that were sources of protein and relatively easily harvested had to have been sufficiently diminished that primitive agricultural practices were adopted. Fire allowed smaller animals (deer, antelope, wild cattle) an increased resource base (grasslands) that sustained the hunting economy for a while. Second, swidden agriculture arose and would have lasted for an indeterminate number of generations, possibly followed by a more settled agriculture. Third, increased population density would have introduced epidemic diseases that cause the human population to cycle. Fourth, a reversion back to hunting-gathering would mean a slower rate of population growth because mothers in hunting-gathering societies can only care for one child every five or so years. (People who are constantly on the move have to carry small children; mothers with a newborn and a two- or three-year-old would have to make unpleasant choices.) So the reversion to hunting-gathering would not end after just a few generations. Finally, the transition to agriculture would begin again with the human society acquiring the lost skills of swidden agriculture and animal domestication. From the prospective of an individual human, this process took an immensely long time. However, sometime around 15,000 years ago in the Fertile Crescent human settlements emerged that have been continuously occupied ever since.[11]

The point of the preceding discussion is to emphasize that environmental changes that affect "sustainability" were part and parcel of human experience for the past 40,000 to 50,000 years. To say that these changes degraded the environment raises an obvious question: to whom? Throughout history, in the past, present, and future, sustainability depended, depends, and will depend on the population, skills, and capital accessible at that time. Some have termed the transition to agriculture as humanity's biggest mistake; not only is this misanthropic, it is somewhat self-contradictory. Only a civilization that records the history of humanity could produce someone who is capable of thinking that the past was more desirable than the present. It seems unlikely that Paleolithic hunter-gatherers would ever have had the ability (or the time) to contemplate the distant past; by necessity their lives were dominated by the immediate present, contemplating the past beyond a couple dozen or so years would be analogous to present-day humans living in the fifth dimension—literally incomprehensible.

The blooming of Paleolithic culture that took place about 50,000 or so years ago did not ensure increasing living standards over the ages, nor did permanent settlements persist after their first appearance. To explain why, we have to go back to the early *Homo sapiens* and their hominid ancestors. For literally millions of years, the hominid economy was one of foraging. It is true that early humans improved on skills and hunting techniques over the eons, but hominids left no discernible footprints on the natural ecology until the Paleolithic "renaissance." This is significant because it means that hominid population growth was so low that it altered neither the number of species nor other aspects of nature. The reason why population growth was low was because fertile women could give birth and care for a child only once every five years or so. Hunting-gathering peoples were constantly on the move; to be safe, children had to be with their mothers (or some other caring adult) at all times. In hunting-gathering societies, mothers have to carry small children while traveling constantly, searching for and gathering foods. Women who had an infant and a toddler were almost sure to lose one (or both) to the environment or to inadequate nutrition (mothers would typically breast-feed children until well past the toddler stage). Consequently, women who had few years between births were likely to have had fewer surviving children than women who gave birth once every, say, five or more years.

Over generations, natural selection would alter the population's gene pool to increase the relative frequency of genes that produce greater infertility in women who are lactating. Similarly, natural selection will tend to reduce the frequency of genes that are associated with multiple births. Evolution also affects cultural practices; in a hunting-gathering society, a culture that reduces the chances of lactating women becoming pregnant would have survival value. Individuals who abided by such practices would be more likely to reproduce successfully. This implies that early humanity had "naturally" low birth rates. With the Paleolithic blooming, the resource constraint on population growth would have relaxed, but we would not expect an immediate demographic change. About 40,000 or so years ago, the Paleolithic population grew more rapidly than before, but not what twenty-first century humans would call rapid. Biology and culture ensured that the Paleolithic populations did not explode.

But grow they did, and with the growth of population came increased human density, permanent settlements, and an environment in which a multitude of diseases proliferated. The diseases reduced population directly by causing death, and indirectly by increasing morbidity (illness/sickness) that reduced fertility (sick women have fewer surviving children).

What we envision is a scenario whose essence is captured in figure 2.1. (As in all of the book's schematic diagrams, the direction of the arrows in figure 2.1 indicate the flow of causality from an originating box to a target box; the algebraic signs indicate the impact of the change in the originating box on the target box, holding all other factors constant.) Starting at the top, an increase in population increases density; increased density has two effects, one is that denser populations have more diseases; the second is that it creates permanent human settlements and agriculture (agriculture becomes more attractive than foraging). Permanent settlements encourage innovations that increase culture; offsetting these beneficial effects, a sedentary population encourages the growth of infectious diseases. Infectious diseases cause death and/or morbidity, which in turn reduce population. The decrease in population may be offset by the acquisition of skills and technology that permanent settlements provide.

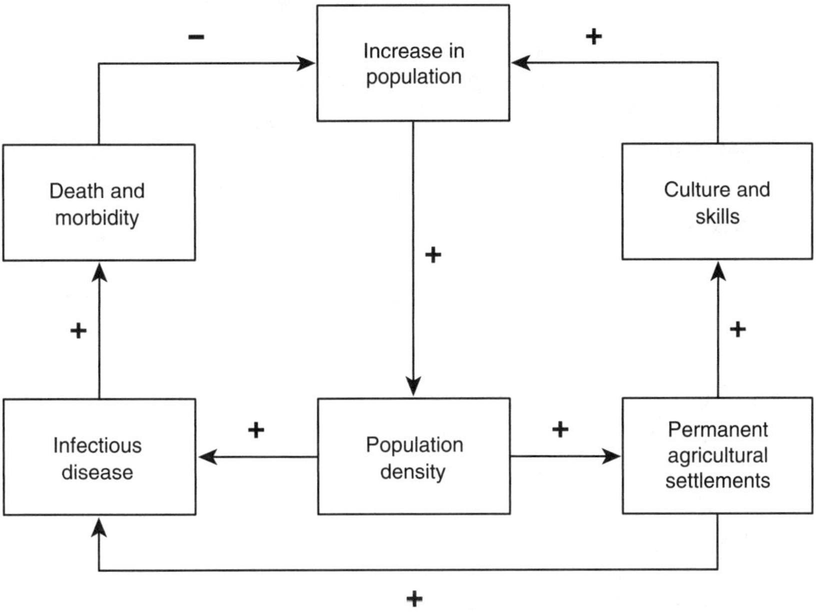

Figure 2.1
Demographic changes and Paleolithic transition

With an increase in population, permanent agricultural settlements appear and proliferate. The settlements have two effects. (1) There is an increase in skills and culture that increase output and have a positive feedback effect on population. And (2) the disease environment becomes more deleterious, which causes an increase in death and morbidity that in turn has a negative feedback effect on population. The ultimate outcome is ambiguous because, if population falls sufficiently, hunting-gathering becomes a more attractive lifestyle. As long as diseases were deadly enough to reduce the human population sufficiently, the human community would cycle between wandering hunter-gatherers and societies where agriculture plays a greater role. Permanent settlements had ambiguous effects on Paleolithic peoples. On the one hand, they provided increased output, increased human numbers, and gave an impetus to civilization. On the other hand, permanent settlements subjected humanity to diseases that theretofore had been rare or unknown; these diseases reduced population, civilization, and made hunting-gathering a more attractive lifestyle. Humanity cycled that way for millennia, but at least by about 14,000 to 15,000 years ago permanent settlements did not vanish; agriculture was here to stay. The reason cyclical stasis did not persist was due to evolutionary processes.

The events depicted in figure 2.1 took place over millennia, and time changes all things. The changes we are concerned with are the impacts that these events had on the human population. We expect that the constant culling of the human population would have had two effects; one effect would be to produce a population that is genetically more resistant to these diseases. The second effect would be cultural; humanity would gradually acquire a collection of practices that both reduced the chances of infection and, if infected, ameliorated its severity.

Starting with the gene pool, we expect that over generations those people who were most susceptible to infectious diseases either to die without reproducing or to leave few descendants. Over generations, the population would become more representative of people who had constitutions that made them less vulnerable to infection and more resistant to the diseases of permanent settlements. The cyclical changes in the human population caused by the changing living conditions and changing disease environments altered the human gene pool.

The events depicted in figure 2.1 also affected cultural practices that ameliorated the diseases of permanent settlements. A process of trial and error (which is what evolution is) would produce a number of natural medicines that treated the diseases more or less effectively. Living styles also affect health; practices such as a reliance on spring or well water rather than ground water, marriage rules, birthing and lactation practices, rules on the disposal of human and animal waste products, care of the sick, cooking and meal preparation, and a host of other activities can affect the health of a population. The practices that had a positive effect on health would tend to persist relative to those that had the opposite effect or no effect. People who acquired the cultural practices that lessened the infectious disease penalty would leave more descendants.

Recurrent bouts of disease and permanent settlements also altered the evolutionary success of genes that affected fertility. In permanent settlements, small children are less of a burden to women than in nomadic foraging societies. In nascent agricultural societies, planting, weeding, food preparation and storage, home maintenance, and garment making are typically "women's work." Infants and toddlers are less of a handicap in doing these tasks than the tasks required of women in societies where there are no permanent settlements. Unlike their counterparts in hunting-gathering societies, women in permanent settlements who have smaller intervals between births do not experience extreme child mortality. Consequently, women with smaller birth intervals between pregnancies in permanent settlements are likely to have more surviving descendants than their counterparts in hunting-gathering societies. Like genes that conferred resistance to the diseases of settlements, genes and practices that reduced birth intervals and increased fertility would similarly bestow an evolutionary advantage to their possessors in permanent settlements. Similarly, genes that confer a measure of resistance to diseases gave people an evolutionary advantage; over evolutionary time, the relative frequencies of these genes would have increased in societies subject to cyclical exposure to these diseases.

The genes that conferred greater fertility and resistance to diseases persisted in the gene pool even when diseases reduced the population sufficiently enough to make a hunting-gathering lifestyle a more attractive option. The reduced population would have a gene pool that had fewer alleles (alternative forms of a gene) that made people more susceptible to disease because a disproportionate number of these people would have died without reproducing. The people reproducing would, in all likelihood, be more resistant to disease. The surviving breeding population would provide a gene pool that was different from that which the population had prior to the epidemics. The changing gene pool made the population slightly more resistant to epidemic disease; subsequent population growth made agriculture and permanent settlements a more attractive way of surviving.

Epidemic diseases can cull the gene pool dramatically. Genes that confer resistance would become substantially over-represented during epidemics. These genes come at a "cost"; they could have other effects in different environments that reduce their evolutionary success. But these effects would have noticeable impact on the gene pool only over many generations, by which time the population may be large enough to be forced to return to agriculture and permanent settlements. Figure 2.2 is a representation of this scenario. The vertical axis represents the frequency (with a maximum of 100 percent and a minimum of 0) of an allele in the gene pool that gives some resistance to diseases of settlement or enhances fertility. On the horizontal axis is time; since we are referring to evolutionary processes, the units of time are generations or centuries. The shaded areas moving along the horizontal axis represent periods when agriculture is ascendant. The peaks of relative

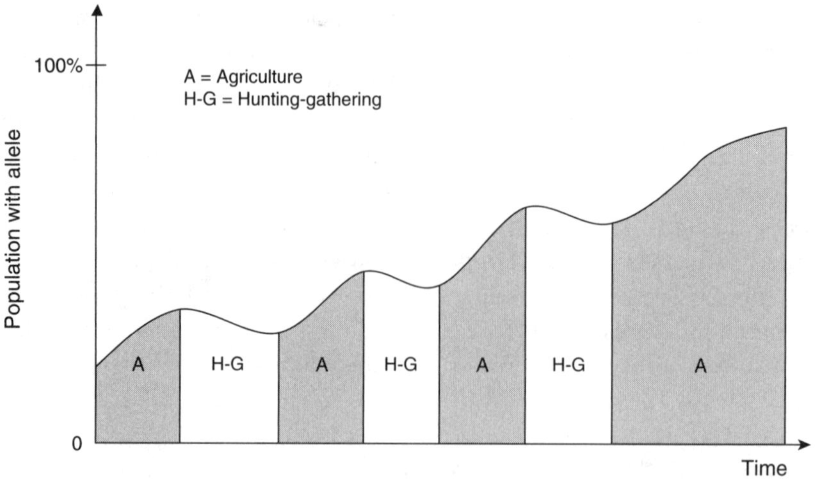

Figure 2.2
Changing allele frequencies in different Paleolithic societies

frequencies coincide with the end of agricultural ascendance. The peak of agriculture coincides with a decline in population caused by diseases; it is followed by a period when hunting-gathering is ascendant, the unshaded areas. The decline from the peak of the frequency of an allele during a period of hunting-gathering is less severe than the increase when agricultural settlements are on the ascendance. This is because of the aforementioned severity of genetic culling in a disease environment of permanent settlements relative to that of nomadic foragers. There are an indeterminate number of cycles culminating in the final period when there is no reversion to hunting-gathering. The relative frequency of the allele becomes asymptotic to a maximum relative frequency (always less than 100 percent) as agricultural settlements become a permanent fixture on the landscape.

Permanent settlements had other profound effects on humanity besides altering the relative frequency of alleles. Because of deleterious disease environments, primitive agricultural settlements had higher death rates than hunter-gatherer societies. Given what we know about Paleolithic hunter-gatherer societies, they had very low rates of population growth. So, if death rates were higher in settled (agricultural) societies and their populations grew, this means that birth rates among primitive agriculturalists had to have been substantially higher than the very low birth rates of hunter-gatherers.[12]

The increase in birth rates did not happen instantaneously. In primitive agricultural societies, women who had short intervals between pregnancies were more likely to have more surviving descendents than women who had longer intervals between pregnancies. In periods when agriculture was in decline, the reverse would be true; shorter intervals would produce fewer descendents while longer ones would produce more. The cycling between agriculture and hunting-gathering would produce ambiguous results over time. However, it is indisputable that primitive agriculture and permanent settlements did eventually endure and hunting-gathering societies were pushed into lands that had low levels of agricultural productivity. Eventually birth rates in primitive agricultural societies must have increased sufficiently to offset the increased death rates that accompanied permanent primitive settlements.

The important points are that (1) death rates in primitive settlements were typically higher than those of hunter-gatherers and (2) birth rates in primitive settlements must have been higher; otherwise, primitive settlements would not have prevailed. Permanent settlements not only lasted, they grew, and again this means a birth rate higher than the death rate. The more deleterious the environment, the higher the birth rate had to be. High death and birth rates have an enormous impact on the age distribution of populations. Populations with these characteristics have an age distribution shaped like a pyramid. Many children are born but few reach adulthood. This means that the dependent portion of the population is relatively large and remains that way. There are few producing adults and many nonproducing infants and children. Resources per capita are few; the population is poor because people are dying, and few are working. This turns the Malthusian doctrine upside down. In this scenario death causes poverty, while the Malthusians say poverty causes death. This is our alternative to the Malthusian scenario; it is more consistent with history (demographic and medical) than the Malthusian story. Inadequate food supplies by themselves do not cause massive die-offs. High death rates during famines are typically caused by people migrating to where they perceive food is in greater abundance. Large numbers of people congregate and infectious diseases spread; during famines people typically die from infections like typhus, cholera, typhoid fever, diarrheal diseases, influenza, and other infections. Typically they do not die of insufficient nutrition but infectious diseases (Livi-Bacci 1991, 1992, 2000). Any increased morbidity that accompanies the disease environment also will have negative effects on productivity; this will exacerbate the effects of disease and increase poverty.

It is true that inadequate nutrition may reduce the effectiveness of the human immune system in combating disease; as a consequence those who already have compromised immune systems (the infirm, the elderly, and the very young) are disproportionately likely to die. It also is true that famines contribute to migration and crowding that accelerate the spread of infectious diseases. All these caveats aside, we would not expect to see famines kill many healthy adults; long-term declines in population are due to rising death rates that are invariably associated with infectious diseases.

Permanent settlements and the general increase in the density of the human population created a disease environment that increased death rates. In spite of this, the human population increased substantially from 12,000 years ago to the present (2011); the expansion in human numbers was sporadic with more than a few centuries witnessing massive population declines. Regardless, the expansion of human numbers means that over time the birth rate must have increased relative to that of the Paleolithic Age to compensate for the higher death rates caused by the disease environment, and to allow for the increase in human numbers.

Figure 2.3 illustrates the process of demographic change affecting the human economy. Ignore the bottom two boxes ("Increase in birth rates" and "Dependency") for the time being. Starting at the top, an increase in death rates (due to infectious diseases) leads to both a decrease in population and lower incomes. Incomes fall because there is a decline in per capita output as markets shrink and become less specialized. Lower incomes reduce birth rates which have a negative impact on population. If this is all that happened then population would decline until society reverted to hunting-gathering. But populations did stabilize and increase despite the excess mortality that permanent settlements imposed on humanity. Now looking at the lower portion of figure 2.3 (lower left), this means that birth rates did increase. The increase in birth rates is depicted as being caused by events outside the purview of figure 2.3. (The causes of increased births can be attributed to genetic and cultural changes.) The increase in birth rates increases population but also increases the percentage of the population that is dependent, and that in turn lowers income. Again, this explanation turns the Malthusian view upside down; here death causes poverty, not vice versa.

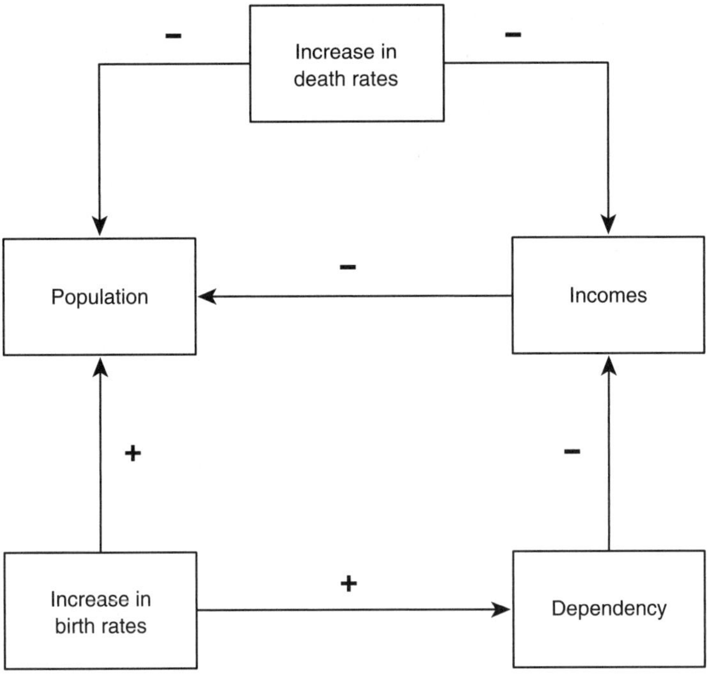

Figure 2.3
Changing demographic regimes

There is some evidence that living standards in the beginning of the sixteenth century were no higher than that of antiquity (Clark 2007). Whether correct or not, stagnating living standards is consistent with both explanations—that poverty causes illness and death (Malthus) or illness and death causes poverty. We wish to emphasize that the bubonic plagues (Justinian Plague 541 to 542 and the Black Death 1347 to 1350) that caused major declines in the European population were infectious diseases unrelated to famine. A Malthusian "crisis" would not cause a sudden die-off; it would cause a relatively stable population or a slowly declining one.

Permanent settlements led to urban living and "civilizations"—societies whose political controls are centered in cities. The words civilization and cities have more than etymology in common; societies based on cities develop more rapidly economically than other non–city-based societies because they have more people in a relatively small space. This allows for the accumulation of capital (both physical and intellectual), increased productivity due to increased specialization, and a lower cost of protection from brigands, barbarians, and foes of all kinds. These advantages came with costs; an increasing biomass (humans, animals, waste products, food, and vermin) provides an environment conducive to pathogens and the spread of diseases. The human population housed in urban agglomerations fluctuated along with fluctuations in the disease environment and human adaptations to it. Human adaptations were typically not conscious, but a product of biological and cultural selection. For example, drinking beverages with boiling water or with an alcoholic content of 4 percent (or more) were effective ways of avoiding water-borne pathogens. The people who drank these beverages might not have known their beverages were safer than river water; nevertheless, whether by taste or intuition, a preference for these beverages developed in various societies. In the Orient, hot beverages were prophylactic against pathogens as were beer and wine in Europe.

These preferences were also more likely to be culturally transmitted to descendants. Dead people cannot tell their children to drink water, and the probability of dying was significantly higher for people who were resistant to the charms of tea and/or alcohol. Biological evolution also worked on populations, alleles that made one very susceptible to water-borne pathogens were more likely to be culled relative to alleles that conferred some resistance.

Still, population growth from antiquity to the beginning of the modern era (circa 1500) was subject to catastrophic declines. As McNeill (1976) points out, these catastrophic declines were in some part due to economic progress. As societies developed, trade links sprang up and with trade in goods and people came another more nefarious trade of pathogens. The Pax Romana allowed the spread of diseases throughout the Empire; this was arguably a major factor in the collapse of the Roman Empire. The visitation of the plague (pneumonic and bubonic) in Europe devastated its population in two distinctive periods that are cataloged as the Justinian Plague and the Black Death.

The history of humanity from antiquity into the early modern period (circa 1700) is explicable in both a Malthusian model and by our framework. The differences between explanations are revealed by history. We argue that people were poor because (1) they were sick and sick people have lower productivities than healthy people, (2) high death rates led to high rates of dependency and lower rates of output per capita, and (3) high death rates produced a younger and more violent population. Young men have a comparative advantage in warfare and violence; a population with the vast majority of people being less than 25 is more likely to be violent than a population with a greater mean age (Heinsohn 2006). The ceaseless violence from the fall of Rome to the early modern period can be, in part, attributed to the age structure, which, in turn is ultimately attributable to the disease ecology. High death rates also meant that investments in human capital had a low rate of return, and in societies with high levels of illiterate peoples some skills and techniques were invariably lost because of untimely deaths. This contributed to economic regression.

The European Voyages of Discovery

The assumptions that the biological environment is unchanging and that the ecology is exogenous to human actions are spectacularly incorrect when it comes to the Voyages of Discovery. The voyages led to the subsequent settlement of the New World with Old World peoples (African and European), animals, plants, and pathogens. The North American ecology that arose out of these migrations was endogenous to human actions. The Old World peoples, plants, and animals that came to North America set in motion interchanges of organisms and, in particular, disease pathogens that fundamentally altered the ecology of its various geographic regions. The changes in the disease ecologies were not uniform; conditions of climate and geography affected which diseases would predominate in the various regions. Altered disease ecologies affected the economic possibilities of settlers. The biological world places constraints on human choices. Before the late-nineteenth century advances in public health, sanitation, and medical science (about 1880 to 1900), the local and regional disease environments that evolved as settlement took place, and later the integration of these spatially distinct disease pools, had considerable consequences for Old World peoples (Africans and Europeans) and their American descendants throughout the New World.

In this book, we concentrate on the fundamental role played by microorganisms, evolution, and infectious parasitic diseases in the economic development of the United States in both the colonial and postcolonial eras, until circa 1900. Recognition of the economic and biological consequences and interactions of the African and European migrations to what became the United States has important implications for the interpretation of American economic history prior to the twentieth century. This biological and economic examination of the historical development of America indicates the importance of the physical environment in understanding the history of the health, life, and employment of Africans, Europeans, and their descendents. The concentration on the biological world suggests an interpretation of the economic history of African slavery in America that alters many of the prevailing views of American slavery. Recognizing the interactions of infectious parasitic diseases with economics yields important conclusions concerning the expansion of African slavery in America, the regional concentration of slaves in the South, the productive efficiency of slavery, and slave living standards.

Concluding Thoughts on the History of Early Humans

What can we conclude from the history of our ancestors, both historic and prehistoric? One conclusion is that the growth of the Earth's human population cannot follow the trend of the last 150 or so years because, if it did, in the foreseeable future simple compounded growth would have the human population so large there would be more than ten people per square meter of the Earth's surface (including the oceans). Nevertheless, we still can have a positive, but lower rate of population growth.[13]

In the recent past, cities served as "black holes" for population (McNeill 2007, p. 326). The death rates of cities up until the latter half of the nineteenth century exceeded their birth rates such that only a constant flow of migrants from the countryside prevented them from collapsing. Death rates in cities have plummeted, and in many countries, they are now lower than rural death rates. But as McNeill (2007) points out, the birth rates in cities have fallen almost as much or more than the death rates. Urban birth rates have fallen because modern women are very much like their Paleolithic progenitors. Modern women earn their living outside the home environs just like Paleolithic women, but having a small child in tow is probably a relatively larger handicap to a modern woman's career. Female work outside the home reduces birth rates, and they are further reduced by the trends in many countries to have more families headed by women without partners. Monogamous heterosexual families produce more children per woman than alternative groupings; familiarity breeds. The increase in market-based female earnings means that single women may successfully reproduce, but statistically they produce fewer children than their counterparts in stable heterosexual unions. Birth rates for modern women dwelling in large cities may be lower than those of our Paleolithic ancestors for the same reason: cost. Children in the modern world are increasingly burdensome (costly) for women working outside the home.

Another conclusion we draw from the history of humanity is that demography does shape our destinies. High death rates cause poverty; and demographically young populations are likely to be more unstable than demographically older populations. Political and economic commentators are prone to worry about the stability of an undemocratic China in the contemporary world; we disagree. China's one-child policy has ensured that for the foreseeable future China will have a rapidly aging population and a high mean age. This is a recipe for stability. Populations with a low mean age rate are more likely to be politically unstable whether they are democratic like India, or undemocratic like Saudi Arabia. An ingredient for societal instability is whenever young men constitute a relatively large percentage of the population. Young men make history more interesting, and add bite to the ancient Chinese curse: "May you live in interesting times."

3 Diseases and Long-Run Economic Growth

Evolution has provided humans with their senses, and we are bound by them. In the English language "inconsequential" is a synonym for "small"—the conflation of the minute with the insignificant is explicable by evolutionary selection. Things that are small are typically not immediate threats to life, so evolutionary selection has had our senses concentrate more on things that were larger and could immediately threaten existence. The invisible, by definition, would not be subject to physical (as distinct from cultural or genetic) evolution. Our senses delude us and provide a false feeling of security. These preconceptions hinder our understanding of history and lead us into a great deal of misunderstanding. The minute and/or invisible have had inordinate and still unappreciated effects on history and human society. In chapter 2, we presented an outline of history emphasizing the impact of pathogens on human society. The prevailing disease ecology was of paramount importance throughout human history until the medical and scientific discoveries of the late nineteenth century.

Here we explain the changing role of infectious diseases over time within an explanation (model) of long-run economic growth that contains cycles (feedback effects), one "virtuous," the other "vicious." Our explanation of long-run economic growth combines the effects of population growth, fundamental principles of microbiology, and public health. We discuss alternative explanations of long-run economic growth based on the insights of Adam Smith and Thomas Malthus. Our own explanation, emphasizing the impact of pathogens, combines the Smithian and Malthusian insights to elaborate an explanation of long-run economic growth that is consistent with history, science, and economic principles. In our explanation, we posit a virtuous economic growth cycle offset by a vicious biological cycle. These cycles were embedded in the process of long-run economic growth (rising incomes) prior to the twentieth century. In the pre-twentieth century world, increasing per capita output inevitably contributed to another process that led to the spread of diseases and lowered incomes. The exact temporal sequence was stochastic, but it was predictable in the long run. These pathogenic infections had significant effects on history, economic development, and the well-being of humanity.

Virtuous and Vicious Cycles of Long-Run Economic Growth

We begin with a highly simplified model of economic growth in an exchange economy.[1] As populations increase, markets expand and the expanded markets induce greater specialization, which in turn increases output and productivity. (Wages are positively related to the increased output that is attributable to an additional worker times the additional revenue that the increased output produces.) This is in essence Adam Smith's observation that specialization is limited by the extent (size) of the market. Growing markets and incomes increase the demand for all sorts of services. We emphasize the demand for transport services (broadly construed to include resources devoted to facilitating exchange) because they (1) are easily explicable, (2) have feedback effects on the size of markets (which propels the cycle), and (3) are an important aspect in determining the size of the market and the concomitant specialization in economic activities.[2]

An increase in demand and the absolute amount of goods traded makes profitable a series of investments in the transportation sector. These investments include (but are not limited to) warehouses, wharves, ports, roads, lighthouses, specialized financial services, firms specialized in the provision of inputs to the expanding transport sector, canals, and the creation of institutions (laws and customs) that create, define, and enforce contract law. In order to make the argument more intuitive and less abstract, we simplify even further on the inland shipment of materials. There are many different ways to transport material given the resources available.[3] For example, in the nineteenth century, material could be transported by human hands, in backpacks, by gravity chutes, by mule or horse, by wagon, railroads, canals, or other means. Which technique was used depended on which was cheaper, and that in turn depended on the absolute physical volume shipped. It does not make economic sense to build a railroad to deliver one pound of sand to a market 10 miles away; it is cheaper hiring someone to carry it. But if you wish to transport 100 million tons of sand a distance of 10 miles with the technology and costs prevailing in mid-nineteenth century England, then hiring people to carry it would be disastrously expensive compared to the costs of delivery using a specially constructed road or rail line. Typically the costs of transport are determined by two parts, fixed costs and operating costs; more specialized facilities have high fixed costs and lower operating costs. Only if the volume of freight is large will the average costs (operating costs plus fixed costs divided by total volume of freight) be lower than techniques that use no (or less costly) specialized facilities and have high operating costs.

There are two basic economic points here: (1) there is no free lunch. If you want low operating costs, you have to pay high fixed costs; alternatively, if you want low fixed costs, then operating (or variable) costs are high. And (2) specialization and increasing productivity are limited by the size of the market. As markets expand, the creation of a network of high fixed-cost modes of transport with low variable costs becomes economic. Given the volume of traffic, these high fixed-cost, low variable-cost modes allow substantial reductions in the overall average cost of transportation. The costs of inland transportation in the United States in the mid-nineteenth century were from 1/5 to less than 1/10 the ton-mile charges prevalent in the 1820s as canals were built. Canals were not constructed in the United States until late in the eighteenth century, and no canal of major importance was completed before the 1820s; yet canals were known and constructed since early antiquity. The reason that their construction was effectively delayed until the nineteenth century was that the size of the American market was not large enough to make them economically viable. With the growth of population, both the absolute size of the market and the absolute volume of freight grew; only then were canals financially viable in the United States. The construction of canals resulted in a substantial widening of the market, which induced more growth and had feedback effects on the transport sector.

This explanation of economic growth is derivative from Adam Smith; the major difference between our explanation of economic growth and Adam Smith's is that we explicitly incorporate feedback effects. Increases in population increase market size, and the increased market size affects how production is organized. Increased specialization leads to rising output (and wages) per worker, as production costs fall. Besides its intuitive appeal, we emphasize developments in transport because of transportation's role in the transmittal of diseases.

Increased market size leads to more specialized modes of transport that have lower average costs *given the increased volume* of goods (and passengers) they carry. The reduction in the average costs of transport leads to increases in the size of markets that stimulate still more investments in specialized transport services, and further declines in costs. This is the virtuous cycle of economic growth. Extensive economic growth increases market size; increasing market size leads to more specialization and greater output per worker. Increasing incomes propel further increases in market size as people buy more goods and services (rather than make them at home or do without) with their increasing incomes.

Before the twentieth century, this virtuous cycle of "Smithian" economic growth was attenuated by a vicious biological ("Malthusian") cycle. Increased market size provided a resource for the pathogens that prey on humanity. In the centuries before the twentieth, a significant increase in human density was *always* associated with substantial increases of biological resources for microparasites. With increased human densities came animals that provided transportation and food. Both humans and their animals excreted waste products that were not subject to sanitary disposal. Waste products contaminated water supplies, foods, housing, and soils, and exposed people to the microbes they harbored. This created ideal breeding grounds for opportunistic infestations by newly introduced microbial pathogens. Along with increased animal populations came plant foods that fed both humans and their beasts. In the absence of modern storage and packaging, plant foods attracted their own set of microbes and vermin that harbored and spread pathogens. The result was that the total biomass available to pathogens increased exponentially because of (1) the increases in income, human numbers, and density; (2) a disproportionate increase in domestic animals associated with the increasing population *and* increasing incomes; (3) the increased organic wastes that humans and their animals generated; (4) the increase in plant food stored next to humans and their animals; and (5) the vermin the increased biomass attracted.

We explicitly note the paradoxical role of increased incomes in the transmission of diseases. Increased income led to an increase in demand for both more food and "higher quality" foods. ("Higher quality" here refers to foods derived from animals such as meat, milk, and cheese.) The increases in the urban populations and incomes led to a more than proportional increase in the demand for animal products. This in turn led to a more than proportional increase in the urban biomass available to disease-causing microbes as the animals, plant foods, and the waste products associated with them increased. Increasing incomes had a positive effect on the biomass, such that the total increase in the biomass was disproportionally greater than the increase in the human population.

The increased biomass surrounding human communities allowed pathogens to become more abundant; increased human densities also facilitated the transmission of infectious diseases among humans. As infectious diseases became more rapidly transmitted and widespread, more people were sick more often. The decline in transport times and costs abetted the process; the consequences were an increase in diseases throughout the trade networks. The resultant increase in human morbidity and mortality associated with these pathogens had their impact throughout the entire world as globalization proceeded until the improvements in medicine, sanitation, and public health curtailed infectious diseases toward the end of the nineteenth century.

Our explanation of long-run economic growth emphasizes the connections between population growth and economic development, including developments in transportation. We now present a more formal (austere) model of our thinking and concentrate on explaining the relationships between a denser biomass and the transmission of infectious parasitic diseases in a model of long-run economic growth.

Three Models of Long-Run Economic Growth

A Smithian Model of Long-Run Economic Growth

Adam Smith recognized that specialization enhances productivity, but that the size of the market constrains specialization. An absolutely large market engenders greater specialization, and consequently productivity and income. We take this as a starting point and examine it within the framework and interpretation presented in Stigler (1951). Our model is a variant of the Smith–Stigler model; the Stigler model concerns firm behavior, while ours is an economy-wide model where the cost functions are for economy-wide production functions. While the use of economy-wide cost functions rather than individual firm functions is not critical to understanding the Smithian model, it is critical in examining the Malthusian doctrine.

Consider a closed economy with no technological change; the stock of technology is fixed and known; yet not all technology is economi-

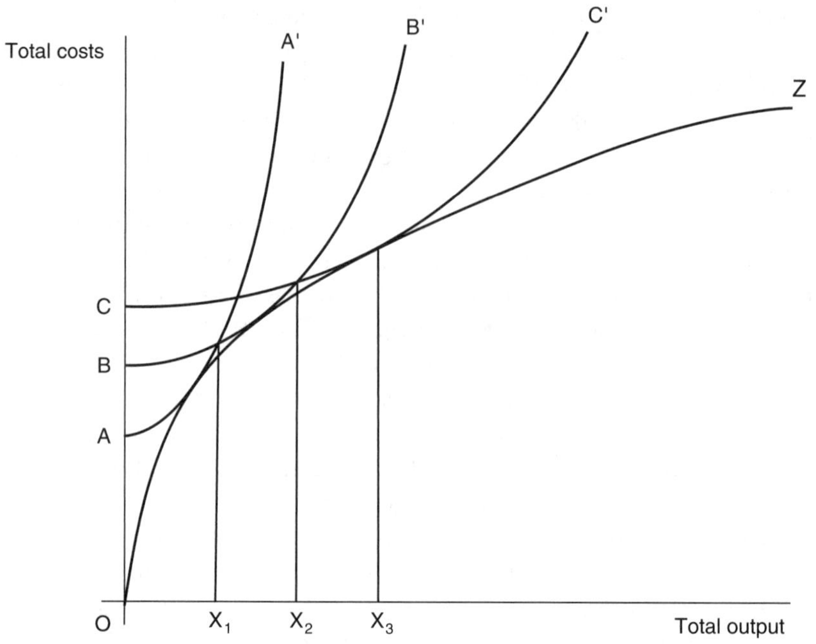

Figure 3.1
Production techniques and the size of the market

cally feasible.[4] Techniques that require substantial fixed costs and incur relatively low variable costs are not feasible in markets below some minimum size. Figure 3.1 illustrates these features: The curves *AA′*, *BB′*, and *CC′* represent the economy-wide cost functions. These economy-wide aggregates are not specific to a firm. For each of the cost curves, total output is on the horizontal axis and total costs (measured in labor units) are on the vertical axis; capital inputs are fixed for each cost curve at a different level as shown by the height of their intersection with the vertical axis. For example, the curve *BB′* has total non–labor fixed costs of *OB* units of labor. Economies of scale (decreasing average or unit costs) exist on each cost curve because of the existence of the fixed costs *OA*, *OB*, and *OC*, respectively, for each of the functions; each cost curve has a continuously increasing slope.

Average cost per unit of output (measured in labor units) in figure 3.1 is measured by the slope of a straight line from the origin to any point on a specific cost curve. Average productivity per unit of input (measured in labor units) would be the inverse of this slope. (We show this later in figure 3.2.) Notice that although there are continuously increasing marginal costs (as measured by the slope of each specific function; each of the curves get progressively steeper as output increases); average costs initially fall and then increase.

The use of labor inputs as the unit in which to measure fixed costs and variable costs has a long tradition and it yields some distinct advantages (for the history of labor theories of value in economics, see Blaugh 1997). First, it allows us to equate costs and living standards (as measured in output per unit of labor) in a perfect inverse function. Second, "total costs" in labor units allow us to examine the Malthusian model on its own terms. Third, as an empirical matter, the rise, or fall, in living standards over time is the stuff of economic history and development.

There are a variety of techniques available to produce output. Figure 3.1 illustrates only three of the possible techniques. For the sake of exposition, the diagram can be thought of as depicting the cost functions for transportation (measured in ton-miles). Curve *AA′* represents the costs of hauling by pack train, curve *BB′* by wagon train, and curve *CC′* by railroad. Only if the market generates a critical mass of more than X_1 output will pack trains (*AA′*) be abandoned in favor of wagons (*BB′*). A volume of transportation greater than X_2 makes railroads (*CC′*) more economic than wagons. At the "critical masses" (outputs X_1 and X_2), the costs for competing techniques are the same, beyond those outputs it becomes economical to switch to the higher fixed-cost/lower variable-cost techniques. Beyond each critical mass, the higher fixed-cost technique yields a lower average cost per unit.[5]

The curve *OZ* is formed by the locus of all the minimum total costs for *given outputs* using different techniques. Accordingly, *OZ* represents the least total-cost method of production for given levels of output when techniques are allowed to vary. It can be considered the long-run total-cost curve formed by the minimum points for outputs using specific, efficient techniques. As it is drawn, *OZ* is a continuous function; implying that there is an optimum total cost function for *each* output. This assumption is not necessary for the argument. All that is necessary is that each discrete change in output has associated with it a total cost function with greater fixed costs and lower marginal costs. A continuous function, however, has the advantage of being described with familiar and accessible mathematics.

This model is representative of Adam Smith's thesis: population growth leads to larger market size, which in turn leads to more specialized techniques (higher fixed costs and lower variable costs) and

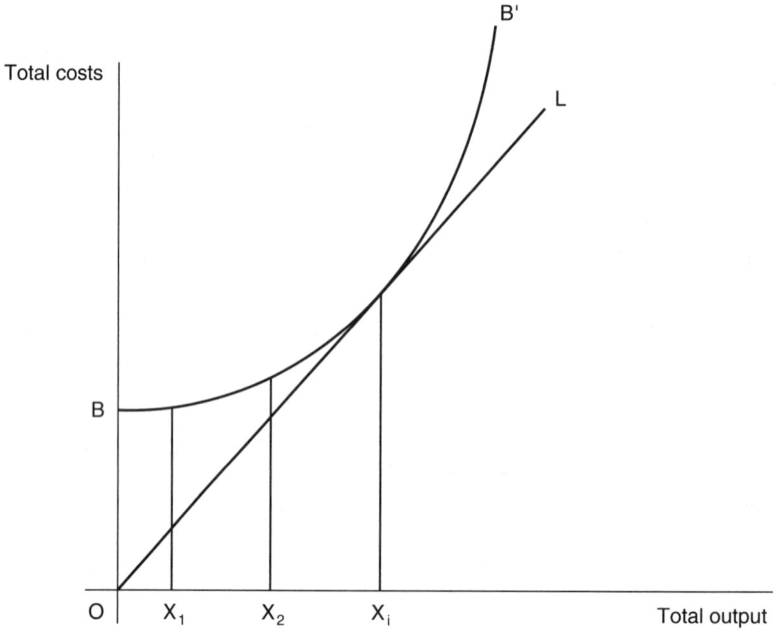

Figure 3.2
Fixed production technique and output

increased productivity. This results in the demand curve for resources shifting to the right leading to higher real wage rates as both the marginal and the average productivity of labor rise.

A Pure Malthusian Model of Long-Run Economic Growth

A straightforward Malthusian model may be illustrated with figure 3.2, which is figure 3.1 with all of the "short-run" cost curves eliminated except *BB*′. For illustrative purposes, we examine curve *BB*′. Since the slope of it is continuously increasing, diminishing returns (that is, increasing marginal costs) exist throughout the entire range of *BB*′ (and all other specific cost curves). This is the "pure" Malthusian case. A less "pure" one would have a range of increasing returns and then decreasing returns to scale. The specification chosen here is less restrictive and, because the curves are *economy-wide* cost curves, has greater fidelity to the Malthusian doctrine. In figure 3.2 average costs are falling (or alternatively, living standards rising) up to output X_i on the cost function *BB*′. The output X_i has the lowest average cost (highest average productivity); average costs (the slope of the straight line *OL*) are at a minimum for technique *BB′* (*OL* is just tangent to *BB′*) at output X_i, beyond X_i average costs rise. The range of outputs beyond X_i *and* on curve *BB′* represent the Malthusian range of increasing average costs as output expands. While the lowest average cost for technique *BB′* occurs at X_i, referring back to figure 3.1, the critical point—the output level where it becomes cheaper to produce using technique *CC′* rather than *BB′*—occurs at the smaller output, X_2; X_i will be at an output in the range of X_3, where the production technique *CC′* is just tangent to the long-run optimum curve *OZ* in figure 3.1.

The obvious difference between the Malthusian and Smithian models is that the Malthusian doctrine holds techniques constant, whereas the Smithian doctrine allows the use of more specialized techniques that are economical at higher volumes of output. Framed in this manner, the Smithian model is more dynamic in that it allows switching techniques. However, the Smithian model is innocent of biological dynamics. The Malthusian model has an intuition that increasing numbers can lead to impoverishment.

Whether technology is "fixed" or not under these conditions is debatable. North (1968) and Rosenberg (1982) address the meaning of technological change. In discussing productivity increases in North Atlantic shipping in the eighteenth century, North argues there was no technological change because the techniques that were used in the mid-eighteenth century had been available (but not used in the North Atlantic trade) a hundred years earlier. Rosenberg contends that it was the adoption of the technology that allowed productivity to increase; consequently it *was* technological change. North's point is that the availability (or the lack thereof) of technology did not constrain shippers from adopting the technology earlier than they did. What did constrain shippers was that, for a variety of reasons (one being market size), the optimum mid-eighteenth century technology was noneconomic in 1680. Rosenberg's argument, in its essence, is tautological: if an increase in productivity is related to the adoption of a technology, it is by definition technological change. North's position is more commonsensical: technological changes apply to developments that were previously physically impossible. The advantage of North's position is that it allows one to distinguish between changes due to relative factor prices (or market growth), and changes due to the relaxation of physical constraints.

Purists may object to the Smithian model because it does not hold the technology used constant, thus violating the strict interpretation of "holding all other factors constant" in the Malthusian theory. But if population density enters into production decisions, and we insist on a strict interpretation of "holding all other factors constant," then Malthusian theory is internally inconsistent. An increase in population would lead to an increase in density, thus violating the proviso to hold other factors constant, unless the amount of resources change, which also violates the proviso to hold other factors constant. As a result, the crucial issue is empirical: Does population density enter into the choice of technologies?

At the risk of belaboring the obvious, there is abundant empirical evidence that population and market density both affect how production is organized. Subway systems (undergrounds), pipelines, jumbo jets, sidewalks, and railroads are just some examples of density and market-size dependent techniques. The theoretical (and empirical) literature in economics of standard "U-shaped" long-run average cost curves for competitive firms, and downward sloping long-run average cost curves for firms that are "natural" monopolies, rests on economies of scale. There is no dispute: Both market size and population density influence real-world technologies.

A Combined Model of Long-Run Economic Growth

Our combined model of long-run economic growth embeds the Malthusian intuition within the framework of a closed Smithian economy. The crucial facet of our combined model is the relationship of population growth with an increase in human density per square mile. With a denser biomass of humanity, microorganisms that prey on humanity will become more abundant, and increasing human density allows the transmission of infectious diseases to occur more rapidly. The knowledge of the correlation of population densities with diseases is well known in the biological literature (Varley, Gradwell, and Hassell 1973; Wilson, Miles, and Parker 1984). Perhaps the best indication of its acceptance is that the relationship between disease, deaths, and population has been formulated into "Farr's Law." According to LeRiche and Milner (1971, p. 276), "This 'law' states that there is a linear relationship between population density and death rate, using the logarithms of the life-table death rates as the ordinate and the density expressed as persons per square mile as the abscissa." Lee (1987, p. 451) disputes the exact specification of "Farr's Law," nevertheless he too observes a negative relationship between human density and the reproduction rate. Rather than an exact specification, "Farr's Law" should be thought of as a Law of Density; as density increases a species' morbidity and mortality increase. A straightforward statement on the impact of population on disease can be found in Fox, Hall, and Elveback (1970, p. 102): "Very simply, increasing the density of population favors the spread of infectious agents to man, whether from human or nonhuman sources and whether by direct or indirect means."

Increased human densities also are highly correlated with increased densities of domestic animals. Combined, these increased densities will increase the diseases that infect humanity. Some major zoonotic diseases (originating in animal populations but transmitted to humans) that result from increased animal and human densities are anthrax, botulism, brucellosis, hemorrhagic fevers, plague, leptospirosis, rabies, salmonella, tetanus, trichinosis, and toxoplasmosis. Some major diseases (most having zoonotic origins) that are now considered nonzoonotic as they have been modified over the millennia so that they no longer depend on direct animal to human contact to spread are chicken pox, cholera, ergotism, hookworm, influenza, malaria, measles, mumps, onchocerciasis (river blindness), polio, rubella, and schistosomiasis.[6]

These listings of diseases are not exhaustive, nor can they ever be as knowledge is incomplete and pathogens and their hosts are constantly evolving. Evolving microorganisms ensure that humanity will be constantly exposed to "new" diseases.[7] An examination of the table of contents of textbooks devoted to infectious diseases reveals literally scores of infections that are communicable to or between humans. The listed diseases are thought to be "major" in their impact on the human community. Zoonotic diseases are infections that are typically not chronic to humans. An infected human either recovers or does not from an exposure to a zoonose; the human is typically not the source for further human infections. "Typically" has to be inserted in these statements because under some conditions a zoonotic disease can be spread by humans to other humans; pneumonic plague is a good example of an initial zoonotic infection that can be spread to the lungs and then be passed human to human.

Increased density leads to increased diseases and infections. This results in increasing rates of morbidity and mortality. Increasing mortality lowers population, which lowers output via the reverse of the Smithian cycle outlined above. Offsetting the Smithian virtuous cycle will be a mortality-induced decrease in density that ultimately reduces morbidity and mortality. Morbidity adds complexity to the model, but it is important to the explanation. Increased density increases morbidity as well as mortality. If the microorganisms invading the human body do not lead to a relatively rapid demise, we would expect the debilitated people still to engage in productive activities albeit at a lower level of efficiency. Recall the effects of infectious diseases on the developing brain (and body) of infants and children (Eppig, Fincher, and Thornhill 2010); over time (intellectually and physically) stunted individuals will comprise the bulk of the labor force in the disease-rich Malthusian environment. Given that a unit of infected human labor is less productive than before the organism appeared (uninfected human labor), income from labor activities per human (uncorrected for quality) would decrease.

The long-run equilibrium for our combined model is not transparent. An increase in population may lead to an increase or decrease in the equilibrium wage rate and in income per capita depending on (1) the increase in productivity due to increased specialization and (2) the offsetting reduction in productivity due to increased morbidity. Although there is no unambiguous equilibrium, the main features of the model are notable: morbidity, mortality, and economic growth are all endogenous to the model. Before sanitation, clean water, and modern medical procedures were introduced, an increasing human biomass per unit of land inevitably led (after some lags) to increased human morbidity and mortality.

Abstracting from the historical transportation developments, figure 3.3 illustrates a schematic outline of our combined model. Starting with the middle box and moving upward, population growth can increase per capita incomes and wages via the "virtuous" Smithian cycle (population growth's positive impact on market size and specialization, which impacts positively on incomes). Alternatively, starting with the middle box and moving downward, the impact of population growth on increasing population density leads to a "vicious" cycle of increased morbidity that may actually lower incomes below what had been attained before population growth began. The increase in morbidity reduces the productivity of humans, or alternatively, the amount of effort a person can produce. The increased density also increases mortality, which then reduces population. These latter consequences are identified as the vicious Malthusian cycle.

The schema in figure 3.3 is purposely simple. Omitted are other variables that affect the elements included in the model. For example,

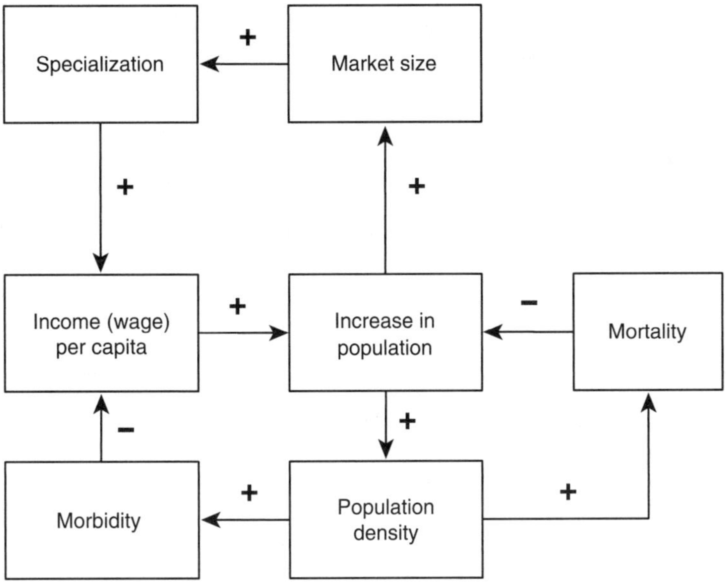

Figure 3.3
Combined model of long-run economic growth

an increase in population density is related to increases in morbidity and mortality; ignored are a host of other factors that mitigate or accentuate its impact. Among the omitted factors are (1) temperature, (2) humidity, (3) consumption patterns, (4) societal behavior that affects the transmission of diseases, and (5) diet.[8]

Wrigley and Schofield (1981) in their history of the English population have similar models (also see Wrigley 1986). However, their models have neither economic growth nor morbidity or mortality as endogenous variables. They do recognize that diseases and high death rates are associated with urbanization, but they do not connect the cause of higher real incomes being the increased market size; that is, population density (Wrigley and Schofield 1981, pp. 415, 463). It appears that in their models economic growth and high wages appear exogenously in "a less healthy environment" (p. 415). Although they do have some intimations of the model presented here, in their explicit models, they treat economic growth as exogenous, and they are Malthusians in their treatment of population growth. To them, population growth lowers real incomes because the price of food is bid up. The link between population growth and lowered real incomes is

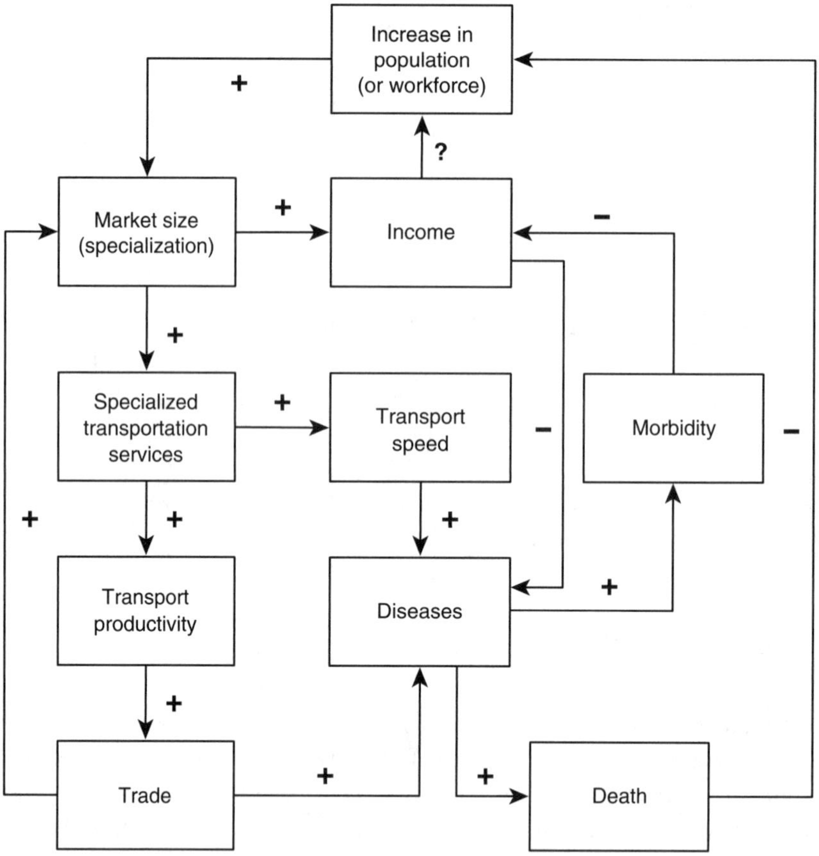

Figure 3.4
Interactions of transport improvements, diseases, and the economy

broken in the Wrigley and Schofield (1981, pp. 474, 478) models for the early and late nineteenth century; prior to the nineteenth century, their models are Malthusian—increased population growth lowers living standards.[9]

The Combined Model with Transportation Developments Included

Figure 3.4 is illustrative of our thinking on the linkages between population growth, developments in transportation, and the economics of diseases. As in our other schematic diagrams, the algebraic signs associated with the avenues of causation indicate the impact that the causal variable has on its target. Starting at the top and working through figure 3.4, note that an increase in population (or the workforce) increases market size and specialization. We focus on the effects of greater specialization on transport. The increase in specialized transport services has two effects: one is to increase the speed of transport; the other is to increase productivity (lower costs per unit). The increased productivity increases the volume of traded goods, which has two effects: (1) it has a feedback effect that increases the size of the market and specialization and (2) it increases the number and variety of diseases transported. The increased speed and regularity of transport services also affect diseases positively because shorter voyage times allow infectious pathogens to survive and to be transmitted more frequently than would have happened with slower transportation.

Transport speed is important in the transmission of diseases because many disease-causing pathogens cannot survive long outside a host body.[10] For example, measles has an incubation period of 8 to 12 days and is contagious for 7 to 9 days (Cliff, Haggert, and Smallman-Raynor 1998, p. 89). Consequently, the probability that the measles virus could survive an ocean voyage of 54 days on an extremely crowded ship, such as the Mayflower, would be remote. The passengers and crew would be rapidly infected and either dead or cured (and not infectious) by the end of the voyage. (A person who has recovered from measles has lifetime immunity and is not infectious.) The same is true for other diseases whose incubation and infectious periods are relatively short, *and* whose victims do not become (relatively) asymptomatic carriers. Typhoid fever is an example of a disease that can infest someone who shows no visible sign of the disease yet harbor it and can spread it. (Typhoid Mary is a notorious example of this in the literature of diseases.) Regardless of these considerations, the reduction in the costs (including money, time, and rigors) of transportation increases the frequency of people and other infectious agents (ticks, lice, mosquitoes, among others) traveling long distances.

With respect to figure 3.4, increasing market size leads to specialized transport services that yield greater speeds and volumes of transport. These increase the transmission of diseases, which increase morbidity and mortality. But the final outcome of increasing specialization on morbidity and mortality is uncertain because an increase in specialization increases income, which *reduces* the susceptibility of people to diseases and their outcomes. Increasing incomes can reduce diseases in a number of ways: (1) the additional resources of a family or individual allowed the consumption of better food and discarding of leftovers obtained earlier but not consumed. In an era that lacked refrigeration, leftovers generated a high risk of food poisoning. (2) More money allowed the family to obtain bigger living quarters; the increase in the space per member of the living unit reduced the transmission of infectious diseases. (3) Additional income allowed the purchase of more clothing and cleaning, and those reduced the transmission of arthropod-borne diseases. And (4) more money allowed the purchase of other goods and services (quinine, clean water, waste removal, among others) that reduced the probability that members of the living unit will contract an infectious disease. However, before the late nineteenth century, increased incomes were not sufficient to reduce the increased morbidity and mortality associated with cities and urbanization. Before modern sanitation, purified water supplies, food preservation, refrigeration, and other such developments, an increase in income may have ameliorated some of the effects of increased density on diseases and their consequences, but in no way did it completely offset these consequences. Increased density, then, was conjoined with increased morbidity and mortality.

In a series of papers, Fogel (1986, 1991, 1992, 1995) argues that better nutrition was instrumental in reducing morbidity and mortality. His argument is not inconsistent with the one presented here, although we place a much greater weight on amelioration of diseases and, as a result, on sanitation and other public health measures. Taking explicit exception to Fogel's nutrition hypothesis are Tsoulouhas (1992) and Johansson (1994). Tsoulouhas finds that technological change is endogenously related to population growth and thus better explains the reduction in morbidity and mortality, and Johansson emphasizes the absence of any link between nutrition (and/or income) and morbidity and mortality prior to the twentieth century.[11]

A Nineteenth-Century Example: The "Antebellum Puzzle" and Diseases

The scholarly literature on living standards in the pre–Civil War United States has two contradictory strands. One is that income (both total and per capita) in the United States increased from soon after the War of 1812 through 1860. The other strand is that America experienced a long-term decline in the biological standard of living, based on anthropometric evidence of a decrease in the heights of Americans starting with (circa) 1830s birth cohorts.[12] Data supporting both propositions appear to be well founded, so there is an "Antebellum Puzzle": Why did human heights decline as income rose? One explanation suggests that when welfare or well-being is assessed historically, traditional measures of income might be inadequate. The reason is that traditional monetary measures of the level of income may overestimate the true growth of income, or they may not accurately measure the distribution of income, especially, the distribution of food resources, over the entire population. The proponents of anthropometrics argue that in some cases anthropometric measures are superior measures of welfare or well-being.

An alternative explanation for the so-called Antebellum Puzzle of increasing incomes and falling human heights, and the one we espouse, is that the disease environment deteriorated even as incomes rose during the nineteenth century. The deteriorating disease environment affected the biological standard of living and, as a result, average heights fell. Before the nineteenth century, local and regional disease pools predominated. But with the turn of the century, these local and regional diseases, both from within the nation and from abroad, became more widespread throughout the United States causing a decline in the biological standard of living. The spread of diseases was a worldwide phenomenon of the nineteenth century, paradoxically reducing the health status of populations as incomes increased at unprecedented rates of sustained growth. The American experience was one reflection of this phenomenon.

The integration of local and regional disease pools took place for a number of reasons; we highlight six of them. (1) The rapid expansion of the cotton South and the system of plantation agriculture cultivated by an enslaved African and African-American labor force spread diseases. (2) The growth in population, increased population densities, and the increased biomass (both human and nonhuman) facilitated the transmission of disease-bearing pathogens. (3) The growth of great cities (apart from the general increase in populations) allowed diseases to exist where before they would not have long survived. Cities provided a habitat and a focal point for diseases that had previously been unknown or episodic in the United States. (4) The declines in the rigors, time, and money costs of transportation allowed the sick, infected, and asymptomatic to travel across vast distances, infecting people along their routes and at their final destinations. (5) Beginning in the early nineteenth century, declines in transport costs and times initiated the migrations of peoples across continents and oceans; these migrations (both domestic and foreign) exposed natives and migrants to new disease ecologies that adversely affected both. The migrants were exposed to diseases that were new to them, but native to the ecologies of their new homes. And the migrants brought *their* diseases with them, adversely affecting the natives. (The word "migrant" is not literally accurate; tourists, sailors, merchants, and other people who traveled long distances also spread diseases.) (6) The declines in transport costs and times also led to a vast increase in the absolute volume of trade; this also brought diseases to both the established and newly settled areas of the United States. Falling mean heights and rising real incomes are now explicable, and the Antebellum Puzzle evaporates.[13]

Concluding Thoughts on Diseases and Long-Run Economic Growth

Ambiguities abound in all aspects of life. Specialization increases human productivity, output, and living standards and is limited by the size of the market. Increasing populations and incomes, reductions in transport costs and times, and changes in technology enable markets to increase enormously. Increasing market size carries with it increased specialization and its concomitant benefits that have the effect of enhancing the agents that caused the increased market size. But the virtuous cycle of increasing market size, population, and income (or progress) was cemented in a Faustian bargain with parasites and pathogens.

Before the era of modern sanitation, public health, and low-cost potable water, increases in human populations and economic activities were accompanied by increases in the pathogens that attack and parasitize humans. The integration of the global economy in the nineteenth and twentieth centuries also integrated diseases globally. The nineteenth century was a watershed; in that century, diseases spread and proliferated enormously. Cholera escaped from its confines in the Indian subcontinent so that by 1800 it was in Europe and it crossed the Atlantic soon thereafter. "Diarrheal diseases" (an appellation that is used because there are too many different pathogens that cause the symptom to have each one separately identified) spread and were killers throughout the world. Tuberculosis ("consumption") took on an added virulence within the confines of densely populated great cities. Sexually transmitted diseases also proliferated in the anonymity of urban conglomerations. Other diseases wrecked havoc and caused devastation in populations that had little or no previous exposure to them.

All these diseases were extraordinary burdens on humanity. Countervailing these developments were advances in science, health, medicine, and sanitation. Before the nineteenth century, it was obvious to virtually all knowledgeable observers that great cities were pest holes devouring people. Before the nineteenth century, death and disease were constant, albeit unwelcome, companions in the major cities of ancient Rome, Byzantium, Venice, London, and Paris. The nineteenth century differed from these earlier times, building on the framework established in the eighteenth century—the Enlightenment, or the Age of Reason. In the nineteenth century, humanity witnessed a systematic and effective attack on the spread of pathogens that afflicted humanity. As one of the agents of the attack on disease, Louis Pasteur said, "Fortune favors a prepared mind." The nineteenth century mind was prepared in a variety of ways to initiate advances against human disease. The Enlightenment taught people to ask questions rather than deferring to "God's will"; the microscope, modern chemistry, statistics, and the scientific method of empiricism were all necessary preconditions for a sustained counter attack on infectious disease. We should not, however, forget that the population was large enough and rich enough to afford and allow people to specialize and study "esoteric" subjects such as the life cycle of parasitic diseases. Economics has played a part, and by no means a minor role, in the pageant of humanity's labors against disease and premature death.

4 The Colonists' Choice of Agricultural Labor in Early America

Following the European Voyages of Discovery, the New World was ultimately populated with Old World peoples, pathogens, plants, and animals. The African and European peoples who settled in North America set in motion interchanges of organisms that critically altered its regional disease ecologies. The changes in disease ecologies were not uniform; climate and geography affected which diseases would predominate in the various regions of North America, and these changes affected the economic possibilities of settlers. Consequently, an explanation of the settlement of America requires the integration of economic motives, the ecological consequences of economic actions, and the feedback effects of a changed ecology on economic possibilities.

Here we provide our explanation (model) of the colonists' choice of servile labor in Early America.[1] The options available to colonialists in seventeenth and eighteenth-century British North America were between African slaves and European indentured servants. Servile labor (both indentured servants and slaves) has to be economically and financially viable in the long run or it will not last. Furthermore, businesses that do not return to entrepreneurs all their costs, including "normal" returns (profits) to invested assets and in-kind inputs (such as labor and management skills) will cease operating in the long run. All inputs into the production process will receive, at the minimum, their opportunity costs or they will migrate to other employments; this is true for physical capital and labor, and it is true for both servile and nonservile labor.

Economic Considerations in the Choice of Servile Labor

"Firms" in the British North American colonies primarily consisted of commercial farmers (planters) who were in the business of providing agricultural goods primarily to the markets in Britain and secondarily to other markets. In the early British colonies, commercial farmers were heavily engaged in the production of sugar in the West Indies and tobacco in the Upper South. These enterprises depended on bound servile labor, indentured servants (almost exclusively of European ancestry) and slaves (almost exclusively of African ancestry). Whether a colonial planter chose to use slaves or servants as labor depended on the relative costs and revenues of employing them. We explain in simplified terms the economics involved in a colonial planter's decision.

Economic models can be used to predict the behavior of profit-seeking firms. Given that New World planters were competitive (price takers) in both the markets to which they sold and in markets from which they bought, then, in the long run, competition would force down prices to the minimum of the typical firm's (planter's) average costs. These costs include normal returns to inputs (labor, capital, land, and enterprise). When the market price equals average cost (at the profit-maximizing rate of output) the firm stays in the market and continues producing because all factors of production (inputs) are earning what they reasonably could expect to be earning in their next best alternative. In the economist's jargon, all inputs are earning their opportunity costs when a firm operates at the minimum of its average costs.

If, at a market price for the output where other firms are just covering opportunity costs, an individual firm uses an innovation (technique or input) that yields economic profits (returns greater than opportunity costs), one would expect that other firms would emulate the profitable one and the innovating process would spread throughout the industry. As more and more firms in the sector (agriculture) adopt these procedures, there would be an increase in product supply at the initial price (where opportunity costs were just being met for all firms except the one earning the economic profits). Eventually only firms that use the technique or inputs that the innovative firm introduced will be able to cover average costs, because the increase in output caused by the spread of the lower cost innovation results in an increase in supply and lower market prices.[2]

There are reasons why innovative firms (in this case, planters) in a competitive (price-taking) industry may not worry about keeping innovations secret. If a neighbor adopts the low-cost methods, the increase in output that comes about because of the adoption will have a negligible effect on the market price of the output being produced. In competitive price-taking markets, no individual producer or a small set of producers can affect the market price of the output. For example, an individual tobacco producer, or a combination of a handful of them, in the Chesapeake region of eighteenth-century colonial America would have had no an appreciable impact on the price of tobacco in Europe. The combined output of a handful of colonial producers could not affect market conditions sufficiently to move prices.

Competition for profits leads firms to adopt profitable innovations, and the innovations lead to an increase in output that causes a reduction in price. After the innovation is fully digested only firms using the innovating techniques will be covering opportunity costs (making normal profits); firms that resist the innovations will be unprofitable and fail to exist in the long run. In terms of the provision of labor to the British North American colonies, if servants and slaves are equally productive (after deducting their maintenance costs), then in the long run profit-maximizing colonialists will exclusively utilize the cheaper source of labor. This analysis presents a problem because the British colonialists used both servants and slaves even though servants were, on average, cheaper for much of the colonial era.

Financial Considerations in the Choice of Servile Labor: The Costs of Slaves and Servants

To a colonial planter, bound servile labor is just another form of capital; like physical capital (land, equipment, animals, structures, and so forth), indentured servants or slaves are durable inputs that provide streams of net revenue into the future (total revenues attributable to the assets less the costs of upkeep and maintenance). To acquire a servant or slave a colonial planter has to bear the acquisition cost (or purchase price) of servile labor in the present, but he receives most of the revenues that the labor yields in future years. Because indentured servants and slaves are long-lived—they are productive beyond the present period—the concept of present value is necessary to understand the demand for servile labor. Present value allows colonial planters to determine what the stream of net revenue that servile labor produces in the future is worth *now*. To decide whether to purchase bound labor, and what type of labor (indentured servants or slaves), the planter must compare an outlay made now with a stream of net revenues extending years into the future. To make this comparison, the planter has to (implicitly, if not explicitly) determine the present discounted value of the stream of net revenues that the servile labor produces throughout its working period, typically extending years into the future.[3]

The present value of any durable asset depends on (1) the annual amount of net revenue that the asset produces (the productivity or quality of the asset), (2) when the revenues are received (for example, one year from the present or ten years), (3) how many years the stream of future revenues is received (the durability of the asset), and (4) the interest rate (the opportunity cost of capital).[4] Knowing the discounted present value of future receipts allows their comparison with expenditures in the present. The value of any amount (£1) in the present is always more than the value of the same amount (£1) received in the future; this is because there is an opportunity cost for the use of capital over time.

We begin by clarifying and simplifying several issues in the development of our model of the choice of servile labor. First, the New World planters were price takers. This means no individual producer could affect (1) interest rates (the opportunity cost of capital), (2) the prices of the inputs they purchased (here we are concerned with the prices of slaves and servants used in the production of crops—we are explicitly confining the analysis to unskilled agricultural labor), and (3) the prices of the outputs they produced (primarily, sugar and tobacco). These observations are an accurate depiction of the observational reality that prevailed in the financial, labor, and output markets in the colonial period. No individual planter could affect the market prices for inputs or outputs by altering how much he individually would buy or sell. In terms of basic economics, the supply curves of inputs (labor) bought by the individual firms (farmers and planters) were horizontal at the going market prices (they were perfectly elastic). Similarly, the demand curves for the outputs that were produced were horizontal to the individual firm at their market prices. The market demand and supply curves were appropriately sloped, but the individual producer was too small an economic actor to affect prices.

Second, for now we assume that the net productivity of the two types of labor (servants and slaves) was the same. The assumption of equal net productivities means that either the maintenance costs (the costs of clothing, food, and shelter, among others) of slaves and servants were identical or that the type of labor with greater productivity also had sufficiently greater maintenance costs to ensure that net yields (earnings) were the same. Later on, we argue that an assumption of equal productivities of the two types of labor is incorrect, and is contradicted by biological, financial, and medical evidence. The reason we begin with the assumption of equal productivities is to highlight the implications of the assumption.

Third, we assume average uncertainty; this means that planters knew the average (mean) price of the output produced and the average (mean) economic life of all assets including labor. This is a simplifying assumption that allows us to concentrate on the economic and financial decision-making with certain knowledge. Any other assumption would be arbitrary and make the economic and financial calculations intractable.

Now suppose a colonial planter knew (1) the net revenue stream for labor (by assumption, the net productivities of slaves and servants are identical), (2) how many years the revenue stream will last for each type of labor, (3) the price of slaves and the price of servants, and (4) the market rate of interest. Knowing these parameters, it becomes a relatively simple exercise to determine the relative profitability of slaves versus servants. For example, suppose that a servant can be employed for 5 years, costs £10, generates a net income of £2.5 per year, and the interest rate is 10 percent per annum; next suppose a slave costs £20, lives for 20 years, generates the same net income of £2.5 per year, and the interest rate is the same 10 percent per annum. It is now a matter of calculating the present values of the two income streams (one for servants and one for slaves) and comparing the values to their acquisition costs (prices).[5] The discounted present value for a slave earning £2.5 per year for 20 years is £21.28 at an interest rate of 10 percent; for a servant working for 5 years, the present value of its income stream is £9.48. In this example, the purchase of a slave is economically viable because the present value of its net revenues are greater than its purchase price, while the purchase of a servant is uneconomic because its purchase price is greater than the present value of its net revenues (£9.48). The purchase prices of labor (£10 for a servant and £20 for a slave) represent the costs of acquisition; the net present values (£9.48 for a servant and £21.28 for a slave) are equal to the present value of their future earnings.[6]

Notice the critical nature of the interest rate. Suppose that a slave works and lives for 100 years and that the price of the slave rises to £30. In this situation, the purchase of a slave is uneconomic because the present value of the 100 years of earnings (slightly less than £25) is less than the cost of the slave. Increasing the working life of a slave 400 percent (fivefold) does not offset a 50 percent increase in the price of the slave. This is because revenues to be received in the distant future are more highly discounted relative to prices and costs paid immediately. Since slaves were purchased in the present, every £1 paid for a slave now (year $t = 0$) has a present value of £1, and this is much greater than the present value of £1 received, for example, 25 years from now (year $t = 25$). The present value of £1 to be received in 25 years is only £.09 at a 10 percent interest rate. If instead the interest rate were 5 percent, the present value of £1 received 25 years in the future increases to £.295 now.

Historically we know within reasonable bounds slave prices, servant prices, and interest rates. Slave prices fluctuated relatively more than servant prices while interest rates fluctuated less than the prices of labor. Throughout most of the existence of the North American slave trade the prices of slaves were substantial, averaging about £20 for most of the seventeenth century, £25 to the mid-eighteenth century, and over £35 from the mid-eighteenth century to the American Revolutionary War. Table 4.1 and figure 4.1 reproduce Bean's (1975) estimates of five-year average British-American slave prices from 1633–37 to 1773–75.[7] In table 4.1, we also include the most recent data on slave prices available from Eltis, Lewis, and Richardson (2005, p. 679); these data are based on the sale prices of 228,877 enslaved Africans sold between 1674 and 1807. The data represent sales of males normalized for sale in Jamaica. Eltis, Lewis, and Richardson reduced the prices of slaves sold in what became the United States by 5 percent because shipping costs to the mainland colonies were higher than to Jamaica and their slave prices are normalized for sale in Jamaica. (Their data are explained more completely in Eltis and Richardson 2004, pp. 183–85.) The Eltis, Lewis, and Richardson (2005) time series is not as complete for the seventeenth century as Bean's, but it is the most recent, and the data are based on the largest number of actual slave sales. Despite the time difference between when the two studies were conducted (one is 1975, the other is 2005), the data are in close agreement. (The five-year periods for each price observation do not exactly overlap for the two sets of data.) We rely on the Bean data because they offer a more complete coverage of the colonial time period and we wanted a series that was gathered in a consistent manner. The slave prices in Eltis, Lewis, and Richardson (2005), however, are in constant pounds, normalized for prime age males (as are the Bean data), and they are based on a very

Table 4.1
Five-year average slave prices in the British colonies, normalized for males in Jamaica

Bean data			Eltis, Lewis, and Richardson data		
Years	Price in £ sterling		Years	Price in £ sterling	
1633–1637	£50.00	(1)			
1638–1642	£16.50	(3)			
1643–1647	£17.03	(2)			
1648–1652	—	—			
1653–1657	£31.00	(1)			
1658–1662	£21.12	(3)			
1663–1667	£21.13	(13)			
1668–1672	£20.28	(14)			
1673–1677	£22.05	(11)	1674	£18.51	(732)
1678–1682	£19.31	(26)	1675–1679	£18.15	(9,108)
1683–1687	£19.56	(9)	1680–1684	£18.37	(9,413)
1688–1692	£23.07	(3)	1685–1689	£20.25	(9,302)
1693–1697	£24.72	(7)	1690–1694	£19.76	(5,882)
1698–1702	£23.52	(19)	1695–1699	£20.32	(5,870)
1703–1707	£26.42	(18)	1700–1704	£23.39	(13,837)
1708–1712	£23.64	(21)	1705–1709	£27.38	(10,104)
1713–1717	£29.33	(4)	1710–1714	£22.55	(1,110)
1718–1722	£21.98	(6)	1715–1719	£18.98	(1,725)
1723–1727	£24.55	(15)	1720–1724	£27.41	(6,809)
1728–1732	£24.08	(12)	1725–1729	£32.59	(2,250)
1733–1737	£21.97	(2)	1730–1734	£25.18	(2,563)
1738–1742	£28.13	(4)	1735–1739	£32.68	(5,288)
1743–1747	£31.56	(6)	1740–1744	£28.46	(8,537)
1748–1752	£26.96	(5)	1745–1749	£28.63	(3,851)
1753–1757	£33.88	(22)	1750–1754	£35.88	(6,793)
1758–1762	£32.86	(7)	1755–1759	£34.09	(13,485)
1763–1767	£35.34	(19)	1760–1764	£32.33	(4,865)
1768–1772	£39.82	(20)	1765–1769	£39.22	(6,386)
1773–1775	£42.91	(14)	1770–1774	£43.45	(16,274)
			1775–1779	£43.28	(17,692)
			1780–1784	£40.17	(7,549)
			1785–1789	£55.57	(23,361)
			1790–1794	£52.65	(26,771)
			1795–1799	£43.86	(7,004)

Sources: Bean (1975); Eltis, Lewis, and Richardson (2005).
Note: While both the Bean and the Eltis, Lewis, and Richardson slave prices are reported as five-year averages, the last slave price reported by Bean is actually for a three-year average and the first slave price reported by Eltis, Lewis, and Richardson is actually for one year only. In the Bean data, the "number of sources" is in parentheses and refers to the number of reference materials that Bean used to derive slave prices. Typically each source reports on the sale of many slaves. In the Eltis, Lewis, and Richardson data, the "number of slaves sold" is in parentheses.

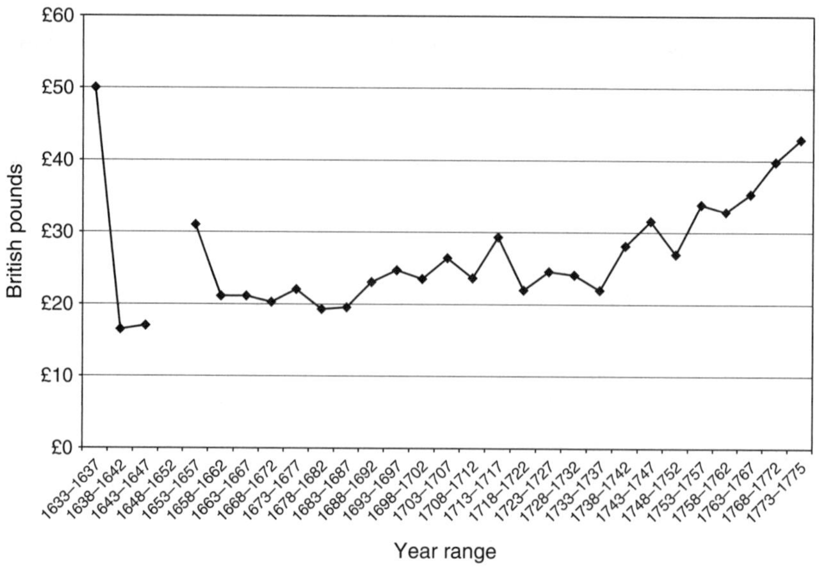

Figure 4.1
British and American slave prices: five-year average prices between 1633–1637 and 1773–1775. Note: The slave prices are reported as five-year averages except for Bean's last reported price, which is the average for a three-year period only. Source: Bean (1975)

large amount of data. Regardless, if we were to use the Eltis, Lewis, and Richardson (2005) data rather than the Bean (1975) data, it would have an immaterial effect on the trend in slave prices.

The prices of indentured servants are more problematic than those of slaves.[8] Servants voluntarily indentured themselves to pay for their passage to the New World. The costs of transporting an indentured servant or a paying passenger were virtually identical.[9] Because the price of passage was relatively high, indentured servants, in effect, had to borrow to finance their voyages. To repay the shipper, servants agreed to bind (indenture) themselves for a fixed period of time. Since the cost that all servants borrowed to undertake the voyage was the same (transportation costs per servant did not vary regardless of their ages and skills), the individual characteristics that affected each servant's productivity was reflected in the length of time that the servant had to endure to pay off the costs of the voyage. Servant productivities varied by the servant's skills, sex, and health (among other factors); consequently, the length of the indentureship reflected not only the costs of the passage across the Atlantic but the estimated productivity of the individual servant. Before agreeing to indenture themselves, servants bargained with the shipper over the length of their indentureship. These negotiations resulted in longer indentureships for younger and unskilled servants, and shorter ones for healthy and skilled servants.

In order to compare the financial merits of acquiring a servant versus a slave, one has to know servant prices. Grubb (2000, p. 103) lists the mean prices of indentured servants for Philadelphia and Baltimore for various years. In Philadelphia for a sample of 471 servants for the years 1745 to 1746, the mean price was £8.56 with a mean indentureship of 4.41 years; during the years 1771 to 1773, the mean price was £8.58 for a sample of 956 servants with a mean indentureship of 3.99 years. In Baltimore, Grubb (2000, p. 103) reports that the mean price for a sample of 125 servants for the years 1767 to 1768 was £8.82 (data on the length of the contract were not available). These mean prices, though, were affected by the characteristics of the servants, their destinations, and the time of year.[10] Galenson (1981a, pp. 97–106) also reports on servant contracts in colonial America, estimating that the mean indenture contract for an illiterate 20-year-old male bound for Pennsylvania (his reference category) was 56 months for the 1718 to 1759 period. He likewise estimates the effects of age, gender, location, and skill levels on the length of the contract, with an additional four months added on for being 18 years old. In his discussion of servant prices, Galenson (1981a) indicates that the mean price of servants with four years (48 months) remaining on their contract was £8.95, the median £9, and the modal price £10 (p. 100).

The price we use is £12. This price is an adjustment to the servant prices found in Galenson (1981a) and Grubb (2000). Using Galenson's mean price of £8.95 (the highest of the various mean prices) as a starting point, and increasing it by 25 percent to adjust for an 18-year-old having to serve 25 percent longer (60 months rather than 48), yields a servant price for an 18-year-old male of £11 (£11.18 to be exact). Atack and Passell (1994, p. 45) contend that £11 was the price that a purchaser had to pay a shipper for a servant with the following characteristics: an illiterate male, 18 years old, unskilled, and suitable for agricultural labor (an appropriate comparison to the alternative of the purchase of the typical African slave); the length of indentureship for a servant with these characteristics in colonial Pennsylvania was five years. The prices of servants reported in the literature, however, are biased downward as measures of the cost of servants because they do not reflect the "freedom dues" and other benefits (typically clothes) that were more than occasionally awarded to servants at the completion of their indentureship. Since these benefits were awarded at the completion of the indentureship, the benefits have to be discounted to get their present value. The acquisition of a servant required an outlay of currency at the time of purchase (we use £11) and another outlay (freedom dues) five years later. To adjust for these freedom dues, an additional £1 was added to the £11 price that the purchaser had to pay to approximate the present value of the freedom dues that were paid to the servant after completion of the indentureship.[11] Servant prices were relatively constant, while slave prices fluctuated substantially. With a servant price of £12, a slave priced at £20 cost 66 percent more than a servant; at a £25 price the slave cost 100 percent more than a servant and at £35 the slave cost nearly 200 percent more than a servant.

Interest rates do and did fluctuate. The best compendium for what we know about colonial interest rates comes from Homer and Sylla (1991); their summary table for the colonial period has interest rates in colonial British North America varying from 5 to 10 percent per year (p. 279). The lowest rates mentioned in Homer and Sylla are not market rates but regulated or government-set interest rates. Benjamin Franklin is quoted as saying that prevailing interest rates in Philadelphia were 6 to 10 percent. We cannot say with any certainty what interest rate prevailed at a specific time, so we have made calculations using interest rates varying from 5 to 10 percent. We are reasonably confident that colonial interest rates were within these bounds. The reader can assess how sensitive the calculation of profitability is to changes in the interest rate with our data.

Summarizing, in order to compare the relative financial merits of acquiring a servant or a slave, one has to know (1) the interest rate that applies to the purchase of agricultural capital, (2) the prices of slaves and servants, (3) the net revenues each produces, and (4) the length of time that servants and slaves would be producing revenue. Now, once again, suppose that the annual net revenue of slaves is constant and identical to that of servants, and the interest (discount) rate applied to the acquisition of a slave or a servant is also the same. The average price of slaves varied over time. For convenience, we analyze four alternative prices for slaves: (1) a (low) price of £20 consistent with the approximate average of British-American slave prices during much of the seventeenth century, (2) a price of £25 consistent with the price prevailing in the eighteenth century to circa 1750, (3) a price of £30 that

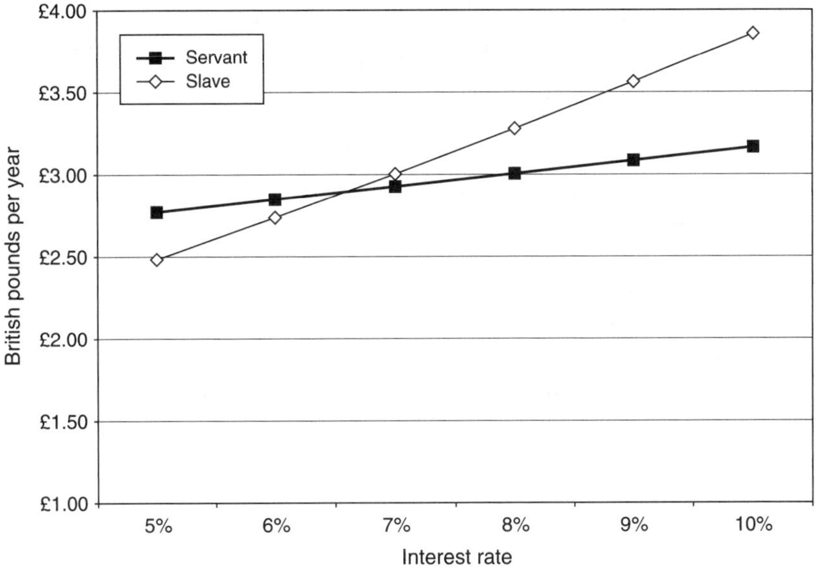

Figure 4.2
Annual returns necessary to amortize a slave or servant at various interest rates: Slave price = £35, slave work life = 25 years; servant price = £12, servant work life = 5 years

is used for comparison, and (4) a (high) price of £35 consistent with prevailing prices post-1750 to the beginning of the Revolutionary War.[12]

We analyze five contingencies for the length of time a slave laborer provided net revenues: 7 years, 12 years, 16 years, 20 years, and 25 years. Seven years is the estimated life expectancy of newly arrived African slaves in the West Indies; we use this later to elaborate on the health effects of tropical regions. Twelve years corresponds to some estimated slave life expectancies after arrival in New England in the early to mid-eighteenth century, 16 years corresponds to some estimated life expectancies of slaves after arrival in the Philadelphia area, and 20 and 25 years are considered a moderate upper bound and an extreme upper bound, respectively. Obviously, the longer a slave works the more financially advantageous an investment in a slave is at any given interest rate.

Figure 4.2 shows what we are trying to accomplish in its simplest form. In figure 4.2, we have only two labor options: one is the purchase of a slave for £35 who has a working life of 25 years (the line with diamonds on it); the second is the purchase of an indentured servant for £12 whose indentureship lasts for 5 years (the line with boxes on it). The vertical axis measures the annual returns necessary to amortize (to repay the principal plus interest) the capital investment in labor over its working life (British pounds is the unit of measure). The horizontal axis represents various interest rates. The line with diamonds represents the annual returns required to repay the purchase price and interest of a slave with a price of £35 and a working life of 25 years (see table A.4, col. $E_0 = 25$, in appendix A).[13] For example, at an interest rate of 8 percent, a slave must yield £3.279 of net revenue per year to repay (amortize the principal and interest) an investment of £35 in slave capital. The line with boxes shows the net returns required to repay an investment of £12 in an indentured servant whose indentureship is for five years. Where the boxed line lies below the diamonded line delineates the interest rates where investments in servant capital are more profitable than those in slave capital. Conversely, interest rates where the amortization payments for slave capital (diamonded line) are below those of servant capital (boxed line) are those interest rates where slave capital is more profitable. The intersection point of the slave and servant lines is the critical interest rate where the relative profitability of an investment in the two forms of human capital change.

Figures 4.3 through 4.6 illustrate the relationship between interest rates, the length of service, and the minimum net returns per year that have to be earned for a slave or a servant to be profitable. The calculated net returns per year are for slave prices of £20 (figure 4.3), £25 (figure 4.4), £30 (figure 4.5), and £35 (figure 4.6); and for a servant price of £12 (in each figure). (The calculated net returns for all cases are reported in tables A.1 through A.5 in appendix A.) Each figure shows the returns that had to be achieved per year at a given interest rate for the slave purchase to be completely amortized (the original investment repaid plus interest charges) at the specified rate of interest. The calculations were carried out for interest rates of 5 through 10 percent. Different slave life expectancies (expected working lives) are shown as different line segments labeled E_7, E_{12}, E_{16}, E_{20}, and E_{25} for the length of services 7, 12, 16, 20, and 25 years, respectively. Each figure also depicts the annual amount necessary to amortize a servant, whose price is £12 and indentureship is 5 years, at varying interest rates; the servant line is the boxed line in each figure.

Figures 4.3 through 4.6 reveal in basic terms the details of the financial aspects of investment in servile labor in British North America. The figures show that at the same interest rate it was only at very low slave prices, or alternatively, at moderate slave prices it was only at relatively

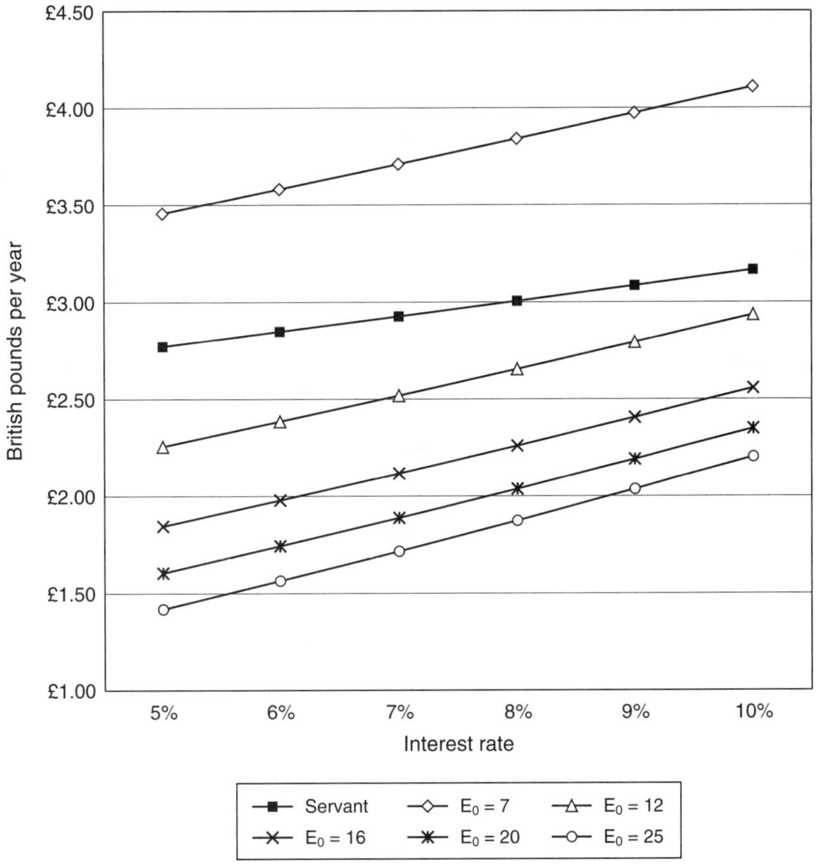

Figure 4.3
Annual returns necessary to amortize a slave or servant at various interest rates: Slave price = £20, slave work life = E_0 years; servant price = £12, servant work life = 5 years

low interest rates, that the profitability of a slave was as high as that of a servant. (Note that the line segment E_7 for a seven-year slave life—the life expectancy of a slave in the West Indies—is unambiguously the least profitable in each figure at all indicated interest rates; the case of the West Indies is discussed below.) Under an assumption of profit seeking, if servants were more profitable, then only servants would be purchased, and conversely if slaves were more profitable, only slaves would be purchased.

The figures indicate that under the regime of the actual prices of slaves and servants that prevailed during most of the seventeenth and eighteenth centuries, the purchase of a slave was not profitable under

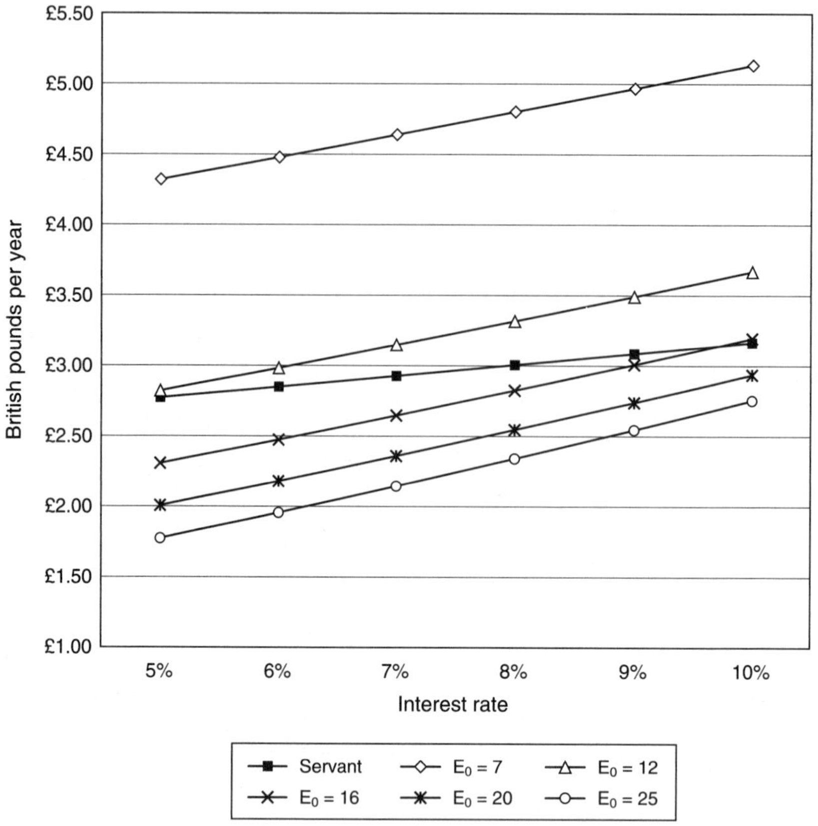

Figure 4.4
Annual returns necessary to amortize a slave or servant at various interest rates: Slave price = £25, slave work life = E_0 years; servant price = £12, servant work life = 5 years

the assumption of equal productivities of slave and servant labor (see also tables A.1 though A.5 in appendix A). Here observational reality intrudes. Our analysis implies that only if the present value of slaves and of servants were equal at the prevailing market rate of interest would both servants and slaves be imported; this is very unlikely given the changing prices of slaves and changing interest rates. Yet historically we know that both slaves and servants were imported and employed throughout the colonial period; thus the predicted outcome of only observing either slave or servant imports (not both) at a particular time is contradicted. Recall that these predictions are made under the assumption that servants and slaves were equally productive; we believe this assumption is false. Historical market data are not

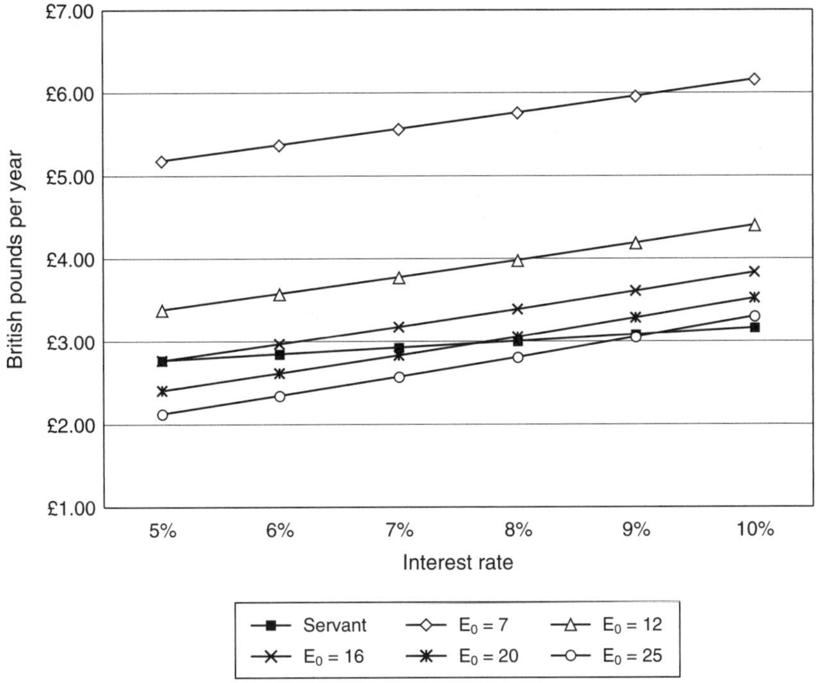

Figure 4.5
Annual returns necessary to amortize a slave or servant at various interest rates: Slave price = £30, slave work life = E_0 years; servant price = £12, servant work life = 5 years

consistent with the assumption's implications, and because there are many observations that exist for servant prices, slave prices, and interest rates during the colonial era, the overwhelmingly likely reason why slaves were purchased despite their higher prices is that slaves were more productive than servants in certain regional environments of British America.

The calculated returns for slave labor in the West Indies (E_0 = 7) shown in figures 4.3 through 4.6 and reported in appendix A (tables A.1 through A.4) are illustrative. If we assume that European servants had the same productivity in the West Indies as African slaves *and* that servants lived out their indentureships, then there is no reason profit-seeking planters would consider slave labor. The payments to amortize the purchase of slave labor in the West Indies dwarf those for servants at all interest rates. Even supposing that servants had a preference for not going to the West Indies, involuntary servants (convicts) would be sent there if someone were willing to buy them. There were some con-

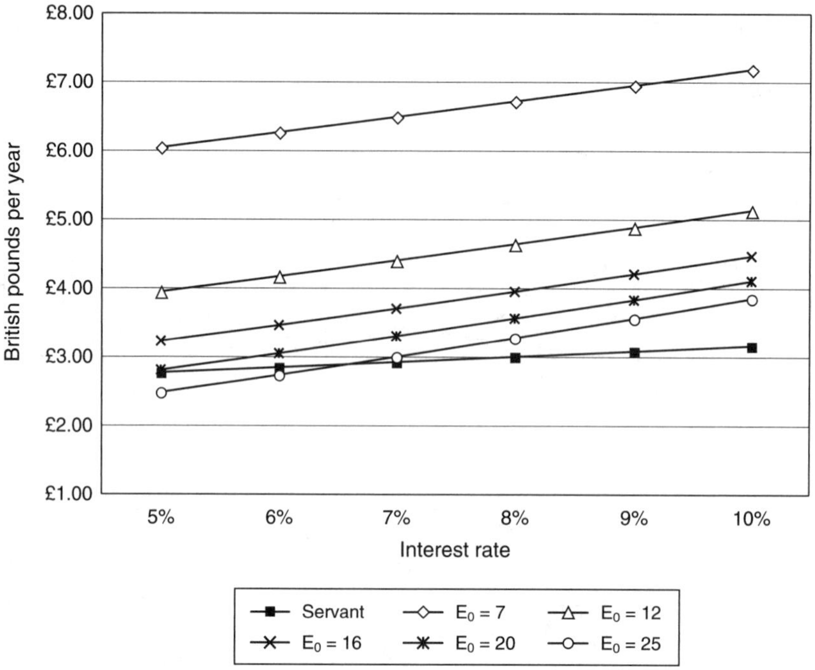

Figure 4.6
Annual returns necessary to amortize a slave or servant at various interest rates: Slave price = £35, slave work life = E_0 years; servant price = £12, servant work life = 5 years

victs sent to the British West Indian colonies, but the majority were sent to and purchased in the North American mainland colonies. This is indicative that slaves, despite their higher capital costs, were more profitable in tropical disease environments than were European servants; African slaves were more productive there.

The Role of the Disease Environment in the Choice of Servile Labor

A profit-seeking colonial planter would have compared the expected purchase price of servile labor to the expected present value of its stream of future net revenues (earnings). The planter would have acquired an indentured servant (or a slave) if the expected present value of the net revenue stream was greater than the expected purchase price. In addition to the standard factors (age, experience, skills, and so forth) that affect labor productivity, the productivity of servile labor and its expected net revenue stream in colonial America depended on the health and life expectancy of the laborer, because labor productivity, at least in part, was dependent on the risk of illness (morbidity) and the risk of death (mortality). In turn, the morbidity and mortality of slaves (Africans) and servants (Europeans) depended critically on the disease ecology in which they lived and worked in the New World. Disease ecologies were region specific to the New World.[14]

Microbiology and evolutionary theory explain why morbidity and mortality differed across populations of different ancestral heritages and differed regionally and locally. Africans and Europeans had disparate biological reactions to the different disease (microparasite) environments that evolved across regions of the British New World. While disease environments and populations interact over time, particular disease organisms are not universal. Diseases evolve in specific environments; an organism that is virulent to humans in one locality or at a particular time may be mild or nonexistent in another location or time. Human populations also evolve and are specific to given areas: a population native to a given region has lived and reproduced in the disease environment specific to that area. Natives of a region will tend to be relatively resistant to the diseases that predominate in their local environment and relatively susceptible to the disease environment of a different and distant location.

Once Africans and Europeans were introduced into the Americas, and their numbers grew beyond a threshold level, a biological process was set in motion that led to irreversible changes in the disease environment across the North American New World. The biological process involved the introduction of Old World pathogens carried over by Africans and Europeans; some of these pathogens survived and became endemic in areas where the environment was suitable for them. As a result different regional disease environments evolved. In New England, cold-weather diseases predominated, primarily those involving upper respiratory infections. The disease environment changed to a mixture of cold-weather and warm-weather diseases as one traveled south on the mainland. In the southern mainland colonies, the disease environment was a mixture of the diseases that were in New England and in the tropical Caribbean. In the Caribbean, the disease environment consisted almost entirely of warm-weather diseases, primarily various fevers and intestinal nematodes. This process was path dependent: the initial labor supply choices, whether because of accident or design, changed the biological environment irreversibly.[15]

The changed disease environment had economic consequences for colonial America; the productivity of labor, and the lifetime productivity of Africans and Europeans changed after both migrated. The altered disease ecology led to regional differences in morbidity and mortality based on a population's ancestral heritage. Over time the current and the lifetime productivity of Africans and Europeans became sufficiently dissimilar across different regions in America that they could no longer be regarded as close substitutes in unskilled agricultural tasks in the same region. This view of changing labor productivity is in sharp contrast to the existing literature on the transition to slaves in the Caribbean and Chesapeake. The literature treats African slaves and European servants generally as close substitutes in unskilled agricultural tasks—only relative costs mattered for the choice of labor.[16] Yet this assumption is contradicted by the data that show that despite widely disparate relative prices, both servants and slaves were imported throughout the colonial period as agricultural laborers, albeit—and this is the crucial point—not in the same geographies.

Specifying the exact temporal sequence of changing morbidity and mortality requires information and data that do not exist. An exact explanation necessitates placing our economic and biological model of the choice of servile labor in a dynamic framework, which in turn requires specifying the exact biological interaction and time sequence of the introduction of the Old World diseases into different regions of the North American New World. This specificity is unknown and perhaps unknowable. Nevertheless, we can indicate the factors that generally affected the interaction and time sequence and, by inference, reproduction and selection. Changes in the morbidity and mortality rates for Africans and Europeans would have depended on (1) the location where they lived, (2) the nature of their acquired immunities before they arrived in the New World, (3) how morbidity and mortality rates change in response to the current and past patterns of the employment of Africans and Europeans, and (4) any relevant exogenous factors.[17] The evolutionary process that leads to changes in morbidity and mortality rates over time is, among other factors, a function of the interactions among different populations (and again, by inference, reproduction and selection) and disease environments. The specifics of the actual biological and historical consequences that resulted from the European Voyages of Discovery to British North America and the subsequent labor choices of colonial planters are examined in the next chapter.

Concluding Thoughts on the Choice of Colonial Labor

The migration of Old World biological organisms (humans, diseases, and parasites) changed the New World ecologies, which in turn altered the rates of morbidity, mortality, and labor productivity for the populations that went to the various regional environments of colonial America. These consequences in combination with economic factors (in particular, interest rates and relative prices of servile labor) provide the evidence for our explanation of the subsequent choices of agricultural labor and the regional concentration of peoples of different ethnicities (ancestral heritages) in seventeenth-century British North America. The results of these labor choices materially affected the history of the United States from its colonial origins, through the Civil War (the bloodiest war fought in the Western Hemisphere), continuing to the present. Contemplating the effects of minute, mindless organisms upon history should be enough to contradict any thoughts that "we are masters of our fate." Human hubris is invisible under microscopic examination.

5 The Initial Location of Africans and Europeans in Early America

The Voyages of Discovery and the interchange of biological organisms between the Old and New Worlds begin our in depth discussion of the roles that microbiology, evolutionary theory, and diseases have on our interpretation of the history and economic development of America.[1] We explain the initial use of Europeans in colonial British North American agriculture, the eventual use and predominance of Africans (blacks) in the tropics (the Caribbean) and subtropics (the southern mainland) of colonial America, and the continued use and predominance of Europeans (whites) in the more temperate regions (the northern mainland) of colonial America.

The migration of Old World peoples—the term "Old World" refers to the Eurasian land mass, Africa, and the islands peripheral to these continents—to the New World set in motion an evolutionary process that led to very different regional disease ecologies in the Americas post-Contact. Our explanation for the predominance of blacks in the Caribbean and the southern mainland and whites in the northern mainland is in the existence of biological and epidemiological differences between populations in different regional disease environments. The explanation emphasizes the interactions among economics, changing populations, and disease environments. Diseases act on populations by causing sickness and death. But specific diseases do not afflict all ethnic (racial) groups equally; therein lies our story.[2]

The Consequences of Contact between the Old and New Worlds

Contact between the Old and New Worlds altered the ecological environments in both Eastern and Western Hemispheres. The hemispheres had been isolated from one another for geological ages except for the times during the Ice Ages when the Bering Land Bridge was in existence. The peoples who populated the New World in the sixteenth and seventeenth centuries were the descendants of the Ice Age migrants (American Aborigines or American Indians) and the more recent Old World migrants of Africans and Europeans, along with mixtures of these people. The demographic experience of these populations varied regionally.

Native Americans

The first human inhabitants of the New World are generally believed to have migrated from northeastern Asia (Siberia) to the North American continent. Wallace (cited in Bishop 1993, p. 1), using evidence derived from DNA analysis, argues that humans also migrated from Polynesia to the Americas, but little is known about these migrants. The Siberian migrants crossed over on the Bering Land Bridge that connected northeastern Asia to the Alaskan peninsula, or along the near-shore coastal waters to its south, during the last Ice Age glacial about 15,000 or more years ago.[3] Humans migrated south until finally Aboriginal Americans inhabited essentially all of North and South America. The only major uninhabited exception was Barbados, the most eastern island in the West Indies.

They came relatively free of disease. The absence of disease was a result of the frigid climate, the small absolute size of the migrant bands, and the absence of domestic animals except the dog. Hunter-gatherer groups usually number from 25 to 75 individuals; this means that for most infectious diseases the absolute number of human beings in any tribal group was not large enough to enable infectious diseases to survive. The lack of domesticated animals prevented the Amerindians from contracting most zoonotic diseases. (Measles, influenza, and chicken pox are examples of diseases that have crossed over from animal populations to infect humans.) Ice Age temperature ensured that airborne pathogens quickly died if they had no host. (In hot and humid climates, the tropics, some airborne pathogens can survive for days without a host.) As a result of these factors, prehistoric humanity was relatively disease free compared to civilized humanity—living in dense, permanent clusters (McNeill 1976).

After the end of the last Ice Age glacial and the subsequent disappearance of the Land Bridge, Aboriginal Americans were almost completely isolated from contact with the Old World and remained relatively (compared to the Old World) disease free for the millennia prior to Contact. Isolation had two significant effects: (1) New World populations exhibited much less genetic diversity than Old World populations, and (2) the lack of domestic animals and communications with other peoples meant that the New World had a disease environment much less complex than the Old World. For millennia, Old World peoples had exchanged diseases and contracted diseases from domesticated animals and wildlife. This process had almost no counterpart in the New World. When animals were domesticated in the Old World, zoonoses (chicken pox, measles, probably smallpox, and yellow fever, among others) were passed from animal populations to human populations. Over centuries, they were transformed from epidemic diseases that affected all age groups to endemic or so-called childhood diseases in Old World human populations.[4] The isolation of the New World meant that when these diseases were introduced into the New World they were epidemic ("killer") diseases. Many other diseases were transmitted from Old World peoples to the New World; there were few major diseases (maybe only one, syphilis) that were endemic in the New World that were unknown in the Old (Diamond 1997; McNeill 1976). Consequently, when interactions on a regular basis with the Eastern Hemisphere began, there was an almost immediate population implosion of Aboriginal Americans due to "virgin soil" epidemics. Because of the *relatively* benign disease ecologies of the New World, there was no corresponding population implosion in the Old World.

We emphasize the word "relatively." The New World was not disease free (Buikstra 1993; Karasch 1993). Indeed, there are substantial disputes over the possible American origins of various pathogens; the best known of these is syphilis. In a recent study, Harper, Ocampo, Steiner, et al. (2008) indicate that New World origins of syphilis, rather than Eurasia or Africa, are consistent with DNA examinations of bacteria in the syphilis/yaws family. Regardless of its origins, in the Old World syphilis was a rapidly fatal disease for many of its victims when first introduced into late fifteenth-century (circa 1495) Europe; over time both the pathogen and the populations adapted to one another.

The Voyages of Discovery brought diseases to the New World to which Aboriginal Americans had no previous exposure. Columbus's second voyage to the New World in 1493 started an epidemic that began the extinction of the Caribbean Aborigines. Guerra (1988) contends that this epidemic was influenza contracted from the swine Columbus acquired when he stopped for provisions in the Canary Islands. Regardless what it was, it killed: Guerra (1988, p. 319) estimates the aboriginal population of Hispaniola declined from over one million to just 10,000 from 1492 to 1517. These estimates imply that the mean annual decline in the Amerindian population from 1492 to 1517 was a little over 18 percent per year. Dobyns (1983) dates the first New World smallpox epidemic at about 1516. Consequently, most of the decline in the aboriginal population of Hispaniola took place *before* the introduction of smallpox.

Native peoples of the Caribbean, Mesoamerican, and Andean civilizations were devastated by exposure to Old World diseases.[5] The tropical pathogens imported from the Old World (along with measles, smallpox, and influenza) were especially devastating to the inhabitants of the tropical and semitropical regions of the Americas. Brooks (1993) offers a revisionist version of the impact of smallpox, contending that smallpox was neither as contagious nor deadly as other scholars would have us believe. Brooks has been severely criticized by McCaa (1995), who uses the sources that Brooks relied on to undermine Brooks's hypothesis. Regardless of these differences, over the period 1518 to 1568, the data favored by Brooks give an annual decrease in population in Mesoamerica of over 2 percent; over two centuries this would produce a population decline of considerably greater than 95 percent! As a result, except for isolated areas in the Amazon and Orinoco River basins, no pure Aboriginal Americans exist in the tropics of the New World.

Recently, the pre-Contact population estimates of Aboriginal Americans have been subject to a continuous stream of upward revisions. In particular, the pre-Contact population of the Amazon aboriginals has been revised upward substantially; some partisans in the dispute even have suggested that parts of the Amazon were as densely populated as the fifteenth century's Old World rice civilizations.[6]

Many scholars believe that for most practical purposes, pre-Contact Americas were virtually a virgin soil for Old World diseases.[7] Others contend that the New World was more exposed to diseases than the "virgin soil" scholars portray; the recent DNA analysis of syphilis that points to its New World origins lends some credence to this school. Still syphilis is the only New World disease that was a major infection for Old World peoples; conversely, there were many Old World diseases that had significant effects and were new to the indigenous Americans. The catalog of pathogens brought from the Old to the New World is lengthy, but not complete; discoveries are still being made. A nonexhaustive list includes smallpox, influenza, measles, malaria, yellow fever, pneumonia, intestinal parasites, ectoparasites, dengue fever, onchocerciasis, trachoma, and leprosy; not all of these diseases are unanimously accepted. Cockburn (1980, p. 159) believes that hookworm was definitely resident in the New World prior to 1492 because of microscopic evidence found in Andean mummies. Hurtado, Hurtado, and Hill (2004, p. 173) dispute this, arguing that contemporary indigenous American peoples "are hyperinfested with helminthes and ectoparasites"; carrying a heavy disease load relative to others is not consistent with them having a long evolutionary history of exposure to these parasites.

The epidemics that devastated the New World also affected the relative mix of Native Americans. Those who had developed relatively densely populated societies based primarily on agriculture were adversely affected relative to the societies that were less developed and more nomadic (hunter-gatherers). Prior to Contact, the nomadic tribes were marginal and inconsequential relative to the total aboriginal population. The densely populated societies of the New World facilitated the spread of Old World pathogens that effectively destroyed the relatively developed aboriginal societies. Societies that followed a more nomadic lifestyle and used natural resources less intensively were less severely affected. Fewer people meant less hunting, and less hunting meant that populations of fish and game exploded. Given the short (relative to humans) generational time in game animal populations, the increase in the wildlife available to surviving Native Americans subsequent to Contact was substantial. Some Old World animals (cattle, horses, sheep, and swine) that were imported became feral and endemic to the American landscape, providing additional food resources. Skeletal remains show that Native Americans prior to Contact were very short and suffered from bone deformities associated with overwork and/or nutritional deficiencies. Post-Contact skeletal remains, although much fewer in number, show that Native Americans had fewer deformities and were substantially taller (Larsen, Crosby, Griffin, et al. 2002).

Figure 5.1 illustrates our conception of the effects that Contact with the Old World had on the native populations of the New World. Contact devastated the Aboriginal American populations. The arrows in figure 5.1 indicate the direction of causality and the algebraic signs indicate the historical effect that occurred as a consequence of Contact; the size of the arrows proxies what we estimate to be the magnitude of the effects. Starting from the top, Contact reduced the total population of

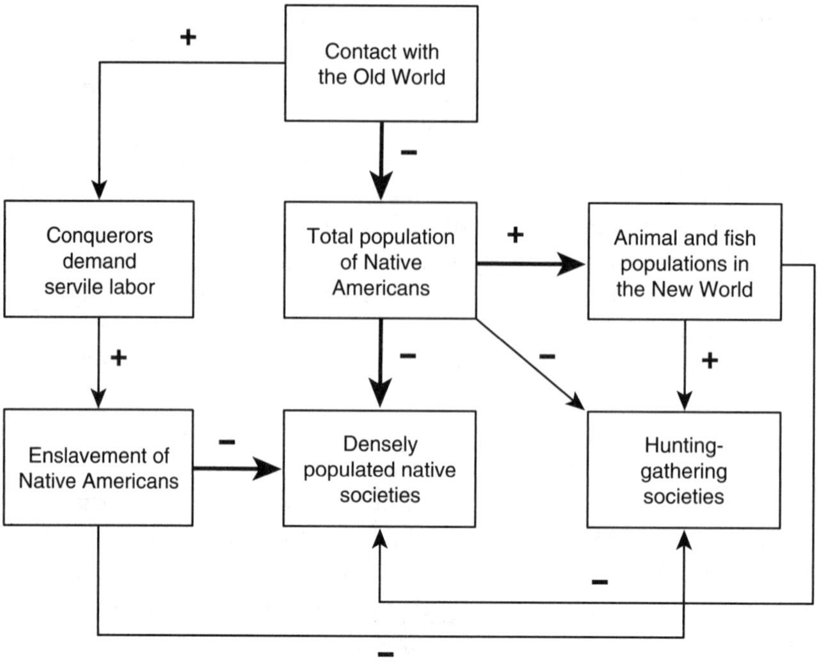

Figure 5.1
Effects of Contact on New World Native American populations

Native Americans, and the large decline in population had sizeable adverse effects on densely populated societies (as indicated by the larger black arrows connecting the boxes) relative to less densely populated societies. Contact also increased the demand for labor on the part of the conquerors, which led to the enslavement of the Native Americans. In turn, enslavement had a sizable adverse effect on densely populated societies relative to the more nomadic hunter-gatherer societies.[8] Nomadic societies became more attractive to Native Americans who had lived in relatively sedentary agricultural communities because of the increase in animal populations; this is shown in figure 5.1 by the negative effect that an increase in animal and fish populations had on the "Densely populated native societies." To emphasize a point, besides the increase in animals native to North America, feral Old World species augmented the supplies of animal proteins available. Depending on hunting for a major portion of one's food is typically a very attractive option to relatively primitive agriculturalists. Europeans also were attracted to the lifestyle of hunting civilizations. There are numerous accounts of Europeans joining native societies because they found the lifestyle attractive. People became agriculturalists in lieu of hunting only when game supplies were reduced.[9]

The demographic experience of Native Americans in the mainland North American colonies was similar; populations decreased rapidly after British settlement (this was in addition to the earlier massive die off that occurred almost immediately post-Contact). Smallpox was the ubiquitous and frequently deadly common denominator to all disease environments in the post-Contact New World. However, with the significant exception of smallpox, the Old World pathogens that afflicted the natives on the British colonial mainland were not identical to those in the Caribbean. In addition, the disease ecology in the mainland colonies varied as the climate varied. In New England, cold-weather diseases predominated; diseases such as influenza, tuberculosis, pleurisy, pneumonia, and other lung infections. The disease environment changed from that of primarily cold-weather diseases to a mixture of cold-weather and warm-weather diseases as one traveled south from New England on the mainland. In the colonies of Virginia, Maryland, and North and South Carolina, there were no diseases that were distinctly "their" diseases; instead the disease environment was more like an amalgam of the diseases that were in New England and in the tropics. These diseases were neither as virulent as in their native climates, nor were the human inhabitants as severely afflicted by any one disease; still there were more diseases to cause sickness and death. In the tropical regions of British America, the disease environment consisted almost entirely of warm-weather diseases: malaria, yellow fever, dengue fever, hookworm, schistosomiasis, and the ubiquitous smallpox.

Smallpox was an exclusively human disease; there were no nonhuman reservoirs or vectors for smallpox. Consequently, when smallpox was introduced into a region or people, it was always through human intervention. This explains smallpox's lack of regional or geographic specificity. Smallpox was a truly human disease; it went wherever people migrated (Crosby 1993b).

Given enough time the population of Native Americans could have recovered from the introduction of Old World pathogens to become, once again, the dominant ethnic group of the Americas. But the Aboriginal American population was not given sufficient time: diseases, enslavement, and the attractions of hunting-gathering lifestyles combined to ensure that Native American civilizations did not have time enough to recover. In the three plus centuries of the colonial period, growing populations of Africans and Europeans and their descendants displaced Native Americans as dominant ethnic groups in the New World.

Genetic Homogeneity: The Chromosomal Evidence Microbiology, DNA analysis, and evolutionary theory offer explanations for the devastating impact Old World diseases had on the New World population. The peoples of the New World were, relative to Old World populations, genetically homogeneous. There are historical reasons for the lack of genetic diversity in the peoples of the New World (Wang, Lewis, Jakobsson, et al. 2007). After migrating from Siberia during the last Ice Age glacial, Aboriginal Americans were isolated for millennia from other humans. Their isolation from the Old World led to a genetically homogeneous population; their lack of genetic diversity is supported by evidence from an examination of immune systems. The locus (chromosomal position) of a part of the immune system, the major histocompatibility complex antigens (termed Class I and Class II MHC glycoproteins) has been identified. The chromosomal position establishes that Class I and Class II MHC glycoproteins are transmitted genetically. An individual's immune system relies on these glycoproteins to identify and assist in the destruction of pathogens. (There is a Class III MHC glycoprotein that encodes for other immune components; since it is not critical to our analysis, it is not discussed here.)

How the body defends itself depends on the nature of the pathogen. Large bacteria and helminthic (parasitic worm) infections are present outside the cell (extra cellular). These pathogens are directly attacked by the immune system. The system deploys antibodies (soluble antigen receptors) that bind directly to the pathogen and act as a signal for other parts of the immune system to aid in the pathogen's destruction. Smaller bacteria, protozoa, ricksettia, and viruses establish their infections inside the cells of humans. To attack these intercellular pathogens is the function of MHC glycoproteins. All cells carry MHC molecules on themselves; on a cell infected by a pathogen, the MHC molecules display a fragment of the pathogen that acts as a signal for further action by the body's immune system. How the immune system wards off invaders depends on a subset of the MHC glycoproteins, which are genes, and are referred to as human leukocyte antigens (HLA); these are genes that attack various bodily invaders. There are large numbers of HLA alleles (alternative forms of a gene) that can concentrate on specific types of invaders. Although Class I and Class II MHC glycoproteins (and their genetic subcomponents, HLA) are not completely understood, it appears that Class I MHC glycoproteins attack invading microorganisms while Class II MHC glycoproteins control damaged or mutant cells within the body (Black 1992, 2004; Englehard 1994).

Class I and Class II MHC glycoproteins are recognized as the body's defenders against cellular invasion. Evolutionary selection favors viral (and other pathogenic) infections that survive the immune system's counter attack. Pathogens are subject to culling by the body's immune system; pathogens that survive and reproduce in the body have been relatively effective in subverting attacks by the host's immune system. A particular strain of a pathogen can be relatively successful in combating the onslaughts of a specific individual who has a limited set of Class I and Class II MHC glycoproteins. If sick people infect genetically related individuals with pathogens that survived attacks by their human immune system, then the pathogens are pre-adapted to the defense mechanisms of their new hosts. This is because both the new victim and the source victim have very similar Class I and Class II MHC glycoproteins as a result of their common genetic heritage.

An individual can have up to six different kinds of Class I MHC glycoproteins; *populations*, in general, have many more types of Class I MHC glycoproteins than an individual. Engelhard (1994, p. 56) states that over 100 forms of MHC glycoproteins have been identified; the number of HLA alleles is vast and continually being upgraded. Here we focus on MHC glycoproteins, while recognizing that the HLA are the proximate defenders of the human body. In recent studies, 40 different types of Class I MHC glycoproteins have been identified in a population of sub-Saharan Africans, 37 in a population of Europeans, 34 in a population of East Asians, but only 17 in a population of North American Indians, and 10 in a population of South American Indians (Black 1992, 2004). The lack of genetic diversity among North and South American Aborigines meant that a pathogen could spread more rapidly through New World populations than through Old World populations. This explains the devastating impact of Old World diseases.

Consequences of Genetic Homogeneity Black (1992, p. 1739) reports that as recently as the 1970s isolated people in the Amazon experienced mortality rates of as high as 75 percent when exposed to relatively common diseases—measles, mumps, and influenza. The isolation of the New World aborigines that kept them free of Old World pathogens also led to their devastation for a related reason. It meant that their ancestors were not selected for their resistance to smallpox, measles, mumps, yellow fever, and influenza, among other diseases. Ramenofsky (1993, p. 322) estimates that approximately 14 diseases were introduced into the Americas between 1500 and 1700.

The argument is one of population genetics, not individual genetics: two individuals from different populations may face the same risk (probability of death), but the *population* that has the greater genetic diversity within it will be at less risk. With a South American Indian population that has 10 Class I MHC glycoproteins, the chances are 32 percent that a virus passing between two people will not encounter a new type of Class I MHC glycoprotein. Among sub-Saharan Africans with 40 different Class I MHC glycoproteins, the chances of a virus not encountering a different Class I MHC is 0.5 percent (Black 1992, p. 1739). This means that pathogens are much more virulent among peoples with little Class I MHC diversity (American Aborigines) than among populations with a relatively large number of different Class I MHC glycolproteins (Africans and Europeans). Hurtado and Salzano (2004, table 11.1, pp. 213–15) show a case mortality rate (percentage of individuals with a disease that die) of 17.7 percent for a measles epidemic among the Yanomamo people (South American Amazon natives) in the 1960s.

An additional problem is that many diseases that kill adults are relatively mild when afflicting children. Yellow fever, measles, chicken pox, and mumps are examples of diseases that mildly impact children but are mortal threats when contracted as an adult (Cooper and Kiple 1993; Kim-Farley 1993). American Indians faced three reinforcing disasters because of epidemics: The obvious first was that many adults died; the second was that with the adult deaths, children, who would have survived with care, perished without adult care; and the third was the death of so many prime-aged adults reduced the resources available to the populations and left them vulnerable to starvation, conquest, and assimilation. Adults similarly died from lack of nursing—that is, from dehydration and disease brought on by the lack of sanitation (Dollar 1977).[10]

Although fewer data exist on morbidity, in general, we expect that the indigenous American populations were very sickly. It is likely there was a positive correlation between morbidity and mortality rates for the types of Old World diseases to which the natives were susceptible.

This would reduce their effectiveness in supplying agricultural labor. As a result, the increased morbidity and mortality of American Indians caused by Old World diseases decreased their lifetime productivity, and consequently decreased the demand for them as unskilled agricultural workers. The negative implications for natives after Contact was so deleterious that the demand for Native Americans as bound servile agricultural labor became negligible in the mainland British North American colonies. The existence of a slave trade in American Indians in the Carolinas in the late seventeenth and early eighteenth centuries proves the point. It failed to survive because Native American populations were declining and the demand for them was decreasing because of their excessive morbidity and mortality (Gallay 2002).

The decline in New World populations presented the Old World conquerors with a dilemma: How were they to get labor to exploit the resources available in the New World? The thought of doing the work themselves was not palatable to the conquerors. A variety of solutions to the problem of labor supply in the New World were attempted. The Conquistadors and subsequent invaders first tried the immediate expedient of enslaving distant Aboriginal Americans after the nearby ones died; after these Aboriginal Americans also died (similar to the local natives, they typically died of Old World pathogens), other sources were used. Various ethnic and religious groups were sent as servile labor from the Old World. "Servile" includes indentured servants who negotiated their contracts and other laborers who were not free to negotiate their own contracts. Some of the latter were slaves, prisoners of war or conscience, and convicts. The result of these "experiments" was that by the middle of the eighteenth century populations of differing racial (ethnic) backgrounds were geographically divided. In general, in the temperate regions of the conquered Americas, Europeans predominated; Africans predominated in the tropical regions. Only in the high mountain regions and high plains (and in the unconquered areas) did Native Americans predominate. In the late twentieth century, Latin American (South America and Mesoamerica) peoples that were identified as indigenous accounted for 3.3 percent of the total Latin American population; only Peru (40.8 percent), Ecuador (43.8 percent), and Bolivia (56.8 percent) had an indigenous population of more than 15 percent of the total population (Hurtado, Hurtado, and Hill 2004, p. 167).

These are generalities, the specifics of demographic change depended on geography and history along with biology. In the United States, the land east of the Mississippi is usually considered a temperate region, but there are certainly significant variations in climate within this area. In this region, the more one travels from north to south, the more the climate variables make the area a "warm-weather" region. In this context, we conceive of climates and regions as a continuum between "cold weather" and "warm weather": the more frost free days there are, the more likely the climate of a region approaches the "warm weather" category or classification. A more nuanced statement concerning geographical divisions and ethnic groups is that Europeans predominated in "cold-weather" regions and Africans predominated in "warm-weather" regions of the conquered Americas. The experiences of Old World populations in the New World disease ecologies differed radically from the disasters suffered by the indigenous American populations.

Africans and Europeans

The Caribbean and Tropical Africa The demographic experience of Africans and Europeans in the tropics of the British New World (the Caribbean), and in tropical Africa, differed from their experience on the British colonial mainland. Involvement in tropical Africa brought Europeans into contact with pathogens for which they had little or no prior exposure. The African pathogens that most afflicted Europeans were hookworm, malaria, and yellow fever, which along with other tropical pathogens, combined to produce phenomenal rates of mortality and morbidity for Europeans in tropical Africa. Examples of other tropical diseases that adversely affected Europeans relative to Africans and thus affected the choice of labor supply were yaws, dengue fever, and schistosomiasis. If we were to include the impact of all of these diseases, it would reinforce our contention about the relative impact of tropical diseases. After tropical pathogens were established in the Caribbean, death rates for non–West Africans in the Caribbean were a multiple of the rates of people of African origins until well after the mid-nineteenth century. Tropical diseases served to eliminate substantial numbers of Europeans from the sugar-producing regions of the New World tropics, resulting in present-day populations in the former Caribbean colonies of Britain, France, and Holland that are primarily of African origins. The former colonies of Spain (Cuba, Puerto Rico, and Santo Domingo) are exceptions. These islands have retained a substantial European contingent in their populations. There are various explanations for this, among the explanations are an Iberian resistance to African diseases; the settlement of cities, which allowed people of European ancestry to avoid malaria and become resistant to yellow fever; and the laggard development of full-scale sugar planting on these islands.

Hookworm, malaria, yellow fever, and other Old World tropical diseases were introduced to the Caribbean after the Voyages of Discovery. Hookworm of the *Necator americanus* variety (one of the two primary hookworms that afflict humans, the other is *Ancylostoma duodenale*) was almost certainly introduced when Africans were first brought to the New World (in the late fifteenth and early sixteenth centuries), but its effects are hard to trace. This is because hookworm is a debilitating disease but not frequently deadly. An individual with a severe case is likely to die of something else. And the etiology of hookworm in the New World was unknown and unstudied until the early twentieth century (Ettling 1981). Similarly, malaria was introduced almost certainly shortly after the first Voyages of Discovery in the late fifteenth century, but because its symptoms can be confused with other fevers, it is hard to date its introduction exactly (Kiple 1984, 1993).

While specific dating of the introduction of hookworm and malaria is not possible, the first yellow fever epidemic affecting Europeans in the Caribbean has been studied and is dated at 1647 in Barbados (Findlay 1941, p. 144). Prior to the mid-seventeenth century, Barbados and the Caribbean in general were not regarded as particularly unhealthy for Europeans. Henry Colt, a British "tourist" in the West Indies in the early seventeenth century, was struck by the absence of disease (Findlay 1941, p. 151). Evidence from other Europeans during the first 150 years after the Voyages of Discovery suggests that the disease environment of the Caribbean was unremarkable for Europeans. Prior to 1647, yellow fever was unknown; after 1647, it became endemic. The permanent establishment of tropical West African pathogens, and the subsequent increase in European mortality rates circa 1650, are consistent with the employment of primarily European servants until the late 1640s and the switch to primarily African slaves during the 1650s in Barbados, and the Caribbean in general. Kiple and Higgins (1992) suggest that yellow fever was what changed the sugar-producing Caribbean's population from European to African (for a history of Caribbean sugar plantations, see Dunn 1972).

The importance of yellow fever in affecting labor choices outside the sugar-producing Caribbean is debatable. First, it is a disease whose vector, the mosquito *Aedes aegypti*, has a limited flight range estimated to be a maximum of a few hundred yards and is considered a disease that thrives in centers of dense human populations (sugar plantations or urban areas). Second, the case mortality rate is debatable (estimates range from 20 to 70 percent with a much lower mortality rate for children), and a victim of yellow fever who recovers enjoys lifetime immunity (Cooper and Kiple 1993, p. 1100). Third, the generations of Europeans growing up in the Caribbean would have acquired immunity to the disease by childhood exposure, as did the Spaniards of Cuba and Puerto Rico. Thus, yellow fever alone does not adequately explain the transition from a European to an African agricultural labor force in the non–sugar-producing Caribbean.[11]

Although neither hookworm nor malaria is as deadly as yellow fever, both are debilitating, and their study is instructive. (We postpone the discussion of hookworm until we discuss the Chesapeake region because hookworm's discovery and history are inextricably linked with the American South.) Four varieties of malaria have been discovered; one, falciparum malaria (*Plasmodium falciparum*), is frequently deadly. The other types are less deadly (but still debilitating) and more geographically diverse than *P. falciparum*. Exposure to one variety of malaria gives no immunity to the other varieties, but attacks of other varieties may be less virulent in people who have suffered from previous malarial attacks. We concentrate on *P. falciparum* because it is the variety of malaria that is most frequently deadly. It is death that is most effective in increasing the relative frequencies of HLA alleles, which resist a disease in a population. The mechanism is that people with resistance are more likely to survive long enough to reproduce, while those who lack resistance are more likely to die before reproducing. Thus, killing diseases are more effective in altering the genetic composition of a population than are high-morbidity diseases. *P. falciparum* is endemic to the tropics of West Africa, and within the human populations in Africa innate resistance has evolved. A substantial portion of the tropical West African population has the sickle cell trait and/or other blood abnormalities that provide protection against malarial attacks. These traits are uncommon in populations not exposed to *P. falciparum* but do occur in both African and non-African populations where malaria and *P. falciparum* are endemic (Kiple and King 1981, pp. 17–22).

The reasons for the extraordinarily high susceptibility of Europeans to tropical diseases and African resistance to them lie in microbiology and evolutionary theory: in an environment with endemic hookworm, malaria, and yellow fever innate resistance is pro-adaptive. A gene that confers resistance to these pathogens will allow the humans who possess it to lead longer and healthier lives, other factors the same. The "other factors the same" condition usually does not hold when speaking about the impact of genes. Genes typically have more than one effect on the body; these phenotypic effects have long been noted. Darwin called them "correlations" and wrote that they can be "quite whimsical: thus cats with blue eyes are invariably deaf; . . . [h]airless dogs have imperfect teeth; . . . pigeons with feathered feet have skin between their outer toes" (as quoted in Cronin 1991, p. 60). Some phenotypic changes will have positive survival value, others negative, and some may have no effect. A statement that is more consistent with the typical effects of genes would be that a gene that confers resistance to the prevailing disease organisms in a given environment, and whose other phenotypic effects do not completely offset their survival advantage, will spread in the relevant population. Each generation that carries this gene will, in all probability, leave more descendants than their peers who do not possess the gene. Over generations and millennia, the gene will tend to become more frequent in the population. The epidemiological results of this process are dramatic.

Acquired childhood immunities also play a part. In an environment where a disease is endemic, the immune system will have had early childhood exposure to the disease-bearing microorganisms. As a result, the immune system will be able to quickly produce antibodies to any subsequent exposure.

Figure 5.2 illustrates the impact of the Old World migrations on the disease ecology in the warmer regions of the New World. As before, the arrows in the schematic diagram indicate the direction of causality. Starting from the top, Europeans' demand for agricultural labor in the British New World leads to migrations of Europeans and importations of African slaves to America. Africans and the ships that transported them carry warm-weather diseases (hookworm, malaria, yellow fever, and other tropical pathogens) with them. With chance and sufficient time, these diseases become endemic. The warm-weather diseases adversely impact European agricultural laborers who become sickly and possibly die. Imported African slaves were very likely to have had previous exposure to the warm-weather diseases imported from the tropics of West Africa and consequently would have had acquired immunities; they also were very likely to have inherited some innate

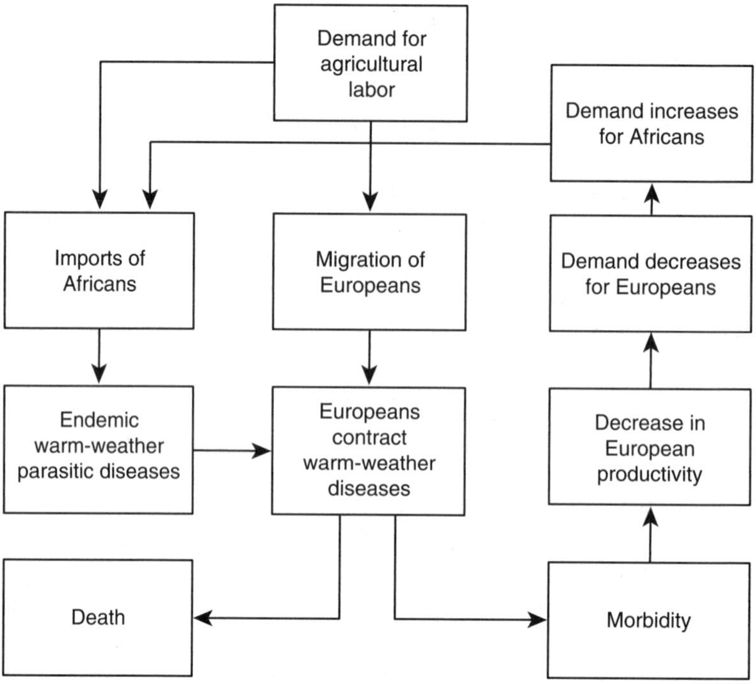

Figure 5.2
Effects of migration on the disease ecology in the warmer regions of British America

immunities from their West African parents. The relatively greater illnesses and deaths among the Europeans would reduce their productivity relative to that of African slaves and, as a result, reduce the demand for Europeans as agricultural field hands. This then increases the demand for Africans as agricultural field hands, increasing slave importations. This feedback restarts the cycle, leading to a decline in the number of Europeans and their descendants living in the tropics of the British New World (the Caribbean).

Data collected by Curtin (1968) allows a comparison of the death rates of troops of differing ethnic origins in the British Army. Curtin's data, which are summarized in table 5.1, are deaths rates for European troops (those enlisted in Europe and presumably primarily from the United Kingdom) and African troops (those enlisted in Africa or from captured slave ships leaving Africa). While the data are for the early 1800s, they are nevertheless relevant for earlier times. Since only fragmentary data exist for earlier periods, the assertion that Curtin's data

Table 5.1
Death rates per 1,000 troops of different origins in the British Army

Location (years)	European troops	African troops
Jamaica (1803–1817)	127	49
Jamaica (1817–1836)	130	30
Windward and Leeward (1803–1816)	138	—
Windward and Leeward (1817–1836)	—	40
Sierra Leone (1817–1836)	483	—
Gold Coast (1823–1826)	683	—
West Africa (1819–1836)	—	32

Source: Curtin (1968, tables 1–3).

are apropos demands a foundation. Recall the earlier discussion of human immune systems. The MHC glycoproteins that individuals possess are inherited from their parents. In a closed population succeeding generations will have the same number of different glycoproteins in their immune systems as the ancestor population had, unless only a small and biased sample of the ancestor population produced offspring. We know that the European population from the seventeenth through the nineteenth centuries was not closed; it incorporated people from all over the world into it; Asians, Africans, and American Indians did interbreed with elements of the European population. Additionally, there is absolutely no reason to believe that only a small and biased sample of the population reproduced. This means that, if anything, the European population of nineteenth-century Europe had a greater variety of MHC glycoproteins than its ancestor populations of the seventeenth and eighteenth centuries. If we consider only the British population as the relevant population, the argument is much stronger. From 1650 to 1850, the British population incorporated into it people from all over the world *and* people from other areas of Europe. Consequently, it would be extraordinarily unlikely that the British population in 1850 had a smaller variety of MHC glycoproteins than the British population of 1650.

The result is that, immunologically speaking, the nineteenth-century European population had the same, or greater, resistance to diseases than its seventeenth-century ancestor population. Consequently, Curtin's nineteenth century data are, if anything, a lower bound for the European experience in tropical environments in earlier times. This implication would have to be modified if the nature of medical care deteriorated over time or the disease environment became more deleterious. There is no evidence for the former, and this book argues against the latter.

Table 5.1 suggests that Africa was close to a death sentence for Europeans; the Caribbean, while better than Africa for Europeans, was decidedly unhealthful. African troops in tropical areas did better than European troops. (Repeating and stressing a point, these were *African* troops in the British Army.) Curtin (1968, p. 206) also includes mortality data for Jamaican born slaves (over three years old) of African ancestry for the years 1803 to 1817. He reports a death rate of 25 per thousand, a lower death rate than the lowest death rate for African troops serving in the West Indies. Perhaps surprisingly, African troops in the New World had mortality rates that were, on average, only approximately 25 percent higher than their mortality in Africa. The death rate for European troops in the Caribbean was at least eight times higher than the estimated rate of 15.3 per thousand in the United Kingdom (Curtin 1968, p. 202). The differential between African and European mortality rates is a result of the disease environment that prevailed in the tropics of the New World after contact with Africa was established on a regular basis. The disease environment was closely related to that of tropical Africa, to which Africans had been pre-adapted by natural selection and childhood immunities.

Curtin's data are based on British Parliamentary records and are acknowledged to be the best currently available. There are other estimates based on good data that, while also for years subsequent to the founding of the first colonies, should be considered lower bounds as well. Steckel and Jensen (1986) present reliable estimates of death rates for slave (African) and crew (European) during loading of the enslaved in Africa and during the voyages; these data are for the late eighteenth century. Steckel and Jensen's (1986, pp. 60–62) reported death rate for Africans while loading the slave cargo is 45.3 per thousand, and during the voyage 115.7 per thousand; the crew (primarily of European ancestry) death rates are 237.9 during loading and 207.4 during the passage. Davies (1975) provides another source of reliable data for the 1665 to 1722 period. Davies's (1975, pp. 93–95) data come from the records of the Royal African Company; the data show first-year death rates for Europeans newly arrived in West Africa. The mean annual first-year death rate for these data is 62.8 percent (628 per thousand); the range in observation is from a low of 54.0 percent to a high of 66.7 percent. Davies (1975, p. 93) also notes that of the new European arrivals during the period: "one man in three died in the first four months in Africa, more than three men in five in the first year."

Less precise and more impressionistic estimates for the death rates of Europeans in the tropics are available from a variety of other sources; they suggest that, if anything, the death rates for European troops in the Caribbean that Curtin presents—roughly from 120 to 140 deaths per thousand troops per year—are too low. Rogoziński (1992, p. 167) estimates that of the roughly 20,000 British troops that invaded Saint-Dominique (Haiti) beginning in September 1793 and continuing until 1798: "Almost 13,000 men died—perhaps 1,000 in battle, the rest of malaria and yellow fever." Twelve thousand deaths from disease over a five-year period imply a death rate of approximately 200 per thousand per year.[12] Writing about the later French invasion of Saint-Dominique, Rogoziński (1992, p. 172) states that of the 20,000 French troops that had landed by February of 1802: "By the middle of April half of the soldiers were dead or sick of yellow fever."

On the African side during the eighteenth century, Miller (1988, p. 286) writes that: "They [men of European birth] settled in the commercial quarter of the lower city [Luanda in Angola]; then within weeks or months the majority was carried off to the European graveyard. . . . The pervasiveness of death . . . in Luanda . . . set the tumultuous style of business in a city that truly merited the sobriquet of the 'white man's grave.'" The earlier experiences of Europeans with Africa were just as deadly; in the sixteenth century, the papal ambassador to Portugal accused the Portuguese Crown of violating the ban on the execution of Catholic prelates by simply exiling the offending churchmen to Africa "knowing that within a short time they would be dead" (Thornton 1992, p. 142).

McDaniel (1994) has argued that it was childhood-acquired immunities, not any innate resistance, that made West Africans more resistant to the diseases of tropical West Africa. Employing data from the migration of African-Americans to Liberia during the nineteenth century, McDaniel (1994, p. 106) reports crude death rates ranging from a high of 143 per thousand during the 1820 to 1828 period to a low of 70.7 per thousand during the 1836 to 1843 period. McDaniel uses these data to argue that innate resistance to diseases was not important, and that tropical West Africans do not have any inherent biological resistances to these diseases. The data that McDaniel presents indicate that the highest death rate for African-Americans in Liberia (143 per thousand) was less than one-third of the lowest death rate for Europeans in Africa

(483 per thousand) reported in table 5.1. Except for the initial experience during the years 1820 to 1828, the death rate for African-Americans in Liberia was substantially less than for European troops in the West Indies during the same period (see table 5.1). McDaniel's (1994, p. 106) mortality data for African-Americans in Liberia for the entire 1820 to 1843 period average 83 deaths per thousand; the simple mean death rate for European troops in the West Indies reported in table 5.1 is 132 per thousand. These data indicate that African-Americans in Liberia had 49 (37 percent) fewer deaths per thousand than did European troops in the British West Indies. Also note from table 5.1 that the simple mean death rate for African troops in the West Indies is 40 per thousand, less than one-third that of European troops (132 per thousand). The data indicate that while acquired antibodies may have played a part in the resistance of Africans in Africa to the local disease ecology, the relative resilience of African-Americans (born and raised in the New World) to the disease ecology of nineteenth-century Liberia was genetically transmitted.

McDaniel's (1994) case is further undermined by his own observation elsewhere that African-Americans of mixed ancestry (African and European) did much worse in Liberia than those of unmixed African ancestry (McDaniel 1995). "Contemporary observers suggested that mulattos were the leaders [of Liberian society] but believed that they suffered from excess mortality" (McDaniel 1995, p. 58). McDaniel (1995, p. 58) also observes that the migrants to Liberia "may have received assistance from their former masters because of past service." An explanation for these payments other than "past service" would be that they were blood relatives: the children and grandchildren of slaveowners.

While McDaniel's (1994, 1995) evidence supports our contention of innate resistance and undermines his contention of none, the data are not entirely adequate to address the acquired immunity/innate resistance issue. Many of the migrants were of mixed ancestry, and death rates were not identified by ancestry. Indeed, given the absence of DNA testing, it is impossible to settle the issue once and for all because the only classification available in the nineteenth century would have been by appearance. Yet the visible physical characteristics of individuals may be entirely unrelated to their inherited immune system; thus, an individual who appears "African" may have a set of MHC glycoproteins that are more closely "European" than "African."[13]

Quite obviously, the death rates of Africans in Africa were substantially lower than those of Europeans in Africa; otherwise, there would have been no Africans. The African slave trade opened the tropics of the New World to African pathogens. These diseases (dengue fever, hookworm, malaria, and yellow fever are prominent examples) afflicted Europeans more severely than Africans. Diseases and an African labor force reinforced themselves: the African slave trade brought into the New World tropical African pathogens and made European agricultural labor a less viable option in regions where these pathogens flourished.[14]

The British Colonial Mainland: The North The demographic experiences of Africans, Europeans, and their descendants in the British mainland colonies were not only different from that in the Caribbean but also differed across areas of the mainland because the combination of diseases on the mainland varied regionally, and the diseases had differential effects on Africans, Europeans, and their descendants. Klepp (1994) provides evidence on differences in mortality of peoples of different ancestral origins during the eighteenth century. While Klepp focuses on eighteenth-century Philadelphia, her study sheds light on the differential impact that diseases had on different peoples and allows us to explain the predominance of Europeans in the northern colonies. Table 5.2 summarizes Klepp's (1994) evidence as well as the mortality rates presented in Warren (1997). Combining Klepp's crude death rate data for cold-weather diseases (measles, pleurisy/influenza, and whooping cough) and smallpox in Philadelphia, the simple mean crude death rate during epidemic years for Africans and African-Americans (blacks) was 87 percent higher than the death rate during epidemic years for Europeans and European-Americans (whites) (see table 5.2, row 5). During epidemics of non–cold-weather diseases (yellow fever, diphtheria/croup, dengue fever, scarlet fever/scarlatina, and typhus/typhoid fever), the black mortality rate was only 10 percent higher than that of whites (see table 5.2, row 6).

Klepp (1994, p. 479) argues that black mortality reached a seasonal peak in the winter months, whereas white mortality reached a seasonal peak during the summer months. Her data imply that although white mortality was substantially lower than black mortality for the entire year in Philadelphia (see table 5.2, rows 7, 8, and 10), white mortality was considerably higher than black mortality in the summer season (row 9). Klepp includes data for the New England area as well. She estimates that blacks had an excess mortality of over 100 percent above that of whites in Boston during the middle of the eighteenth

Table 5.2
Eighteenth- and nineteenth-century death rates per 1,000 blacks and whites: Various American cities

Location and disease type	Years	Season	Blacks	Whites
Boston				
All diseases	All years (1725–1744)	Entire	80.0	32.0
All diseases	All years (1730–1774)	Entire	65.4	33.7
All diseases	All years (1854–1875)	Entire	34.4	24.1
Providence, RI				
All diseases	All years (1855–1890)	Entire	32.8	19.4
Philadelphia				
Cold-weather diseases	Epidemic years (1722–1775)	Entire	88.8	47.5
Non–cold-weather diseases	Epidemic years (1722–1775)	Entire	55.2	50.2
All diseases	All years (1729–1744)	Entire	78.0	50.0
All diseases	All years (1746–1774)	Entire	66.0	47.0
All diseases	All years (1722–1775)	Summer	36.0	60.0
All diseases	All years (1821–1840)	Entire	40.4	24.1
Baltimore				
All diseases	All years (1817–1880)	Entire	32.1	23.9
Charleston				
All diseases	All years (1822–1848)	Entire	26.2	26.1

Source: Klepp (1994); Warren (1997).

century. From these data the absence of African slavery as a significant economic institution in the New England colonies of British North America is explicable—in regions with cold climates, cold-weather diseases predominated and Africans died at disproportionate rates relative to Europeans. Warren's (1997) mortality data for the nineteenth century are for: Providence, Baltimore, and Charleston, and are consistent with Klepp's conclusions concerning regional differences in the mortality rates of blacks and whites. Warren's estimates indicate that blacks died at a rate that was 70 percent higher than the white rate in Providence; they died at a 34 percent higher rate than whites in Baltimore; and, despite blacks' obviously lower income, lower

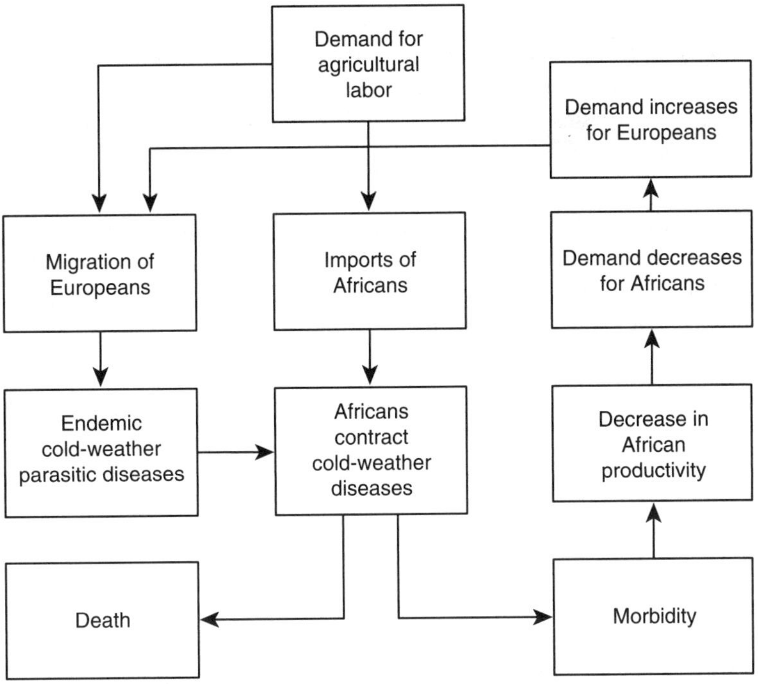

Figure 5.3
Effects of migration on the disease ecology in the colder regions of British America

standard of living, and bias against them in the provision of public services in the antebellum South, they died at an (essentially) identical rate as whites in Charleston.

Figure 5.3 illustrates the impact of the Old World migrations on the disease ecology in the colder regions of the New World. Again, starting from the top, Europeans' demand for agricultural labor in the colonies leads to migrations of Europeans and importations of African slaves. With European settlers come measles, whooping cough, pleurisy/influenza, other lung infections, and in general, cold-weather diseases. With chance and sufficient time, these Old World cold-weather diseases become endemic to the northern regions of colonial British North America. Because they lack both innate and acquired immunities to cold-weather diseases, people of African ancestry contract relatively more of these diseases. Consequently, they are more sickly and die at greater rates than people of northwestern European ancestry. The relatively greater illnesses and mortality among Africans reduce their productivity and the demand for them as agricultural labor. This increases the demand for Europeans as agricultural labor. As a result, there is an increase in the migration of European indentured servants. This feedback restarts the cycle, leading to a decline in the number of Africans and their descendants living in the northern colonies of the British American mainland.

McCusker and Menard (1985, p. 222) provide estimates of the number of African-Americans living in the British mainland colonies that are consistent with our disease story. They report that the percentage of African-Americans in colonial New England stabilized at about 2 percent of the total population (the percentage in 1700 was 1.8, the percentage in 1780 was 2.0); in the middle colonies, it stabilized at about 6 percent (6.8 percent in 1700 and 5.9 percent in 1780). The percentage of African-Americans in the South did not stabilize: in the upper South it grew from 13.1 percent in 1700 to 38.6 percent in 1780 and in the lower South it grew from 17.6 percent to 41.2 percent from 1700 to 1780.

We can now illustrate the economic case for the relative absence of Africans in the northern colonies. Klepp's (1994, p. 477, n. 13) crude death rate data for Boston for 1725 to 1744 of 80 deaths per 1,000 for blacks and 32 deaths per 1,000 for whites, imply a life expectancy of 12 years for blacks and a life expectancy of 29 years for whites when the data are truncated at 100 years. An indenture contract was considerably less than the life expectancy of an indentured European, it usually ranged from four to seven years. Recall from the discussion in chapter 4 that the exact length of an indenture contract was a function of age, gender, location, and skills, where an illiterate 18-year-old male bound for Pennsylvania could expect to serve five years. Because reliable data for indentured servants bound for New England are not available, we chose to utilize data about servants for the northern-most colony for which reliable data exist for the early eighteenth century. We use the price of an illiterate 18-year-old male because that age and skill category would represent the appropriate comparison to the typical imported African slave.

As noted earlier, colonial interest rates are not known with precision, but a good estimate for relatively safe mortgages is 8 percent. Homer and Sylla (1991, pp. 274–75) indicate that colonies passed maximum interest rate laws ranging from 5 percent in Virginia to 8 percent in Massachusetts, noting that "While such legislation does not tell what the prevailing rates were in the colonies, it does indicate the rates that leading citizens considered normal or reasonable. According to

Benjamin Franklin, commercial interest rates in Pennsylvania in the latter half of the eighteenth century were between 6 and 10 percent." We take 8 percent as an appropriate rate, being the midpoint of Franklin's range. Also recall from chapter 4 that we estimated the delivered price of the illiterate 18-year-old male servant to be £12, and here we estimate the purchase price of a slave during the early eighteenth century (1725 to 1744) to be £26. (For the years 1723/27 to 1743/47, the unweighted mean of the slave prices presented in table 4.1, column 2, in chapter 4 is £26.06.) We note that the £26 price used here is well below the slave prices that prevailed during the *second* half of the eighteenth century. But recall that if we used higher slave prices, that would make the choice of a servant more profitable, other factors the same.

Using these estimates, we can calculate the expected annual returns over costs for European servants and African slaves, given the same productivities, as agricultural labor in the northern colonies. Given the market price of bound servile labor would equal the present value of the expected stream of net revenue produced by the servile labor, we calculate that a servant would have to return only £3.005 per year while a slave would have to yield £3.45 per year (or 15 percent more) for its entire expected life to justify the higher purchase price.[15] Recall that people of African ancestry were sicklier in the cold-weather disease environment of the North. These calculations favor purchasing a European servant in the northern colonies; servants did not require as high a yield as African slaves to be profitable. Risk aversion also would favor servants over slaves because the initial investment was less than the price of a slave, and the risk of death was less with a servant. Under these circumstances, we would not expect African slaves to be competitive with European servants in the North, and they were not.

While these estimates do not address the issue of the absolute profitability of indentured servants or slaves, they do suggest that investments in European indentured servants were more profitable than investments in African slaves in the northern colonies. To calculate the absolute profitability of indentured servants and slaves, we must know (1) the acquisition cost of indentured servants and slaves, (2) the rate at which the investment in each is being discounted, (3) the length of time the investment in each lasts, and (4) the net revenues generated by each type of servile labor. All the data are known except for the last. And the argument in this book is that the net revenues generated by African slaves in agriculture differed regionally from those of European indentured servants.

Another indication of the relative profitability of African and European servile labor across regions of the mainland colonies is to estimate the annual imports of each type of labor into each region. The data assembled by Perkins (1980, p. 154) show the regional distribution of slaves and indentured servants in 1774. While the total stock of slaves exceeded the number of indentured servants in the Middle and New England colonies, the annual number of imports of indentured servants substantially exceeded the annual imports of slaves into these colonies.

With a few assumptions we are able to calculate annual imports. We assume that the expected life of a slave was 12 years and the length of an indentured servant contract was 5 years. We also assume that the natural growth rates of the servant and slave stocks were zero. Indentured servants obviously did not reproduce as indentured servants; and an assumption of no reproduction on the part of slaves biases the estimated imports of slaves upward because some did reproduce. In the Middle colonies (New York, New Jersey, Pennsylvania, and Delaware), the stock of slaves was 34,172 and that of indentured servants 21,374. The annual number of imported servants, under our assumptions, would have been 4,275 (1/5 of 21,374) and the number of imported slaves 2,848 (1/12 of 34,172).

Similar calculations for New England (Connecticut, New Hampshire, Massachusetts, and Rhode Island) reveal that annual imports of indentured servants would have been 2,371 and imports of slaves would have been 1,137. The estimates indicate that for each slave imported into New England a little over two indentured servants were imported, and in the Middle colonies the ratio of indentured servant to slave imports was a little over one and a half to one. As one would expect, the calculations suggest completely different outcomes in the southern colonies (Georgia, Maryland, North Carolina, South Carolina, and Virginia). Under the same assumptions, albeit biased upward for slave imports, the data suggest that for each indentured servant imported there were a little over nine slaves imported.

In regions with cold climates, investments in white indentured servants, given the same productivities, were more profitable than were black slaves at the prices that prevailed in the eighteenth century. We expect that the assumption of equal productivities in cold climates to be invalid. Given the disparity in death rates and the nature of many cold-weather diseases to linger (causing high morbidity), it is unlikely that in agriculture Africans were as productive as Europeans in the northern colonies. The disease environment almost precludes that as a possibility.

In a related issue, Hanes (1996) argues that slaves were preferred for employment in personal service (domestic servants) because people used in such service had to be aware of the idiosyncrasies of their masters. Since slaves were permanent (as long as they lived), training costs were reduced by using slaves rather than indentured servants. Personal servants perpetually bound (slaves) would have a greater knowledge of their overlords various tastes and idiosyncrasies; this would have made them more valuable than a constantly changing stock of free labor. As a result, the demand for personal servants may explain the continuing (small) demand for slaves in the North. The slavery that did exist in late-colonial New England and New York was largely confined to domestics with the exception of New York City and parts of Rhode Island. Also there is some literary evidence that African slaves in the North were employed more in personal service than their counterparts in the southern colonies. Nonetheless, our argument addresses the use of labor of different ethnicities (ancestral heritages) in the agricultural sector, not their use as domestic servants.

The British Colonial Mainland: The South In the tobacco-growing regions of the Chesapeake and into the Carolinas, the environment is more favorable to the transmission of warm-weather diseases. These diseases, their seasonal virulence, and the significant differential impact on Africans and Europeans explain the eventual predominance of Africans as the agricultural labor force in these regions. We concentrate on the Chesapeake region for three reasons. (1) The data and evidence that exist are better for this region than any other region where African servile labor was a major force. (2) The reason for the transition from European to African servile labor for agricultural tasks in this region has been widely studied and has a substantial literature. And (3) in the Chesapeake, there is a very interesting anomaly—the evidence indicates that in the early years in the Chesapeake region mortality rates for blacks were greater than those for whites (Fogel 1989; Klepp 1994). Fogel (1989, p. 125) actually reports a negative natural growth rate for blacks in the early eighteenth century, while whites had a positive natural increase.

The issue then is to explain the existence and evolutionary success of African labor in the period 1680 to 1720 in the Chesapeake region in the face of appreciably higher death rates for blacks. Our explanation involves the seasonality of diseases, the differences between rates of morbidity and mortality, and the spread of hookworm and malaria.

In the agricultural cycle any illness that strikes the labor force during the late summer or early fall harvest season can have a devastating effect on the economic well-being of the agriculturalist. Because the environment favors warm-weather diseases as one travels further south in the Northern Hemisphere, the ethnic differences in seasonal mortality rates would have been as great in the Chesapeake as in Philadelphia. Consequently, part of the conundrum of choosing Africans over Europeans despite the lower life expectancies of Africans can be explained by the seasonality of disease in the South. African-Americans got sick (and died) disproportionately in the winter months—the slack time in agriculture—while European-Americans were brought down in the summer months—at the peak of the agricultural cycle. The economic productivity of Africans relative to Europeans in agricultural pursuits in British North America was greater in the summer and early fall because of the regional predominance of warm-weather diseases.

A number of parasitic diseases afflicted the American South. The climate allowed warm-weather diseases that were endemic to tropical Africa to flourish in the long Chesapeake summers. Some of these diseases preexisted, and others became serious health problems only after Contact with the Old World. Over time some Old World diseases became endemic to the southern disease ecology and made the South disease ridden to people of *European* ancestry relative to the more northern regions of America. Warm-weather diseases were a major factor in the southern disease environment that affected the economy and differentially affected whites during the slave era. Of these, the primary ones are malaria, yellow fever, dengue fever, hookworm, and schistosomiasis. All of these were (and are) found in tropical West Africa and were widespread and abundant. The climate and sandy soils of the South, as well as the plantation system, were relatively conducive to the maintenance and spread of many infectious parasitic diseases. There were other such diseases that are not known to have differential effects on ethnic groups that also thrived in the South because of its climate and soils; some of these include amoebic dysentery and the helminthes, roundworm, threadworm, whipworm, and tapeworm. The South also had the ubiquitous smallpox.

The best documented and studied of the diseases that had disparate impacts on peoples of African and European ancestry are hookworm, malaria, and yellow fever. Both hookworm and malaria have a low case mortality rate but cause a great deal of sickness. Both are of considerable importance in explaining the ultimate dominance of African slavery in the Chesapeake and, by extension, the entire American South. As for yellow fever, because its vector, the mosquito *Aedes aegypti*, thrives in centers of very dense human populations compared to the malaria mosquito *Anopheles genus*, it had little impact on agricultural field labor in the Chesapeake. And, except for the occasional epidemics in the cities that did exist in colonial North America (New York in 1688, Philadelphia and Charleston in 1690, Boston in 1691, and Philadelphia in 1762), yellow fever was not a major factor in the demographic history of the *colonial* South.

Natives of tropical West Africa tend to have both a genetic resistance and acquired childhood antibodies to the various forms of malaria, while the natives of northwestern Europe lack these bodily defenses. This is not entirely correct because the "ague" or the vivax type of malaria (*Plasmodium vivax*) was present in seventeenth- and eighteenth-century Europe (Kiple and King 1981, pp. 12–23). This may have allowed some eighteenth-century Europeans to have acquired resistance to strains of *Plasmodium vivax*, but they did not have an innate (genetic) resistance to malaria. Innate immunities are caused by differential reproductive success; only diseases that selectively kill elements of a population have major effects on the populations' gene pool. *P. vivax* is very infrequently fatal, while *P. falciparum* is the most lethal of the malarial diseases. *P. falciparum* was never endemic to Britain; consequently, the pressures of evolutionary selection for resistance to malaria did not exist in Britain in the millennia before the modern era. Furthermore, Kiple and King (1981, p. 16) note that any acquired immunities would be limited to a specific strain of a variety of malaria because different varieties and strains, of which there are many, are not immunologically similar.

When Africans were brought to the Chesapeake in substantial numbers in the late seventeenth century, unwittingly malaria of the *P. falciparum* variety was also imported. An individual may be infected with the malaria plasmodia but, for all practical purposes, be asymptomatic. Yet these infected people carry within themselves fully virulent malaria. (The African forms of malaria are, primarily, *Plasmodium falciparum*, and secondarily, *Plasmodium malariae*.) The natives of tropical West Africa are likely (relative to non–West Africans) to have the sickling trait. This is a probabilistic statement. The probability of a West African carrying the sickle-cell trait approaches 40 percent in some populations (Dunn 1993, pp. 855–62; Kiple and King 1981, p. 17). The sickling trait allows the human body to exist and function almost normally while bearing the plasmodia parasites. In tropical West Africa malaria is endemic, people born and raised there have, very likely, been exposed to many strains of *P. falciparum* by puberty. Some natives of tropical West Africa could have escaped being bitten by malarial-bearing mosquitoes, but the probability would not be high, and their numbers would be statistically and economically insignificant. While the Africans brought to the Chesapeake region could have been inured to the ravages of malaria by the sickling trait, other blood abnormalities, or previous exposures, they still could serve as reservoirs of the disease that allowed the mosquitoes to transmit it to others.[16]

In the summer, mosquitoes were and are ubiquitous in the Chesapeake region. Mosquitoes transmitted malaria from Africans to Europeans and the Europeans took sick; some died, but the case mortality rate for malaria was low. We do not distinguish between the various types of malaria here because pre–twentieth-century medicine could not accurately distinguish between them. And the available data typically make no mention of the varieties of malaria. While data on morbidity and mortality for malaria in the Chesapeake for the 1680 to 1720 period do not exist, Duffy (1988) has a general discussion of malaria morbidity in the American South. And Curtin (1989, pp. 174–77) reports the causes of morbidity and mortality for British (European) troops in the British West Indies during the nineteenth and early twentieth centuries. Curtin's (1989) data indicate that the case mortality rate for malaria in the Caribbean was approximately 1.6 percent.[17] Furthermore, Curtin (1989, p. 133) states that prior to 1840 the case mortality rate for malaria in Madras, India, was 60 percent higher than after 1840. Suppose it also was 60 percent higher in the Western Hemisphere. That implies the pre-1840 case mortality rate for malaria would have been slightly more than 2.5 percent in the Caribbean. (We multiplied 1.58—Curtin's actual mean percentage of case mortality—by 1.6 to get 2.53 percent.)

The case mortality rate for Europeans in the Caribbean was probably higher than the case mortality rate for Europeans in the Chesapeake because malaria was more prevalent in the Caribbean and it was a year-long disease, not a seasonal disease as it was in the Chesapeake. The number of and different types of plasmodia protozoa in the victim's blood stream determine the case mortality for malaria. Given that malaria was more prevalent and year round, a victim in the Caribbean was more likely to be bitten by greater numbers of infectious mosquitoes carrying a greater variety of plasmodia types than a victim in the Chesapeake.

Although 2.5 percent is likely to be an upper bound estimate of the malaria case mortality rate in the Chesapeake for the 1680 to 1720 period, how probable is it? Suppose the morbidity rate for malaria in the Chesapeake was 200 cases per thousand. (This also is likely to be an upper bound estimate; Curtin's 1989, pp. 174–80, morbidity rate for European troops in the Caribbean ranges from over 300 cases per thousand to 90 cases per thousand.) The arithmetic implies that malaria could have contributed, at most, an additional five deaths per thousand (2.5 percent of 200) to the European and European-American death rate. Walsh and Menard (1974, p. 224) estimate that, for the late seventeenth century, males at age 20 in New England had a life expectancy of between 10 and 26 more years than males in Maryland (the Chesapeake). An additional five more deaths per thousand does not explain this gap. Accordingly, the evidence from the death rate data that do exist makes estimates of a case mortality rate of 2.5 percent and a morbidity rate of 200 per thousand for malaria in the Chesapeake more than plausible. (Rutman and Rutman 1976 have a similar accounting in their study.) The estimates are more than plausible because, given what we know about the disease ecologies of the two regions (New England and the Chesapeake) and how they changed, it would be implausible if malaria alone accounted for all or most of the gap. The estimates suggest that malaria could have been doing a lot of damage to the productivity of whites in the Chesapeake (high morbidity) but still not make a dent in the difference in crude death rates across regions (low case mortality). Consequently, to quantitative economic historians, who often insist, "If it can't be counted, it didn't exist," the impact of malaria might be invisible if mortality rates are the only data included in the metric.

The history of hookworm in America is more obscure than that of malaria. Hookworm was not recognized as a major problem in the United States until 1902 when Charles Wardell Stiles conducted microscopic studies on hookworm among the southern population and found it to be endemic in the South. Hookworm is an infestation of intestinal nematodes that is a seasonal, warm-weather disease that parasitize humans. The type of hookworm infecting the American South is infrequently fatal, but it can be debilitating. How debilitating hookworm is depends on a variety of factors: general health, nutrition, physical activity, and parasite load. The same parasite load in a poorly nourished population that engages in heavy physical exertions, compared to a well nourished one, can have severe effects; on the poorly nourished population, these effects include chronic sluggishness, weakness, exhaustion, and, in extreme cases, even cerebral hemorrhage.

Hookworm disease has ethnically (racially) disparate effects: natives of and descendants of people from tropical West Africa resist it better and tolerate a given parasite load better than do natives of and descendants of people from northwestern Europe. The exact scientific reason that people of tropical West African ancestry have greater resistance to hookworm is unclear. That they do was recognized almost as early as the disease (Stiles 1909). Indeed, in one study of descendants of people from tropical West Africa residing in the Caribbean, it was found that people infected with hookworm had higher productivity than the non-infected (Weisbrod, Andreano, Baldwin, et al. 1973, p. 76).

The impact of hookworm on people of northwestern European ancestry is different. Brinkley's (1994, pp. 113–14) findings suggest that in areas in the American South with ideal conditions for the propagation of the hookworm nematode, the percentage of whites in the area had a *significant and negative* impact on per capita agricultural income in 1910. His findings also indicate that locations that likely had heavy hookworm infestation in the post–Civil War South—an area in which people of African ancestry were systematically discriminated against—were places where "A county composed of 100 percent blacks would have a higher income of between \$10.50 and \$23.80 than a county of 100 percent whites, *ceteris paribus*" (Brinkley 1994, p. 114). Brinkley (1994, p. 84) also cites estimates by medical doctors of hookworm's affect on the reduction in early twentieth-century agriculture productivity that range between 20 and 70 percent with 40 percent being the most common estimate (see also Brinkley 1995, 1997). The exact reduction in the productivity of agricultural workers, however, is not the central issue here, what we do know is that hookworm reduced productivity differentially: people of European ancestry suffered more severely than people of African ancestry. There is every reason to believe that this ethnic disparity also existed in the centuries that preceded the twentieth century.[18]

We can summarize our explanation for the transition to African agricultural field workers in the Chesapeake with the help of figure 5.4, which is a combination of figures 5.2 and 5.3. We begin with the importation of African slaves into the Chesapeake in the seventeenth century (the top box in figure 5.4). Africans carry hookworm, malaria, and other tropical pathogens, within themselves. After the number of Africans increase beyond a threshold level, tropical diseases become endemic. Mosquitoes then transmit the malaria to the Europeans, and the hookworm nematode finds hosts among the Europeans as do other

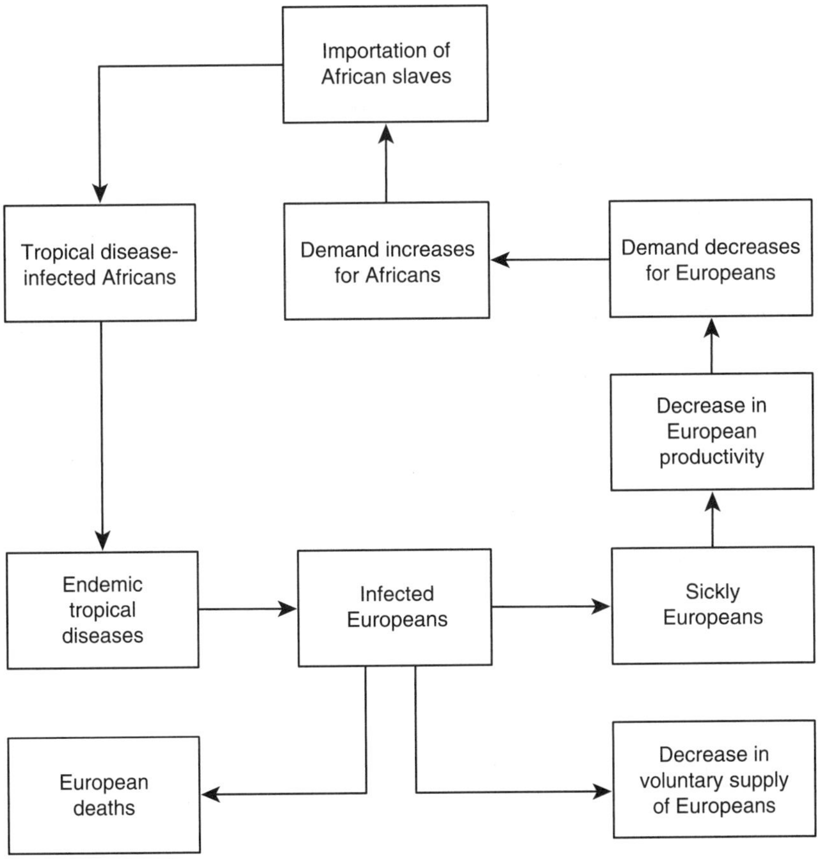

Figure 5.4
Interaction of the disease ecology and economics in the early Chesapeake

tropical pathogens. The Europeans are relatively sickly and die (not very probable), or are sickly (highly probable) during warm weather and the harvest seasons when tropical pathogens flourish. The relatively greater illness among Europeans would decrease the supply of those willing to voluntarily indenture themselves as agricultural field hands in the Chesapeake region (the bottom right-hand side box in figure 5.4). The illness among Europeans likewise decreases their agricultural productivity, which reduces the demand for Europeans as agricultural field hands. This increases the demand for Africans, leading to increased importation of African slaves, which restarts the cycle and leads to a relative decline in the number of Europeans and their descendants living in the southern colonies of the British American mainland.

In the British North American colonies of South Carolina and Georgia, hookworm and malaria were similarly associated with the introduction of African slavery. In South Carolina, Childs (1940, p. 263) argues that with the regular importation of African slaves, malaria had become endemic by the late 1690s; Wood (1975, pp. 62–69) notes that high mortality rates among whites discouraged their immigration to South Carolina at the end of the seventeenth century. Georgia, initially established as a free colony (where slavery was prohibited), did not become malarious until after its charter was altered in 1752 and slavery was established. Cates (1980, p. 153) writes: "Rapid expansion of slavery in the 1750s and 1760s [in Georgia] introduced large numbers of malaria infected Negroes to the colony. Thus, the very changes that most colonists felt were necessary to a prosperous and vital society produced an environment favorable to the growth and dispersal of parasites that would prey on it." Hookworm and malaria transformed the American South; once introduced, they became endemic. Given the knowledge of the time, these changes were irreversible.

Concluding Thoughts on the Initial Location of Africans and Europeans

History is written from an anthropocentric viewpoint. As humans, this should not cause us much concern except when nonhuman organisms materially impinge on the course of human events. The discovery of the New World and the interchanges of biological organisms (human and nonhuman) was one of those events. Prior to Contact, the New

World was relatively disease free. Immediately after Contact, the disease environments of its different climatic and geographic regions began the process of transformation into mirror images of their Old World counterparts. The African slave trade opened the New World to Africans and the diseases of tropical West Africa. This affected the patterns of settlement in the New World.

The value of servile labor depended on the discounted stream of income produced. In the Caribbean, the stream of earnings produced by an African was, on average, at least twice as long as that of a European because of the African's greater life expectancy. The European's income stream in turn was markedly longer than that of a Native American. The African also was likely to be healthier. Unless native or European servile labor was substantially cheaper, or their productivity in the same occupation was substantially greater than their African counterparts, neither would survive economically in competition with Africans in the New World tropics.

The biological susceptibility of northwestern Europeans to the disease environment that eventually prevailed in the New World tropics substantially reduced their life expectancy and capability for work. Given the alternative of enslaved Africans, European labor, servile or free, could not be supplied at a price low enough to be a viable alternative. The native populations fared even worse. The reason for these ethnic differences is that the disease environment that eventually prevailed in the tropics more closely resembled that of tropical West Africa rather than that of northwestern Europe or the pre–Contact New World. For millennia generations of West Africans had been exposed to virtually all tropical diseases. West African peoples had immune systems that had been selectively culled by the environment for the greatest resistance to tropical pathogens. The surviving and reproducing Africans of tropical West Africa produced a population that was, relative to Europeans, much more resistant to the onslaught of tropical diseases.

On the mainland of the North American continent, the environment became less favorable for tropical pathogens as one moved north. Cold-weather diseases were sufficient to make the northern colonies relatively unattractive for African slavery. In the Chesapeake, a combination of warm-weather diseases and agricultural seasonality were sufficient to make African slavery thrive. Further south, the introduction of African slaves changed the disease environment so that African slavery was the most economic form of labor given the institutions that existed.

How well does this disease story fit with the existing historical chronology? Economic historians have frequently written about the transition from European indentured servants to African slaves in British North America. Their explanations are driven by relative price differences: In the late seventeenth and early eighteenth centuries, the price of indentured servants rose relative to the price of slaves. Our explanation is perfectly consistent with this: a relative price shock induces the large-scale importation of African slaves. The timing of the price shock coincides with and is at least partially explained by the ending of the Royal African Company's monopoly of the English slave trade and a series of European wars that disrupted the markets for both African slaves and European indentured servants. The wars made African slaves cheaper to the English by disrupting the French and Spanish slave trades, and simultaneously raised the price of unskilled Europeans to the New World settlers because the wars increased the demand for soldiers, and thus raised the price for young, unskilled males—the type of person most likely to become an indentured servant (Grubb and Stitt 1994).

But we tell the remainder of the story, and resolve the dilemma of why Chesapeake plantation owners did not switch back to indentured servants when the price of African slaves rose relative to Europeans later in the eighteenth century, and why slavery was not viable in the northern regions. Once tropical diseases became endemic to the warm-weather areas of the New World, the economic calculus changed: Europeans were no longer good substitutes for Africans in agricultural field labor. Repeating a point previously made, these effects were irreversible and thus path dependent given scientific knowledge at the time.

Past and present historians have noted the "unsuitability" of European labor in the tropics and subtropics of the New World. In contrast, economic historians have made the (often implicit) simplifying assumption that Africans and Europeans were similarly productive and thus substitutable. The assumption of (approximately) homogeneous labor led economic historians to concentrate on changes in the supply of indentured servants and slaves in explaining the switch to African slaves in the New World. What we do is call attention to the differential reaction of peoples of different ancestral origins to the Old World pathogens introduced into the New World that led to changes in the demand for servants and slaves. A somewhat paradoxical result is that African slavery was a curse to not only the enslaved African, but also to the Europeans (and their descendants) in the New World where the environment was conducive for the growth and transmission of warm-weather diseases. Only after a significant African slave trade was established did the British American New World disease environment begin to resemble that of tropical West Africa. The changed environment made the American South a pest house, and the New World's tropics a graveyard for Europeans.

6 Slavery and Diseases in the Antebellum American South

As an economic institution American slavery was certainly privately profitable.[1] Slavery easily passed the most rigorous evolutionary test: survival. American slavery existed and thrived for over two hundred years; it was only extinguished in 1865 after the bloodiest conflict fought in the Western Hemisphere. Prior to the Civil War, slavery had spread throughout the reaches of the American South. It was entrenched as far north as Kentucky and Missouri; in the West, it had spread across Texas and was a contentious issue in the debates over statehood for New Mexico. For over two centuries, slaveowners profited immensely from their ownership of human chattel, and they were willing to plunge the American nation into war rather than contemplate any possible attenuation of their "peculiar institution." Regardless, these facts do not prove that slavery was profitable (efficient) to the *entire* non-enslaved Southern society, neither do they disprove that it was only slaveowners who profited from slavery with the rest of Southern society bearing the brunt of slavery's costs. Whether slavery was profitable to the entire non-enslaved population of the South is an issue unto itself demanding a complete listing of all the costs that slavery imposed on the South that were not paid by the owners of slaves.

Some costs of slavery were known to be borne by the entire society, not just by slaveowners; other costs that fell on the broader society were incompletely recognized, and some were completely unrecognized. Included in the costs borne by the entire South were (1) the costs of the legal system that defined and delineated property rights in humans, (2) the costs of the judicial and law enforcement systems that implemented the laws, and (3) the costs of the restrictions that the laws and customs of slavery imposed on the rights and privileges of the non-enslaved. These costs are widely ignored in the literature on slavery. Prior to the Civil War, mere discussions about the morals, ethics, and feasibility of slavery in the South that did not reflect well on slavery were hazardous to people who entertained them. Extrajudicial capital punishment (lynching) existed in the South before the Civil War; only before the Civil War its victims were mostly white, and many were lynched because of their antislavery views. The restrictions on human freedoms that upholding slavery entailed were no small sum either. For example, whites and blacks could not legally marry, and those who married without legal sanction could not send their children to school. The second Roman Catholic Bishop of Portland, Maine, James A. Healy was a child of such a mixed union. Healy and his siblings were separated from their parents in Georgia to receive an education in the North. These marital restrictions on freedom and choice are eerily suggestive of Nazi Germany.[2]

These everyday restrictions and expenses were all real costs of slavery, no less real were the costs imposed by the disease pools that slavery introduced and perpetuated in the American South. Two different forces made the southern disease environment different from that of the other states before the Civil War. One was climate, which differed by degree from that of the North; the other was slavery. It was slavery that made profitable the plantation economy (large landholdings cultivated primarily by non-family labor) that dominated much of southern agricultural output. Slavery and the plantation economy differed in kind from the way agricultural output and labor markets were organized in the North. Biological, epidemiological, and historical evidence document the role of the plantation South in the maintenance and spread of pathogens, and the debilitating effects of infectious parasitic diseases in the South.

In our discussion of the profitability (efficiency) of slavery, we accede to the common (yet morally reprehensible) practice of excluding the welfare of slaves from the calculus. We do this because if the welfare of slaves is included in the calculus, then the profitability and efficiency of slavery is trivially obvious: slavery was unprofitable and inefficient. If the benefits to slaves of slavery exceeded the costs to them, there would have been no need for physical compulsion (slavery); voluntary contractual arrangements could have replaced chattel slavery. People are willing to and do work under degrading, deplorable, and dangerous conditions if they are sufficiently compensated. Professional "sports" such as alligator wrestling and cage fighting are blatant examples of people sacrificing their dignity, and physical and mental well-being for fame and fortune. One might cast aspersions on the judgment and/or mental abilities of the participants, but there is no physical compulsion that forces them to undertake these activities; they are not slaves in any literal sense of the word.

After the Civil War, plantation owners found that they could not afford to pay freedmen enough to work as they did when they were slaves; this meant that the resumption of plantation-type agricultural production failed because the extra revenues generated by working under slave-like conditions (gang labor) were insufficient to compensate a free labor force to work under those conditions. The wages that had to be paid to a free labor force to work as it did before emancipation far outweighed the extra revenues the labor would have produced in plantation agriculture. Share cropping, tenant farming, and other forms of agricultural organizations were the institutional response to the financial impossibility of using pre-war production techniques (gang labor) with an emancipated labor force. This gives us the obvious conclusion: if the welfare of the enslaved is included in the calculus, slavery is patently unprofitable. The value of leisure (freedom) and more desirable work conditions were greater than the extra revenue generated by working people like slaves.

In this chapter, we examine the antebellum southern disease environment and the interactions between diseases and slavery. This involves assessing the impact of the primary "southern" diseases and their disparate effects on people of different ancestral heritages (ethnicities), identifying the interactions with the slave system, and exploring how this affected slavery and its profitability. We assess the role of slavery and the plantation system in the spread and perpetuation of infectious parasitic diseases throughout the southern populations—black and white—and discuss the impact of these diseases on health, human development, productivity, and society.[3]

African-American Slavery and Diseases

We begin with an observation that is medically and scientifically uncontroversial: diseases have different impacts on people of different ethnicities. Regardless of its acceptance by the medical and scientific communities, this statement still raises hackles in the social sciences; it appears to be a matter of morality for many social scientists to believe that there *should* be no genetic traits that differ markedly between ethnic (racial) groups. Stampp (1956) is a prominent example of this school of thought. In the absence of any evidence, and with only moral indignation supporting his case, he bluntly asserted his *belief* that there is no difference in ethnic susceptibilities to diseases: "The slave of tradition was a physically robust specimen who suffered from few of the ailments which beset the white man. A tradition with less substance to it has seldom existed. In the South, disease did not discriminate among men because of the color of their skins; wherever it was unhealthy for whites to live it was also unhealthful for Negroes" (Stampp 1956, p. 296). Charitable critics may say this statement is literally true: diseases do not discriminate on the basis of skin pigmentation but on other criteria (Duffy blood type, sickle cell trait, sweating response, and so forth). But even here a recent study by Pierson (2008) suggests that vitamin deficiency diseases (specifically, lack of vitamin D) differentially affected darker skinned people.

Stampp's beliefs are contradicted by evidence and objective reality. In the context of the antebellum South, there were identifiable diseases that had disparate impacts on the black and white southern populations. The warm southern environment and the plantation system of relatively clustered dense rural populations were particularly conducive to the perpetuation and spread of infectious pathogens. Plantation slavery played a significant role in creating and maintaining a distinctive southern disease ecology that, in turn, affected both the southern economy and society.

Even before the Civil War, slavery in America was a constant source of scholarly and public interest. In the present era, African-American slavery has simultaneously disgusted scholars and seduced them into expending scholarly efforts into researching it. In 1974, the hallmark addition to the continual flow of scholarship on slavery was the book *Time on the Cross* by Robert William Fogel and Stanley L. Engerman. This book intensified slavery debates, enflamed scholarly passions, and spurred interest among scholars and wider audiences. Both book and authors crossed over from academic venues to the general media. Book reviews appeared in all major newspapers in the United States, and Fogel conducted both radio and television interviews and appeared on nightly talk shows. Publicity and notoriety spurred an avalanche of scholarly (and nonscholarly) articles, books, and manuscripts on slavery. One of the more contentious issues that arose was that of slave living standards and the adequacy of slave diets. Indeed the heat of the debate on slave living standards can be appraised by the headline in *The New York Review of Books* (May 2, 1974) when it featured *Time on the Cross* in its lead book review. The review by C. Vann Woodward was headlined "The Jolly Institution." Interest in slave living standards metamorphosed into an interest in the role of nutrition and its effects on slave health and human development. Physiological measurements (termed anthropometrics) were used to address the question of the adequacy of slave diets, as it was maintained that the average stature (height) of a population is a relatively good proxy for the net nutrition of the population and can serve as a substitute for explicit evidence on diet when it is missing.[4]

Part of the emphasis on anthropometrics was the availability of large datasets containing physical measurements of enslaved Americans. These measurements, for instance, were required as a component of the prohibition of the international slave trade that was enacted by Congress on March 2, 1807, and took effect January 1, 1808. To ensure that no slaves in the antebellum era's coastwise trade were smuggled in from abroad, all slaves boarding and disembarking ships in ocean ports of the United States beginning in 1808 had to have a manifest detailing their physical characteristics lodged at the customs house of the ports of origin and destination. These coastwise manifests recorded estimates of slave ages, heights, weights, sex, and other physical characteristics; the records could then be used to ascertain whether any of the slaves in the coastal waters of the United States had been smuggled into American ports. The data are enormous (over 146,000 individual observations); consequently, the slave manifests provide fairly reliable estimates of the physical characteristics of slaves who were shipped on the coastal waters of the United States. Another large dataset containing measurements of the heights (and other personal characteristics) of nineteenth-century southern blacks, a substantial portion of who were former slaves, come from Union Army records during the Civil War. These data also are enormous, over 186,000 black males enlisted in the Union Army from late 1862 to 1865. While not containing as many observations as the preceding datasets, there are other substantial sources that detail the physical characteristics of nineteenth-century southern blacks (most of whom were born and raised slaves); among these are convict (penitentiary) records for various states.

Yet like most data, the data on slave (black) heights can mislead the unwary. The data have to be standardized to make sense of them; an obvious example is that the data have to be standardized for age and sex—because males are typically taller than females, and adults taller than children—to assess height. What also is normal is that height data are reported by year of birth; this is termed birth cohort. Even so the data are not revealing unless taken in historical context with an appreciation of the nuances that the entire dataset entails. A good example is that some of the anthropometric data indicate that the mean height of various slave cohorts was increasing during parts of the antebellum period and decreasing during other parts; other data indicate that the mean height of black Tennessee convicts born in the 1830s was increasing; still other data indicate that the heights of black Georgia convicts born in the 1830s and 1840s were stable (if not slightly increasing). But these findings have misled scholars to conclude that diets, not diseases, were certainly the more important influence on slave heights (see Komlos and Coclanis 1997; Rees, Komlos, van Long, and Woitek 2003; Sunder 2004).

The anthropometric data, though, are inadequate to answer the diet versus disease question for at least two reasons. First, the height findings derived from the data themselves are ambiguous about the exact time profile of slave heights; they indicate both fluctuations in heights as well as some (contradictory) time trends depending on the slave and birth cohorts examined and the data used.[5] Second, there are historical reasons. In the years between the end of the Revolutionary War (1783) and before the ban on the international slave trade (1808), extraordinarily large numbers of African slaves were imported into the United States.[6] Slave imports during this period dwarf that of any other similar period. The most recent direct estimate of slave imports for 1783 to 1810 puts imports at 170,300 slaves (McMillin 2004, pp. 30–48, and tables 7, 9); accepted estimates of total slave imports into the United States (or what became the United States) from colonial times to 1810 are between 600,000 and 660,000 slaves. This means that between 26 and 28 percent of all slave imports were brought into the country in less than thirty years.[7]

There are two reasons that make the absolute number of slaves imported important in the interpretation of slave heights. First, people born in tropical West Africa during the eighteenth and early nineteenth centuries were much shorter than their American-born descendants. Kiple and Kiple (1980, p. 786) summarize this issue: "Research conducted by Fogel, Engerman, and Higman concerning the height of some 25,000 Trinidadian slaves indicates that newly imported Africans were significantly shorter than Creole-born slaves. Fraginals has found the same to be true for Cuba. First-generation Creole slaves were significantly taller than freshly imported Africans." This means that the average slave height was depressed by the addition of African-born slaves. So the large number of slave imports from 1783 until the trade ban in 1808 would have brought down the mean heights of slaves in any data that included slaves born before 1808. But this is arithmetic; it does not indicate deteriorating diets in the United States.[8]

Second, and more important, the number of slaves imported is significant because with the importation of Africans came an increasing number of pathogens to which American-born slaves had no, or few, acquired immunities. The spread of these diseases to American-born slaves during the years when these pathogens were most rampant (1783 to 1808) would have affected American slave children born during those years and affected their adult heights. This can help explain the sharp increase in the heights of male and female slaves, aged 12 to 17, in the birth cohorts born circa 1817 to 1830 (Steckel 1979, p. 377). A milder disease ecology, because of the decline in "new" African diseases in their childhood, also can help explain the increasing heights of the adult male slaves born between circa 1805 and 1820 (Steckel 1979, p. 377), the stable heights of adult male black Georgia convicts born in the second half of the 1830s and in the 1840s (Komlos and Coclanis 1997, p. 439–40), and the increasing heights of adult male black Tennessee convicts born in the 1830s (Sunder 2004, pp. 80–81, 84–85). Alternatively, the increasing heights could be attributed to better diets, or they could be due to both diets and an ameliorating disease ecology. The possibility also exists that there were other entirely different reasons for the increasing heights. The data alone do not reveal truth; to unravel the connections, we have to use all the knowledge available, and still hope that we are right and not missing something. Still attributing increasing slave heights to slave diets may be entirely incorrect. Slave diets in the United States could have been unchanged and the mean heights of slaves would have risen as the proportion of African-born slaves in the coastal shipping data fell, and as the disease ecology in America ameliorated.

Regardless of these considerations, from the anthropometric findings, scholars suggest that adult male slaves were given adequate sustenance, but slave infants and children (and perhaps females) were severely malnourished (Steckel 1986b, 1992). The data indicate that adult slaves were only slightly shorter than contemporaneous whites; slave children were extraordinarily short, and slaves had relatively high rates of neonatal and infant mortality (Fogel 1986; Steckel 1986b, 1992). The obvious question is: If adult slaves were relatively healthy, then why were slave infants and children severely malnourished?

Steckel (1986b, 1992) addresses this issue, arguing that slaveowners systematically deprived infants and children of a nutritious diet.

We offer an alternative explanation: it was not the diets of slave children, but a combination of the plantation system and diseases that caused much of the phenomena of relatively healthy adults and sickly infants and children. Of course, there were synergies between diets and diseases in slave health; inadequate slave diets increased susceptibility to diseases and existing diseases in slaves affected their appetites and eating habits; these interactions led to inadequate diets. More precisely, *both* diets and diseases mattered. We emphasize the role of infectious parasitic diseases in the plantation South because heretofore such diseases have been given a subsidiary role in the history of the American economy. The role of infectious parasitic diseases in slave health is fundamental to a complete history of antebellum slavery, including the issues surrounding the biological standard of living of slave infants, children, and their caregivers, as well as the economics of slave productivity.[9]

Yellow Fever and the Southern Urban Disease Environment

Some diseases that were relatively common in the South ("southern" diseases) were less common in the North. As noted in the previous chapter, the further south one travels in the United States the more the climate is conducive to the maintenance and spread of pathogens that depend on warm weather for survival, or the survival of their vectors (most usually arthropods). Yellow fever, while never endemic to the United States, was one of the parasitic diseases that was initially imported with the slave trade, and we believe was instrumental in shaping southern society.

To repeat points made earlier, yellow fever is typically a disease of urban or very dense populations, and an individual once infected with yellow fever has life-long immunity to re-infection. It is an acute viral disease that has a relatively brief duration in humans. It does not exist during cold periods because its vector (the mosquito *Aedes aegypti*) cannot survive freezing cold and is inactive in cool weather. *A. aegypti* has a range of less than a few hundred meters and can only survive a few days without water; consequently, it is usually active in wet and warm areas such as the American southeast. Without continuously warm weather, yellow fever cannot become endemic. It was endemic in the Caribbean islands and tropical South America, where it is still endemic in monkey populations. Currently, it spreads from monkey populations to the occasional human, but modern medicine and vaccinations have reduced yellow fever to a minor public health menace. In nineteenth-century America, yellow fever epidemics were most severe in urban environments; it has been absent from the American landscape since 1905, but its mosquito vector is still abundant and widespread.

Yellow fever was imported into the port cities of the antebellum South, particularly when the international slave trade was in its noxious bloom. Along with tropical produce, yellow fever was episodically introduced into southern port cities after the prohibition of the international slave trade in 1808. Children infected by the disease seem to suffer less and die less frequently than adults. Southerners who grew up and lived in or near port cities (New Orleans, Charleston, Mobile, Savannah, and Wilmington) were likely to have had a childhood exposure that made them immune to yellow fever. People of tropical West African ancestry were (and are) relatively resistant to yellow fever. While the physiological basis for African resistance to yellow fever has not been identified, tropical West Africans and their descendants are much less susceptible to death from yellow fever than non-Africans. What this means is that the people who were especially susceptible to yellow fever were recent arrivals to southern port cities not of West African ancestry. Northerners and European immigrants were the peoples who fit in this category; the death rate of yellow fever among recent arrivals was so appalling that it was given the appellation, the "strangers' disease." Pritchett and Tunali (1995, p. 519) estimate that non-Americans constituted 89.5 percent of all fatalities in the 1853 yellow fever epidemic in New Orleans; in contrast, African-Americans constituted just 1.2 percent of the fatalities and whites born in New Orleans 3.3 percent. Pritchett and Tunali (1995, p. 519) also estimate that the mortality rate in New Orleans for foreign-born whites from all diseases in 1853 was 148 per thousand, contrasted to 24 per thousand for New Orleans-born whites.

The differential in death rates is even more impressive when one accounts for the presumed age and health of immigrants. The population of people who emigrated in the nineteenth century was not an unbiased sample of the originating population; immigrants tend to be lumped between the ages of 18 and 40, and they tend to be healthy. Given the rigors of long-distance travel in the nineteenth century, we expect these traits in immigrants to be even more pronounced. This means that a relatively young and healthy population died at a rate six times higher than that of the native white population (including infants, the elderly, and the sickly), according to Pritchett and Tunali's estimates; in 1853, an immigrant to New Orleans had a better than 1 chance in 7 of dying. Moreover a little over a decade later, in New Orleans in 1867, black troops in the Union Army who had no previous exposure to yellow fever (and consequently no acquired immunities) suffered a mortality rate of 73 per thousand when they contracted yellow fever; their white counterparts died at a rate of 256 per thousand (Kiple and King 1981, p. 45).

Part of the excess mortality of immigrants was due to living conditions; immigrants tended to live in crowded conditions without many amenities; in short, slum-like housing. Standing pools of water (New Orleans had no sewers) served as breeding grounds for yellow fever's mosquito vector; this explains part of the excess mortality of immigrants. Another part can be explained by their relative poverty; the staple southern diet of the poor consisted of cornmeal, molasses, and pork fatback. This diet can and did cause pellagra, a disease of nutritional (niacin) deficiency. Immigrant nutritional resources would have been depleted by the long ocean voyage and exacerbated by their adoption of the diet of the southern poor; sickly people are more likely to suffer more severely when attacked by another disease.

The urban South was decidedly unhealthful for newcomers that were not of West African ancestry. This had a profound impact on southern culture and American history. Besides yellow fever in southern urban areas, there were the ubiquitous diseases common to most nineteenth-century American cities. Among the more common urban diseases were some that are the childhood diseases of today—measles, whooping cough, diphtheria—in addition to cholera, dysentery, and tuberculosis. While it might seem that these ubiquitous urban diseases would have had no particular differential effect on European immigrants or northern migrants in the South, this is not correct. Given the southern climate relative to that from which the immigrants and migrants came, the specific strains of pathogens that thrived in southern cities in the nineteenth century were relatively virulent throughout more of the year than in the North or in Europe.

Death and disease, and the competition from slave labor, made the South unattractive to European immigrants and northern migrants. Low levels of such newcomers had the effect of homogenizing the white society of the South. The politically active immigrants who fled

European tyrannical rulers and secret police did not typically go to the South; those who did go south (and survived) were too few in numbers to question the southern system of slavery and aristocracy. This, and the low numbers of northern migrants, allowed the belief that the institution of racial slavery was natural and just to flourish in the South because there were no substantial elements in the white population who spoke in opposition. All true (white) southerners supported the system; a relatively homogeneous population allowed the easy suppression of heterodox opinions. This was unlike the North; immigrants there were relatively common, and a myriad of opinions on slavery and race, while not welcomed, were tolerated for the most part. Southerners viewed the election of Lincoln as a kind of blasphemy; no right thinking (white) man would question the morality of slavery.

In the North in 1860, there was no overwhelming desire for war to free slaves. There was an emotional attachment to the concepts of one country and a shared history. It was only the southern actions to dissolve the Union by force that galvanized the North to go to war. And why was the South so unyielding? It was because *everyone* knew that slavery was beneficial and right. A substantial portion of southern belligerence and intransigence can be attributed to the southern disease environment that visited illness and death so abundantly on northerners and European immigrants who may have had radically different views on the ethics of African slavery.

Slave Plantations and the Southern Rural Disease Environment

The living conditions of most African-American slaves were very different from those of other agriculturalists in the pre–Civil War United States. The ownership of slaves was relatively concentrated. In 1850 for the entire South, 21.6 percent of all slaves were owned by people who owned 50 or more slaves; in 1860, the percentage was 24.9 percent. In the lower South, the percentages were 30.6 percent in 1850 and 33.2 percent in 1860 (Gray 1958, vol. 1, p. 530). There is a caveat; these data are for slaveowners, not slaves resident per plantation. However, the source of the data, Gray (1958, vol. 1, p. 530), states that "While a single large slaveholding might be distributed among several different plantations, this was undoubtedly exceptional." Relying on Gray, we can interpret these data for the most part as slaves per plantation, except for the largest slaveowners, say owners with 200 or more slaves. For the entire South though, owners with 200 or more slaves accounted for only 2.2 percent of all slaves in 1850 and only 2.4 percent in 1860 (Gray 1958, vol. 1, p. 530). Gray (1958, vol. 1, pp. 529–35) also has data on the size of slave holdings; for the entire South, the median number of slaves held was 20.6 in 1850 and 23.0 in 1860; for the lower South, the median number of slave holdings was 30.9 in 1850 and 32.5 in 1860.

The resident slave population on plantations was for the most part kept in compact areas ("slave quarters"), close but not adjacent to the dwellings of the white residents. In nineteenth-century America, the housing of slaves represented a highly unusual form of farm housing. Non-slave agricultural communities had a much more dispersed population, with the distance between residences vastly greater than that between slave cabins. Free farms had many fewer acres and workers (both family members and any hired workers) per farm relative to slave plantations; free agricultural workers typically lived on or very close to the land they cultivated. In contrast, the density of the slave population and housing was unique in nineteenth-century agriculture because on large slave plantations the slave quarters typically had multiple families and many slaves per acre.

The slave quarters that have survived into the twenty-first century are outliers; the typical shoddily built structures were much more likely to have been torn down and/or abandoned relative to more substantial structures. Nevertheless, from surviving structures and documentary material, it appears that slave quarters were constructed with between 15 to 30 cabins per acre. A little arithmetic supports this observation. The typical slave cabin is reported to have been 800 square feet. Suppose, to error on the side of caution, we double it to 1,600 square feet and give an additional 1,000 square feet of grounds between cabins; our "typical" slave cabin then occupies 2,600 square feet (including grounds). This gives a separation of about 20 feet between each cabin. From casual observation of surviving slave quarters, this seems about right. There are 43,560 square feet in an acre; consequently, these dimensions imply approximately 17 slave cabins per acre (17 cabins times 2,600 square feet per cabin equals 44,200 square feet). If each cabin housed a family of five, then 20 cabins would have housed 100 people. The 20 cabins would require 2,600 square feet each, for a total of 52,000 square feet or approximately 1.19 acres. As a result, a plantation with 100 slaves could have housed them on just over one acre.

The animals and food storage of the slave quarters were similarly confined and concentrated in a relatively small area. Defecation, urination, disposing of waste products, and cooking invite environmental pollution and infestation by pathogens. Somewhat ameliorating the increased hazards associated with crowding and pollution was that slaveowners could more readily absorb the fixed costs associated with a "public works" infrastructure. For example, wells could be dug and lined with brick and mortar to prevent ground water and animal contamination, and privies could be built some distance away from housing. In contrast, many small farms in the South, both before and after the Civil War, had no dedicated facilities for the disposal of human wastes; their sanitary facilities were bushes or secluded outposts.

We focus on the diseases that were both endemic to the southern plantation system and had disparate effects on African-American and European-American peoples. Hookworm and malaria are given special consideration later in the chapter because (1) they have disparate effects on African-Americans and European-Americans that have been documented, (2) they were both widespread in the antebellum rural South, (3) they affect adult productivity even though they have relatively low levels of case mortality, and (4) they both have a substantial historical, medical, and scientific literature that allows for their investigation and analysis.[10]

Nutritional and Parasitic Diseases on Southern Plantations

The diseases of the slave quarters can be broken into two parts—nutritional and parasitic. Nutritional diseases of the slave quarters were significant and relatively widespread. The nutritional diseases in the slave quarters were caused by ignorance rather than malice; this should not be taken to imply that slaveowners were benevolent. Slaves were very valuable and expensive assets. Any deliberate nutritional deprivation would have been economically stupid. Nevertheless, there were nutritional deficiencies in the slave quarters and some of these deficiencies manifested themselves in the form of illnesses.

Probably the most prevalent of the nutritional diseases was pellagra, but pellagra was not identified as a nutritional disease until the first half of the twentieth century. Pellagra is caused by lack of niacin (B_3). People whose diets rely heavily on corn (maize) are particularly susceptible to it because untreated corn is deficient in niacin.[11] Symptomatic of pellagra are the "four D's": diarrhea, dermatitis, dementia, and death; other symptoms include sensitivity to sunlight, aggression, red skin lesions, insomnia, weakness, mental confusion, and paralysis of extremities. Kiple and Kiple (1977) argue that pellagra, although not identified as a specific disease, was widespread in the slave population of the antebellum South.

There are difficulties in identifying pellagra; the difficulties are because pellagra advances in stages that are not easily recognized as one clinical manifestation. Kiple and Kiple (1977) maintain that pellagra manifested itself seasonally; its early symptoms appearing in late winter and early spring when slave diets were most monotonous and most dependent on corn meal. They argue that "black tongue" and other diseases that were identified by the southern medical establishment were simply manifestations of pellagra in its various stages. The case they make for the prevalence of pellagra in the antebellum South is compelling; their arguments are even more convincing because in the early twentieth century pellagra was found to be endemic among the poorer peoples in the South.

Knowledge of the prevalence of other nutritional diseases is less well documented than pellagra. Protein deficiencies can cause kwashiorkor (protein malnutrition; indicated generally by fatigue, irritability, lethargy, growth failure, diarrhea, dermatitis, and mental retardation); other specific vitamin and mineral deficiencies also can cause mental retardation, physical deformities, and reduced growth. While a single incidence of vitamin-protein-calorie malnutrition may not cause permanent disability, an entire regime of childhood malnutrition will have permanent effects (Das and Pivato 1976; Das and Soysa 1978). Except for iodine deficiencies (goiter and cretinism), most nutritional diseases would have been eliminated or, at least alleviated, by the more abundant and varied diet that accompanies the warm-weather months of the year. As noted earlier, Pierson (2008) suggests that darker skinned African-Americans were more susceptible to diseases associated with vitamin D (the "sunshine" vitamin) deficiency. To repeat a point, the diseases caused by nutritional deficiencies were due to neither malice nor avarice: slaveowners could have been morally obtuse, but they would not have deliberately hazarded slave capital valued at over a thousand dollars and compromised slave productivity to save a few dollars per year (see Lebergott 1984, pp. 210–35). Still, nutritional diseases were a hazard in the slave quarters, but they were not infectious, unlike parasitic diseases.

Parasitic diseases are those that are caused by foreign organisms entering the human body; these organisms include viruses, fungi, protozoa, bacteria, and multicellular parasites. The human body contains a multitude of organisms that are nonhuman. Indeed, it has been estimated that the amount of nonhuman DNA in a human body vastly exceeds that attributable to *Homo sapiens*. (So when people use the term "we" rather than "I" it can be interpreted literally.) The vast majority of these organisms do not cause illness in humans; some are symbionts (mutually beneficial), others are commensals (nonharmful parasites), and others become pathogenic only during specific circumstances.

All the diseases caused by foreign organisms (parasites) have not been identified; the acquisition of knowledge is ongoing, and what we know today may be undone tomorrow. The history of stomach ulcers is illustrative of the growing realization of the importance of microorganisms. Twenty years ago (in 1990) the prevailing medical view was that stomach ulcers were known to be caused by stress and diet. Barry Marshall, a relatively obscure (at least to the medical establishment and to the authors of medical textbooks) internist in Australia, had in the 1980s co-authored papers showing that a bacterium (*Helicobacter pylori*) was associated with gastric ulcers and that the ulcers responded to antibiotics. Only after the renowned medical organ, *The National Enquirer* (March 13, 1990), publicized his work did the medical establishment pay heed (cited in Ewald 2000, p. 233). Today antibiotics are the usual treatment for gastric ulcers. In this vein some forms of cancer have been shown to be caused by viruses; the importance of microorganisms is undergoing a transformation in the causal factors of diseases (Ewald 2000).

Parasitic diseases are infectious; just how they are transmitted depends on the organism. Some are transmitted by soil or water pollution, others have arthropod vectors, and others are communicable from other humans. We have difficulties listing all the parasitic diseases of the slave quarters because such diseases are superabundant and we cannot completely identify which diseases were present and when, and which were not. Microorganisms as a causal factor in disease were not recognized until the works of Louis Pasteur, Robert Koch, Charles Laveran, Ronald Ross, Charles Finlay, and the other pioneer microbiologists of the late nineteenth and early twentieth centuries. But we do know that parasitic agents existed before they were identified, and that diarrhea, which was common in the South, is a symptom that is widely associated with parasitic and water-borne diseases.

Diseases that are soil transmitted, water-borne, and/or density dependent would have been much more abundant in plantation slave quarters than on family farms in similar climatic and geographic circumstances. These diseases are so ubiquitous that they are frequently not identified by the causal parasite or scientific name, but by symptom; they are lumped together and characterized as diarrheal diseases. We cannot attempt an even modestly comprehensive list of parasitic diseases because there are just too many pathogens and they are (and were) evolving too rapidly to assemble a comprehensive catalog of them.

To illustrate the problem for water-borne diseases, the Center for Disease Control in the United States estimated that 58 percent of all cases of water-borne infections in the United States for the years 1991 to 1998 had no identified causal agent (Cullimore 2008, p. 29). The public health authorities in the United States at the end of the twentieth century were competent and conscientious; the reason that so many infections were not matched with pathogens is that the task is not possible given the state of knowledge. Nevertheless, some parasitic diseases related to human density (in addition to hookworm and malaria) that are mentioned prominently in the literature and were likely to have been in and around antebellum slave quarters are hepatitis A, infectious hepatitis, viral gastroenteritis, *Campylobacter*, *Escherichia (E.) coli*, leptospirosis, Salmonella enteric fever, rotavirus, Shigella, cholera, yersiniosis, amebiasis, *Giardia lamblia*, and enterobiasis. Most of these diseases are due to fecal pollution. Besides hookworm, other helminthic infections of tropical origin also would, in all probability, have been more abundant in plantation slave quarters than on family farms, as they are spread through fecally polluted soils and water, and are density dependent. The most common of the other parasitic worms in the antebellum South were *Ascaris* (large roundworm) and *Trichuris* (whipworm). While neither as abundant nor as widespread as hookworm, the available evidence suggests that large roundworm and whipworm infections were relatively common in the antebellum South.[12]

Although the significance, both medical and economic, of large roundworm and whipworm infections is tertiary to that of hookworm, it is not trivial and the two parasitic worms have many similarities with hookworm.[13] The survival, maintenance, and spread of large roundworm and whipworm are similar to hookworm. Both predominate in areas of poor sanitation where there is fecal pollution. Individuals acquire the parasites when they inadvertently ingest fecally contaminated soil or consume contaminated food or water. Because of their behavior, infants and young children are more commonly and more heavily infected in poor, rural areas with warm humid climates and moist sandy soils. (Neonates also can acquire the worms in the placenta.) Both parasites eventually end up in the human's intestine where they live on the host's tissue secretions. Many of their symptoms and consequences also are similar to hookworm but typically not as severe because they do not suck the hosts' blood (and its nutrients) as do hookworms. Individuals with either large roundworm or whipworm infections usually are asymptomatic. When they are not, they are likely to have abdominal cramps, fever, coughing and wheezing, nausea, and vomiting.

For large roundworm infections, a heavy worm load can block the intestine, resulting in severe pain and vomiting, and may lead to cachexia (general ill health, malnutrition, weight loss, wasting of muscle, loss of appetite, and physical weakness). Heavy worm loads also are associated with iron-deficiency anemia and impairments of growth and cognition (mental retardation). Children infected with heavy loads may not grow or gain weight normally. For whipworm infections, the common symptoms are present only for individuals with very heavy worm loads, and there are no pulmonary symptoms because, unlike large roundworms and hookworms, there is no pulmonary migration with whipworms. A large number of whipworms in the colon can lead to loss of appetite, chronic diarrhea, and dysentery. Exceptionally large whipworm loads, especially in children, may lead to weight loss, bleeding from the intestine, iron-deficiency anemia, and stunted growth.

Recent research suggests that another helminth also could have been in southern slave plantations. Hotez and Wilkins (2009) argue that infection with the roundworms *Toxocara canis* and *Toxocara cati* is the most common intestinal infection among Americans today; they are especially prevalent in poor rural and urban areas in the American South and among African-Americans. As with other parasitic worms, *T. canis* and *T. cati* are spread when humans inadvertently ingest fecally contaminated soils, but in this case it is zoonotic transmission; it is the feces of dogs and cats, respectively, that contain *Toxocara* eggs and larvae. The most common clinical features of infection are wheezing, pulmonary infiltrates, and eosinophilia (a blood abnormality commonly associated with helminthic infections). As these features also are characteristic of childhood asthma, it has been hypothesized that *Toxocara* infection and childhood asthma are linked; Hotez and Wilkins (2009) note that the two have been linked in a handful of studies.

Toxocara infection also has been linked with mental retardation and developmental delays. Given conditions on southern plantations and the prevalence of dogs in the antebellum South, it seems likely that, at least, *T. canis* infection could have been common among the resident plantation population.

We emphasize that the slave quarters of nineteenth-century America were highly suited for the transmission of parasitic diseases, and that the increased density of the biomass provided ecological niches for pathogenic infestation. Microbes are ubiquitous; so the appropriate question is not "where are there microbes," but "where are the places from which microbes are absent?" Everywhere there are humans there are microbes, and indeed we harbor multitudes of them inside our bodies; bodily functions of all animals release microbes that may become pathogenic outside of their normal environment. The interactions of diseases within the human body can create negative synergies that may exacerbate the consequences of disease. For example, individuals afflicted with pellagra *and* hookworm are much sicker than if they had just one or the other (Kunitz 1988; Martin and Humphreys 2006). The same is true of individuals infected with cholera *and* hookworm (Harris, Podolsky, Bhuiyan, et al. 2009). Moreover, having one disease often makes treatment and recovery from another disease more problematic.

When we consider the health effects of slave plantations, the interactions among diseases magnifies the negative consequences of the plantation system. Slavery exacerbated the disease situation; low living standards, poor sanitation, and dense human and animal populations made the slave quarters a haven for many pathogens that adversely affected human health. While we concentrate on the affects of these pathogens on the enslaved population, the pathogens were opportunistic, afflicting all to a greater or lesser degree. Large slave plantations served as disease reservoirs that aided the survival of pathogens and assisted in their transmission from the plantation to the wider world. Within the plantation South, slavery and diseases interacted and had profound effects.

We illustrate how we conceive of the biohazards that surrounded the inhabitants of the slave quarters on large plantations in figure 6.1. The figure illustrates our thinking; the arrows in figure 6.1 indicate the direction of causality. Starting at the top, large-scale slave plantations led to (1) increased rural human density, (2) poorly constructed and dense slave housing, (3) slave infants and young children concentrated

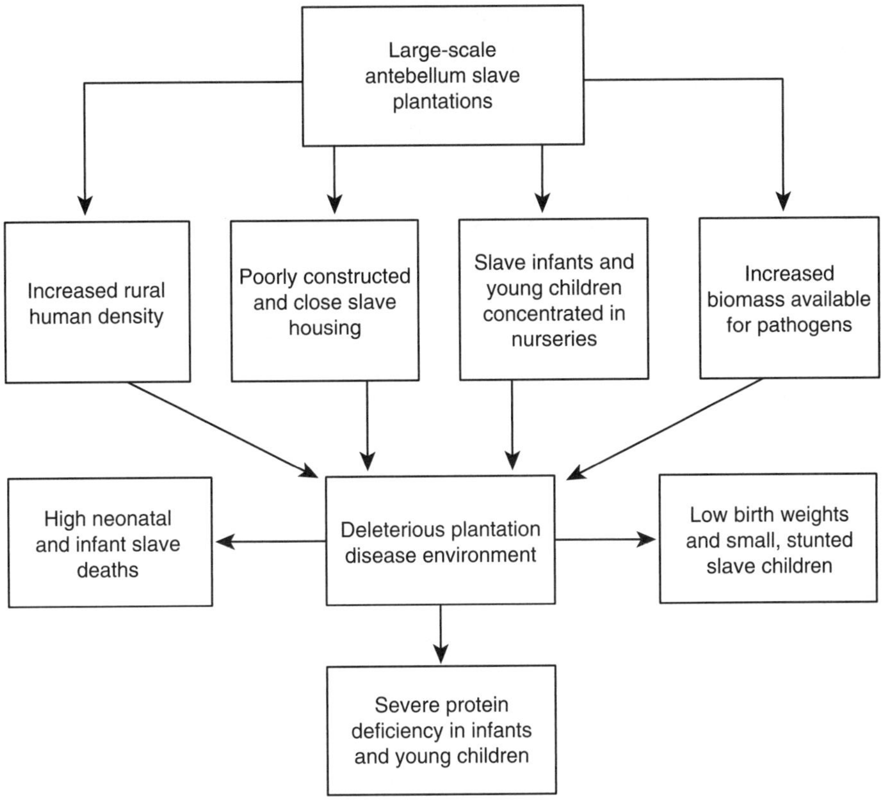

Figure 6.1
Interactions of antebellum agriculture and slave health

in nurseries, and (4) a general increase in the biomass available for pathogens. Slave children who had not yet learned to control their bowel functions defecated around the slave quarters. Coprophagous animals (dogs, chickens, and swine) further disseminated the fecal biohazards. These conditions produced a plantation-specific disease ecology conducive to the establishment and propagation of pathogens that arise from fecal contamination of soil and water, zoonoses from the farm animals, food-borne diseases, parasites, and a host of other conditions associated with poor living standards, inadequate sewage and water, and animals and humans confined to a small area. Given these conditions, plantation water supplies would have been frequently contaminated by runoff and poor sanitation. All of this led to a deleterious plantation disease environment. These disease conditions would have affected slave infants and young children more severely than older children and adults because their immune system had not been exposed to the infections common on the plantations; consequently, they had no ready supply of antibodies to combat these infections.

The results of the plantation disease environment and infections were (1) low birth weight babies and small, stunted children, (2) high neonatal and infant mortality, and (3) the effects of severe protein deficiency—hypoalbuminemia (inadequate protein) and kwashiorkor in infants and young children afflicted with the pathogens abundant in and about the slave quarters.

Relative to living conditions in the twenty-first century, slave living conditions were abysmal. Still this is a book about history, and relative to early nineteenth-century conditions, slave living conditions were better than some and worse than others.[14] A point we wish to make here is that the living conditions of slaves likely were improving throughout the nineteenth century's slave era. Improvements would have been due to (1) an amelioration of the disease environment associated with the end of the international slave trade, (2) an increase in knowledge in providing medical care, sewage disposal, and water on large plantations, (3) an increase in slave "income" due to increasing productivity, and (4) rational behavior as the price of slaves increased substantially with increasing productivity and the end of slave imports. So, while conditions were not up to standards anyone reading this book would like to experience, they were improving.

The two diseases that we discuss in detail below, hookworm and malaria, were initially brought to the American South as a by-product of the Old World migrations. There is speculation that hookworm and some types of malaria appeared in other locations by the time of the Voyages of Discovery; but generally they are considered to be of tropical African origin. These infectious parasitic diseases can place severe burdens on their victims. In the South, the diseases differentially affected the white and black populations and their life cycles.

Before the Civil War, many of the enslaved blacks were concentrated on plantations; infants and young children were placed in plantation crèches ("nurseries" or "day care centers") under the care of older children, pregnant women, and elderly slaves. The combination of slavery and large-scale plantation agriculture created pockets of relatively dense rural populations that allowed the maintenance and spread of malaria. Malaria during pregnancy, infancy, and childhood adversely affected younger slaves, who, while they might have had some innate immunity, had no acquired immunities. (More discussion of the two types of immunities appears later in the chapter.) The environment of slave crèches also was conducive to the spread of hookworm, as was the practice of allowing children to go barefoot. Hookworm placed stresses on slave children, reduced the nutritional value of a given diet, and reduced appetites. Moderate to severe hookworm infection would lead to low slave birth weights, short stature, extraordinarily small slave children, and high neonatal and infant mortality. These symptoms that the anthropometric literature attributes to inadequate diets also are consistent with the plantation South's disease environment.

White infants and children were much less likely to be raised in conditions that were as conducive to the breeding and transmittal of disease. White children typically had fewer of the pathogens common to the plantation than slave infants and children because they were not subject to the disease environment that existed in the slave quarters 24 hours per day. The diseases also affected black and white adults differently. When slaves entered the adult workforce, they were taken from the disease breeding grounds of the slave quarters and "day care centers" and sent into the relatively (for blacks) healthy fields, while whites who went into the fields found a disease environment that was typically worse than that of their childhood. The antebellum agricultural labor force of the South was composed of two populations, white and black, both diseased; with the adult white population more sickly where the disease environment supported warm-weather pathogens that flourished in hot weather.

Plantation slavery allowed reservoirs of parasitic diseases to exist. Human hookworm and malaria require human hosts to complete their life cycles. Without a critical mass of both carriers and potentially infected humans, these diseases could not have existed. Slave plantations concentrated human beings into close proximity with one another; the increased density on plantations insured the diseases' survival and transmission. Endemic to the plantation South these diseases spread to nonplantation populations.[15]

Disparate Impact of Diseases on Ethnic Groups

Repeating a major theme of this book, diseases do not have the same impact on people of different ethnic (ancestral) backgrounds; there are two reasons for this: acquired and innate immunities. Acquired immunities are obtained when an individual contracts the disease. Individuals who recover have immune systems that are primed to resist subsequent re-infections by the same pathogen. In an environment where the pathogen is endemic, acquired immunities may make the disease a childhood infection with a few adults contracting it. Some common diseases (yellow fever, mumps, measles, and chickenpox) appear to affect children much less severely than adults. But appearances may be deceiving, and in fact disease may not affect children less severely. The empirical evidence for the resistance of children to some "childhood" diseases may be because, in an environment where these diseases are endemic (the diseases are a common feature of life, so adults who were born in the area typically had exposure to the disease as children), there are disease-free adults to care for sick children. If both adults and children are stricken, as in epidemics, many children perish simply for the lack of adequate care. For example, diarrhea causes dehydration, and the effects of dehydration are a function of body mass; because of their small size infants can easily die from a loss of fluids in less than 24 hours.

Innate resistance is the product of evolutionary selection. Both pathogens and humans are native to specific geographic environments. Human populations become accommodated to the disease environments in which they reside generation after generation. Depending on a variety of factors (virulence, nonhuman hosts, and the method of transmission), pathogens can evolve into less deadly forms (Ewald 1994). It is widely thought that syphilis is less virulent now than in early sixteenth-century Europe in part because it's more deadly forms were culled from the bacterial population (McNeill 1976). The genetic characteristics that make an individual more resistant to the onslaught of pathogens will spread among members of the population as the individual humans with that characteristic survive longer and have more surviving and successfully reproducing children. Genetic characteristics are innate. They are transmitted by parents to the fertilized egg and are in the individual at birth; they are not acquired after exposure to a pathogen. People who do not possess genetic traits that convey resistance to disease pathogens are at a disadvantage in environments that harbor the pathogens.

A single gene, as noted, typically has more than one phenotypic effect; these effects may have positive, negative, or no impact on reproductive success. Genes react with one another and with the external environment to shape phenotypic effects. Genes that confer resistance to pathogens that abound in a particular disease ecology and whose *net* effect on reproduction is positive (they have no offsetting phenotypic effects that *in toto* reduce reproductive success), are proadaptive; they will spread through the population. Conversely, in environments that do not harbor diseases to which the specific genes confer resistance, the phenotypic effects will typically prove maladaptive; populations that have these genes will have less reproductive success than populations that do not possess them. The sickle cell gene is illustrative of this process; where malaria is highly endemic, populations that carry the sickle cell trait have more reproductive success than populations without it because the trait confers substantial resistance to malaria, and malaria places heavy burdens of increased morbidity and mortality on nonresistant populations. In environments that are not malarious, populations that have the sickle cell trait have less reproductive success because when both parents have the trait, on average, one-quarter of their children will have sickle cell disease and die young. In a malarious environment, these deaths are less burdensome than the toll that malaria extracts from a nonresistant population. This illustrates that the relative frequency of genes in a population is subject to changes over time; these changes depend on, among other things, the disease ecology, evolution, and human responses to the prevalence of diseases.

Slaves in the antebellum South were of predominately tropical West African heritage, but not entirely. Africans from other regions were sometimes brought to the North American continent; also there were subsequent unions between people of tropical West African ancestry and individuals of other ancestry. As evidence of these unions, Wahl (1996, p. 21) has a vignette concerning a "blonde, blue-eyed, light-skinned slave" in the pre–Civil War South, obviously a slave whose American ancestry was more "European" than "African" due to sexual unions between African slaves and whites in the New World. Free labor in the antebellum South was of predominately northwestern European ancestry. Even accounting for unions of people of different ancestral heritages, any innate resistance that tropical West Africans had to specific pathogens would have been overrepresented in the enslaved population relative to other Americans. There is ample evidence that people of tropical West African ancestry (blacks) are, and were, more resistant to infection by hookworm and malaria than are people of northwestern European ancestry (whites).

Hookworm

The Disparate Impact of Hookworm

Hookworm disease is caused by an infection of parasitic nematodes (genus *Strongyloidea*). The two major hookworms that afflict humans are *Ancylostoma duodenale* and *Necator americanus*. While these genera differ in their habitat, mode of transmission, and other significant details, their effects on humans are similar (see Breeden 1988; Ettling 1981; Savitt and Young 1988).

As noted in chapter 5, hookworm was not identified as a major problem in the United States until 1902 when stool samples drawn from the southern population that September were microscopically examined by Charles Wardell Stiles; the samples indicated that hookworm was endemic to the South. The presence of endemic hookworm among the southern population was then given wide publicity in a paper presented by Stiles at a scientific conference in December 1902. But it appears to have taken several years for medical authorities to accept the fact of endemic hookworm (Chernow 2004, pp. 487–88). Compounding the error of not recognizing the disease, the type of hookworm infecting southern Americans was identified as native to America and named *Necator americanus* (American killer). The scientific appellation remained even after it was discovered that *Necator americanus* was endemic to tropical West Africa, parts of the Middle East and southern Europe, and the Indian subcontinent.

In reaction to Stiles's work, "[n]o less than eight investigators surveyed all or part of the southern lowlands. . . . In every instance, the results were the same; each researcher uncovered numerous cases of the disease and provided concrete evidence that hookworm was indeed a condition from which many in the South suffered" (Marcus 1988, p. 91). The Rockefeller Sanitary Commission for the Eradication of Hookworm Disease, organized in late 1909 and lasting until March 1914, estimated that more than 43 percent of all southerners were infected with hookworm in the early 1900s, or 7.5 million people out of a population of approximately 17.5 million. Brinkley (1994, p. 84) also reports an estimate of hookworm infestation, estimating that 39 percent of the southern labor force was infected in 1909.

But the impact of hookworm is not the same for people of different ancestry. Clear empirical regularities exist that show, relative to other ethnic groups, descendants of tropical West Africans have less infection in the same hookworm environment (Chandler 1929; Dock and Bass

1910; Smillie and Augustine 1925). Descendants of West Africans also appear to tolerate a given parasite load better than descendants of people from northwestern Europe (Weisbrod, Andreano, Baldwin, et al. 1973, p. 76). The scientific basis of this relative resistance of people of West African ancestry is not known, though evidence has emerged suggesting that genetic factors may partially account for human susceptibility to hookworm infection (Williams-Blangero, Blangero, and Bradley 1997). The apparent reason for the lack of a scientific basis is that the medical and scientific communities in the United States and other developed countries devoted relatively few resources to the study of hookworm and other parasitic diseases after World War II until recently. The seeming eradication of hookworm disease from the developed world by World War II is probably the reason for the lack of resources engaged in its study. In the entire world, however, estimates indicate that over one billion people are still afflicted with hookworm (Hotez and Pritchard 1995, p. 68; Schad 1991, p. 179).

Early evidence indicating ethnic differences in hookworm disease in the United States comes from the examination and treatment of infections among southern men enlisted in the United States Army during the early twentieth century. Knowlton (1919) found that soldiers classified as white from the Carolinas and Florida had about four times the worm burden as soldiers classified as colored (black) from the same states. The study conducted at Camp Jackson, South Carolina, found 69 cases of hookworm infection among the white soldiers and only 18 hookworm cases among the colored soldiers; the average worm count for the white soldiers was more than 4 times greater than the average for the colored soldiers, 155.3 worms versus 38.3 worms, respectively (Knowlton 1919, pp. 701, 703). In other early twentieth-century United States Army hookworm studies, Frick (1919), Kofoid and Tucker (1921), Lucke (1919), and Siler and Cole (1917) all reported similar findings for colored and white southern soldiers, with the white soldiers having substantially more hookworm infection and worm counts in each study.

In a study of southern civilians, Smillie and Augustine (1925) showed that children classified as white had substantially more hookworm than those classified as colored (black). Table 6.1 reports their data on Alabama children aged six to sixteen. Smillie and Augustine's (1925) summary of their own findings is: "Our results clearly show that when the two races are living under almost identical conditions of sanitation, economic status, occupation, soil, temperature, etc., the whites may

Table 6.1
Prevalence and intensity of hookworm infection by ethnicity in Alabama and Covington County, Alabama, 1922

	Amount of hookworm infection					
	No infection	Very light (1–25 worms)	Light (26–100 worms)	Moderate (101–500 worms)	Heavy (501–1,000 worms)	Very heavy (1,001–3,000 worms)
Percentage of white children infected (6- to 16-year-olds)						
Alabama (n = 1,284)						
Rural	37.1	12.6	16.7	26.0	4.1	3.3
Urban	63.8	11.9	17.7	5.1	1.0	0.7
Covington County						
Rural (n = 444)	3.6	15.3	24.5	42.5	7.7	6.3
Urban (n = 220)	55.9	15.0	22.0	5.9	1.0	0.0
Percentage of "colored" children infected (6- to 16-year-olds)						
Alabama (n = 550)						
Rural	76.1	13.8	6.1	3.0	0.3	0.3
Urban	64.8	19.1	10.4	4.3	1.2	0.0
Covington County						
Rural (n = 117)	39.0	30.9	20.6	8.0	0.9	0.0
Urban (n = 97)	45.2	28.3	18.9	3.2	2.0	1.0

Source: Smillie and Augustine (1925).
Note: The number in parentheses (n) is the number of children examined.

have a heavy infestation whereas the negroes have a very light infestation" (p. 1962).

The data in table 6.1 are for 1922. They should not be confused with nineteenth-century experiences. Before the Civil War, the majority of African-Americans living in the rural South in 1860 were grouped together on plantations of twenty or more slaves. In the lower South, more than 60 percent of all slaves lived on such plantations (Gray 1958, vol. 1, p. 530), with infants and young children likely kept together in crèches, resulting in greater exposure to hookworms. After the Civil War, African-Americans living in the rural South were apt to live in cabins separated from their neighbors by the surrounding fields. The decreased density of African-Americans resident in the rural South *after* the Civil War would have reduced their exposure to hookworm disease.

In contrast, there is evidence of severe consequences of hookworm exposure among more susceptible northern whites resident in the South *during* the Civil War years. Northern Union soldiers who were prisoners at the notorious Confederate Military Prison in Andersonville, Georgia, died at extreme levels, even for Andersonville, in 1864. Cross (2003) attributes much of this extreme mortality to intensely endemic hookworm at Andersonville in the summer of 1864. In one case, 224 (or 59 percent) of 379 northern whites from the Vermont Brigade of the Army of the Potomac, who were captured June 23, 1864, and imprisoned at Andersonville, died during captivity or subsequently as a direct result of their prison experience. In another case, 34 (or 69 percent) of 49 northern whites from Company A, 5th Rhode Island Heavy Artillery, who were captured May 5, 1864, died at Andersonville or afterward in southern captivity elsewhere.

The differences in hookworm infections between the black and white Alabama children are depicted in figure 6.2, which is a visual illustration of the means of the data in table 6.1. They reveal some interesting anomalies. White children had vastly more hookworm in rural areas than colored children; yet in urban areas, colored children had more hookworm than in rural areas and in Covington County even more hookworm than white children. Our explanation for the ethnic disparity between rural and urban divisions is that in urban areas people of African ancestry were poorer and deprived of public services relative to their counterparts of European ancestry. African-American children residing in tightly packed living quarters, with poor sanitation and probably going barefoot much of the year, were subject to constant

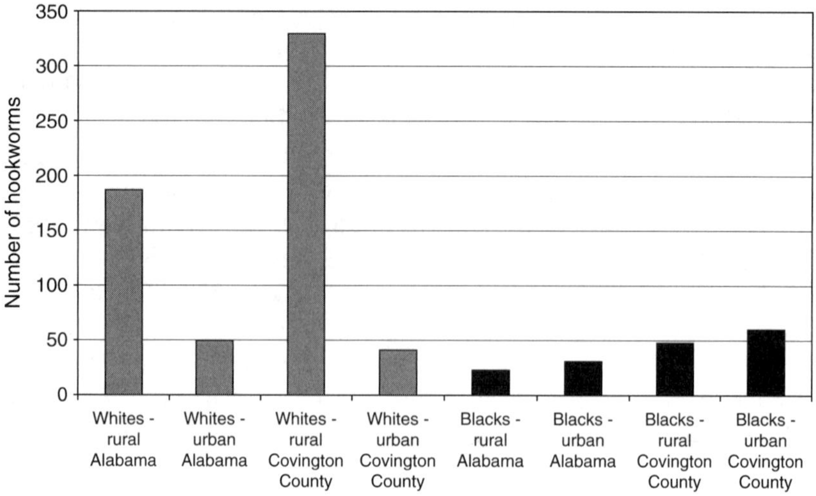

Figure 6.2.
Mean hookworm burden for blacks and whites in Alabama and Covington County, Alabama, 1922. Source: Smillie and Augustine (1925)

hookworm infestation. People of tropical West African ancestry are relatively resistant to hookworm infestation, but in an environment where hookworm is pervasive, they too will be infested with the parasites.

Nevertheless, urban white children had living conditions that were less amenable to the transmission of hookworm than their rural counterparts. With relatively good sanitation and wearing shoes, they were spared the hookworm burden that afflicted whites in the countryside and blacks in the cities. The relative differences between white and black children with respect to the impact of hookworm in urban environments can be attributed to economic conditions and to discrimination in the provision of sanitation, roads, and other public services to nonwhite urban areas.

The Rockefeller Foundation–sponsored International Health Board (IHB) conducted a series of hookworm inspections in 1920 to 1923 to determine the continuing presence of hookworm in the American South. Unlike earlier Rockefeller-sponsored hookworm inspections in the 1910s, those conducted in the 1920s reported hookworm infection among individuals by "race" for selected counties in eleven southern states. Surviving summary statistics for these county inspections indicate that the white infection rate was greater than the black rate in 57 of 60 counties surveyed ("Resurveys, Southern States" 1920–23).

Elsewhere, we examined the data for 542 black and white residents of 1922 Marion County, South Carolina, one of the handful of counties for which the IHB raw data survived (Coelho and McGuire 2006). The study indicates a large, statistically significant difference in hookworm infection between African-Americans (blacks) and European-Americans (whites) in Marion County in 1922. Controlling for other demographic factors, we estimate that an otherwise average white was 2.8 times more likely to be hookworm infected compared to an otherwise average black. The estimated probability of testing positive for hookworm is 56.1 percent for an average white and only 20.3 percent for an average black, an incremental effect of "race" of 35.8 percentage points. Consistent with the results for Marion County, Martin (1972) reports that in a survey of residents of rural southeastern Georgia in mid-1969, whites had a hookworm infection rate of 16 percent while blacks had an 8 percent infection rate.

The Spread of Hookworm

Hookworms attach themselves to the human intestine and obtain nourishment by sucking their host's blood and other nutrients. The hookworm arrives in the small intestine by a circuitous route. Hookworm larvae in the soil penetrate the skin of their host. The penetration is frequently through the feet of people walking barefoot, or through the hands and arms of people in contact with the ground such as farmers and miners. *Ancylostoma duodenale* also can be transmitted by nursing mothers to their children; this route of infection is not available to *Necator americanus*.[16] The host's body reacts to hookworm larvae by "causing dermatitis labeled 'ground itch' or 'dew poison' in the southern United States" (Ettling 1993, p. 784). Hookworms make their way through the blood stream into the lungs. The worms are then coughed up, and if the mucosa containing them is swallowed, the hookworms have their route to the small intestine. After they are attached, hookworms live one to five years, grow, and mate (hookworms are sexual). The hookworm eggs produced by the female are passed with the fecal matter of their host.

Once attached and fertilized inside the human gut, the female hookworm commences her egg production. The female hookworm is a prodigious egg layer. "Frequently cited estimates of egg output range from 9,000 to 25,000 eggs/female per day" (Schad 1991, p. 33). Wherever its human host (victim) goes, hookworms go, and when the human defecates, large numbers of eggs are deposited along with the feces. The deposited eggs produce larvae that molt twice before they can infect another host. Depending on circumstances, the hookworm larvae can live for a few days to months before finding a host. Some hookworm larvae under laboratory conditions, with constant temperature and humidity, are remarkably long-lived. Some larvae survived more than two months (Smith 1990, pp. 97–99). The optimal conditions for long-term larvae survival are protection from direct sunlight, a moist (but not liquid) environment, and a temperature between 15°C and 35°C (59°F to 95°F).

The life cycle of the hookworm is fairly straightforward (see Chandler 1929, pp. 91–98). The hookworm eggs deposited in the feces typically consist of four cells and are not infectious. The eggs mature into an embryonic stage (under favorable conditions this takes over 48 hours), and then into a larval stage (approximately another 48 hours). Before the larvae can become infectious, they must mature further, typically an additional four to five days. Consequently, under normal conditions, from the time the eggs are passed in the feces to the time hookworm larvae are infective is about eight to nine days (two days in the egg stage, two in the initial embryonic stage, and four to five days in the second larval stage).

Given the primitive state of sanitation in the pre-modern, rural American South, hookworm was common. Sanitary privies were rare in the rural South prior to the twentieth century; toilet facilities in rural areas were frequently just secluded bushes (Dock and Bass 1910, pp. 86–93). Free-roaming coprophagous animals (pigs, chickens, ducks, dogs, and some wild life) could eat feces and pass viable hookworm eggs out in their own feces. "[In the typical county privy] [t]he animals root and scratch the feces, and then scatter them about over the ground. Not only this, but they often eat feces. If the feces eaten by such animals contain hookworm ova, they pass undigested and are thus widely distributed" (Dock and Bass 1910, pp. 86–87). Once established, hookworm became permanent in the rural South because of (1) climate favorable to hookworm that existed throughout much of the year, (2) lack of sanitary privies, and (3) non-use of shoes in much of the rural South in warm weather. The African slave trade introduced hookworm into North America; it spread wherever infected people went. Because of its life expectancy attached to the human intestine, from one to five years and fecundity (the female laying eggs at the rate of up to 25,000 eggs per day), the result was endemic hookworm throughout much of the antebellum South.

The Health Effects of Hookworm

Hookworm disease causes a number of medical problems. Depending on the number of worms attached and sucking, the signs of disease that are commonly associated with hookworm are anorexia, abdominal pain, nausea, headache, rash, weakness, fever, vomiting, diarrhea, dysentery, and intestinal bleeding. Figure 6.3 reproduces Crompton and Stephenson's (1990, p. 235) outline of the symptoms, effects, and outcomes of hookworm disease in human populations. This should not be interpreted as a listing of predetermined outcomes; the clinical impact of hookworm disease depends on how many hookworms are attached, the nutritional and health status of its victims, and the host's ability to fight off hookworm. Age, living conditions, climate, cultural practices, and other diseases affect the rate of hookworm infection and its impact.

It is instructive to observe that hookworm disease can cause anorexia, diarrhea, and vomiting, which contribute further to the malnutrition of its victims. "[A]norexia caused by hookworm infections in children may be an important cause of loss of weight and failure to thrive. All of these early manifestations of hookworm disease can cause a great deal of morbidity but with no anemia" (Nelson 1990, p. 420). Because of their smaller size, the same number of hookworm in children is more deleterious to their health than to adults. The hookworm symptoms can contribute significantly to anemia and hypoalbuminemia.

> Hypoalbumimenia is common [among hookworm victims]. As a direct consequence of infection it is probably explained by the fact that the worms abstract more fluid than the measurement of blood loss indicates, in other words, that they cause a true protein-losing enteropathy. The degree to which the patient becomes hypoalbumimenic depends, on the one hand, on the volume of fluid lost and the concentration of albumin which it contains, and on the other, on the capacity to increase the rate of synthesis in compensation. . . . The small albumin pool and maximal synthetic capacity of children may explain why hypoalbumimenia may dominate the clinical picture in infants (Migasena and Gilles 1991, p. 186).

Hookworm reduces the net nutrition available to its host for a number of reasons. The hookworm-infected human has a smaller intake of nutrients because of symptomatic anorexia and loss of

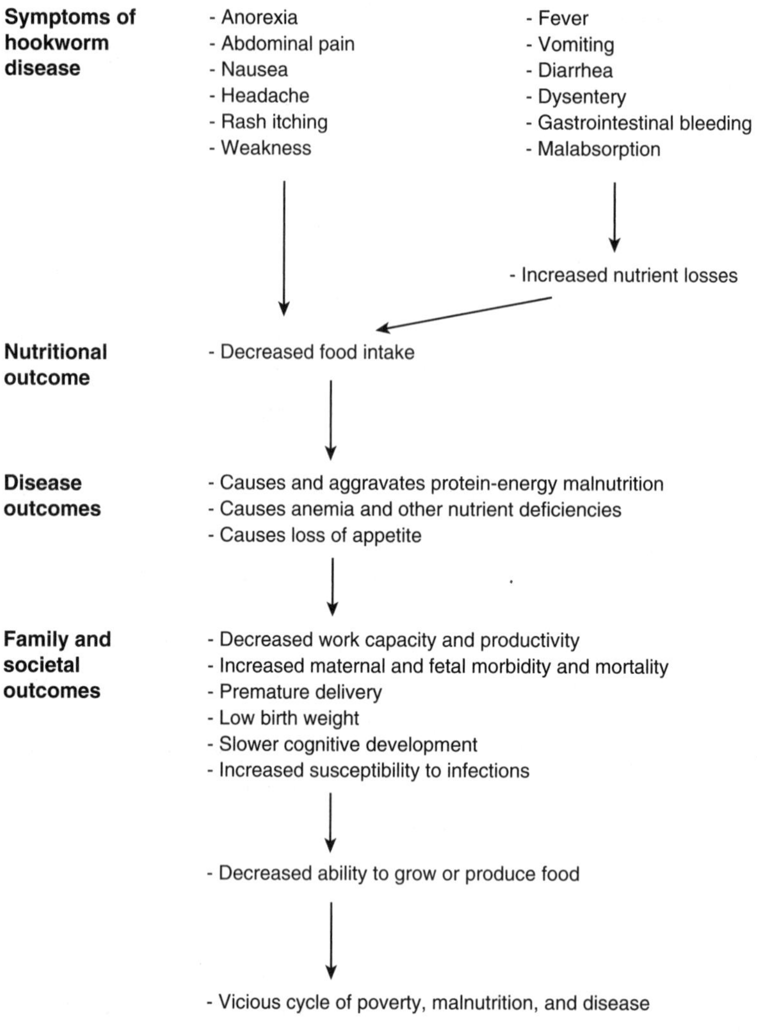

Figure 6.3
Effects and consequences of hookworm disease in human populations. Source: Crompton and Stephenson 1990, p. 235, reprinted with permission)

appetite caused by the disease. The food that the host does manage to ingest has its nutritional value further reduced by symptomatic diarrhea and vomiting associated with hookworm disease. Finally, hookworms reduce the net nutrition available to the host by the red blood cells and other fluids that hookworms consume.

The deleterious effects of hookworm disease on physiological development and growth were indicated at least a century ago. Dock and Bass (1910, pp. 115–17) estimated that adult men in the American South in 1910 who were thought to have had long-term hookworm infection weighed 8.25 pounds less and were 2.33 inches shorter than men not infected with hookworm. Strong (1916) and Kelley (1917) likewise reported negative growth effects of hookworm infection on southern children in the early twentieth century. Smillie and Augustine (1926, tables 1 and 3, charts 1–2, pp. 154–59) determined that southern white adolescences (14- to 15-year-olds and 16- to 17-year-olds) who were found to have heavy hookworm infections (more than 500 worms) weighted about 9 to 14 pounds less and were about 2 inches shorter than similar adolescences with no hookworms.

The negative effects of hookworm disease on human health and physical development have been well documented for contemporary populations as well. In the last thirty years, numerous studies have investigated the interrelationships among various parasitic diseases in highly endemic environments and their impact on the development, physical fitness, and appetite of children.[17] The major focus of these studies is to measure the influence of different treatments on improving the physical development and health of children; the studies provide valuable evidence on the influence of a reduction in the prevalence and intensity of hookworm, roundworm, and whipworm (the three most common intestinal worm infections), as well as other diseases. Bundy, Kremer, Bleakley, et al. (2009) recently concluded that such deworming programs provide economic benefits that greatly exceed their costs.

Separating the impact of individual diseases can be difficult because in highly endemic areas people are often afflicted with multiple helminthic infections, as well as malaria and schistosomiasis. Consequently, when any parasitic burden is decreased, other infections may be continuing, and re-infection is an additional problem. Despite these disentangling problems, a lengthy series of studies of Kenyan school children indicated significant improvements in the children's growth and health.[18] In one study of primary school boys in Kenya, the findings indicate that after treatment for several intestinal worm infections there was significant improvement in physical fitness, growth, and appetite (Stephenson, Latham, Adams, et al. 1993b). The improvements were measurable despite persistent exposure to re-infection and a less than complete cure after treatment. Four months after treatment, the hookworm prevalence rate fell significantly from 98 to 44 percent, roundworm prevalence fell from 98 to 85 percent (not statistically significant), and whipworm prevalence fell significantly from 41 to 18 percent; there also were significant reductions in the *intensity* of all three helminthes as measured by fecal egg counts. The treated Kenyan schoolboys gained on average 167 percent more in weight and 43 percent more in height than an untreated control group. There were significant improvements in the aerobic capacity of the treated boys as well; fitness scores, resting heart rates, and heart rates after exercise all increased. (The untreated group showed no improvement in the fitness test and no significant changes in the two heart rate measurements.) The reduction in intestinal worms also affected the potential nutritional intake of the schoolboys. "The most important new finding . . . is the significant improvement in perceived and measured appetite" for the treated boys, and "in the prevention and control of malnutrition and its functional sequelae, it is often just as important to improve children's desire to eat" as it is to grow or buy more food (Stephenson, Latham, Adams, et al. 1993b, p. 1044).

In a study of iron-deficiency anemia among African children, an analysis of several thousand Zanzibari school children shows that while infections with malaria, hookworms, and other tropical worms "were all associated with worse iron status; the association with hookworms was strongest by far" (Stoltzfus, Chwaya, Tielsch, et al. 1997, p. 153). The study indicates that the intensity of the hookworm infection was the strongest variable in explaining anemia and accounted for 25 percent of all anemia cases, 35 percent of iron-deficiency anemia, and 73 percent of severe anemia in the Zanzibari school children.

In another study, designed specifically to determine the magnitude of stunting caused by hookworm disease, Foo (1990) collected anthropometric and parasitological data in Malaysia in the 1980s for Indian and Malay school children. The data show significant differences in anthropometric measurements between those children moderately infected with hookworm and those not infected, holding other factors the same. The infected 7-year-old Indian children were on average 2.4 centimeters (0.95 inch) shorter than those without hookworm; stunting among the 7- to 9-year-old Malay children was much greater; those with hookworm were on average 3.8 centimeters (1.5 inch) shorter than those not infected. Both groups of hookworm-infected children also were lighter and had lower hemoglobin values than those not infected. Foo's (1990) findings also indicate the anthropometric and hemoglobin deficits were both significantly related to the intensity of hookworm infection.

The deleterious cognitive effects of hookworm disease in infants and children also have been documented in several different populations. A major factor in reduced cognitive development in school-age children and in children less than five years old—primarily in the southern United States in the early twentieth century and in tropical Africa and South Central Asia in more recent times—is hookworm disease and its associated anemia and malnutrition—as well as infection with the other helminthes, *Ascaris* (large roundworm) and *Trichuris* (whipworm). Research suggests that an entire childhood of hookworm disease and its associated malnutrition can have permanent effects on the mental capabilities of children. Hookworm infestation among infants and developing children can be particularly devastating cognitively because the growth process, and the growing brain, in particular, demands substantial nutrients; infestation both reduces the nutrition available and diverts some of it to the immune system that is combating the parasites. Repeating a point made earlier: "From an energetic standpoint, a developing human will have difficulty building a brain and fighting off infectious diseases at the same time, as both are very metabolically costly tasks" (Eppig, Fincher, and Thornhill 2010, p. 1).[19]

The Health Effects of Hookworm in the Antebellum American South

Clearly, hookworm was endemic in the American South in the years before 1902 when it was first recognized as widely endemic. While the first known case of hookworm in the United States was not until 1893 and only nine cases in total were known before it was recognized to be endemic (Marcus 1988, pp. 81, 89), we do know that parasitic diseases do not take hold and become highly endemic overnight. Given that hookworm's effects are so gradual, hookworm is not normally recognized symptomatically. Nevertheless, there is evidence suggesting that hookworm was prevalent in the South before it was identified as endemic.

In the antebellum American South, plantations concentrated slaves into relatively close quarters with infants and young children even more concentrated in crèches that facilitated the spread of disease. The concentration of young children continues to contribute to disease to this day: "The rate of diarrhea for non–toilet-trained infants in day care centers in urban areas of the United States [in the 1990s] is comparable to the rate of illnesses seen in Third World countries" (DuPont 1993, p. 676). Young slave children, diaperless and wandering around barefoot, wearing only shirts, defecated randomly. Diarrhea made the situation even more favorable to the transmission of hookworm. Hookworm transmission typically occurred during the warmer months of the year and caused increased morbidity and mortality in slave children throughout the year.

The environment of endemic hookworm affected the health and net nutrition of slaves. Steckel (1992) reports that slaves were small relative to twentieth-century norms. In fact, "At age 1 the slaves were nearly Lilliputians" (Steckel 1986a, p. 177). Steckel (1992) attributes the remarkably small stature of slave children to the diet of slaves during infancy and childhood, which he believes was severely protein deficient because it was not profitable to feed slave babies and young children a nutritious diet. Aside from any moral qualms slaveowners may have had, to be plausible and make *economic* sense Steckel's view depends on a number of *necessary* conditions. First, the differential costs of an adequate diet versus an inadequate one. Second, real interest rates would have been such that the present value of current savings on food is greater than any losses caused by inadequate diets on slave prices, productivity, and a lower future stock of slaves. (It is worth noting that Steckel acknowledges that taller slaves were worth more than were shorter slaves; accordingly, a rational slaveowner would consider the decline in the market value of slaves, approximately "1.5 percent per inch of height"(Steckel 1999, p. 48) in any decision to reduce expenditures on food.) Third, any declines in the present value of workforce productivity would have been modest due to slaves caring for sick children, or mourning over dead infants and young children. Fourth, little or no transfers of food resources would have come from older slaves to infants and young children. Steckel (1992) reports that slaves underwent a growth spurt after they left the children's quarters to work in the fields, attributing the spurt to the better diet that field workers had relative to children. But this suggests that slaves who were more than adequately fed—they were doing fieldwork *and* undergoing a growth spurt—did not share some of their abundance with their younger siblings or their own children. This is a behavioral trait among adolescent and adult slaves counter to that documented in all other populations in deprived situations. And, fifth, the morale of the plantation workforce would have been unaffected, or if it was affected it did not impact the present value of labor productivity.

Even if all these conditions were met, the disease environment still would have extracted its toll. Slavery was a morally repugnant institution. Yet moral repugnance does not mean that slaveowners systematically deprived infants and young children of adequate diets. For a variety of reasons they could have starved infants and young children, but there is a simpler, and more compelling reason for low birth weights, stunted children, high neonatal and infant mortality, and a late-adolescent growth spurt. The reason is disease; the catalog of diseases that afflicted the slave quarters is long and as yet still incomplete. Endemic hookworm disease alone could have been the cause of these phenomena; repeating a point, slave nurseries also were nurseries for hookworm infections. Regardless of the amount of food provided, severe hookworm disease would have had deleterious effects on the net nutrition of pregnant women, infants, and young children, resulting in (1) an increase in neonatal and infant mortality, (2) low birth weight babies, (3) small stature children, and (4) the effects of severe protein deficiency (anemia, hypoalbuminemia, and kwashiorkor).

Starting with pregnant slaves, if owners put them in tasks that were less physically demanding than fieldwork, those who were assigned to the care of infants and young children would be at severe risk of hookworm disease. Pregnant slaves and their fetus would be in a worse environment in and around the slave quarters than in the fields. For the future newborns it may be a worse environment even when including the effects of maternal work on the fetus.[20] The lack of bowel control in children in "day care," and the shaded environment of slave nurseries, would increase the probability of hookworm infection in the pregnant women assigned to care for the children. If the women went barefoot, the risks of infection would be compounded. Pregnant women with hookworm disease give birth to smaller babies and nurse them less well relative to women who have no hookworm burden (Brooker, Hotez, and Bundy 2008). Steckel's (1992) estimates on stillbirths, neonatal and infant mortality, and birth weights, which are derived from the heights of slave children, are all consistent with hookworm disease, as is the evidence on stunted children. People of tropical West African ancestry are more resistant to hookworm infection than other peoples; however, we emphasize this is *relative*. People of African ancestry are still afflicted by hookworm, and hookworm disease in African children can have severe consequences.[21]

Steckel (2000; 2009) has questioned a claim of ours about the deleterious effects of hookworm on the heights of slave children. Using estimates of the average height of antebellum slave children, modern height standards, and contemporary estimates of the impact of hookworm on the heights of Indian and Malay children, we argued elsewhere (Coelho and McGuire 2000) that hookworm infection during infancy and early childhood may account for as much as 31 percent (3.12 centimeters, or 1.23 inch) of the implied 10.1 centimeters (or 3.98 inches) mean height deficit that slave children had compared to modern height standards. Steckel (2000) maintains that our estimate is overstated by a factor of ten, basing his conclusion in part on a modern intervention study that examines child growth over a given period of time after ridding children of a significant amount of hookworms. We believe that Steckel (2000, 2009) ignores what amounts to the effects of a lifetime of exposure to hookworm during the crucial growth years for slave infants and young children when he claims that a temporally brief intervention study indicates that hookworm infection accounts for only a tiny proportion of slave children's stunting. To approximate the amount of stunting due to hookworm in slave children, Steckel (2000) relies on the only intervention study (Stoltzfus, Albonico, Tielsch, et al. 1997), among many intervention studies, that indicates a small impact of treatment—one year after treatment for hookworms the heights of African school children improved only 0.3 centimeter (0.12 inch), one-tenth of our 3.12-centimeter estimate of stunting. While we are aware of the advantages of intervention studies for estimating temporal hookworm stunting and that the Indian and Malay study upon which we relied raises the problem of controlling for confounding factors and also notes the advantages of intervention studies itself (Foo 1990, p. 11), we still believe our 3.12-centimeter estimate is likely a lower bound for antebellum slave stunting for a number of reasons.

First, as noted, many historical and modern studies of the physical effects of hookworm infection indicate sizable amounts of stunting.[22] Second, antebellum slaves were sicklier than contemporary Indians and Malaysians (and most other contemporary populations). As a result, hookworm infection would have had more adverse effects on the sicklier slaves. Third, in our view, Steckel (2000) confused the measured effect of a de-worming program on child growth with the effects of a lifetime of hookworm infection on child growth. He confused a one-year effect in one modern treatment study with the effect of years of infection on slave child heights. In intervention studies the researchers give some dosage of a therapeutic substance to a study group of children and a placebo (or no treatment) to another group; they measure the observed effects on growth sometime after the substance is expected to take effect, and then compare the growth of the treated children to that of the placebo (or no treatment) group. These "growth effects" are typically a centimeter or so. How large the effects are depends on the efficacy of the substance as an anti-helminth, the size of the dosage, the number of treatments, the duration of the study, and the rate of re-infection. If a study reports a "growth effect" of 0.3 centimeter, for example, over one year for a treated group, it means that one year after the study began the subjects given the treatment dosage grew 0.3 centimeter more than the placebo (or no treatment) group. The 0.3 centimeter should not be interpreted as the total effects of hookworm on child growth over many years unless one believes that the effects on stature of a childhood of exposure to hookworm can be offset by one year's "growth effect" after de-worming. We know of no reputable expert in the field who makes that contention.[23]

We believe that Steckel (2000, 2009) confuses the "growth effect" in modern intervention studies with the antebellum "catch up growth" that began in slave adolescence and continued during the teen years and early adulthood and allowed maturing slaves to recover several inches of growth. The antebellum "catch up growth" was the result of many years of living and working in a reduced hookworm environment compared to the worm-rich environment of infancy and early childhood; the catch up was not the result of only a few months or a year's growth because of having fewer worms.

When slave children were sent from the slave quarters to do farm work, they were freed from an environment highly conducive to the spread of hookworm (and other diseases). Slaves sent to work were typically given shoes that inhibited hookworm infection. Going barefoot in the rural American South was common among children and lower income people during warm-weather months, but going barefoot would have been *less* likely while engaged in physical labor. And those slaves who were sent to cotton fields were sent to a physical environment that was inhospitable to the survival of hookworm larvae (Chandler 1929, p. 186). But sawmill camps were hospitable to the transmission of hookworm. So whether the health of a particular slave child was enhanced by promotion to adult work depended on where he or she went; if sent to the cotton fields, it was enhanced. If hookworm were responsible for their small stature, children promoted to adult field work in early adolescence, or before, would have experienced a nutritionally induced growth spurt in subsequent years as the hookworm burden decreased. Because an attached hookworm has a life expectancy of one to five years in the human intestine, an individual with a heavy hookworm burden who is not re-infected will be cured over time as the worms age and die. Recall that among other benefits, a reduction in the prevalence and intensity of hookworm produces a significant improvement in appetite.

Slaves wearing shoes and working in the fields would have a much-reduced exposure to hookworm infection. Some adult practices such as chewing tobacco and spitting inhibit hookworm infection; because hookworm gains entrance to the intestine when the human swallows the worm-bearing mucosa coughed up from the lungs, constant spitting (as from tobacco chewing) reduces or eliminates this mode of infection (Dock and Bass 1910, p. 147). Older slaves could have acquired immunities to hookworm because a childhood of constant exposure to hookworm primed their immune systems to resist infections. Working, wearing shoes, adult lifestyles, and previous exposures all contributed to the reduction in the hookworm burden a field-working slave would have borne. Only when exposed to the children's play area and where coprophagous animals were roaming would a field slave have had a high risk of hookworm disease.[24]

In their cabins, if adult slaves took their shoes off, neither wooden nor earthen floors would allow the easy transmittal of hookworm. Wood floors in slave cabins would be prophylactic and dirt floors are not necessarily "dirty." Vlach (1993, p. 165) states that "[a] packed earthen floor can, if properly maintained, become as hard and smooth as concrete." Regardless of the type of floors in slave cabins, because hookworm eggs do not mature for eight to nine days after passing, it would be highly unlikely that hookworm would have been transmitted from the floors of slave cabins. Adult slaves would not have been likely to leave feces lying on their cabin floors for eight to nine days.

Malaria

The Disparate Impact of Malaria

Malaria is an infectious parasitic protozoan (genus *Plasmodium*) disease. There are four types of malaria protozoa—*Plasmodium falciparum*, *Plasmodium malariae* (quartan), *Plasmodium virax*, and *Plasmodium ovale*—that cause the disease of malaria in humans, though only the first three are commonly found in humans. The most threatening to human life is *P. falciparum*. Before modern nomenclature was developed, *P. falciparum* was frequently referred to as "malignant malaria." In contrast, the others were commonly call "benign malaria." The use of the term "benign" may be questioned given that the case mortality rate for these types is above zero, and they cause significant suffering and hardship.

People of tropical West Africa ancestry show a remarkable resistance to malarial infection. The genetic defenses to *P. falciparum* are the ones that are most effective; evolution works by selectively increasing the genes in a population that enhance the probability of having surviving offspring; death halts reproduction. *Plasmodium falciparum* is the most deadly version of malaria, and it is endemic to tropical West Africa. The sickle cell trait is the best known of the innate defenses that evolved to combat *P. falciparum*. And not surprisingly the sickle cell trait is relatively abundant in tropical West Africa, and among people of West African ancestry. Malaria is considered endemic if "over a succession of years there is a constant measurable incidence of cases due to natural local transmission. The term *epidemic* malaria is applied when the incidence of cases in an area rises rapidly and markedly above its seasonal level" (Sambasivan 1979, p. 281, emphasis in original). Malariologists classify endemicity into four categories. From the least to the most severe, they are hypoendemic, mesoendemic, hyperendemic, and holoendemic malaria. Much of tropical African is considered holoendemic.

Kiple and King (1981, p. 17) write that "so long as the possessor of this [sickle cell] trait is heterozygous (inherited from one parent only), he or she does not develop deadly sickle cell anemia." When the individual is homozygous (the gene is inherited from both parents) for the sickle cell gene, the result is sickle cell anemia. The resistance that the heterozygous sickle cell trait confers to populations against malaria disease offsets the evolutionary disadvantage of sickle cell anemia. Although sickle cell anemia does confer resistance to *P. falciparum*, many with sickle cell anemia die by adolescence (Kiple and King 1981, p. 17). When infected with *P. falciparum*, individuals with the sickle cell trait exhibit lower parasite counts than individuals without the trait, and are much less frequently beset with deadly complications such as blackwater fever or cerebral malaria (Kiple and King 1981, p. 18). The exact prevalence of the sickling trait among antebellum American blacks is not known with exactitude, still based on prevalence rates among contemporary West African and African-American populations medical authorities have estimated that at least 22 percent of Africans first brought here possessed the trait (Savitt 1989, p. 331).

The sickle cell blood abnormality is illustrative of the cost–benefit analysis that evolution employs. People who are heterozygous for the sickle cell trait have a substantial resistance to malaria and will do much better in an endemic malarious environment than people without this trait. But people who are sickle cell homozygous develop sickle cell anemia and typically die before reaching maturity. The arithmetic is grim, parents who are heterozygous for the sickle cell trait, on average, will have one-fourth of all their children homozygous for sickle cell; they will develop sickle cell anemia and are destined for an early death. The environment has to be highly malarious and deadly for a gene that confers resistance to malaria, yet kills one-fourth of its breeding population, to spread over a large segment of the gene pool. The toll it extracts is large; this is why the sickle cell trait is vanishingly small in populations (and their descendants) who did not live in highly malarious environments.

A second innate trait that populations of tropical West African ancestry have relative to others is "a blood enzyme deficiency bearing the somewhat forbidding name glucose-6-phosphate dehydrogenase deficiency . . . better known as G6PD deficiency . . . many variants of G6PD deficiency (over 100) have been discovered with more turning up all the time" (Kiple and King 1981, p. 19). Savitt (1989, p. 331) indicates that about 20 percent of West Africans possess G6PD deficiency, and estimates that between 30 and 40 percent of African slaves would have possessed either the sickle cell trait or G6PD deficiency. According to Kiple and King (1981, p. 19), "As with the sickling trait . . . [this] deficiency [glucose -6- phosphate dehydrogenase] is one . . . for which there is definitive evidence of stabilization by selection with geographic incidence pointing to malaria as the selective factor . . . The trait has been observed among Sephardic Jews, Greeks, Iranians, and other areas in which falciparum malaria is (or was) endemic."

A third innate trait that populations of tropical West African ancestry possess is deficiency of Duffy blood group antigens, F_{ya} and F_{yb}; the scientific evidence indicates that the Duffy antigens act as outside receptors for *P. vivax*. Without the Duffy antigens, *P. vivax* parasites cannot intrude humans (Allison 1961; Crutcher and Hoffman 1996).

Savitt (1989, p. 330) maintains that among contemporary populations approximately 90 percent of West Africans and about 70 percent of African-Americans lack the Duffy antigens.

There also are acquired immunities to malaria, but because malaria protozoa reproduce sexually, the human immune system has difficulty combating malarial pathogens (Dunn 1993, pp. 858–59; Kiple and King 1981, pp. 12–23). The sexual reproduction changes genetic markers that immune systems bore in on when a foreign substance invades the body. As a result, each variety of malaria has a large number of strains that the human immune system may not immediately recognize as invaders, even if it had been previously infected by the same variety (but a different strain). An individual growing up in tropical West Africa is very likely to have had many exposures to different varieties and strains of malaria. Although this would not impact their New World descendants, the slave South did have malaria, and while not as abundant as in tropical West Africa, the existing forms and intensity, especially on plantations, would have conferred some acquired immunities to people who survived its initial onslaughts.

While references to malaria in Europe have been dated as far back as the mid-Pleistocene epoch and it was endemic to northwestern Europe until about the mid-nineteenth century, *P. Falciparum* (the most frequently deadly form of malaria) was never endemic there. Because evolution works by culling the breeding population, the lack of the relatively deadly *P. Falciparum* did not allow malaria's existence there to confer on northwestern European populations the type of innate resistance that existed in West African populations. The prevalence of the sickling trait, G6PD deficiency, and Duffy blood antigen deficiency are, and were, much rarer in northwestern Europeans than among tropical West African populations. While good estimates of the prevalence of these traits among northwestern European populations for the nineteenth and earlier centuries are not available, from examining contemporary populations the historical prevalence among individuals of European ancestry can be inferred to be quite low relative to peoples of West African ancestry. Recent estimates of the prevalence of the sickle cell trait for whites and blacks in the United States are about 250 per 100,000 for whites and about 6,500 to 7,000 per 100,000 for blacks; the prevalence of the sickling trait today among American whites is about 1/20 the prevalence among American blacks (National Library of Medicine 1998). Additional evidence comes from Marks and Gross (1959) who show the differences in the prevalence of G6PD deficiency among twentieth-century blacks and whites in the United States.

Historical records suggest the reason for less innate resistance to malaria among northwestern Europeans is that northern Europe had a lower incidence of endemic malaria, and the types and strains of malaria were substantially less varied and deadly than in tropical West Africa (Bruce-Chwatt and de Zulueta 1980). The northern European climate was one factor affecting the incidence of malaria; malaria was not a year-round phenomenon there as it was, and is, in much of tropical West Africa. Ample historical epidemiological evidence supports the conclusion of less innate resistance among northwestern Europeans: Europeans involved in the early African slave trade suffered extraordinary mortality rates from malaria and other tropical diseases; their mortality rates in Africa during this period were on the order of fifteen to twenty times those of Africans (see chapter 5).

Malaria in northwestern Europe consisted primarily of *P. vivax* and to a lesser extent *P. malariae*. As noted, *P. falciparum* was not endemic there nor was *P. ovale* a factor. Sizable rates of prevalence of the sickle cell trait and G6PD deficiency among a population are dependent on people living and reproducing within an environment of intensely endemic (hyper- or holoendemic) and stable *P. falciparum*. *Plasmodium falciparum* is the most deadly of the malarial diseases; consequently, it has the greatest impact in evolutionary selection. A substantial proportion of a population being deficient in the Duffy blood group antigens is the result of people living and reproducing within an environment of intensely endemic and stable *P. vivax* (Bruce-Chwatt 1980). Epidemiologists classify malaria as stable in an area if it is intense, robust, and difficult to interrupt. Stable malaria accordingly is thought of as continuous throughout the year. Malaria transmission that is endemic to an area but lacks these traits would be referred to as unstable, and intermittent. Malaria becomes less stable as endemicity declines.

With respect to any acquired immunities, Europeans were less likely to be protected by them. As Kiple and King (1981, p. 16) explain, "although immunity once acquired, [to vivax, the primary type of malaria protozoa found in northwestern Europe] renders the host more or less refractory to a reinoculation with the same parasite (homologous acquired immunity) all strains of the same species (and there are many) are not immunologically similar. Therefore, despite premunition (immunity to a specific strain), one remains liable to infection of other strains, particularly those of a more virulent [non-vivax] nature."

The Spread of Malaria

The life cycle of malaria is more complex than that of hookworm and is intimately involved with its vector and hosts, mosquito (genus *Anopheles*) and humans (see Oaks, Mitchell, Pearson, and Carpenter 1991, pp. 25–30). The female anopheline mosquito, seeking a blood meal, bites a human whose blood harbors infectious malaria gametocytes. The gametocytes are both male and female, and they mate and reproduce in the mosquito's gut. The newly produced protozoa undergo several stages inside the mosquito until they reach the insect's salivary gland and the sporozoites, the product of the protozoan sexual reproduction, are injected into another human. There the protozoa may be dormant (hypnozoite) or active, when active it finds its way to the liver and undergoes more transformations emerging as schizonts that release merozoites into the blood stream. The merozoites and the immune system's reaction to them cause symptomatic malaria. Some of the merozoites in the blood differentiate sexually into male and female; these are the gametocytes that can reproduce only inside the mosquito's gut. When another anopheline mosquito bites the infected person, the cycle begins again with the gametocytes being imbibed with the blood meal.

The larvae of a mosquito infected with malaria are free from malaria. So the malarial protozoa depend on human hosts for their survival. Because nonhuman animals do not contract most forms of malaria, they cannot serve as malarial reservoirs. Humans must serve as the reservoir with the exception of *P. ovale*, which is believed to have avian hosts in its African homeland. In places where there are killing frosts, most mosquitoes die over the winter, only their larvae (malaria free) survive. So a mass of infected humans must be available to start the cycle again. Humans maintain the cycle in two ways. One is by harboring dormant liver-stage protozoa that become active. (They can be dormant for years; this is termed relapse.) The other is by an outbreak of gametocytes caused by surviving blood-stage protozoa. This is termed recrudescence. *Plasmodium malariae* and *P. virax* can lie dormant within the human body, reappear, and cause the disease malaria even decades after the original attack. Wills (1996, p. 151) reports that a British veteran of the Asian campaigns of World War II who contracted malaria in the 1940s had it reappear in his body starting in 1987.

While other types of malaria can persist in the human body for years, *P. falciparum* cannot; at the most it survives 18 months (more typically 9 months). After these months, survivors of *P. falciparum* will have had the plasmodia purged from their bodies. Since the mosquito vector must imbibe the plasmodia from a malarious person in order to spread the disease, *P. falciparum* does not usually survive areas where there are killing frosts. Plantation slavery allowed *P. falciparum* to persist by providing a large number of potential human carriers living in a malarious environment. The potential carriers were of tropical West African ancestry who were relatively resistant to it; this means that they can be infected but the effects will be relatively mild; in some cases they can be asymptomatic carriers. These conditions increase the probability that there will be malarious people infected with the falciparum version of malaria to host new generations of mosquito vectors. Large slave plantations provided a reservoir for *P. falciparum* in the cold-weather (mosquito-free) months, from which malaria could spread with the return of warmth and mosquitoes. Malaria (presumably *P. falciparum*) was a significant cause of death in both the North and South before the Civil War. As a cause of death in the non-southern United States, malaria declined substantially after the war; we attribute a large part of this decline to the demise of the plantation system and its role as a malaria reservoir.

The spread of malaria in nineteenth-century America is not well documented. The biological and medical sciences did not identify the malaria protozoa until 1880 and even then its identification was not well accepted for a number of years. The mosquito vector was not identified until 1898, and the protozoan life cycle was not discovered until well into the twentieth century. Nevertheless, we can identify the symptoms of classic malaria (intermittent and recurring fever, chills, and low case mortality) throughout nineteenth-century America. Medical identification of malaria was certainly less accurate in the nineteenth century than in the twentieth. So when the American military reports that Fort Leavenworth, Kansas, had 629 cases of malaria per 1,000 men during the 1830s (Drake [1850, 1854] 1964, p. 707), this report may be biased downward or upward. A downward bias would be imparted if nineteenth-century medical practitioners incorrectly diagnosed malaria as typhus, typho-malaria fever, congestive fever, or some other idiosyncratic term. Alternatively, an upward bias would be imparted if instead practitioners misdiagnosed typhoid fever or typhus as malaria.

Malaria appears to have been widespread in the antebellum American South and Midwest, declining in both areas after the Civil War. Before the United States banned the importation of slaves in 1808, imports of African slaves from Africa brought with them many varieties of malaria protozoa, especially *P. falciparum* (Blanton 1930; Childs 1940; Curtin 1968; Rutman and Rutman 1976). In the nineteenth century, the growth of large-scale slave plantations in the South and the reduction in transportation costs and time facilitated the spread of malaria throughout the South and into the Midwest. On plantations with large numbers of slaves, the enslaved were housed in densely populated slave quarters. The availability of human hosts (slaves) that typically survived the disease enabled malaria to survive the winter months and spread when mosquitoes were once again abundant. Surviving a bout of malaria was enhanced by the use of quinine; it was widely known and efficacious in combating malaria. The financial resources of large plantation owners would have ensured that the cost of quinine would not have been an obstacle to its use. The value of a slave was substantially greater than the cost of quinine.

Anopheline mosquitoes were the vectors and incubators of malaria; with the right conditions, mosquitoes and malaria flourished in nineteenth-century America. The "right" conditions for malaria are a climate and geography conducive for harboring many mosquitoes and a relatively dense population of infected and non-infected people. The ideal climate and geography would be consistently humid lowland areas, temperatures between 17°C and 32–34°C (63°F and 90–93°F), standing water (typically freshwater pools or marshes), and average monthly rainfall in the range of 80 millimeters (3.15 inches) to provide a source for the standing water and humidity. Many mosquitoes were necessary because the mosquitoes must harbor the malarial pathogens for a number of days before the vector is infectious, before that, the mosquito is infected but not infectious. For *P. falciparum* in the mosquito *Anopheles gambiae*, the incubation period of the pathogen is eleven days and the life expectancy of *A. gambiae* in the wild is estimated to range from eight to about fifteen and one half days. This results in a rate of prevalence (the percentage of infectious mosquitoes) of malaria in mosquitoes of less than 2 percent (Anderson and May 1991, pp. 387–88).

A relatively dense population is necessary for the spread of malaria because if the number of infectious vectors is low, and if malaria is to remain an endemic disease, this means there has to be a relatively large number of people around to propagate the infection. Since female mosquitoes simply want a blood meal, they do not have to bite humans. Other mammals will do as well or better because horses, cows, and pigs, for example, are less successful in swatting mosquitoes than are humans. And if a nonhuman animal is bitten, malaria is not transmitted. How many and how dense the human population has to be depends on other factors such as the availability of nonhuman mammals, herding practices, the quality of human housing, and agricultural developments. Because the anopheline vector is primarily a rural mosquito, malaria is usually transmitted in rural areas.

Wesenberg-Lund (1920–21, pp. 161–95) attributes the decline in malaria in parts of northwestern Europe in the mid-nineteenth century to an increase in animal husbandry and the practice of stabling animals some distance from human habitation. The increase in animal husbandry provided the mosquito with alternate food supplies and the stabling of animals allowed mosquitoes to survive the winter. The mosquitoes that "preferred" nonhuman animals would have increased relative to mosquitoes that "preferred" humans, and to the extent that preferences were genetically transmitted between mosquito generations, malaria would have declined over time. Wesenberg-Lund (1920–21, p. 168) reports that the mosquito *A. maculipenis* living in barns did not bite humans. In other areas, *A. maculipenis* bit humans and transmitted malaria. This suggests some mosquitoes may have "preferences" both for and against biting humans.

In the antebellum American South, the slave labor force was kept close together, and animals were penned rather than stabled. Mosquitoes would have been more likely to bite humans under these circumstances than when animals were stabled and humans dispersed. A constant supply of unexposed children in slave compounds assured the survival of malaria on large plantations.

Malaria spread between plantations and from there to the non-slave population by mosquitoes infectious with malaria. This occurred in a number of ways: people with malaria going off the farm, people coming to a malarial-infested farm, or mosquitoes flying or being transported (by winds or inadvertently by humans or animals) into other areas. The reduction in transportation costs and times in the antebellum United States facilitated the spread of malaria. By 1830, the number of days for an upstream passage on a steamboat from New Orleans to Louisville, Kentucky was less than ten days, and the costs of passenger fares had fallen to 26 percent of their 1815 values (Mak and Walton 1972, pp. 630,

639, app. table II, respectively). The advent of the steamboat, allowed people in 1830 to be infected with malaria in the state of Mississippi, take the steamboat to southern Illinois and be there before they knew they had the disease. The latent period for malaria is from nine to sixteen days; once an individual had the disease, they typically remained infectious from two to nine and a half months (Anderson and May 1991, p. 378).[25]

The transmission mechanism of malaria to the Midwest is now transparent: loci of infection were along the lower Mississippi River and its tributaries. As the New South became more settled, and transportation costs and times declined, the disease pools of the American South and Midwest were integrated. Malaria became endemic throughout. With the post–Civil War abandonment of the plantation system and the growth of animal herds and stabling, malaria's hold on the Midwest waned rapidly. Malaria declined more slowly in the South; it was not until after World War II that malaria was no longer a significant factor in the public health of the United States. The use of quinine as both a curative and prophylaxis assisted in the reduction of malaria. Curtin (1989) ascribes the reduction in malarial mortality rates for British troops stationed in various locations in earlier times to the isolation of quinine from the cinchona bark in 1820 and the increasing usage of quinine.

The question remains: How widespread was malaria in the antebellum American South? Because the malaria plasmodium was not recognized until 1880 and medical authorities did not accept it as the causal factor until even later, scientific data directly measuring the amount of malaria prior to 1880 are not available. However, mortality data on deaths by specific causes, including malaria, for the 1850 to 1900 censuses were reported. The 1850 census includes mortality data for the white and slave populations; the 1860 census did not report deaths by "race." From 1870 to 1900, the census resumed reporting mortality for both whites and blacks. We calculated "malarial fever" mortality rates for whites and slaves for 1850 and for whites and blacks for 1870 to 1900 from the data reported in each of these censuses. The mortality rates for fourteen southern and border states are presented in table 6.2. (The accuracy and reliability of the 1850 to 1900 census mortality data, issues involved in the calculation of the malaria mortality rates, and the data sources are discussed in detail in appendix C. Appendix C also presents various mortality rates, which are discussed in chapter 7, for all causes of death and for nearly

Table 6.2
Death rates for malaria per 100,000 in the southern United States

	1850		1870		1880		1890		1900	
State	Whites	Slaves	Whites	Blacks	Whites	Blacks	Whites	Blacks	Whites	Blacks
Alabama	53.9	51.0	57.9	94.6	90.0	120.1	53.0	86.6	39.8	73.3
Arkansas	104.8	57.3	87.8	95.8	153.3	102.4	134.0	139.0	129.8	137.3
Florida	46.6	35.3	141.6	109.1	118.5	104.0	72.5	74.5	60.2	80.9
Georgia	22.4	19.1	52.3	71.5	42.0	33.8	44.4	58.6	36.8	55.7
Kentucky	22.6	13.7	24.7	21.6	44.8	NA	26.5	34.7	14.7	24.6
Louisiana	97.5	18.8	92.8	94.2	102.4	83.1	110.9	104.4	57.7	93.3
Maryland	57.2	59.8	17.7	22.8	28.4	26.0	19.6	27.3	8.7	20.8
Mississippi	64.3	63.3	68.4	82.4	86.6	94.1	91.4	104.1	46.3	75.4
Missouri	59.6	29.7	52.6	44.0	83.0	NA	36.9	52.4	31.3	26.0
North Carolina	47.6	27.8	35.1	52.9	66.1	73.1	27.5	55.8	22.0	39.5
South Carolina	75.0	65.7	28.7	88.7	71.1	74.9	43.5	78.2	29.8	74.5
Tennessee	27.7	18.4	45.0	44.4	55.7	69.9	48.8	85.4	36.0	90.1
Texas	54.5	13.8	104.3	91.5	95.7	86.9	93.0	97.6	34.6	78.9
Virginia	26.4	34.3	17.7	24.6	33.9	45.3	27.5	52.7	14.7	35.4

Source: United States Bureau of the Census (1855, 1872b, 1886, 1896, 1902b).
Note: For 1850, malaria death rates are calculated from the total deaths for "bilious," "congestive," "intermittent," and "recurrent" fevers. For 1860, deaths were not reported separately for whites and slaves. For 1870, malaria death rates are calculated from the total deaths for "intermittent," "recurrent," and "typho-malaria" fevers; other malaria-symptomatic fevers were not reported in 1870. Beginning with the 1880 census, malaria deaths are listed as deaths from "malaria fever" and "bilious," "congestive," "intermittent," and "recurrent" fevers were listed as "malaria fever." For 1880, deaths in Kentucky and Missouri were not reported for blacks.

two dozen major infectious diseases for all states for 1850 to 1900 for which data exist.)

The malaria mortality rates in table 6.2 indicate that during the era of slavery African-Americans likely had lower death rates from malaria than European-Americans, for later years the situation was reversed. The reported death rates from malaria in 1850 among whites were *greater* than those for blacks in all but two slave states (Maryland and Virginia); in 1900, the reported death rates from malaria were *lower* for whites than blacks in all the southern and border states except Missouri (see table 6.2). This anomaly may be explained by the greater resources that slaveowners had in their possession to treat malaria and/or their reluctance to put slave capital in highly malarious areas. In most of the American South, the malaria mortality rates for whites increased up to 1880 and declined thereafter (in nine of the states in table 6.2; in two others states, the mortality rates peaked in 1870), while the death rates for blacks generally continued to increase until 1890 and declined thereafter (in ten of the states in table 6.2).

The mortality rates indicate a nontrivial amount of malaria in the antebellum American South. While direct data on the case mortality rate for malaria in the mid-nineteenth century South do not exist, it can be inferred from other data to have, most likely, ranged from well below one percent to about 1 percent at the most. Using "realistic" case mortality rates, the data in table 6.2 imply a nontrivial proportion of the southern population had malarial attacks during each of the census years listed. For example, in Alabama in 1850, there were 53.9 deaths per 100,000 among whites. Using a "high" but realistic case mortality rate of 1 percent, this implies there were 5,390 malaria cases per 100,000 whites in 1850. (To derive the rate of malarial disease per 100,000 whites, the number of deaths due to malaria per 100,000 whites is divided by the malaria case mortality rate to get the rate of malarial disease: 53.9 divided by 0.01 equals 5,390 per 100,000 whites.) Using a "low" but realistic case mortality rate of 0.2 percent implies, there were 26,950 cases of malaria per 100,000 whites. These estimates suggest that between 5.4 and 27 percent of the white population in 1850 Alabama would have been malarious.

These "realistic" case mortality rates are derived from Curtin (1989). Curtin reports mortality for British troops stationed in various locations during the nineteenth and early twentieth centuries for symptomatic malarial diseases (fevers, and continual and paroxysmal fevers), among other diseases. In the Madras Presidency in India, the combined case mortality rate for these fevers declined from 1.3 percent during the years 1837 to 1846 to 0.79 percent during the 1860 to 1867 period. (These case mortality rates are calculated from the morbidity and crude mortality rates in Curtin 1989, pp. 181–82.) In estimating the case mortality rate for the mid-nineteenth century American South, we take the Curtin data for the Madras Presidency as a benchmark. The American case mortality rate was certainly lower than that of British troops in Madras because Madras is a much more tropical area (approximately thirteen degrees from the Equator) than the American South, the bulk of which is above thirty degrees north. This means that the length of the mosquito season as well as the intensity of mosquito infection were greater in Madras. Consequently, we consider a 1 percent case mortality rate as a realistic "high" estimate. The benchmark for the lower bound case mortality is more problematic. The lowest malarial case mortality rate for British troops in India was 0.2 percent during the years 1886 to 1894. (This case mortality rate is calculated from the morbidity and crude mortality rates in Curtin 1989, p. 185, where data are presented for India not just the Madras Presidency.) If, similar to our "high" mortality rate, we use a "low" rate for the American South that is less than the lowest Indian rate, say, a 0.1 percent case mortality rate, it would make the malarial morbidity rate probably far too high—53,900 per 100,000 whites for Alabama in 1850—for the actual American experience. So, rather than make an adjustment to the lowest calculated case mortality rate for India, we use the unadjusted lowest Indian rate. This gives us what we believe to be a realistic "low" mortality rate of 0.2 percent. (Recall the case mortality rates for malaria in the Chesapeake during colonial times presented in chapter 5.)

The Health Effects of Malaria

The impact of malaria infection on its human victims depends on the severity of the disease and how often it is contracted. Malaria incapacitates by causing fever, chills, and other maladies. The malaria protozoa attack the human host's red blood cells and also attack various organs (primarily, the liver and spleen). In a population that is severely infested with malaria, there are visible effects:

> The term "chronic malaria" is sometimes applied to the condition seen in children who in highly endemic areas suffer from many attacks, often untreated, of malaria. This is seen more often in vivax and quartan infections and results in "malarial cachexia" characterized by stunting of growth, wasting, anemia, and much enlargement of the liver and spleen. The temperature is often normal,

at other times low fever occurs; parasitemia is variable, and the thick blood film may be often negative; only prolonged observation can establish the diagnosis, which is not finally clinched until improvement occurs under appropriate therapy (Bruce-Chwatt 1980, p. 44).

Malaria does have a differential impact on specific segments of a population. Pregnant women and, in particular, women pregnant with their first child are especially vulnerable to malaria as pregnancy suppresses immunities to malaria. The vulnerability of pregnant women is well documented for Africans (Brabin 1983, 1991; Gilles, Lawson, Sibelas, et al. 1969; Fleming 1989). Malarious women give birth to low birth weight babies who are subject to anemia and other illnesses. Because some acquired immunities exist, the incidence and severity of malaria disease decline with age in highly malarious environments. Children consequently are relatively more vulnerable to malaria in such environments because they lack acquired immunities. Figure 6.4 summarizes the symptoms, effects, and outcomes of malaria in humans.

An examination of figure 6.4, and comparison with the outcomes of hookworm in figure 6.3, indicate there are many similarities between the outcomes of malarial and hookworm diseases. The impact of these parasitic diseases on children also is very similar. Both diseases cause symptomatic anorexia and a loss of appetite. In both cases infected children have less desire to eat. Both diseases cause anemia and other nutrient losses. And both malarial and hookworm diseases lead to low birth weights, increased fetal and infant morbidity and mortality, reduced body size of newborns and infants, and stunting of child growth.

Studies of contemporary populations in malarious environments indicate the severe effects that endemic malaria has on human health and development. In a study of malaria disease and fetal growth in a malarious region of Zaire, Meuris, Piko, Eerens, et al. (1993) conclude that malaria in pregnant women had negative effects on their newborns. Among the several hundred expectant mothers studied, circulating malaria parasites, malaria-associated placental lesions, and low hemoglobin levels were observed either individually or together in different combinations. Over 25 percent of the women with both malarial pathological findings had low birth weight (less than 2,500 grams or 5.5 pounds) babies while only 6.5 percent of women without any malarial findings had low birth weight babies. Low birth weight is considered "the greatest single risk factor for neonatal and early infant mortality" (Meuris, Piko, Eerens, et al. 1993, p. 33). The low birth

Symptoms of malarial disease

Acute
- Anorexia
- Nausea
- Vomiting
- Diarrhea
- Prostration
- Malaise
- Chills
- Sweating
- Shaking
- Abdominal pain
- Cough
- Recurrent high fever

Chronic
- Headaches
- Muscle pains
- General poor health
- Loss of appetite

Complications
- Cerebral malaria (state of altered consciousness; coma)
- Renal failure
- Pulmonary edema
- Hypoglycemia
- Severe anemia
- Shock
- Enlargement of spleen and liver

↓

Nutritional outcomes
- Increased urinary nitrogen excretion
- Increased nutrient loss in cases of diarrhea and vomiting
- Decreased food intake

↓

Disease outcomes
- Causes anemia (especially in children)
- Causes increased morbidity and mortality
- Causes loss of appetite

↓

Family and societal outcomes
- Growth retarded newborns
- Childhood growth stunted
- Chronic or relapsing course (recurrent infection)
- General poor health
- Reduced work capacity and productivity

Malaria in pregnancy → Results in

Malaria in pregnancy
- Parasitemia
- Lesions in placenta
- Low hemoglobin

Results in
- Decreased birth weights
- Reduced head circumference
- Reduced birth length
- Reduced ponderal index

Figure 6.4
Effects and consequences of malarial disease in human populations. Sources: Bruce-Chwatt (1980); Meuris, Piko, Eerens, et al. (1993); Oaks, Mitchell, Pearson, and Carpenter (1991); Steketee, Wirima, Hightower, et al. (1996); Strickland and Hunter (1982)

weight differences were significant for both malarial conditions. Moreover, a measure of the size of the Zaire newborns (the ponderal index, a measure of body mass) was significantly smaller for women with the placental lesions.

In a clinical study of the effects of malaria treatment on the anthropometric measurements of newborns in a sample of more than 1,700 Malawians, Steketee, Wirima, Hightower, et al. (1996) find that women with placental blood malaria were 1.7 times more likely to have had low birth weight babies. Placental blood malaria in pregnant women was, among other factors, significantly related to low birth weight babies due to intrauterine growth retardation while umbilical cord blood malaria (fetal) was significantly related to preterm (delivery at less than thirty-seven weeks' gestation) low birth weight babies. The combined incidence of intrauterine growth retardation and preterm low birth weight babies was over 31 percent in firstborns to women with malaria versus 24 percent to women without the malaria; it was over 20 percent (with malaria) versus 10 percent (without malaria) in second-born children, and it was 16.5 percent (with malaria) versus 9 percent (without malaria) in all other births. Steketee, Wirima, Hightower, et al. (1996, p. 40) conclude that "in highly malarious areas, malaria may account for more than 30 percent of preventable [with treatment] LBW [low birth weight]."

In a study of the changes in weight gain and anemia among infants and children six to forty months old in a holoendemic malarial environment in Tanzania, Shiff, Checkley, Winch, et al. (1996) show statistically significant improvements when the subjects were given insecticide-impregnated bed nets. One year after implementation of the program, the infants and children not given bed nets grew, on average, 286 grams (10.1 ounces) less and were twice as likely to be anemic over the five-month study period. The authors conclude that *P. falciparum* has a marked effect on increased anemia and a negative effect on human growth as measured by weight gain. (Strictly speaking, *P. falciparum* reduces the hemoglobin/red cell content of the blood, leading to the clinical condition known as anemia.)

A treatment study of the relationship among schistosomiasis, hookworm, and malarial infections, and the nutritional status of Kenyan primary-school children, indicates the children's growth increased significantly during the first six months of the sixteen-month study after treatment for schistosomiasis (Stephenson, Latham, Kurz, et al. 1986). Growth, as indicated by several anthropometric measures, was much slower in the last ten months of the study. Stephenson, Latham, Kurz, et al. (1986, p. 41) conclude that "the most likely explanation for this phenomenon, of the variables we measured, is the dramatic increase in malarial infection . . . that probably began soon after Exam 2 [after the first six months of the study]."

The Health Effects of Malaria in the Antebellum American South

During the antebellum period in the United States, slaves that did not have any innate immunity to malaria (either due to random genetic mixing or to having a parent that was not refractory) would have suffered in malarious environments. The poorly constructed slave quarters on plantations allowed the mosquito vectors easy access; the high density of large plantations allowed easy transmission from human to mosquito and the reverse. The concentration of slave infants and young children in crèches facilitated the transmission of the malaria pathogens among them and their caretakers—older children, pregnant women, and elderly slaves.

When whites contracted malaria, the consequences would have been more severe because the white population lacked the innate resistance that people of tropical West African ancestry typically had. But the white population would have suffered from fewer mosquito bites. The resident white population of a plantation typically was absent from the slave quarters at the times when mosquitoes' bites were most likely—early mornings and evenings. Many wealthy whites adapted to existing conditions by going away from their plantations during the malaria season, or by sending away the most susceptible members of their families. Plantation whites also were wealthy enough to purchase quinine, which was available as both a remedy and a prophylactic. Consequently, the overall impact of malaria on antebellum plantation whites is problematic.

Antebellum nonplantation whites also would have suffered fewer mosquito bites because they did not live in the relatively high-density plantation environment. Yet for whites residing in areas to which malaria had spread and had become endemic the impact of malaria is more predictable. The impact of malaria on nonplantation (and relatively low-income) whites would have been more severe than on African-American slaves, other factors the same, because whites lacked the innate resistance to malaria that blacks typically possessed. The consequences of chronic malaria among these whites would include, among others, increased morbidity and mortality and, in all probability, reduced productivity in physical labor.

Given the southern climate and geography, poor conditions of slave quarters, and high human densities on large plantations, the southern plantation environment resulted in endemic malaria that affected the health and net nutrition of slaves. We believe the plantation disease environment explains the phenomena that plagued slave plantations: low birth weights, high neonatal and infant mortality, stunted slave children, and the effects of protein deficiency.[26] Endemic malaria was a key element in shaping the plantation disease environment. As with endemic hookworm (and other tropical diseases), slaves in the South were relatively more resistant to malaria infection than others (white southerners and northerners). Nevertheless, in the highly malarious environment of the plantation South, African descendants (slaves) still would have been afflicted with malaria, and malaria in pregnant women, infants, and young children can have severe consequences.

The results of chronic malaria among slave infants, children, and pregnant slaves are consistent with the anthropometric measurements of slaves in the antebellum South: low birth weights, relatively high neonatal and infant death rates, anemic children and mothers, and severely stunted children. Regardless of the food resources available, a malarious population will have, relative to a nonmalarious population, reduced body size and increased morbidity and mortality.

Implications of Endemic Parasitic Diseases in the Antebellum South

The disease environment of the antebellum South affected various elements of the southern population differently. All other factors the same, we expect that warm-weather diseases would more severely affect (1) infants and children relative to adults, (2) whites relative to blacks, (3) women pregnant for their first time relative to other women, (4) residents of areas where tropical pathogens were abundant relative to people who lived in areas that were less conducive to the survival of tropical pathogens, (5) plantation residents relative to nonplantation residents, and (6) whites that were in close proximity to blacks relative to whites who were more isolated from blacks. The disease environment also affected the anthropometric dimensions of the southern populations differently. (But recall our earlier discussion of caveats when drawing implications from the slave height data.) All other factors the same, we expect that (1) plantation slave children would have been stunted, (2) plantation slave adults would have been shorter than normal stature, (3) high-income plantation whites would have been of normal stature, (4) low-income whites in close proximity to blacks and located in hookworm and/or malarial regions of the South (areas that were warm, moist, swampy, and contained humus and/or sandy soils are examples) would have been below normal stature, (5) nonplantation whites located in other regions of the South (the border states and areas that were colder, more upland, drier, and contained clay soils are examples) would have been of normal stature, and (6) nonplantation blacks would have been of normal stature and taller than plantation-born and reared blacks.

There are anthropometric data that are consistent with elements of our story, supporting the hypothesis of the impact of the southern disease environment on human populations. The data analyzed by Bodenhorn (1997), Coclanis and Komlos (1995), Komlos (1992), Margo and Steckel (1982, 1992), and Steckel (1995b) show that living in the South close to the Atlantic coast made black populations shorter. The reason is that the coastal areas are more humid and have fewer killing frosts. The human inhabitants of the coast were subject to pathogenic onslaughts more frequently than were their inland contemporaries.[27]

The hypothesis of endemic hookworm, malaria, and other tropical pathogens in the antebellum southern United States also has implications for the existing evidence on the relative productive efficiency of antebellum American slavery shown in the studies of Fogel and Engerman (1971, 1974a, b, 1977, 1980). The differential susceptibilities between African-Americans and European-Americans to parasitic diseases suggest differential agricultural productivity between the two groups of people in favor of higher productivity for antebellum blacks irrespective of the form of the labor system. This suggests that the entire issue of the relative productivity of slavery must be reexamined.

From the known genetic variations between populations of northwestern European ancestry and tropical West African ancestry concerning susceptibility to malaria, we surmise that some of the measured productivity differences between antebellum free farms and slave plantations in the American South can be explained by the presence of endemic malaria alone. Likewise the historical evidence from the early twentieth century on the impact of hookworm disease on the southern labor force and the significantly lower hookworm prevalence rates among African-Americans suggest that productivity differences due to hookworm in favor of blacks also were likely in the antebellum American South. If black adults (slave labor) were more productive than white adults (free labor) because of their greater resilience to the pathogens that abounded in their environment, then part of the measured differences in productivity between slave plantations and free farms should be attributed to the lower morbidity rates for individuals of West African ancestry, rather than to any inherent efficiencies of the institution of slavery.

The hypothesis of endemic tropical parasitic diseases has implications for the interpretation of the history of the post–Civil War American South as well. Real incomes and wages were lower in the South than in other regions of the United States and they remained below (probably substantially below) that of the rest of the country until after World War II (Easterlin 1961; Roberts 1979). Why? In their examination of regional incomes in nineteenth-century America, Coelho and Shepherd's (1979, p. 78) explanation for the lower southern incomes is that "[we] can only speculate that a combination of the remnants of slavery, Jim Crow laws, and racial discrimination had the effects of increasing supplies of unskilled workers in the South." But this explanation of below-average southern incomes is flawed because it was not simply the preponderance of unskilled labor that drove southern incomes down. The implication from the hypothesis of endemic diseases is that post–Civil War southern incomes remained below other regions because the productivity of southern workers was lower than in the other regions as a result of the southern disease environment. In support of this, the Rockefeller Sanitary Commission "believed that 'inefficient' workers whose productivity was thought to have been reduced by disease could be made more productive simply by ridding them of the parasite [hookworm], thus contributing to the economic and industrial development of the region" (Kunitz 1988, p. 143).

Concluding Thoughts on the Antebellum Southern Disease Environment

The physical world shapes and constrains all human activities. We have focused on the biological environment and parasitic diseases that confronted people living in the pre–Civil War American South. Appropriately slavery also can be viewed as a form of parasitism in which slaveowners, like biological parasites, live off the labors of the enslaved.

Viewed this way slaveowners have incentives to maintain their capital across generations, making undernourishment of slave infants and children both less probable and less profitable. Unlike slavery in ant societies though, American slavery was, by and large, an inherited condition by the nineteenth century.[28]

The diseases that were endemic to the American South and the slave system were not dramatic diseases that kill, but lingering diseases that debilitate. Lingering diseases affect infant and child development, adult heights, mental development, and economic productivity. Humans are prone to believe that their histories and fates are the products of human actions that are amenable to reason. Thus the Shakespearean quote: "The fault, dear Brutus, is not in our stars but in ourselves." In opposition, we contend that much of the economic and social history of the American slave South is the product of uncaring, mindless forces that were unimagined by the contemporaneous human population. The pathogens that were abundant in the American South were not the products of human malevolence. They were the unintended consequences of trade with Africa and the tropical New World. It must be recognized that these pathogens were not equal opportunity diseases. People of tropical West African ancestry were more resistant than were those whose ancestors came from other areas.

Our examination of the biological and historical role of pathogens of tropical West African origin calls for a new interpretation of the economic and social history of American slavery. The evidence presented here calls into question the prevailing views of the inadequacy of the diets of slave infants and children and the relative productive efficiency of slavery. This suggests that an alternative interpretation of the histories of both the pre– and post–Civil War American South might be warranted as well. We envision an interpretation that incorporates the traditional factors of resources, institutions, and profitability along with the minute organisms that, although mindless and unconcerned with human welfare, still impose costs and haunt humanity. We share the world we inhabit with organisms that consider *Homo sapiens* a resource, we may not be able to see them with the naked eye, but their impact on humans has been visible.

7 Evidence on the Spread of Diseases in Nineteenth-Century America

Chapter 3 provided the analytical framework that explained the interactions among the growth of population, economic growth, and the spread of diseases. Here we present historical and biomedical evidence that places the model in the context of nineteenth-century America. The available and pertinent data are on (1) the growth of population, (2) urbanization and population density, (3) transport developments associated with the demographic changes, and (4) the prevalence of infectious diseases across states and time. Some of the data are well known and widely accepted; however, including census mortality data, evidence on diseases is less reliable than that for population and transport. The evidence that does exist is consistent with the conceptual underpinnings that combine an increase in market size and specialization with an increase in infectious diseases.

The emphasis is not in the novelty of our story of the impact of diseases during the nineteenth century, but in the similarity of the nineteenth century with past centuries. Like the nineteenth century, all economic expansions of civilizations in the past were eventually wracked by deteriorating disease environments. The nineteenth century was not unusual because diseases became more widespread; what was unusual in the nineteenth century was the incubation and initiation of developments during the latter half of the century that were to break the age-old linkage between population growth, economic expansion, and a deteriorating disease environment. The story of how and why that linkage broke is an important one, but it is not our story. In this chapter, we provide evidence on how the economic expansion of nineteenth-century America is consistent with our population and disease model of economic growth and is similar to the past as it facilitated the spread of pathogens throughout most of the century.

The Demographic and Transport Evidence

In 1800, the population of the United States was approximately 5.3 million people, and the nation's borders encompassed approximately 864 thousand square miles. Most of the population was clustered along the Atlantic coast with the center of population of the United States located just west of Baltimore (Atack and Passel 1994, p. 244). No region of the United States had a sufficiently dense population to warrant the capital investment required by an extensive canal system. Competition from natural waterways (the Hudson, Connecticut, Potomac, and other rivers) and the lack of concentrated economic activity inhibited the development of canals. The first canal in the United States was in operation before 1800, but the canal (in South Hadley, Massachusetts, built in 1796) was small and was located in a relatively densely settled area that connected populated areas along and to the Connecticut River. With the passage of time a system of inland transportation improvements became feasible with increased population and economic output, the settlement of inland territories, and the concomitant growth of agricultural production.

Canals had been built in antiquity, and canal locks were being built by at least the end of the fifteenth century. Canals were not built earlier in the United States because the size of the American market was inadequate to make the absolutely large financial investments that canals required economically viable. In general, highly specialized investments that require a substantial investment in fixed capital are not economic in markets that are small (relative to the financial commitment) and fragmented. This is why specialized investments in wharves, warehouses, and port facilities in British North America were delayed until the eighteenth century rather than earlier. Walton (1967) and North (1968) attribute most of the growth in productivity of ocean going transport in the eighteenth century to the development of specialized facilities (including protection from piracy) that were noneconomic earlier because the market was too small.

Population growth averaged close to 3 percent per year throughout much of the nineteenth century; at 3 percent, population doubles every 23 years. Table 7.1 shows the growth of the American population during the nineteenth century. The population grew from 5.31 million people in 1800 to 76 million in 1900. The peopling of the interior was even more rapid. The population center of the United States moved from just west of Baltimore in 1800, to nearly 100 miles further west in

Table 7.1
United States population and population density, 1790 to 1900

Year	Total population (in millions)	Population density (per square mile)
1790	3.930	4.5
1800	5.308	6.1
1810	7.240	4.3
1820	9.638	5.5
1830	12.866	7.4
1840	17.069	9.8
1850	23.192	7.9
1860	31.443	10.6
1870	39.818	13.4
1880	50.156	16.9
1890	62.948	21.2
1900	75.995	25.6

Source: Carter, Gartner, Haines, et al. (2006, vol. I, series Aa1–5, pp. 1–26, and n. 1)

Virginia in 1820. By 1860, the population center of the United States was in Ohio; in 1900, it was in the middle of Indiana. In the 100 years of the nineteenth century, the geographic center of the American population moved more than 500 miles west.[1]

These shifts in the population center are for the entire United States; the movement of slaves mirrored that of the free population. With the expansion of the cotton economy and antebellum cotton plantations into the New South, the slave population and the pathogens that slavery harbored followed. In the five states of the New South (Alabama, Arkansas, Florida, Louisiana, and Mississippi), the slave population increased from 145,374 in 1820 to 1,376,297 in 1860, an increase of 847 percent, or approximately 5.8 percent per year. The free population of these states increased from 225,751 in 1820 to 1,663,086 in 1860, an increase of 637 percent, or approximately 5.1 percent per year (North 1961, table 9, p. 129). Data on the interregional movement of slaves between 1790 and 1860 also indicate a dramatic increase in the regional movement of slaves within the South. The changes captured in the data are impressive: 17,000 slaves were shipped interregionally in the 1790s; 31,000 slaves were shipped in the 1800s; 101,000 in the 1810s, 121,000 in the 1820s; 223,000 in the 1830s; 149,000 in the 1840s; and 193,000 in the 1850s (Fogel and Engerman 1974a, p. 46). These movements of people (enslaved and free) contributed to the spread of pathogens and facilitated the nationwide spread of diseases that previously had been local and regional.

The population density of the nation increased rapidly during the nineteenth century. The data on population density in the United States for 1790 to 1900 also are reported in table 7.1. The data indicate that population density in the nation increased by 21 percent between 1800 and 1830, 43 percent between 1830 and 1860, and another 141.5 percent by the turn of the century in 1900. The geographical boundaries of the United States approximately tripled during this era, making the increased density even more impressive. The growth in density varied widely across states though; the population per square mile in Massachusetts in 1800 was 52.69; in 1860, it was 153.14; and in 1900, it was 348.97. In Ohio, the corresponding population densities for the same years are 1.05, 57.43, and 102.05; in Pennsylvania, the corresponding densities are 13.44, 64.82, and 140.57; in Virginia, the corresponding densities are 20.07, 30.29, and 46.05.[2]

Along with increased density came a more than proportional increase in the urban population. In 1800, the percentage of the total population classified as urban was 6.1 percent; in 1830, it was 8.8 percent; in 1860, it was 19.8; and in 1900, 39.8 percent of the population was classified as urban. The rapid growth in the number of urban places and cities can be seen from the data in table 7.2, which reports the number of urban places for various size categories, total number of urban places, and the percentage of the population classified urban for 1800 to 1900. The total number of urban places grew 173 percent from 1800 to 1830, 336 percent from 1830 to 1860, and 344 percent from 1860 to 1900. For larger urban places, the growth in the 50,000 to 100,000 size category was 200 percent from 1800 to 1830, 133 percent from 1830 to 1860, and 471 percent from 1860 to 1900. The increases in population density and urban places and the growth in the size of cites assisted the spread of diseases; these demographic changes allowed pathogens to survive in places where they would not have survived in earlier centuries when humanity peopled the land less densely.

Increasing population and output increased the demand for transportation services. This led to investments in specialized transport services that both lowered the average cost of shipping a given volume of freight and increased the speed of transportation. These investments included the historically familiar canals, steamboats, and roads and the less familiar wharves, harbors, navigation charts, and lighthouses. Within the United States, investments in roads, canals, coastal packet

Table 7.2
Number of urban places and percentage of population urban in nineteenth-century United States

	Number of urban places									
	Size of urban population									
Year	2,000 to 5,000	5,000 to 10,000	10,000 to 25,000	25,000 to 50,000	50,000 to 100,000	100,000 to 250,000	250,000 to 500,000	Over 500,000	Total urban places	Percent of population urban
1800	12	15	3	2	1	0	0	0	33	6.07
1810	18	17	7	2	2	0	0	0	46	7.26
1820	26	22	8	2	2	1	0	0	61	7.19
1830	34	33	16	3	3	1	0	0	90	8.76
1840	46	48	25	7	2	2	1	0	131	10.81
1850	89	85	36	17	4	5	0	1	237	15.41
1860	163	136	58	19	7	6	1	2	392	19.77
1870	309	186	116	27	11	7	5	2	663	24.87
1880	467	249	146	42	15	12	4	4	939	28.17
1890	654	340	230	66	30	17	7	4	1,348	35.12
1900	833	465	281	83	40	23	9	6	1,740	39.76

Source: Number of urban places is from Carter, Gartner, Haines, et al. (2006, vol. I, series Aa684–98, pp. 1–102). Percentage of population urban is calculated from Carter, Gartner, Haines, et al. (2006, vol. I, series Aa2, pp. 1–26, and n. 1) and Carter, Gartner, Haines, et al. (2006, vol. I, series Aa699, pp. 1–104).

Table 7.3
Average freight rates per 100 pounds of cargo between Louisville and New Orleans: Antebellum years

Years	Upstream ($)	Downstream ($)
Before 1820	5.00	1.00
1820 to 1829	1.00	.62
1830 to 1839	.50	.50
1840 to 1849	.25	.30
1850 to 1859	.25	.32

Source: Haites, Mak, and Walton (1975, p. 32), cited in Walton and Rockoff (2010, table 9-2, p. 151).

ships, steamboats, and tugboats led to substantial declines in the costs of transport, and concomitant increases in the volume and frequency of interregional traffic. As the lower Mississippi became settled with slave plantations, they generated an increased demand for shipping services. The subsequent increased specialization in the transport sector led to falling costs. These transport developments were so pervasive and rapid that freight prices on steamboats on the Mississippi for the Louisville–New Orleans route declined extraordinarily quickly. In 1830, an index of freight prices on that route was just 25 percent of its 1815 level; and by 1860, it was just 11 percent of its 1815 level (Mak and Walton 1972, p. 639, app. table II). Table 7.3 presents data on average freight rates for each direction between New Orleans and Louisville in the years prior to the Civil War. Relative to pre-1820 rates, upstream freight rates by 1850 fell 95 percent; downstream freight rates by 1850 fell less, but they were still less than a third of their pre-1820 rates.

Data for freight transport costs in the United States circa 1815 and circa 1860 are presented in table 7.4. The costs of all forms of transport fell substantially between 1815 and 1860. Improvements in roads lowered freight costs in 1860 to about half their 1815 levels. Improvements in sailing ship design and harbor management made ocean shipping the cheapest form of transport; in 1860, the cost of ocean transport was 95 percent less than its costs circa 1815. Improvements in sailing ships on the Great Lakes and competition from steamships gave the Great Lakes the second lowest freight costs in 1860. If we proxy the missing data for shipping on the Great Lakes for 1815 with that of ocean shipping circa 1815 (1 cent per ton-mile), then the estimated decline in shipping costs on the Great Lakes from 1815 to 1860

Table 7.4
Transport costs in the United States circa 1815 and circa 1860: Various types of transportation

Type of transportation	Cost per ton-mile circa 1815 (cents)	Cost per ton-mile circa 1860 (cents)
Road	30.00 or more	15.00 or more
River		
Boat upstream	6.00	—
Raft downstream	1.30	—
On the Mississippi	—	0.37
On the Illinois	—	1.20
Ocean Ship	1.00 or less	0.05 or less
Canal		
On the Erie	—	0.99
On the Pennsylvania Main Line	—	2.40
Ship on the Great Lakes	—	0.10
Railroad		
On the New York Central	—	2.06
On the Erie Railroad	—	1.84

Source: Taylor (1962, app. A, table 2), cited in Atack and Passell (1994, tables 6.1 and 6.3, pp. 148 and 157, respectively).

was 90 percent. In a similar vein, investments in canals had a major impact on transport costs; Daniel Drake claimed that "[C]anals drove down the cost of shipping from about 20 cents per ton-mile in the 1810s and 1820s to 2 or 3 cents per ton-mile in the 1830s" (quoted in Atack and Passell 1994, p. 155).

Antebellum steamboat shipping had an enormous impact on lowering freight rates from 1811 to 1868. As a consequence, total tonnage on the western rivers increased from 400 tons per year in 1811 (at the beginning of the steamboat era) to 14,500 tons in just ten years (1821); by 1846 shipping tonnage had increased to over 100,000 tons (a 633 percent increase over 1821). Fourteen years later in 1860 the annual tonnage on the western rivers was 195,000 tons (an 83 percent increase over 1846). (Annual data on the number of steamboats and total tonnage (or capacity) on the western rivers are presented in table B.1 in appendix B.)

Throughout the antebellum years, accompanying declining transport costs and the increasing movement of goods were dramatic decreases in the times required to carry freight (and passengers). Travel times by inland water transport fell by more than 50 percent on some routes between 1815 and 1840. On the Mississippi, an upstream trip by steamboat from New Orleans to Louisville in 1815 to 1819 took 20 days; by 1840, it took 9.5 days; by 1860, it took just 6.5 days. While the declines in downstream travel times were not as dramatic, they were still sizable; from Louisville to New Orleans travel times for the corresponding years in order were 10 days, 6.6 days, and 5.2 days (Mak and Walton 1972, p. 630, table 2).

Indicative of the magnitude of the "less familiar" types of transport investments is the growth of federal expenditures on rivers and harbors; they grew substantially over the entire century, but not evenly. Beginning with $1,000 in 1822 to nearly $19 million in 1900, yearly federal expenditures fluctuated unevenly through the early 1860s. Much of the investment on transportation through the mid-nineteenth century came from sources other than the federal government (private sources and state and local governments). Still federal expenditures grew from 1822 until 1837 when they reached a pre-Civil War peak of $1,362,000. Subsequently, annual federal expenditures fluctuated with no obvious trend until the end of the Civil War. After 1866, federal expenditures on transportation began a long secular increase that continued to the end of the century. For the twenty years 1867 to 1886, expenditures averaged $6.4 million annually; they averaged $9.8 million annually for the entire post–Civil War period—1867 to 1900. (Annual federal government expenditures in the United States on rivers and harbors for the years 1822 to 1900 are presented in table B.2 in appendix B.)

Investments in transportation infrastructure predate any significant federal expenditure. The first major canal built in the United States, and the one that set off a canal building boom was the Erie Canal, was initiated by the state of New York. Started in 1817 (twenty-one years after completion of the first American canal in South Hadley), construction on the Erie Canal was completed in 1825. The Erie Canal provided low-cost bulk shipping to the nascent economies of the upper Midwest and the Great Lakes. The Erie was built in segments from east to west; segments were opened as soon as they were completed; these segments were immediately profitable. Well before its terminus on Lake Erie was reached, one million dollars per year in tolls were being collected. The entire multimillion-dollar cost of the canal was recouped within a few years of its completion (Atack and Passell 1994, p. 150). The immediate profitability of the canal is consistent with an increase in the size of the market leading to increased specialization; alternatively, the potential demand for transport services preexisted the Canal. The construction of the Erie began only after New York State west of the Hudson River Valley and, more generally, the Great Lakes region had experienced sufficient population growth and settlement to generate a large potential demand for transport services.

From 1837 to 1860, tonnage on the Erie increased 238 percent, from 667,151 tons to just over 2.25 million tons; it increased another 105 percent to just over 4.6 million tons by 1880. Tonnage data indicate the continued growth of shipping between the Great Lakes region and the port of New York. The Civil War era and the years immediately thereafter were enormously profitable for the Erie; the data indicate a massive diversion of trade during the War (and for a few postwar years) from the North–South river network to the East–West route of the Erie Canal. (Annual data on tonnage in the mid-nineteenth century for the Erie division of the New York state canals are presented in table B.3 in appendix B.)

Following the Erie's early success, a host of other canal projects were initiated; the Pennsylvania Main Line, the Schuylkill, the Champlain, the Delaware and Raritan, the Chesapeake and Ohio, the Ohio and Erie, the Miami and Erie, the Wabash and Erie, and the Chicago–La Salle Canals (to name some of the major undertakings). These canals were completed during the three decades subsequent to the Erie's completion. By 1860, the United States had 4,254 miles of completed canals, and the canal era had ended. Canal building stopped because competition from railroads did not allow canals to be profitable. (Only during the years impacted by the Civil War did canal prosperity revive only to disappear again with the return of normalcy.)

Developments in transportation allowed an extraordinary increase in the movement of goods across regions. An example is the development of the Ohio and Erie Canal; the canal's first leg between Cleveland and Akron opened in 1827. The entire canal was completed in 1832, a total distance of 308 miles between Cleveland on Lake Erie and Portsmouth, Ohio on the Ohio River. Within one year of its completion, wheat shipments through Cleveland had increased from 1,000 bushels to 250,000 bushels; seven years later in 1840, wheat shipments through Cleveland were 2.2 million bushels.

The first miles of railroad track were being laid just as canal building was in full bloom in the nation. In 1830, there were twenty-three total miles of railroad track in the United States; in 1840, there were 2,818 miles. The railroad industry expanded rapidly in the 1840s and by 1850 total mileage had increased to 9,021 miles, more than twice the total mileage that canals had in *1860*. There were over 30,000 miles of railroad track in 1860, a 239 percent increase from that of 1850. The growth of the nation's railroad network continued during the post–Civil War decades of the nineteenth century; by 1890, there were 166,703 miles of track, 444 percent more than in 1860. (Annual data on railroad track during the nineteenth century are presented in table B.4 in appendix B.)

In their infancy railroads complemented rather than substituted for canals; in the 1830s, shipping by rail was substantially more expensive than canals for most purposes. When railroads were first constructed, it was where canals were very costly to build or maintain—over hills and mountains, and between ports and cities. Railroads were cheaper to build than canals, but they still had substantial fixed costs; their variable costs, which were lower than other forms of overland transport, were higher than those of canals. This meant that passenger fares and freight rates on the early railroads were lower than other forms of overland transport but not lower than on canals. Consequently, rail mileage in the 1830s and 1840s was concentrated in the densely populated areas of the Northeast where the volume of traffic was greatest and passenger tolls were a significant portion of the income of railroads. (Passenger traffic is, and was, willing to pay a great deal for speed; a 200-mile rail trip took about half a day in 1840; the same trip by canal boat would take over three days.) In the 1840s, more than half the total railroad mileage in the country was concentrated in the Northeast. Continuing improvements in engine efficiency, rails and track, and other innovations gradually reduced the costs of rail traffic. As a result, railroad track mileage and traffic increased substantially. In 1860, developments in rail transport had given railroads at least three distinct advantages over inland water freight: (1) railroads could be constructed in places where canals were impracticable, (2) railroads could be operated year round, and (3) railroads were faster than water transport.

Railroad travel times in 1860 were small fractions of those in 1830. The percentage declines in the time it took to travel long distances (primarily along East–West routes) were greater than the declines for shorter distances. Travel times circa 1860 were about 1/7 to 1/10 of those in 1830, which in turn were about half of those in 1800. In 1857, eastern Ohio was one day's travel from New York City; it had been a seven-day journey in 1830. The travel time to New York City from much of Illinois was two days in 1857 compared to journeys of three weeks in 1830. In the densely populated urban areas of the Northeast, travel times between cities were typically a matter of hours.[3] Increased speed allowed railroads to capture nearly all the higher valued freight from water transport; the speed and comfort of railroads redirected passenger traffic from canals and steamboats to the rails as well.

In trans-Atlantic shipping, declining costs in both time and money affected the immigration of Europeans to the United States. Steerage fares from Europe to the United States fell by almost 70 percent between the 1810s and the 1830s. By the late 1820s, packet ships had regularly scheduled crossings of the Atlantic, and fares were 50 percent less than the fares a decade earlier (the 1810s). These developments aided the movement of peoples and the pathogens that preyed upon them. Two significant changes in immigration to America were (1) a substantial increase in the numbers of people coming to the United States and (2) major changes in the primary countries of origin. Changing origins implies that different (to Americans) pathogens entered the United States in the nineteenth century. Early in the nineteenth century, the number of immigrants was relatively small; in 1820, total foreign immigration was just 8,385 people; in 1830, it was 23,322. By 1840, immigration was 84,006; from 1846 to 1860, immigration averaged over a quarter million people per year (Carter, Gartner, Haines, et al. 2006, vol. 1, series Ad1–2, pp. 1–541). The entire population in 1845 was just over 20 million; consequently, the foreign born added about 1 percent per year to the American population for each year from 1846 to 1860. Immigration reached its pre–Civil War high in 1854 when 427,833 immigrants came. The early Civil War years reduced the flow of immigrants considerably, but by 1863 it was recovering. Immigration averaged more than 365,000 people annually from 1863 to 1900. Nineteenth-century immigration peaked in the 1880s when an average of nearly 525,000 immigrants came each year of the decade, reaching a single year high in 1882 of 788,992. (Annual immigration and annual immigration for the three major countries of origin are presented in table B.5 in appendix B.)

Nineteenth-century developments in transportation, the increase in the volume of freight, and the movements and numbers of people affected the transmission of diseases. In prior centuries, diseases were primarily local and regional. In the nineteenth century, the growth of transport networks, the reduction in transport costs, and the reduction in journey times led to an integration of disease pools: locally, regionally, nationally, and, in some instances, internationally. The diseases that were identified and spread included (among others): cholera, tuberculosis, dysentery, malaria, hookworm, influenza, gastrointestinal diseases, measles, yellow fever, mumps, and smallpox. These diseases had existed before the transport changes of the nineteenth century, but they were generally localized and regional. A widespread, low-cost, and relatively rapid, transport system integrated goods, peoples, and, importantly for our story, diseases. The increasing density and the growth of cities and urbanization further integrated disease pools and facilitated their propagation. Increased virulence accompanied disease strains when "new" diseases or their variants were introduced to areas where they had been absent.

The Biomedical Evidence

US Army Morbidity Data, 1830s

Table 7.5 presents data on malaria morbidity rates for American soldiers in the 1830s. At the time, malaria was known under a variety of names, such as "autumnal, bilious, intermittent, remittent, congestive, miasmatic, malarial, marsh, malignant, chill-fever, ague, fever and ague, dumb ague, and lastly the Fever" (Drake [1850, 1854] 1964, p. 703). The data in table 7.5 are for military posts of the United States Army in coastal areas and the interior of North America; the data are reported by latitude and name of the post in the 1830s. Although the latitudinal location is known for all posts and the location of many is obvious, the exact location of some posts has to be determined from the historical record and maps.

The morbidity rates in table 7.5 indicate that malaria had spread from coastal areas in the southern United States to northern areas along the Mississippi River system. While the prevalence of the disease generally declined the further north a military post was located, other geographical aspects of a post's location also were important to the survival and propagation of the malaria. For example, Fort Towson (in present-day Oklahoma) was more northern than both Fort Mitchell (Alabama) and Fort Jesup (Louisiana), yet it had a malaria morbidity rate that was from four to five and a half times higher than the other two forts. Fort Towson had a substantially higher incidence of malaria in spite of its more northerly location because it was located in a low-lying area a few hundred yards from a small standing lake right in the heart of the Red River basin. (The Red River is a major tributary of the Mississippi.) Fort Jesup was

Table 7.5
Annual malaria morbidity rates per 1,000 troops: US military posts during the 1830s

Location of military post	Annual morbidity rate
Key West, N. latitude 24° 33′	190
Fort Brooks, N. latitude 27° 57′	849
Fort King, N. latitude 29° 12′	1,387
Fort Jackson, N. latitude 29° 29′	1,600
New Orleans Barracks, N. latitude 29° 57′	544
Fort Wood, N. latitude 30° 5′	1,063
Fort Pike, N. latitude 30° 10′	232
Baton Rouge, N. latitude 30° 36′	824
Fort Jesup, N. latitude 31° 30′	302
Fort Mitchell, N. latitude 32° 19′	225
Fort Towson, N. latitude 33° 51′	1,265
Fort Smith, N. latitude 35° 22′	1,161
Fort Gibson, N. latitude 35° 57′	1,435
Jefferson Barracks, N. latitude 38° 28′	475
Fort Leavenworth, N. latitude 39° 20′	629
Fort Armstrong, N. latitude 41° 28′	307
Fort Dearborn, N. latitude 41° 51′	251
Fort Gratiot, N. latitude 43°	803
Fort Crawford, N. latitude 43° 3′	301
Fort Niagara, N. latitude 43° 15′	368
Fort Winnebago, N. latitude 43° 31′	63
Madison Barracks, N. latitude 43° 50′	255
Fort Howard, N. latitude 44° 40′	84
Fort Snelling, N. latitude 44° 53′	62
Fort Mackinack, N. latitude 45° 51′	89
Fort Brady, N. latitude 46° 39′	44

Source: Drake ([1850, 1854] 1964, pp. 706–707).
Note: A malaria morbidity rate greater than 1,000 per 1,000 troops means that soldiers at that military post averaged more than one malarial spell per year per soldier.

located in a part of northern Louisiana about 120 miles west of the Mississippi River; although it has relatively mild winters, it receives measurable snowfall once every five to ten years (and killing frosts more frequently). Fort Mitchell was located about 200 miles north of the Gulf coast near present-day Auburn, Alabama, in a partially hilly area at the edge of the Piedmont plateau. So it too had geography less amenable for the propagation of mosquitoes and the spread of malaria than Fort Towson.

If we allow the incapacitation rates in table 7.5 to approximate the general prevalence of malaria, then the data indicate how pervasive malaria was in the antebellum era. In some areas, the incapacitation rates for presumably relatively healthy young men (they were in the military) exceeded 100 percent (more than 1,000 cases of incapacitation due to malaria per 1,000 troops per year). At these posts, the troops averaged more than one malarial spell per year per soldier. The morbidity rates indicate that the soldiers experienced malarial attacks that removed them from the duty roster some time during the year. The data do not indicate the length of incapacitation.

Census Mortality Data, 1850 to 1900

United States Census data on the number of deaths by specific causes in each state for the years 1850 to 1900 provide further evidence of the spread of infectious diseases during the nineteenth century. From these data, we calculated cause-specific mortality rates for the entire population for nearly two dozen major infectious diseases for the 1850 to 1900 census years for each state for which data exist. We also calculated mortality rates for deaths from all causes for (1) the entire population, (2) four age cohorts—adults (20 years and older), children/adolescents (5–19 years old), young children (1–4 years old), and infants (under 1 year old), (3) two ethnicity cohorts (blacks and whites), and (4) two nativity cohorts (native born and foreign born) for each census year for each state for which data exist. The cause-specific mortality rates for the major infectious diseases are presented in tables C.1 through C.11 in appendix C. The mortality rates for all causes of death for the entire population and the eight different cohorts are presented in tables C.12 through C.16 in appendix C. Appendix C also includes a discussion of issues involved in the calculation of the mortality rates for several of the diseases, an examination of the overall accuracy and reliability of the census mortality data, and a listing of the data sources.

The cause-specific mortality rates indicate that many of the infectious diseases had spread from the locations where they were initially concentrated to other regions of the country. Expanding on the evidence on malaria morbidity presented in table 7.5, the malaria mortality rates indicate that malaria had clearly spread far beyond the South, and by 1850 it was embedded in the Midwest and much of the Northeast. But malaria had reached its peak prevalence in the Northeast by the mid-nineteenth century, from then until the end of the century malaria mortality rates in most northeastern states declined steadily. By 1900, malaria mortality rates were small fractions of their 1850/1860 rates in many states in the Northeast. Similarly, malaria declined in midwestern states during the second half of the nineteenth century; nevertheless, in several midwestern states malaria remained a nontrivial disease until circa 1880/1890. In contrast, malaria in the South remained a relatively major cause of death. Malaria mortality rates in the southern states were several multiples larger than the rates in rest of the country in 1900 (see table C.4).

Deaths from intestinal parasites/worms were concentrated in the Deep South (see tables C.5 and C.9). The data indicate that these diseases also afflicted the border states, parts of the Midwest, and at least two northeastern states; albeit the mortality rates indicate deaths in northern states were small fractions of those in the Deep South. For other diseases, the data indicate their epidemic nature; for example, mortality rates for cholera (all variants) in about two dozen states decreased from 1850 to 1860 to become a small fraction of their 1850 rates (see table C.1). Yellow fever, while not unknown outside of the South, was generally concentrated in southern cities, as indicated by the very high yellow fever mortality rates in Louisiana and South Carolina in 1850, in Texas and Louisiana in 1860, in Florida in 1870, and in Tennessee and Louisiana in 1880, also indicating the epidemic nature of the disease (see table C.9). The data also indicate that several of the infectious diseases appear to have declined throughout the nation, among these were croup (table C.2), dysentery (table C.3), scarlet fever (table C.6), and smallpox (table C.7). Conversely, other diseases appear to have increased, among these were diphtheria (table C.3), consumption/tuberculosis (table C.1), and pneumonia (table C.6).

We also calculated a series of regional mortality rates for the regional populations, and for the eight different cohorts for three regions of the United States for all causes of death and for four major groups of infectious diseases for the 1850 to 1900 census years. These regional rates aid in understanding the differences in the mortality rates for the regional populations and for the various cohorts across states and time for all causes of death and for the nearly two dozen infectious diseases

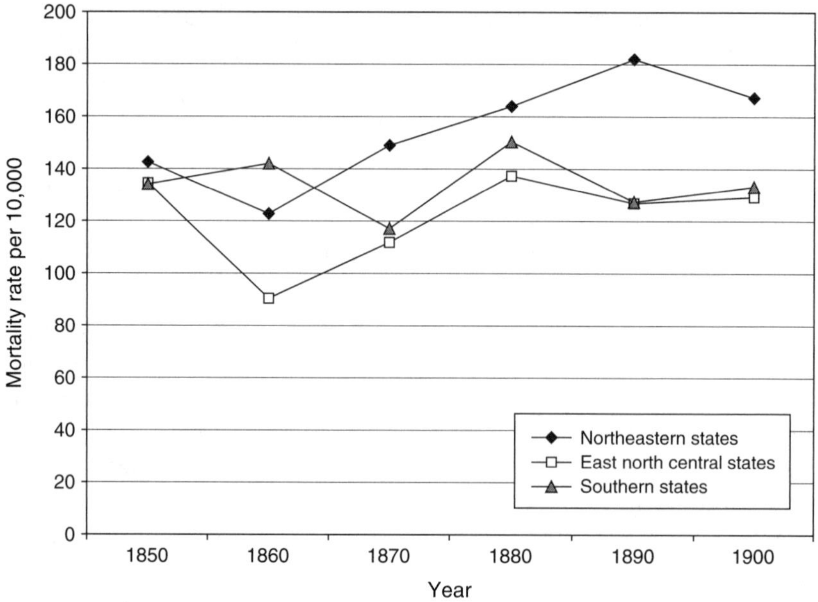

Figure 7.1
Mortality rate for regional populations per 10,000 by region, 1850 to 1900

that were examined. The regional mortality rates were calculated for three regions of the eastern third of the United States: (1) the Northeast (Connecticut, Maine, Massachusetts, New Hampshire, New Jersey, New York, Pennsylvania, Rhode Island, and Vermont), (2) the East North Central (Ohio, Indiana, Illinois, Michigan, and Wisconsin), and (3) the South (Alabama, Arkansas, Florida, Georgia, Kentucky, Louisiana, Mississippi, North Carolina, South Carolina, Tennessee, Virginia, and West Virginia). The four disease groups for which we calculated mortality rates are (1) upper respiratory diseases (consumption/tuberculosis, croup, influenza, pneumonia, "winter fever," and whooping cough), (2) warm-weather fevers (bilious, congestive, intermittent, remittent, malarial, typho-malarial, typhus, and yellow fevers as well as fever, not specified), (3) intestinal parasites/worms (dirt eating, parasites, parasitic diseases, and worms), and (4) gastrointestinal tract diseases (cholera, cholera infantum, cholera morbus, diarrheal diseases, diphtheria, dysentery, and typhoid/enteric fever).[4]

The regional mortality rates for all causes of deaths indicate several interesting patterns. The mortality rates for the regional populations shown in figure 7.1 indicate that overall the Northeast was the least

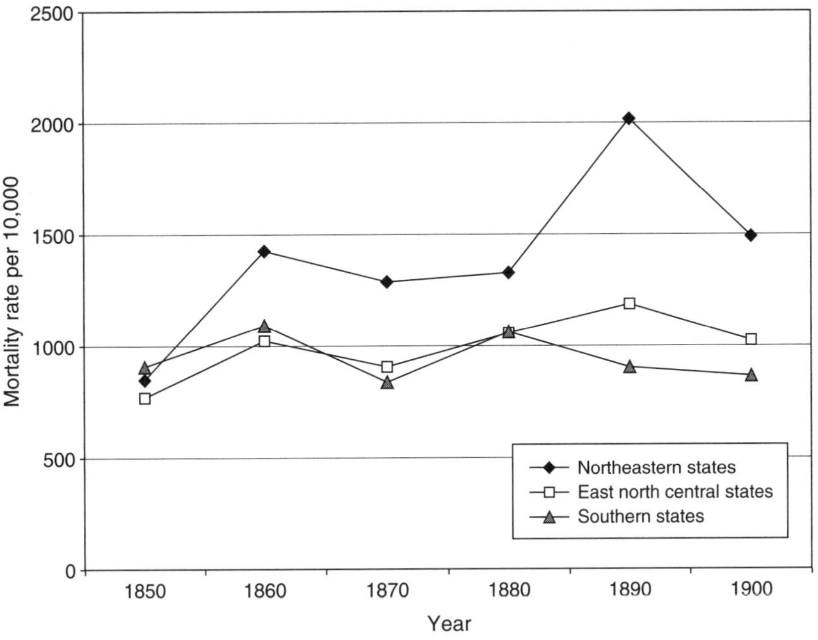

Figure 7.2
Infant mortality rate per 10,000 by region, 1850 to 1900

healthy region with the highest regional death rates. Northeastern death rates increased until at least 1890, ending the century substantially higher than their 1850 level. The data for the other two regions indicate that both regions ended the century with death rates essentially at their 1850 levels. Nearly all of the cohort mortality rates, except for foreign-born individuals, show the northeastern states with the highest mortality. Figures 7.2 and 7.3 depict the regional mortality rates for infants (under 1 year old) and young children (1 to 4 years old), respectively; the figures show that the Northeast had the worst environment for these cohorts. The highest mortality rates in the Northeast are consistent with our story of infectious diseases being a product of economic growth, increasing population, density, urbanization, large cities, and developing transportation networks.[5]

Infant death rates for all causes in all three regions were much higher than the regional rates for other age cohorts, and infant death rates do not appear to have fallen before 1890. The mortality rates for young children were second highest by far; they rose slightly in the Northeast and South, and fell slightly in the East North Central, from 1850 to 1880;

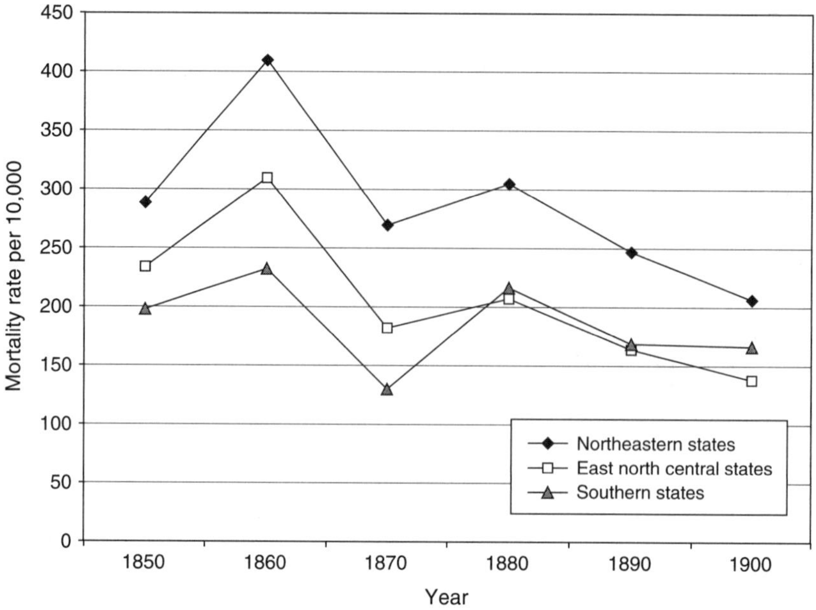

Figure 7.3
Young children mortality rate per 10,000 by region, 1850 to 1900

they declined substantially from 1880 to 1900 in all three regions (see figures 7.2 and 7.3, respectively). The children/adolescents (5 to 19 years old) cohort had the lowest mortality rates. The foreign-born mortality rates generally are higher than the native-born rates, but the census mortality data categorized by nativity are the most problematic of all the population cohorts. In two of the censuses, deaths by nativity were reported only for whites (native-born and foreign-born whites); in another census, deaths by nativity were reported for whites and free "colored" combined (native-born and foreign-born whites and "free colored"); in another census, deaths by nativity were reported for the entire population (native born and foreign born). In the other two censuses, no mortality data were reported on the basis of nativity (see appendix C for more details).

The white and black mortality rates for all causes in the three regions are shown in figures 7.4 and 7.5, respectively.[6] They indicate that during the 1850 to 1900 period blacks had higher mortality rates than whites, and black mortality rates were closest to white rates in 1850. Except for 1850, black death rates were the highest in the Northeast and lowest in the South, and black mortality rates exceeded white rates by the most

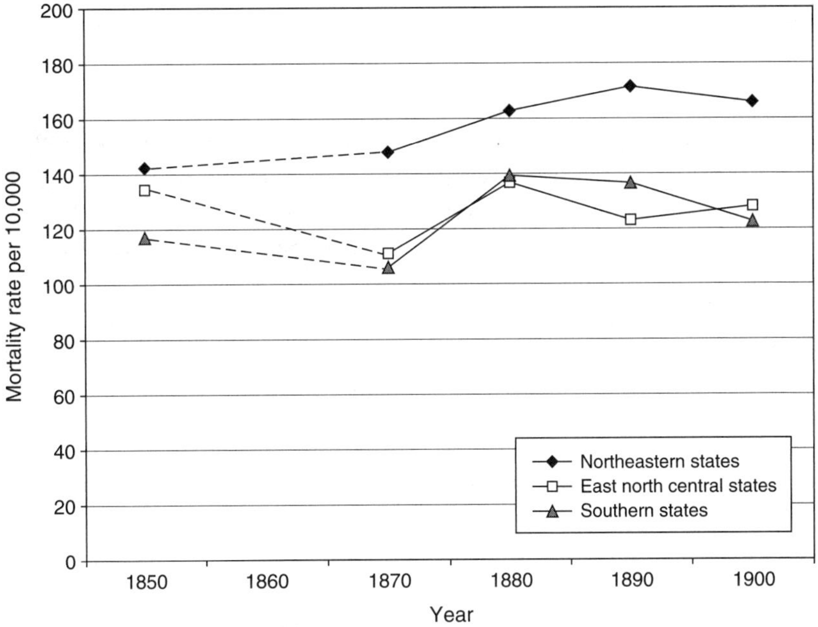

Figure 7.4
White mortality rate per 10,000 by region, 1850 to 1900. Note: No white mortality rate for 1860 was calculated; the 1860 census did not report mortality data based on ethnicity (race).

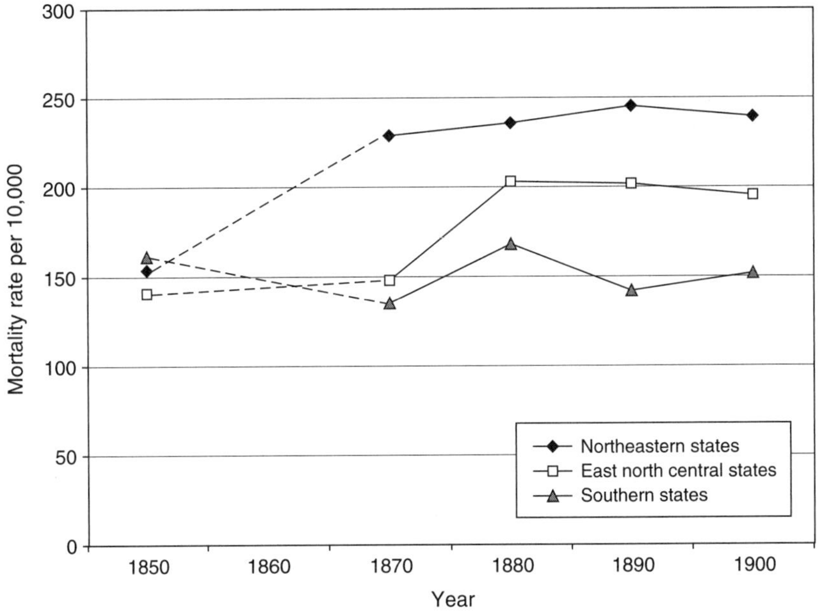

Figure 7.5
Black mortality rate per 10,000 by region, 1850 to 1900. Note: No black mortality rate for 1860 was calculated; the 1860 census did not report mortality data based on ethnicity (race).

in the Northeast and the least in the South. Except for 1850, black and white death rates were much more similar in the South than the other regions (compare figures 7.4 and 7.5). These findings are consistent with both the history of nineteenth-century America and our disease story for the second half of the century. Higher overall mortality for blacks during this period is consistent with inferior economic and living conditions for blacks in the industrial Northeast and the postbellum South (two-thirds of the census years examined come after the Civil War). In the northeastern states, the high black mortality rate and the large gap between the black and white mortality rates is consistent with crowded living quarters (density), urbanization, poor living conditions, and a greater relative susceptibility to "cold-weather" diseases. The similarity of the mortality rates for blacks and whites in the southern states is consistent with a combination of lower susceptibly of blacks to "warm-weather" southern diseases (and the increased susceptibility of whites), the increasing spread of diseases during the nineteenth century, and deteriorating social conditions for blacks in the postbellum South.

The regional mortality rates for the four disease groups indicate important patterns as well. For upper respiratory diseases, figure 7.6 shows the Northeast had the highest mortality rates for the regional populations, while the South and East North Central regions are generally similar. Infants (under 1 year) had the highest susceptibility to upper respiratory diseases with mortality rates triple those of young children (1 to 4 years), who had the second highest mortality rates. Similar to the white and black mortality rates for all causes of deaths, white mortality rates due to upper respiratory diseases, shown in figure 7.7, were much lower than those of blacks, depicted in figure 7.8, in the Northeast and East North Central regions while in the southern states blacks and whites had very similar upper respiratory mortality rates.

Figure 7.9 shows the mortality rates for deaths from intestinal parasites/worms for the regional populations; death rates in the South were several multiples greater than those of the other two regions. While there were some deaths from intestinal parasites/worms in both the Northeast and East North Central regions, they were nearly nonexistent by 1870 in the Northeast. Moreover, all three regions had declining trends from 1850 to 1900. In all three regions, the infant (and young children) mortality rates for intestinal parasites/worms were about forty to fifty times greater than those of adults (see the infant and adult

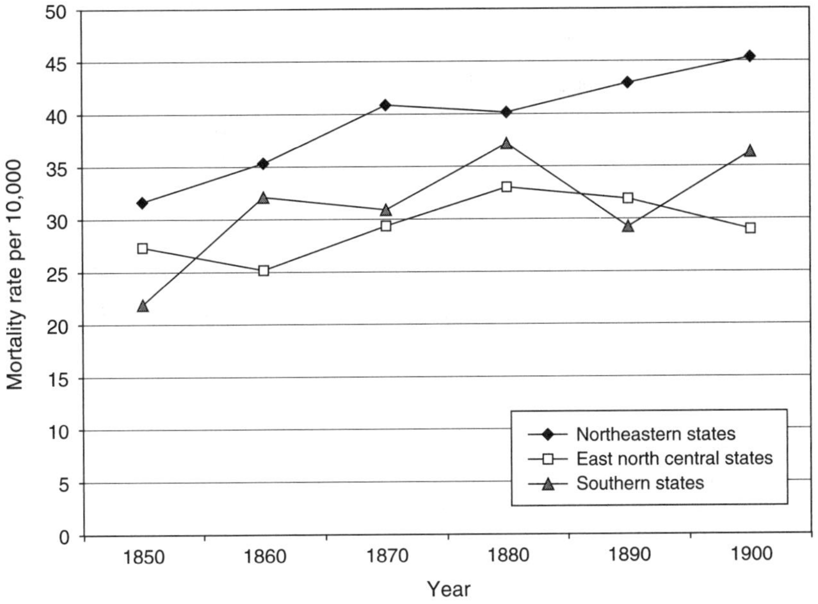

Figure 7.6
Mortality rate for regional populations per 10,000 for upper respiratory diseases by region, 1850 to 1900

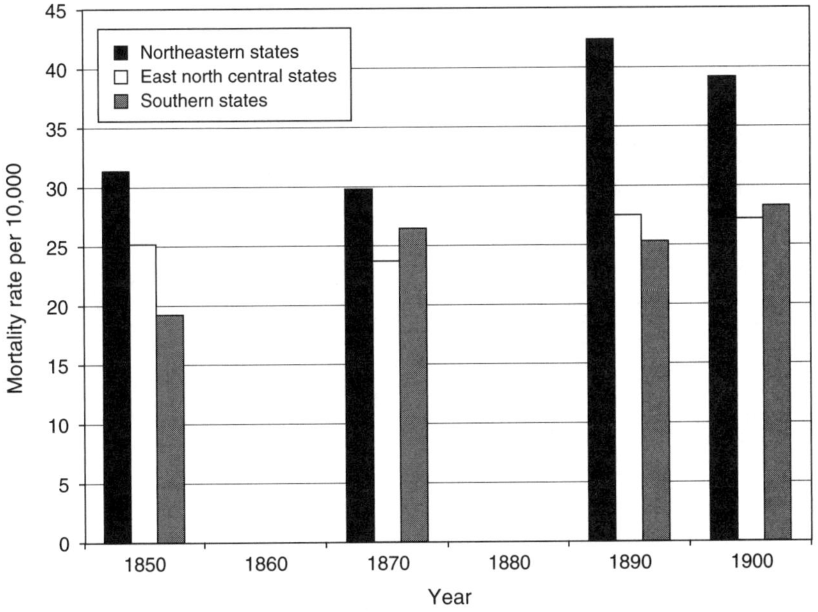

Figure 7.7
White mortality rate per 10,000 for upper respiratory diseases by region, 1850 to 1900

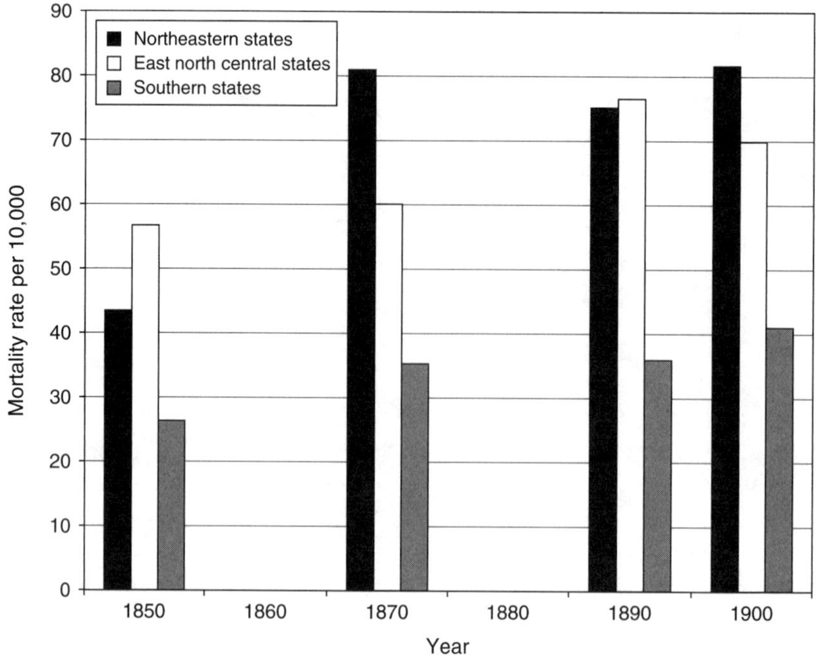

Figure 7.8
Black mortality rate per 10,000 for upper respiratory diseases by region, 1850 to 1900

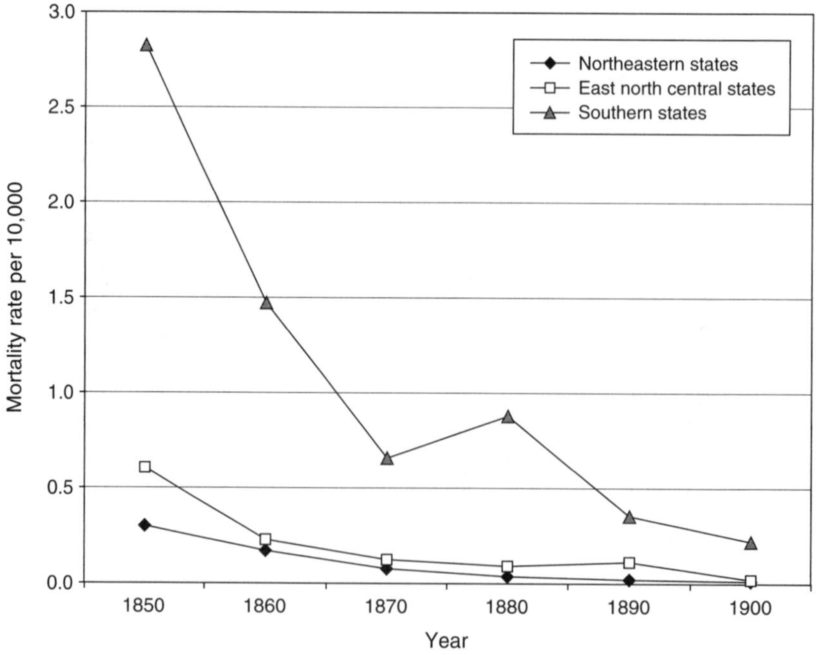

Figure 7.9
Mortality rate for regional populations per 10,000 for intestinal parasites/worms by region, 1850 to 1900

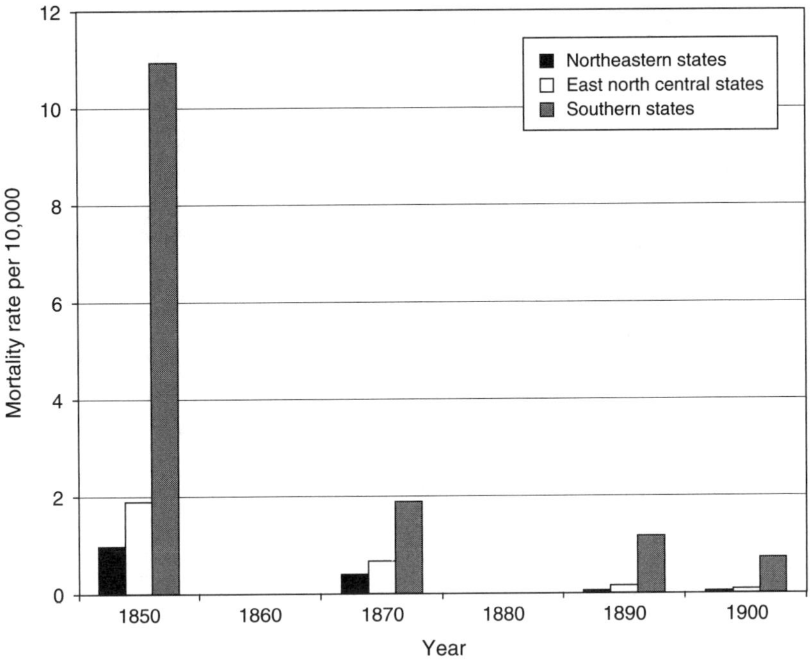

Figure 7.10
Infant mortality rate per 10,000 for intestinal parasites/worms by region, 1850 to 1900

mortality rates in figures 7.10 and 7.11, respectively) and ten to twelve times those for the children/adolescents cohort (not shown). The Census reported on deaths from intestinal parasites/worms by ethnicity (black and white) for only two of the six census years, making any conclusions about black and white mortality rates problematic.

The mortality rates for warm-weather fevers for the regional populations (see figure 7.12) indicate a common trend for 1850 to 1900 in the Northeast and East North Central states. Death rates from these fevers declined throughout the period (with the possible exception of 1880) in both regions until in 1900 they were no longer a major threat. The mortality rate for these fevers fell in the South so that by 1870 it was about a third of its 1850 rate; subsequently, there was a major resurgence in 1880 after which it returned to its (approximately) 1870 level and remained there. Similar to the findings for intestinal parasites/worms, warm-weather fever mortality rates were by far the highest in the southern states, especially for 1870 to 1900 when the southern death rates were two to about six times higher than those in the East North

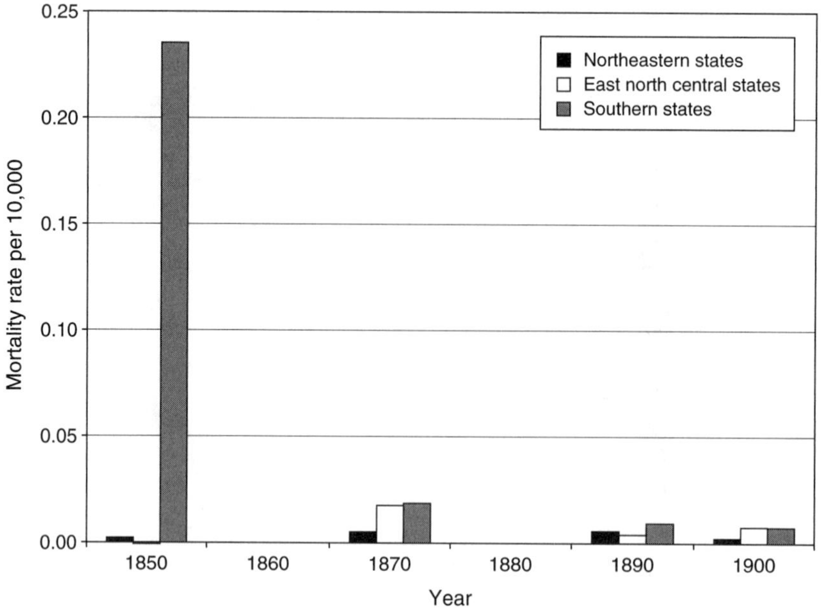

Figure 7.11
Adult mortality rate per 10,000 for intestinal parasites/worms by region, 1850 to 1900

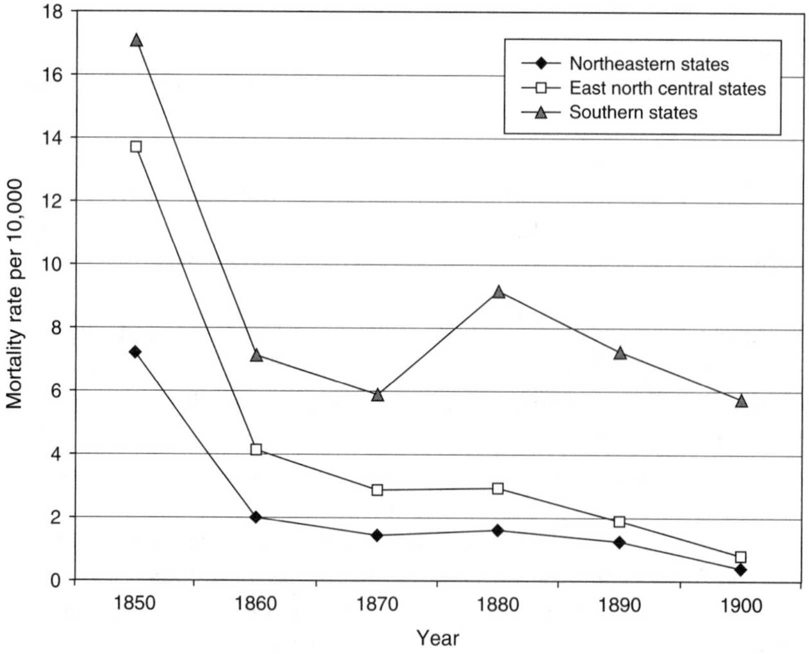

Figure 7.12
Mortality rate for regional populations per 10,000 for warm-weather fevers by region, 1850 to 1900

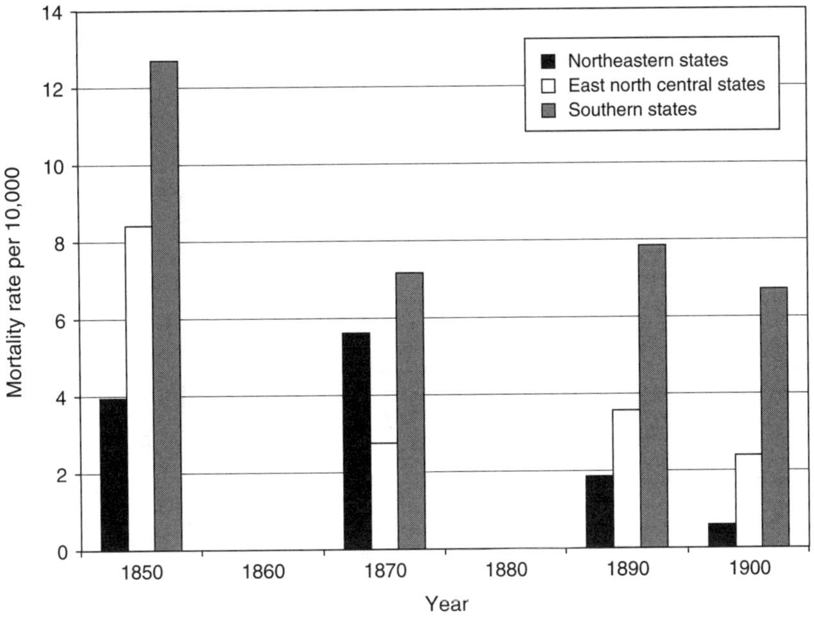

Figure 7.13
Black mortality rate per 10,000 for warm-weather fevers by region, 1850 to 1900

Central states and six to about eleven times higher than those in the northeastern states (see figure 7.12).

Among the age cohorts, infants and young children were by far the most susceptible to deaths from warm-weather fevers in all three regions. For the census years for which warm-weather fever deaths by ethnicity were reported (1850, 1870, 1890, 1900), the mortality rates for blacks (see figure 7.13) were greater than those for whites, except at the beginning of the period; in 1850, white mortality rates (see figure 7.14) were somewhat greater than black rates in all three regions. Because of the problematic nature of the census mortality data based on nativity (noted above), any conclusions about warm-weather fever mortality for native born and foreign born should be viewed cautiously. Nevertheless, the mortality rates for warm-weather fevers are highest for the foreign born in all three regions, except in 1850 in the South. But in the South in 1850, slave deaths were not reported on the basis of nativity and very few foreign-born individuals had settled there. As a result, the South's native-born and foreign-born populations and deaths are not directly comparable to those in the other regions.

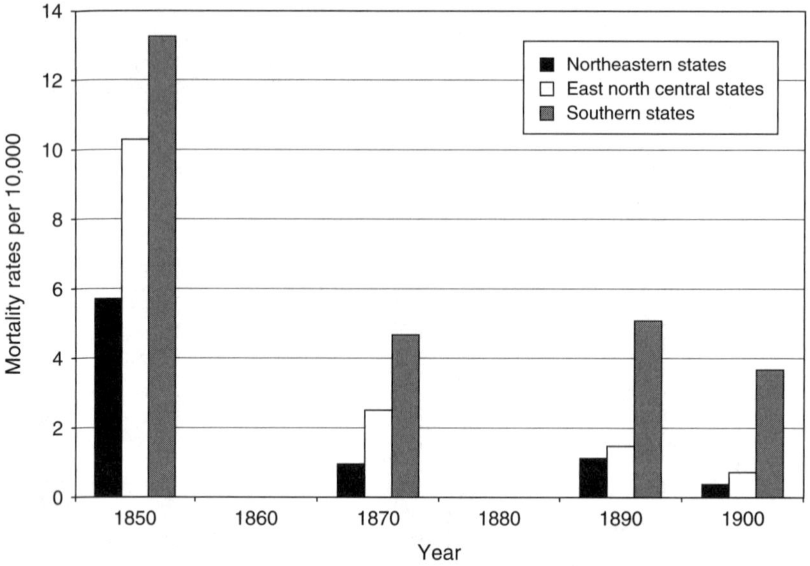

Figure 7.14
White mortality rate per 10,000 for warm-weather fevers by region, 1850 to 1900

The mortality rates for gastrointestinal tract diseases for the regional populations, shown in figure 7.15, indicate the epidemic nature of the individual diseases that make up this group, with two major peaks in the death rates in 1850 and 1880 and major troughs in 1860/1870 and 1900. This pattern shows up as well in the mortality rates for young children, but less so for infants who were somewhat protected from waterborne diseases by relying mostly on mother's milk. Gastrointestinal tract deaths do not appear to be noticeably concentrated in any specific region, except those for infants and young children that are noticeably greater in the Northeast. For whites and blacks, the mortality rates for gastrointestinal tract diseases are the most similar of all the disease groups across the four census years (1850, 1870, 1890, 1900) that have data for all three regions. The mortality rates by nativity are not comparable because too many of the individual gastrointestinal tract diseases were not reported for foreign born in the Census.[7]

The Impact of Infectious Diseases on Infants and Young Children in the Nineteenth Century

The most susceptible elements of a population to infectious diseases are typically infants and young children. Infants who have just been

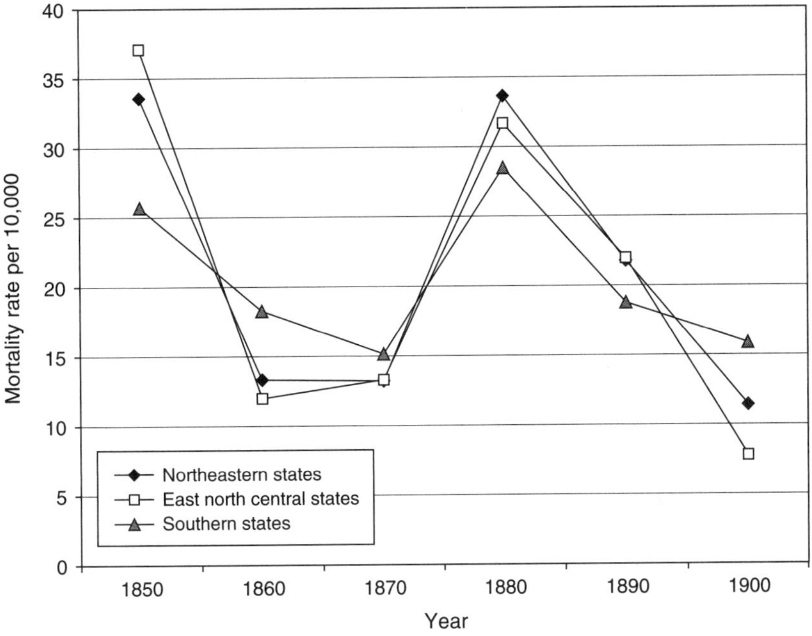

Figure 7.15
Mortality rate for regional populations per 10,000 for gastrointestinal tract diseases by region, 1850 to 1900

weaned or are being weaned are particularly susceptible. For nursing infants, mother's milk provides partial protection from infection for (at least) two reasons. The first is that breast milk directly provides antibodies to the infant (a breast-fed baby is less likely to be infected by diseases than is a non–breast-fed baby). The second reason is that breast-feeding eliminates the use of other foods that may harbor diseases (such as typhoid fever, dysentery, salmonella, and other diarrhea-causing diseases). It should be pointed out that while diarrhea is a symptom not a disease there are many infections of the gastrointestinal track that cause it. Many diarrheal diseases are frequently not identified, and even when they are, they are usually diagnosed as diarrhea rather than caused by a specific pathogen or pathogens. Infants and young children, because of their small size, are very susceptible to diseases that affect their gastrointestinal track. A human baby infected by an organism that causes diarrhea can dehydrate and die within a day. The enhanced susceptibility of newly weaned babies to diarrheal diseases is exacerbated by the infant's lack of exposure to disease-causing pathogens. In older children and adults, previous exposure to diseases primes the immune system with acquired antibodies that resist the same (or similar) invasive pathogens. An infant just weaned from mother's milk has an immune system that lacks such prophylactic devices, so pathogens have a relatively easier time establishing themselves.

Consistent with the greater susceptibility of infants to infectious diseases, our state-level infant mortality rates in table C.14 in appendix C appear to indicate rising trends during the second half of the nineteenth century, at least for the eastern third of the United States. Other infant mortality rates for Baltimore, Maryland, the state of Massachusetts, and the Northeast region are presented in table 7.6; these rates show similar rising trends during the same period. In the second half of the nineteenth century, Baltimore was more populous and densely populated than the average city in the nation. Massachusetts was an industrial state where development and urbanization began earlier, and it was a destination for immigrants. Similarly, the Northeast region was more industrial and urbanized and had more immigrants than the United States as a whole. These are the very characteristics of locations that our disease story of economic growth suggests would have generated higher mortality rates especially among susceptible groups (that is, infants). Because the mortality rates we calculated for the Northeast are based on the census mortality schedules, which certainly underenumerated deaths for infants and for the earlier census years, they have some inherent limitations (see the discussion in appendix C). For example, it seems clear that the 1850 infant mortality rate for the Northeast in table 7.6 is a substantial underestimate compared to the other mortality rates shown in the table. Finally, while the infant mortality rates for the United States that are presented in table 7.6 do not indicate the same increasing trend as indicated by the other mortality rates in the table, they do indicate that the United States rate in 1880 was still over 98 percent of its 1850 rate.

The infant mortality rates in appendix C (table C.14) and table 7.6 are generally consistent with our disease story. The trends in many of the rates in table C.14 for the eastern part of the United States appear to indicate sizable increases, even if 1860 is used as the beginning date. These trends are more readily apparent in the Northeast region infant mortality rates (table 7.6 and figure 7.2). But given the certain underenumeration in 1850, the 1860 mortality rate is the better beginning date for examining mortality trends in the Northeast. The infant

Table 7.6
Various mortality rates per 10,000 for infants under 1 year old: Baltimore, Massachusetts, Northeast region, and the United States

	Location			
Year	Baltimore	Massachusetts	Northeast region	United States
1850	1,670	1,325[a]	849	2,289
1860	1,881	1,337	1,427	1,967
1870	2,780	1,622	1,288	1,845
1880	2,723	1,626	1,328	2,251
1890	2,864	1,666	2,016	1,604
1900	2,422	1,567	1,490	1,290
1910	2,098	1,329	—	1,042
1920	1,761	912	—	858

Source: The Baltimore mortality rates are contained in Howard (1924, table 136, p. 517). The Massachusetts mortality rates are contained in Carter, Gartner, Haines, et al. (2006, vol. I, series Ab928, pp. 1–462). The Northeast region mortality rates are the rates we calculated for the northeastern states from the census mortality reports, the sources of which are listed in appendix C. The US mortality rates are contained in Carter, Gartner, Haines, et al. (2006, vol. I, series Ab920, pp. 1–459).
Note: The Baltimore mortality rates have been converted from deaths per 100,000. The Massachusetts and US mortality rates have been converted from deaths per 1,000.
a. The actual date for this mortality rate is 1851.

mortality rate in the Northeast in 1890 was over 41 percent higher than its 1860 rate, and the rate in 1900 was still 104 percent of its 1860 rate. (Moreover, as discussed in appendix C, infant deaths reported in the 1900 census no longer included stillbirths unlike the earlier censuses.) The Massachusetts data in table 7.6 show a 26 percent increase in infant mortality from midcentury to 1890 (Massachusetts infant mortality actually peaked in 1872 at 1,941 deaths per 10,000); in 1900, the Massachusetts infant mortality rate was still 18 percent above that of 1850; in 1910, it was still as high as that of 1850. The infant mortality rates for Baltimore show a 71.5 percent increase in the death rate from 1850 to 1890; in 1900, the mortality rate in Baltimore was still 45 percent higher than in 1850.[8] (Our mortality rates for young children presented in table C.13 in appendix C do not show similar increases; they actually decline during the period but not by much, at least in the eastern part of the country. The 1890 mortality rate for young children in the Northeast region was still nearly 86 percent of its 1850 rate.)

As discussed in chapter 3, the Antebellum Puzzle is the term encompassing data that show adult heights declining in the birth cohorts of men who fought in the Civil War (born a couple or so decades prior to the war). The mean heights of age cohorts born after midcentury subsequently rose. The term "puzzle" is used because real living standards (as measured by real income per capita) were increasing during the period when adult heights were falling. In addressing this issue in chapter 3, we argued that the puzzle was explicable within the framework of a deteriorating disease environment. Here we add another "puzzle" that can be explained by the disease environment as well: Why were mortality rates of infants in the eastern part of the nation increasing as income per capita rose in the decades following the Civil War? Was there a "Postbellum Puzzle" to accompany the Antebellum Puzzle? The answer to these questions is embedded in the spread of infectious diseases. Infant mortality rates increased in the decades following the Civil War in those locations that were especially likely to have faced a deteriorating disease environment; infants are particularly susceptible to many infectious diseases.[9] Similarly, in the antebellum United States, transport integration and revolution united disease pools even as they led to a more specialized and productive economy. Increasing urbanization facilitated the exchange of pathogens as well as economic exchanges. Cities of hundreds of thousands could only exist within a network of efficient, relatively rapid low-cost transportation that also materially assisted the spread of disease.

Concluding Thoughts on Growth and the Spread of Diseases

The increasing efficiency of transportation distorts nineteenth-century data that are used to measure living standards. In 1800, internal transport in the United States depended on natural waterways and animal power. By 1860, railroads, canals, and streetcars economized on the use of animal power in transport. Per unit of economic output there was literally less "horse" power in transportation in 1860 relative to 1800. Consequently, if the ratio of the stock of grain commodities to the population during the 1800 to 1860 period is examined, as some scholars do, the presumption of "holding other factors constant" is incorrect. The same amount of grain per capita or even a smaller amount may have meant an increase in grain consumption for the *human* population. Thus, it cannot be concluded from data on the stock of grains (or "food") per capita alone whether a change in the amount of "food" led to a change in the biological standard of living.

Similarly, data on prices may give a misleading picture of the standard of living. The nineteenth-century developments in transportation reduced the wedge between what consumers paid for farm output and what farmers received for the output. Because of the transport improvements it is plausible that retail prices could have fallen *while* wholesale and/or farm gate prices rose during the first half of the nineteenth century. The reduction in the costs of transportation leads to higher prices to producers and lower prices to consumers. The wedge between the prices paid by demanders and the prices received by the producers narrowed due to the developments in the transport sector. This is the well-known consequence of any reduction in the costs of trade. As a result, it cannot be concluded from data on wholesale and/or farm gate prices alone whether a change in agricultural (wholesale and/or farm gate) prices led to a change in the biological standard of living.

In previous chapters, we argued that developments in transport are not exogenous; they are instead endogenous to the economy. Increases in specialization and output occur because of an increase in market size, this increase also increases the biological resources available for opportunistic pathogens. No ecological niche goes unoccupied for long. Diseases, morbidity, and increased infant mortality were some of the consequences; these affected measures of health and well-being throughout most of the nineteenth century. It was only with the increase in the knowledge of public health and biology, and improving water and sanitary practices that occurred relatively recently, did infectious parasitic diseases cease their slaughter of the innocents.

8 The Biology and Disease Lesson

The message of this book is that some of the most salient features of history can be explained by (1) differentials in the evolutionary heritage of various peoples, (2) climatic and geographic factors related to the spread of pathogens, and (3) the prevailing institutional background that frame the consequences of deliberate human choices. In this vein, an understanding of the American historical experience without a thorough examination of these elements is seriously flawed. A prominent example is the American Civil War; taking these factors and placing them in historical context, we can say that, in a sense, the American Civil War was attributable to parasitic infections. (Explicit in this argument is that the issue of slavery was a major root of the American Civil War.) Without the differential reactions of peoples of northwestern European and tropical West African ancestries to hookworm, malaria, and other warm-weather pathogens, slavery would neither have been as profitable nor as pervasive. Answering critics who would ask: Do we really believe that nematodes less than a fraction of a centimeter long were instrumental in the bloodiest war ever fought on American soil? The answer is an emphatic *yes*. Therein lies the problem of our message; it is extraordinarily difficult for people to think beyond the dimensions of the everyday; synonyms for small are trivial, inconsequential, and insignificant. This clouds thinking.

Humans are captive in time and space; our imaginations and thoughts are constrained by the dimensions in which we live our lives. Small things—things that can be captured or crushed by a child or that are invisible to unaided human vision—are naturally thought of as inconsequential. "Naturally" here is meant literally; is in our nature to think this way and only constant intellectual vigilance can prevent us from equating small with inconsequential. Constant intellectual vigilance is costly and often relaxed because of the efforts required to maintain it; the result is that world renown medical centers in the twenty-first century suffer from significant rates of easily avoidable nosocomial (originating in hospitals) infections close to a century and a half after Pasteur's researches and the germ theory. Human senses do not naturally regard the unseen as threats. Human senses evolved to protect early humans (and their hominid ancestors) from the very real dangers they faced in the ancestral environment. Dangers from large predators, poisonous animals, and other humans were immediate; because the ancestral environment was not densely populated by humans, the pathogens that prey on humanity today were either rare or nonexistent. Evolutionary processes take literally a thousand years or so (about 50 generations) to begin to affect instinctive behaviors; as a result, we are not naturally fearsome of "new" things (in existence for less than a millennia or so) that pose significant dangers to us in the world in which we live.[1] This creates paradoxes that are frequently commented: in modern high-income nations the dangers to life and limb from automobile accidents are literally thousands of times more likely than the risks from poisonous snakes, yet we jaywalk and fear snakes.

For hundreds of thousands of years the evolving hominid species lived in small groups. These populations were too small and too scattered throughout the earth to provide reservoirs for acute (as distinct from chronic) diseases.[2] Early humans did not keep animal herds, consequently they rarely acquired zoonoses. Skeletal remains of evolving humanity are consistent with this story (indeed in some cases they are the progenitors). Skeletal remains of stone-age peoples suggest that the most recent ancestors of evolving humanity were, relative to primitive agriculturalists, disease free, well fed, and violent.

When history is written, dramatic human actions, foolish or heroic, are the focus of attention; microbes and the minute are typically ignored or given tertiary (or lower) considerations. Before the current age (pre–World War I), military deaths from diseases vastly outnumbered deaths directly caused by combatants; still it is a rare text that emphasizes the impact of diseases in war. Nearly two hundred years ago the Battle of Borodino was "won" by the Napoleonic forces; battlefield deaths at Borodino were large, yet they were dwarfed by the carnage caused by typhus in combination with its vector, the louse. This lesson has been forgotten, if indeed it was ever learned. The popular culture of the twenty-first century regards the louse and other vermin as things that are not fearsome but comic; they are frequently topics of humor, and cartoon films that anthromorphize vermin as furry, funny, lovable objects of entertainment, brave defenders of their liberties against evil villains (typically *Homo sapiens*). Humans do not fear them because innate fearful reactions to them are not embedded into our nature as were the fears of snakes and scorpions. Typhus, plague, AIDS, sexually transmitted diseases, and the other illnesses of civilizations were unknown (or extraordinarily rare occurrences) in the environment in which ancestral humans evolved; furthermore, these diseases escape detection by unaided human senses. Because we are unable to identify them with our senses, evolution has not provided us with an instinctive fear of microbial infection, unlike the instinctive aversions that many have toward snakes and scorpions.

Humanity's concept of time is similarly skewed by our senses and experiences. The Darwinian theory of natural selection faced a great deal of resistance because the time scales inherent in evolutionary selection are so vast compared to our intuitive grasp of time. The human sense of time is similarly limited by what we know and grasp intuitively; our sense of time is bounded in the short run by seconds and in the long run by decades. The processes of evolutionary selection are affected over many generations; almost by definition they are invisible to any specific generation.

An analogous historical example that illustrates the point that glacial processes tend to escape human commentary is that of economic growth. In the British Colonies of North America that became the United States, incomes per capita are estimated to have risen at between 0.3 to 0.5 percent per year during the years 1650 to 1776. At a rate of 0.3 percent per year, incomes double about every 230 years. During the same period England was probably experiencing a slightly slower rate of growth; economic changes were not remarked upon during the eighteenth century. Consequently, it is no wonder that when Samuel Johnson, one of the great intellects of the ages, argued that the reign of Caesar Augustus in ancient Rome was humanity's golden age, no one laughed. He could have actually thought that the arts, manners, and society had reached their apogee in Augustinian Rome. Like almost all of his age, Johnson had no conception of the economic changes and growth that were occurring in his lifetime because they were so small as to be unnoticed by contemporaneous observers. We can imagine a growth rate of 0.3 percent per year continuing over millennia, leading to enormous wealth and economic changes, yet to the human population alive at the time the world is unchanging and static.

Samuel Johnson was not alone in his belief that the world was unchanging (or even deteriorating); Adam Smith, David Hume, Voltaire, and the luminaries of the Enlightenment were all pre-modern in their conception of economic progress. Indeed the very conception of economic progress had to await the arrival of growth rates that had noticeable effects during the life span of an ordinary human. The intellect of the sentimentalist and writer Charles Dickens will never be confused with those of the likes of Johnson, Smith, Hume, and Voltaire; still Dickens writing in the mid-nineteenth century would never have identified Augustinian Rome with the apogee of human achievements. Whatever his intellectual failings, Dickens could not help but be smitten by the economic changes that enveloped his time. Adam Smith, an extraordinarily perceptive observer of the human economy, was unaware of the economic changes that were taking place in his age. Smith published his great work, *The Wealth of Nations*, in the monumental year of 1776; Dickens started publishing in the 1830s. Consequently, we can narrow the years that gave birth to modernity; sometime in the 60 years between Smith's *Wealth of Nations* and Dickens's first writings gave birth to the modern and the concept of material progress.[3]

People are generally unaware of processes that take more than two human generations to have noticeable impacts. Background conditions also matter. Suppose that a society has a demographic regime of high birth and death rates. If the mean birth rate is 35 per thousand and that is accompanied by a death rate of 33 per thousand, the population has a mean growth rate of 0.2 percent per year. If the birth rate is constant, and the death rate falls to 29 per thousand, the change has a material chance of being unremarked and unnoticed by contemporaneous observers (yet the growth rate is now 0.6 percent per year). But over 500 years the effects of this change will be immense. At a growth rate of 0.2 percent, population doubles every 345 years or so; after 500 years the population would have increased by approximately 2.72 times its original size. While at a rate of 0.6 percent per year, population doubles approximately every 115 years; after half a millennium population would have increased by nearly 20 times. The arithmetic is basic and unchallenging; the hard part is thinking in terms of centuries or millennia.

Yet these processes arguably have had the most profound impact on observational reality and history. In this book, we have shown how different biological environments affected evolution. People who have innate resistance to pathogens that predominate in the place where they reside will tend to live longer and have more surviving offspring than those who have no innate resistance. An innate advantage does not have to be large because over millennia evolutionary selection will magnify by orders of magnitude both resistance and the proportion of the population that possesses the trait.[4] The time necessary to achieve these results is not easily comprehensible to humans. "Living memory" is, by definition, bounded by human life expectancy. What we have not witnessed fades like shadows at twilight; one wonders, were they real or imagined? They were very real, and were instrumental in shaping American history.

The conquest of the New World by Old World peoples was almost entirely due to biology and evolutionary selection. The introduction of Old World pathogens into the relatively disease free New World environment caused the aboriginal American population to collapse. Epidemiologists and biologists estimate that it takes five generations for the population of a species to stabilize in the face of an epidemic disease. A human generation prior to the twentieth century was about 20 years. Consequently, five human generations would be about 100 years. Yet in 1620, more than 100 years after Contact, the aboriginal American population had not stabilized; it was still in deep decline. This was because it was not just one disease that afflicted the native inhabitants of the New World but a host of them, some occurring simultaneously, others sequentially. Among them were influenza, smallpox, dysentery, malaria, yellow fever, dengue fever, typhus, tuberculosis, and cholera (the latter two becoming rampant in the nineteenth century). These diseases literally changed the complexion of the New World's peoples.

The Old World peoples were relatively immune to the effects that Old World pathogens had on New World peoples. But all Old World peoples did not have the same innate responses to the diseases that were established in the New World post-Contact. In the tropics of the Americas, people whose ancestry made them relatively resistant to warm-weather diseases lived longer lives and produced more surviving offspring relative to those people whose heritage did not include an immune system that had been shaped by exposure to warm-weather diseases for millennia. People who had an inherited resistance to warm-weather diseases were from warm-weather areas in the Old World; in the historical context they were predominantly from tropical West

Africa. Repeating points we made earlier, it is not because Africans came from areas where the climate was hot. The native Aborigines from equatorial America were after all, from a similar climate. Tropical West Africans were relatively resistant to diseases that came to predominate in the warm-weather area of the New World because the pathogens also were from tropical West Africa. The innate resistance their evolutionary heritage provided Africans gave them a survival advantage over other ethnic groups in tropical America, and this is why African slavery survived there.

Conversely, in the areas in the New World that were subject to frequent killing frosts, tropical pathogens had difficulty establishing themselves. Cold weather and killing frosts were not a deterrent to diseases such as influenza, pleurisy, tuberculosis, and other lung infections, hence the term cold-weather diseases. People from northwestern Europe had an ancestral heritage of generations of exposure to cold-weather diseases. Again, they were relatively resistant to the onslaught of these pathogens, and they and their offspring had a survival advantage relative to the other ethnic groups.

In the context of the historical experience, the disease environment in the tropics was more virulent for a number of reasons. The first reason is that most cold-weather pathogens can survive in warm-weather areas. Cold-weather diseases can frequently exist for years in the human populations in the tropics. Indeed most cold-weather diseases, even the ones with high case mortalities, do not kill quickly because their reservoirs tend to be in human populations.[5] Outside a host they cannot survive killing frosts (nor can most pathogens); consequently, if they are quickly fatal, the pathogens will not survive for long. The reason that cold-weather pathogens do not *thrive* in the tropics is that their victims, because of their weakened state, frequently succumb to an opportunistic warm-weather infection before the cold-weather pathogen has had a chance to spread. Over years, unless continually reintroduced, the cold-weather pathogens will diminish and perhaps vanish. As a consequence, the tropics of the New World were subject to endemic warm-weather diseases and the periodic episodes of cold-weather diseases. In the nontropical areas of the New World, while the occasional outbreak of a warm-weather disease did occur, they were rare and irregular.

Second, the major export staple of the tropical New World was sugar. The production of sugar was subject to economies of scale; large plantations with hundreds of workers (slaves of tropical West African ancestry) were packed together in the slave quarters. The slave quarters facilitated the transmission of pathogens among slave and non-slave populations. Indeed in the tropics of the New World the mortality rates of people of European ancestry were higher than those of African slaves. This was due to the differential effects of the warm-weather pathogens and the efficiency in which they propagated in the slave quarters. From having a reservoir in the slave quarters to spreading to the non-slave population was an easy step. This had deleterious effects on the non-slave population, but what we are emphasizing here is that they had very detrimental effects on the slave population as well. Compared to the South of the United States the slaves of tropical America were decidedly unhealthy. This led to high death rates in the slave populations of tropical America. To replace the declining slave population, more people were brought in from tropical West Africa. Imported with them were old and new versions of virulent diseases, reinforcing the deleterious environment of tropical America.

These events were gradual; death rates even in the tropics and the New World while high were not close to the catastrophic death rates of European troops in tropical West Africa. Where population densities were high (the slave quarters on sugar plantations), and sugar production and slavery predominated, then warm-weather pathogens both deadly and chronic became endemic.

The parasitic diseases that had reservoirs in the human population, hookworm and malaria among the most prominent, did not require tropical conditions to survive. Human hosts harbored parasitic diseases during the season when the weather was inimical to the spread of the parasite. Longer warm-weather seasons were conducive to their spread but not necessary. Malaria spread as far as human hosts and mosquitoes went, and that was as far as the Arctic Circle in Siberia. Hookworm had a harder time in cold climates because even in the summer season most humans wore shoes in the latitudes where cold weather and killing frosts occurred. This was prophylactic against the spread of hookworm, but not entirely. In the deep mines and tunnels where outside temperatures were low, hookworm could and did thrive in the mild temperature that prevailed in deep shafts year round. Thus hookworm earned its sobriquet, the "miner's disease," in nineteenth- and early twentieth-century Europe.

It is instructive to note that hookworm was not discovered to be endemic in Europe until it was found to be widespread among the laborers constructing the Gotthard Rail Tunnel in the Alps in the second half of the nineteenth century.[6] The Gotthard Pass is a frigid area much of the year, and in fact ski resorts are nearby; still hookworm thrived in the depths of the tunnel. When did hookworm first appear in Europe? We do not know but, as we indicated in chapter 6, parasitic diseases do not become established and highly endemic overnight. Angelo Dubini identified hookworm disease in an autopsy of an Italian woman conducted in 1838. The evidence does indicate that hookworm was prevalent in many areas before it was identified as endemic. But like evolutionary processes, hookworm so gradually weakens people that it is not recognized symptomatically, so it may have been common long before Dubini's discovery.

Similarly, the accommodation of humans to disease, or the gradual eradication of diseases, goes unrecognized for the less dramatic persistent parasitic infections. For example, malaria had almost disappeared from northwestern Europe before it was discovered to be a parasitic disease. Even after its protozoa were recognized in 1880, there still was no effective campaign against it; malaria receded into a medical curiosity in northwest Europe even before Ronald Ross identified its mosquito vector in 1897. Changing living standards and changing land uses gradually reduced and finally eliminated malaria from northwest Europe; the decline in malaria was not noticed at the time. Likewise, gradual changes in the environment and the disease ecology are rarely noticed contemporaneously if unaided by conscious human actions. If they are ever noticed, they are noticed retrospectively.

Herein lie the difficulties of our story. The history and changes we have attempted to delineate occurred so gradually that they were invisible to those who were experiencing them. Prominent in our story is the relative economic merits of slaves vis-à-vis indentured servants. In the American South, the relative profitability of slavery over indentured servitude did not manifest itself immediately. Indeed, as shown in chapter 4, if slaves and servants had the same productivity, then throughout much of the slave importing era of American history the annual costs of using indentured servants were lower than those of slaves. Since we know that slaves were bought, then we also can deduce that slaves had a greater productivity in the regions in which they were habitually preferred to servants. But how did the potential slave/indentured servant buyer of the seventeenth and early eighteenth centuries learn this? The answer lies in trial and error. In environments where life expectancy and annual slave productivity were large enough to amortize the purchase price, the buyers of slaves profited, and slavery and slave imports expanded. In environments where life expectancy and annual slave productivity were not large enough to amortize the purchase price, slaveowners made losses, and slavery and slave imports diminished.

These processes were so gradual that contemporary observers did not feel them worthy of much comment. They tend to be invisible to observers distinct in both time and space. Centuries after the fact writers ascribe New England's and northern antipathy and aversion to slavery as rooted in tastes and values. But are tastes and values endogenous to economic success, or are they completely divorced from it? People who do not wish to use slaves, for whatever reason, would be successful relative to slaveowners in regions where slaves have low or negative profitability. Where slavery was profitable, the converse is true. Successful people generally ascribe their success to their superior abilities, morals, and personal characteristics.

Prior to the American Civil War, generations of southerners grew up thinking that success and slavery were obviously correlated. The word "obvious" is deliberate; anyone who could see, saw that. Similarly, conventional wisdom associated success with free labor in the non-South. Chronologically, we know that African slavery in both the North and South preceded the divergence in regional tastes; consequently, the more logical inference is that the financial success or failure of slavery was substantive in the formation of regional tastes. There is no evidence of tastes being instrumental in the financial viability of slavery.

In American history, the reason why African slavery was geographically isolated was because only in the South was it sufficiently profitable to thrive and expand. The reason that it was more profitable in the South rather than the non-South was that the disease environment that eventually predominated in the South differentially favored people of tropical West African ancestry. Because labor of African ethnicity was more productive than labor of northwestern European ancestry, scholars have concluded that slavery was profitable. This is simply confusing cause and effect; it was not slavery that caused labor of African ancestry to be profitable but labor of African ancestry caused slavery to be profitable, or more profitable than it would have been. Without resistance to warm-weather morbid (and mortal) diseases, slavery would not have been as profitable as it was. Indeed the entire issue of slavery's profitability may be in question; in comparing the production and efficiency of free versus slave labor in the antebellum South, how much of slavery's advantage was due to the ancestral advantage that labor of tropical African ancestry had in warm-weather disease environments? And how much was due to the increased output that slave institutions could extract from an enslaved labor force? We know that people of tropical West African ancestry were more resistant to the diseases that infested the American South. Consequently, what proportion of slavery's supposed economic advantage was due to the nature of its workforce in that particular disease environment is an unanswered question. It could have been relatively small (say 10 percent), relatively large (say 60 percent), or even greater than the so-called efficiency advantage of slavery (more than 100 percent). In the latter case, the institution of slavery would have reduced the output that would have been produced by free black labor; granted this is probably an unlikely alternative, but it is a conceptual possibility once we recognize the differential impacts of the disease environment.

Changes in environments, diseases, climates, or languages tend to go unnoticed and unmentioned because they change so slowly that they are rarely noticed. Similarly, economic changes are usually so slow as to be literally unmemorable. People in East Asia, Latin America, Europe, and North America who were over the age of 40 when this book was published (2011) have experienced (1) societal incomes that more than doubled during their lives, (2) increased life expectances (in some areas by decades), and (3) a generally much better life than their counterparts forty years earlier. Yet what do the populace, the media, and the intellectual class offer but gloom and doom. It is not just that bad news sells, but that we are not conscious of changes that took place in our lifetimes because many of these processes are similar to aging: we wake up one morning and wonder when did we become so old? We live our lives a day at a time; the passage of time escapes us. This is the same as it was for all people in different times and places. We are trapped in time; we try to make sense of our experiences with what intellectual capital we have. Once an explanation seems to make sense, it lasts whether it does, or does not, conform to observational reality. Ideas and coherent explanations have long lives, and they tend to overshadow mundane facts and actual history.

We have explained how nineteenth-century American economic growth was facilitated by population growth. Larger markets meant increased specialization. This is a fundamental insight of Adam Smith summarized in his aphorism: "Specialization is limited by the size of the market." Increased population led to (1) increases in productivity (specialization), (2) increases in incomes, and (3) both of these fed back to increased population. This is the virtuous cycle of Smithian growth. Associated with an increase in human population is a concomitant increase in population density and an additional increased biomass consisting of the animals, organic materials, vermin, and waste products associated with human settlements. The increased human and nonhuman biomass was a resource for organisms that are inimical to human health. Some of the organisms (smallpox, plague) have high-case mortalities; these diseases have made their mark on history. Persistent diseases with low-case mortalities (parasitic infections, dietary deficiencies, and some bacterial and viral infections) rarely make the history books; they are like background music, easily ignored and forgotten. They may be ignored and forgotten, but their impact has left their mark both literally and figuratively.

The effects of morbid diseases and the effects of increasing specialization are alike because they are so easy to overlook. Yet our explanation of economic growth in America up to the early twentieth century is consistent with science, history, and theory. We contrast this to the Malthusian theory that increasing population leads to stagnation and immiseration. The Malthusian association of increased population with increased poverty has an intuition that appears to make sense, but on examination, the rationale is flawed. The reason for human poverty and misery is not because resources grow less rapidly than the human population, it is that the population of pathogens increases disproportionately more rapidly with an increase in the human population. A disproportionate increase in the number and variety of pathogens has a deleterious effect on human welfare. Increased pathogens lead to increasing rates of illness and death. Most infections have higher rates of case mortality to infants and children; their smaller bodies and less developed immune systems make children much more susceptible to death.

If there is an increased death rate among the young, the only ways a population can sustain itself are with an increased birth rate and/or migration. In other words, high death rates "cause" high birth rates.[7] This is in stark contrast to the Malthusian model where increased births lead to poverty that in turn increases deaths; we envision an increase in deaths leading to both an increase in birth rates and poverty. In our view, poverty results from increased deaths because more resources are devoted to childbearing and rearing. Many childhood deaths imply a large dependent population that is not engaged in economic production because many of the young never become economically active adults; a relatively large number of people who survive to become adults will have reduced productivity because of physical and mental defects that the disease environment imposed upon them during their formative growing years. It is death and disease that cause poverty, not an excess of people. The Malthusian model relies on the lack of resources to cull the population; the historic facts, however, are the conjoining of high birth rates and high death rates. The difficulty with the poverty explanation for death is that nutritionally deprived women do not have many live births; nutritionally deprived women do have amenorrhea, still births, and spontaneous abortions. Relatively healthy women have more children, but high infant death rates reduce the rate of breast-feeding among women than in comparable societies with lower infant death rates. Breast-feeding tends to reduce the probabilities of conception. In sum, birth rates were high because death rates were high; in the face of a deteriorating disease environment, this is the only way a population can maintain itself. In the face of a high death rate (and in the absence of immigration) societies without a birth rate high enough to compensate for the death rate vanished.

The reduced productivity of the human workforce continually exposed to new diseases was another important factor causing poverty. People are not identical, some are active and healthy, others inactive and disease ridden. The more that a population consists of low-productivity, disease-ridden people, the more that observed wages will reflect their condition. This implies that wage data covering centuries have to be treated with extreme caution. The assumption that the health characteristics of a population are unchanging over the centuries is founded on nothing but hope. Similarly, climatic changes do occur; they are slow to contemporaneous humans, but over centuries these effects are bound to be reflected in data concerned with agriculture.

In the Northern Hemisphere starting in the mid-thirteenth century, a period of global cooling began. There is no definitive timing of the Little Ice Age, but periods ranging over 450 years are identified with the Little Ice Age. We do know that the cooling forced the evacuation of the Norse colonies in Greenland, and caused a massive decline in the Icelandic population. It defies all we know about agriculture to suggest that the Little Ice Age had no effect on labor productivity in the fifteenth, sixteenth, and seventeenth centuries. But, if we compare agricultural wage or productivity data over these centuries, either we have to assume that climate had no effect or that we are making adjustments for it.

Historians who have studied the centuries that encompass the Little Ice Age have been seduced by its gradualness. Climates did not change overnight, nor did the disease environment. But small changes accumulated over centuries had a massive impact. In his time, Malthus associated poverty with an increasing human population. He did not see how climate and disease environments had deteriorated nor was he aware of changing agricultural techniques nor changes in the treatment of diseases. The accommodation of the human immune system to the changed disease environment eventually led to lower death rates. The evolution of climate, agriculture, diseases, and people were so gradual as to be invisible to those experiencing them, and still they remain invisible in our histories.

Gregory Clark's recent book *A Farewell to Alms* (2007) is the latest contribution to the Malthusian literature. It is an undoubted contribution, yet we spend some effort disputing it because it is entirely in the Malthusian tradition, and as such, Clark's story is antithetical to our story. *A Farewell to Alms* ignores the impact of climate and persistent morbid diseases (as opposed to acute diseases) in the economic history of England from the thirteenth through the nineteenth centuries. Clark presents a clear and concise rendition of the Malthusian explanation for the history of Britain, and how Malthusian theory works within Britain's history. His reliance on agricultural real wage data as a proxy for living standards is unfortunate because the data are neither corrected for changing climate nor corrected for the changing levels of morbidity in the agricultural workforce. An assumption that these variables do not change much year to year (the short run) is tenable; the assumption is not tenable over centuries. Nevertheless, Clark's book is intriguing because it has an insight that evolution was at work, and because he has assembled what is probably the most comprehensive argument for applying the Malthusian doctrine to the British experience. His work has to be taken seriously; the hypothesis that increasing births lead to poverty and (increasing) mortality is clearly and carefully specified.

We have some fundamental disagreements with Clark (2007); we believe that history and the data support our explanation of the past. Our disagreements may appear innocuous; however, they are based on fundamental differences. One example is Clark's discussion of the influence of the Suez (and Panama) Canal. Clark states that "The result of these *technological* changes was a significant decline in real transport costs by 1900" (Clark 2007, p. 309; emphasis added). At least for the Suez Canal, we disagree with his characterization of the change as being technological. The Suez Canal could have been, and indeed had been, built again and again since the time of the Pharaohs. Canals at Suez are built at sea level. No locks are necessary, and that is why the technology of canal building was easily within the grasp of Pharaohnic Egypt. Canals with various connecting routes from the Red Sea to the Mediterranean Sea existed in antiquity; Suez canals were periodically constructed, but they did not survive because they did not generate economic returns above their costs. The lack of profits was due to the enormous costs of canal building and maintenance, and the scanty revenues they generated. Revenues were small because the size of the market was too small to support the large investment in specialized capital that canals required. The nineteenth century saw an increase in population, incomes, and the volume of trade that made the construction of the Suez Canal viable. In other words, the Suez Canal is an example of our Smithian virtuous cycle (see chapter 3); its construction by a profit-seeking enterprise shows the beneficence of the cycle associated with increasing populations and incomes.

Another example of a seemingly innocuous statement that Clark makes is actually indicative of a major difference between his view and ours. Clark correctly outlines the nascent industrial progress that Japan and China were making through the nineteenth century, although he misdiagnoses the reasons behind the relatively slow rates of growth between these large Asiatic economies and England. Clark (2007, p. 262) maintains that "though these societies were on the path to an eventual Industrial Revolution, they were progressing more slowly than England, and they had not progressed as far as England by the late nineteenth century, when they ended their self-imposed isolation." The question remains why were they progressing so slowly? If we accept Clark's thesis, it is because of their demographics: populations were increasing too rapidly. Our explanations are different, they are rooted in history and economics. The nineteenth century was disastrous for both China's society and economy; wars, rebellions, and foreign occupation wreaked havoc on China from early in the nineteenth century until the mid-twentieth century. This book has not focused on institutions, but when banditry, murder, and war are ever present, economies are much more likely to regress than progress.

In order to achieve sustained economic progress some semblance of the rule of law has to prevail, whereby trading activities and production can take place without fearing arbitrary confiscations. The rule of law was, at best, sporadic and haphazard throughout China in the nineteenth and twentieth centuries. China's nonperformance in the international growth comparisons can be attributed in whole or part to its chaotic history. Japan, however, is different; it had internal stability and more than a semblance of the rule of law throughout the nineteenth and twentieth centuries. So why was Japan an economic backwater in "the late nineteenth century, when . . . [it] ended . . . [its] self-imposed isolation" (Clark 2007, p. 262). The answer is simple: Japan was an economic backwater *because* of its self-imposed isolation. Autarky is a sure recipe for economic stagnation, whether a country is in Africa, the Americas, or Asia. For all practical purposes, Japan had isolated itself from the rest of the world from the mid-seventeenth century to the mid-nineteenth century. Besides being unable to obtain expertise from the rest of the world, the Japanese economy was unable to specialize in world trade; during this period the Japanese impoverished themselves by abdicating specialization and trade. This explains economic retardation in Japan, but how can we explain why the Japanese were "progressing more slowly than England" in the late nineteenth century? That too is a simple exercise: the statement is simply wrong; the Japanese economy was growing very rapidly after it ended its "self-imposed isolation." This is supported by both historical events and empirical data.

First, if Japan were not growing rapidly in the latter half of the nineteenth century, where did it get the resources to sequentially defeat the Chinese, and then the Russians, in two wars in the late nineteenth and early twentieth centuries? Objective reality contradicts the casual observation that the Japanese had low growth rates in the latter part of the nineteenth century; Japan's economy had to have been expanding rapidly to defeat the much more populous and larger countries that she battled. The cause of accelerated growth was the end of isolation that was forced on the Japanese in 1858. With the end of isolation, Japanese growth accelerated. Second, Huber (1971) long ago estimated that Japanese income increased by approximately 65 percent because of the opening of international trade during the period from 1858 to the mid-

1870s. The reason why Japan's economy grew so rapidly in the latter part of the nineteenth century was because the Japanese were allowing themselves to take advantage of gains from trade that increasing specialization and increased markets allow. Additionally, before 1858, Japan's knowledge of the techniques and sciences that Western countries were developing and using was extraordinarily limited. So not only did Japan gain from exchanging domestically produced goods for foreign goods, it also gained by using different production techniques and knowledge to augment its own production of both goods and services. Prior to 1858, Japan had sacrificed increasing incomes and economic development on behalf of political decisions to isolate the Japanese people from contacts with non-Japanese. The isolation was never complete, but it was effective in suppressing Japanese growth.

Japanese history illustrates our model of long-run economic growth; increasing output leads to increased specialization, and increased productivity and income, but the advantages of trade are most effective in increasing total income when there are substantial differences in factor endowments, be they differences in human capital, physical capital, or natural resources. Under a policy of autarky, a relatively small homogeneous archipelago of islands like Japan is not sufficiently diverse economically to gain as much from increased market size as countries like the United States or China under similarly autarkic policies. It is not that geographically large and diverse countries will not suffer, but they will suffer less than smaller, more homogeneous economies. In the world of today, a policy of autarky would damage the economic interests of the European Union, China, and the United States far less severely than the same policy would damage the economies of Brazil, Canada, and Japan. Size and diversity do matter. In terms of contemporary events, the young people with an excessive amount of ideology, indignation, and ignorance who continually assault trade conferences in the name of anti-globalization are actually advocating policies that will cause impoverishment in small economies. Adam Smith said it well, we say it less elegantly: trade enriches, it does not impoverish nations.

In any story there are nuances; to confine ourselves to one volume and to emphasize our message, we have admittedly neglected qualifying some of our statements that, perhaps, deserve qualifications. In our defense, the importance of evolution, diseases, and their interactions with the human economy and history have been slighted in traditional texts of history and economic history; we have attempted to bring attention to the undeniable impact they have had in molding history.

The Malthusian demographic model has increasing human numbers leading to the impoverishment of the overall human community. Here too objective reality rears its ugly head to slay a beautiful (?) theory. With increasing numbers humanity has become richer and healthier. Malthusian theory is contradicted because increasing numbers do not cause poverty and misery; it is increasing diseases that cause poverty and misery, albeit there is a link between population density and the disease explanation. Put simply, our story is that (1) many more people died of disease than starvation. (2) People were poor because they were chronically ill. (3) Many diseases were "new" to the areas brought by an integrating regime of world trade. (4) High birth rates were a result of the high death rates. (5) Evolution has bestowed on people of different ancestries different inherent immunities that give them partial protection to some (but not all) disease environments. (6) Disease ecologies have changed in the recent past because of inadvertent human actions, and these changes have had profound consequences on human history. And (7) all data have to be interpreted to reflect changes in human productivity due to changing disease ecologies and changing long-run climates.

Concluding Thoughts

People tend to believe that tomorrow will be much like today. As a matter of fact, that is literally true, but we must not commit the Fallacy of Composition. Because today is very similar to yesterday, we cannot assume that the same reasoning applies to years, decades, or even longer. Change is the enduring constant. Evolution pervades us at all times and in all places; yet it happens so gradually that it evades our senses. History and science have to guide us in assessing its effects over time. Today humanity is richer than centuries before, in part because we are healthier, more numerous, have a more beneficent climate, and not coincidentally have a better knowledge of how to manipulate the material world from the macro to the micro levels. Without a large population, we could not have the specialists that abound today making our world healthier and more productive. Take this book. There is the possibility that major parts of our thesis are not correct, but only a large and specialized economy could have two people devoting a good part of their working lives over many years investigating the impact of miniscule organisms on humanity. Not all endeavors will bear fruit, but enough have (and will) to transform the world we inhabit. Paradoxically our story is one of optimism, paradoxical because this book is about pathogens that have afflicted humanity more severely than all the tyrants and cutthroats combined. Our conclusion is that there is nothing in our genes or demographics that imply a destiny of poverty, misery, and destruction. But as "dismal" scientists we must end more ambiguously. Because we have no destiny that leads us to doom and destruction does not mean that it cannot happen.

Appendixes

Appendix A: Earnings Required to Amortize Investments in Slaves and Servants

Table A.1
Net earnings per year required to amortize a £20 investment in a slave (slave price = £20)

Interest rate	$E_0 = 7$	$E_0 = 12$	$E_0 = 16$	$E_0 = 20$	$E_0 = 25$
5%	3.456	2.257	1.845	1.605	1.419
6%	3.582	2.386	1.979	1.745	1.453
7%	3.711	2.518	2.117	1.888	1.612
8%	3.841	2.654	2.260	2.038	1.776
9%	3.974	2.793	2.406	2.191	1.947
10%	4.108	2.935	2.556	2.349	2.122

Source: See text, chapter 4.
Note: E_0 represents working life, in years; earnings are in pounds sterling.

Table A.2
Net earnings per year required to amortize a £25 investment in a slave (slave price = £25)

Interest rate	$E_0 = 7$	$E_0 = 12$	$E_0 = 16$	$E_0 = 20$	$E_0 = 25$
5%	4.320	2.821	2.307	2.006	1.774
6%	4.478	2.982	2.474	2.180	1.956
7%	4.639	3.148	2.646	2.360	2.145
8%	4.802	3.317	2.824	2.546	2.342
9%	4.967	3.491	3.008	2.739	2.545
10%	5.135	3.669	3.195	2.937	2.754

Source: See text, chapter 4.
Note: E_0 represents working life, in years; earnings are in pounds sterling.

Table A.3
Net earnings per year required to amortize a £30 investment in a slave (slave price = £30)

Interest rate	$E_0 = 7$	$E_0 = 12$	$E_0 = 16$	$E_0 = 20$	$E_0 = 25$
5%	5.185	3.385	2.768	2.407	2.129
6%	5.374	3.578	2.969	2.616	2.347
7%	5.567	3.777	3.176	2.832	2.574
8%	5.762	3.981	3.389	3.056	2.810
9%	5.961	4.190	3.609	3.286	3.054
10%	6.162	4.403	3.834	3.524	3.305

Source: See text, chapter 4.
Note: E_0 represents working life, in years; earnings are in pounds sterling.

Table A.4
Net earnings per year required to amortize a £35 investment in a slave (slave price = £35)

Interest rate	$E_0 = 7$	$E_0 = 12$	$E_0 = 16$	$E_0 = 20$	$E_0 = 25$
5%	6.049	3.949	3.229	2.808	2.483
6%	6.270	4.175	3.463	3.051	2.738
7%	6.494	4.407	3.705	3.304	3.003
8%	6.723	4.644	3.954	3.565	3.279
9%	6.954	4.888	4.210	3.834	3.563
10%	7.189	5.137	4.474	4.111	3.856

Source: See text, chapter 4.
Note: E_0 represents working life, in years; earnings are in pounds sterling.

Table A.5
Net earnings per year required to amortize a £12 investment in a servant (servant price = £12)

Interest rate	$E_0 = 5$
5%	2.772
6%	2.849
7%	2.927
8%	3.005
9%	3.085
10%	3.166

Source: See text, chapter 4.
Note: E_0 represents working life, in years; earnings are in pounds sterling.

Appendix B: Nineteenth-Century Transportation and Immigration Data

Table B.1
Number of steamboats in operation and steamboat tonnage on western rivers, 1811 to 1868

Year	Number of steamboats in operation	Tonnage	Year	Number of steamboats in operation	Tonnage
1811	1	400	1840	494	82,600
1812	1	400	1841	504	85,200
1813	2	400	1842	458	76,500
1814	3	700	1843	449	80,000
1815	7	1,500	1844	509	90,300
1816	11	2,300	1845	538	96,200
1817	16	3,000	1846	578	106,300
1818	30	5,800	1847	638	122,400
1819	59	13,000	1848	666	133,400
1820	69	14,200	1849	648	130,100
1821	73	14,500	1850	638	134,600
1822	71	13,400	1851	660	142,900
1823	74	12,500	1852	676	152,900
1824	67	10,500	1853	711	169,300
1825	80	12,500	1854	696	169,000
1826	107	17,300	1855	696	172,700
1827	120	19,700	1856	761	188,100
1828	118	18,900	1857	800	199,600
1829	140	22,300	1858	779	196,400
1830	151	24,600	1859	779	192,800
1831	183	28,700	1860	817	195,000
1832	227	35,200	1861	665	165,100
1833	239	36,800	1862	666	157,300
1834	270	41,000	1863	778	160,200
1835	324	50,100	1864	919	193,200
1836	374	57,400	1865	1,006	228,700
1837	399	63,600	1866	1,028	238,400
1838	391	65,300	1867	976	232,300
1839	480	78,200	1868	874	212,200

Source: Haites, Mak, and Walton (1975, pp. 130–31), cited in Walton and Rockoff (2010, table 9.1, p. 149).

Table B.2
US federal government expenditures for rivers and harbors, 1822 to 1900

Year	Total expenditures (in thousands of $)	Year	Total expenditures (in thousands of $)
1822	1	1862	37
1823	—	1863	65
1824	26	1864	102
1825	40	1865	305
1826	87	1866	295
1827	136	1867	1,217
1828	188	1868	3,457
1829	524	1869	3,545
1830	574	1870	3,528
1831	652	1871	4,421
1832	538	1872	4,962
1833	704	1873	6,312
1834	598	1874	5,704
1835	569	1875	6,434
1836	869	1876	5,736
1837	1,362	1877	4,655
1838	1,054	1878	3,791
1839	780	1879	8,267
1840	145	1880	8,080
1841	79	1881	9,072
1842	82	1882	11,624
1843	111	1883	13,839
1844	313	1884	8,237
1845	529	1885	10,558
1846	219	1886	4,197
1847	44	1887	7,786
1848	24	1888	7,007
1849	26	1889	11,234
1850	42	1890	11,740
1851	70	1891	12,253
1852	40	1892	13,024
1853	489	1893	14,804
1854	937	1894	19,888
1855	791	1895	19,944
1856	161	1896	18,119
1857	268	1897	13,686
1858	427	1898	20,792
1859	290	1899	16,094
1860	228	1900	18,736
1861	172		

Source: Carter, Gartner, Haines, et al. (2006, vol. 4, series Df690–91, pp. 4–883).

Table B.3
Tonnage originating on the Erie division, New York state canals, 1837 to 1880

Year	Tonnage (2,000 pounds per ton)	Year	Tonnage (2,000 pounds per ton)
1837	667,151	1859	1,753,954
1838	744,848	1860	2,253,533
1839	845,007	1861	2,500,782
1840	829,960	1862	3,204,277
1841	906,442	1863	2,955,302
1842	712,310	1864	2,535,792
1843	819,216	1865	2,523,490
1844	945,944	1866	2,896,027
1845	1,038,700	1867	2,920,578
1846	1,264,408	1868	3,346,986
1847	1,661,575	1869	2,845,072
1848	1,599,965	1870	3,083,132
1849	1,622,444	1871	3,580,922
1850	1,635,089	1872	3,562,560
1851	1,955,265	1873	3,602,535
1852	2,129,334	1874	3,097,122
1853	2,196,308	1875	2,787,226
1854	2,224,008	1876	2,418,422
1855	2,202,463	1877	3,254,367
1856	2,107,678	1878	3,608,634
1857	1,566,624	1879	3,820,027
1858	1,767,004	1880	4,608,651

Source: Carter, Gartner, Haines, et al. (2006, vol. 4, series Df696–97, pp. 4–885).

Table B.4
Railroad mileage operated in the United States, 1830 to 1890

Year	Total miles of road operated	Year	Total miles of road operated
1830	23	1861	31,286
1831	95	1862	32,120
1832	229	1863	33,170
1833	380	1864	33,908
1834	633	1865	35,085
1835	1,098	1866	36,801
1836	1,273	1867	39,050
1837	1,497	1868	42,229
1838	1,913	1869	46,844
1839	2,302	1870	52,922
1840	2,818	1871	60,301
1841	3,535	1872	66,171
1842	4,026	1873	70,268
1843	4,185	1874	72,385
1844	4,377	1875	74,096
1845	4,633	1876	76,808
1846	4,930	1877	79,082
1847	5,598	1878	81,747
1848	5,996	1879	86,556
1849	7,365	1880	98,262
1850	9,021	1881	108,108
1851	10,982	1882	114,677
1852	12,908	1883	121,422
1853	15,360	1884	125,345
1854	16,720	1885	128,320
1855	18,374	1886	136,338
1856	22,076	1887	149,214
1857	24,503	1888	156,114
1858	26,968	1889	161,276
1859	28,789	1890	166,703
1860	30,626		

Source: Carter, Gartner, Haines, et al. (2006, vol. 4, series Df874–81, pp. 4–916).

Table B.5
Total foreign immigration to the United States and number of immigrants from top three countries of origin, 1841 to 1900

Year	Total	Country 1	Country 2	Country 3	Year	Total	Country 1	Country 2	Country 3
1841	80,289	37,772 (Ir)	16,188 (B)	15,291 (G)	1871	321,350	85,455 (B)	82,554 (G)	57,439 (Ir)
1842	104,565	51,342 (Ir)	22,005 (B)	20,370 (G)	1872	404,806	141,109 (G)	84,912 (B)	68,732 (Ir)
1843	52,496	19,670 (Ir)	14,441 (G)	8,430 (B)	1873	459,803	149,671 (G)	89,500 (B)	77,344 (Ir)
1844	78,615	33,490 (Ir)	20,731 (G)	14,353 (B)	1874	313,339	87,291 (G)	62,021 (B)	53,707 (Ir)
1845	114,371	44,821 (Ir)	34,355 (G)	19,210 (B)	1875	227,498	47,905 (B)	47,769 (G)	37,957 (Ir)
1846	154,416	57,561 (G)	51,752 (Ir)	22,180 (B)	1876	169,986	31,937 (G)	29,291 (B)	22,781 (Ch)
1847	234,968	105,536 (Ir)	74,281 (G)	23,302 (B)	1877	141,857	29,298 (G)	23,581 (B)	22,137 (C)
1848	226,527	112,934 (Ir)	58,465 (G)	35,159 (B)	1878	138,469	29,313 (G)	22,150 (B)	25,592 (C)
1849	297,024	159,398 (Ir)	60,235 (G)	55,132 (B)	1879	177,826	34,602 (G)	29,955 (B)	31,286 (C)
1850	310,004	133,806 (Ir)	63,182 (G)	41,679 (B)	1880	457,257	99,744 (C)	84,638 (G)	73,273 (B)
1851	379,466	221,253 (Ir)	72,482 (G)	51,487 (B)	1881	669,431	210,485 (G)	125,450 (C)	81,582 (S)
1852	371,603	159,548 (Ir)	145,918 (G)	40,699 (B)	1882	788,992	250,630 (G)	105,326 (S)	102,991 (B)
1853	368,645	162,649 (Ir)	141,946 (G)	37,576 (B)	1883	603,322	194,786 (G)	81,486 (Ir)	76,606 (B)
1854	427,833	215,009 (G)	101,606 (Ir)	58,647 (B)	1884	518,592	179,676 (G)	65,950 (B)	63,344 (Ir)
1855	200,877	71,918 (G)	49,627 (Ir)	47,572 (B)	1885	395,346	124,443 (G)	57,713 (B)	51,795 (Ir)
1856	200,436	71,028 (G)	54,349 (Ir)	44,658 (B)	1886	334,203	84,403 (G)	62,929 (B)	49,619 (Ir)
1857	251,306	91,781 (G)	54,361 (Ir)	58,479 (B)	1887	490,109	106,865 (G)	93,378 (B)	68,370 (Ir)
1858	123,126	45,310 (G)	28,956 (B)	26,873 (Ir)	1888	546,889	109,717 (G)	108,692 (B)	81,924 (S)

Table B.5
(continued)

Year	Total	Country 1	Country 2	Country 3	Year	Total	Country 1	Country 2	Country 3
1859	121,282	41,784 (G)	35,216 (Ir)	26,163 (B)	1889	444,427	99,538 (G)	87,992 (B)	65,557 (Ir)
1860	153,640	54,491 (G)	48,637 (Ir)	29,737 (B)	1890	455,302	92,427 (G)	69,730 (B)	56,199 (O)
1861	91,918	31,661 (G)	23,797 (Ir)	19,675 (B)	1891	560,319	113,554 (G)	76,055 (It)	71,042 (O)
1862	91,985	27,529 (G)	24,639 (B)	23,351 (Ir)	1892	579,663	119,168 (G)	81,511 (R)	76,937 (O)
1863	176,282	66,882 (B)	55,916 (Ir)	33,162 (G)	1893	439,730	78,756 (G)	72,145 (It)	58,945 (S)
1864	193,418	63,523 (Ir)	57,726 (G)	53,428 (B)	1894	285,631	53,989 (G)	42,977 (It)	39,278 (R)
1865	248,120	83,424 (G)	82,465 (B)	29,772 (Ir)	1895	258,536	46,304 (Ir)	35,907 (R)	35,427 (It)
1866	318,568	115,892 (G)	94,924 (B)	36,690 (Ir)	1896	343,267	68,060 (It)	65,103 (O)	51,445 (R)
1867	315,722	133,426 (G)	72,879 (Ir)	52,641 (B)	1897	230,832	59,431 (It)	33,031 (O)	28,421 (Ir)
1868	138,840	55,831 (G)	32,068 (Ir)	24,127 (B)	1898	229,299	58,613 (It)	39,797 (O)	29,828 (R)
1869	352,768	131,042 (G)	84,438 (B)	43,941 (S)	1899	311,715	77,419 (It)	62,491 (O)	60,982 (R)
1870	387,203	118,225 (G)	103,677 (B)	56,996 (Ir)	1900	448,572	114,847 (O)	100,135 (It)	90,787 (R)

Source: Carter, Gartner, Haines, et al. (2006, vol. 1, series Ad90, pp. 1–555, 556; series Ad106–20, pp. 1–560, 1–561; series Ad136–48, pp. 1–566, 1–567; series Ad162–72, pp. 1–571, 1–572).

Note: The letters in parentheses indicate the country of origin, where B = Britain, C = Canada, Ch = China, G = Germany, Ir = Ireland, It = Italy, O = Other, R = Russia (in Europe) and Baltic States (Latvia, Estonia, Lithuania, and Finland), and S = Scandinavia (Denmark, Norway, Sweden, and Iceland). The "Other" category, which is used in the 2006 edition of *Historical Statistics of the United States*, has exactly the same number of immigrants for each year as is indicated as being from Austria-Hungary for the same years in the 1960 edition of *Historical Statistics of the United States* (see United States Bureau of the Census 1960, series C88–114, pp. 56–57).

Appendix C: US Census Mortality, 1850 to 1900

This appendix presents state-level mortality rates calculated from the United States Census mortality data for 1850 to 1900. The appendix includes a discussion of various issues involved in the calculation of the mortality rates for certain diseases, an examination of the accuracy and reliability of the census mortality data, and a listing of the data sources. For specific causes of death for nearly two dozen major infectious diseases, we present cause-specific mortality rates for the entire population for each disease for each census year for each state for which data exist. For all causes of death, we present mortality rates for the entire population as well as mortality rates for (1) four age cohorts—adults (20 years and older), children/adolescents (5 to 19 years), young children (1 to 4 years), and infants (under 1 year), (2) two ethnicity cohorts (whites and blacks), and (3) two nativity cohorts (native born and foreign born) for each census year for each state for which data exist. The mortality rates are reported as rates of death per 10,000 people or per 10,000 of the relevant cohort (adults, children/adolescents, young children, for example). The cause-specific mortality rates for the major infectious diseases are presented in tables C.1 to C.11. The mortality rates for all causes of death for the entire population and for each of the eight cohorts are presented in tables C.12 to C.16.

If no mortality rate is shown for a state for a specific disease, a particular cohort, or the population for a given census year then the census did not report deaths for that state for that category in that year. If a mortality rate of 0.00 is shown for a specific disease or a particular cohort for a particular state, that means the census reported deaths for that category for that state but reported that there were no deaths. The census reported deaths on the basis ethnicity (race) in all census years from 1850 to 1900 except 1860. As a result, no 1860 mortality rates by ethnicity are calculated. The mortality rates reported here for "blacks" for four of the census years (1850, 1870, 1880, and 1900) were calculated from "negro" deaths. For the other census year (1890), the reported "black" mortality rates were calculated from "colored" deaths, which included negroes, Chinese, Japanese, and civilized Indians; the 1890 census did not report separate mortality data for the various ethnic groups. The census reported deaths on the basis of nativity (native born and foreign born) in four census years (1850, 1870, 1890, and 1900). In 1850, the census nativity mortality data were reported for whites and "free colored" but not for slaves. As a result, native-born deaths included both native-born white and native-born "free colored" deaths, and foreign-born deaths included both foreign-born white and foreign-born "free colored" deaths. In 1860 and 1880, no census mortality data were reported on the basis of nativity. In 1870, the census reported nativity mortality data for the entire population (native born and foreign born population), which included whites and "colored." In the 1890 and 1900 censuses, deaths on the basis of nativity were reported for whites only, identifying deaths as native-born white deaths and foreign-born white deaths.

For 1850, the "malarial fever" mortality rates are calculated from the total deaths reported for bilious, congestive, intermittent, and remittent fevers. For 1860, the "malarial fever" mortality rates are calculated from the total deaths for intermittent and remittent fevers; no other malaria-symptomatic fevers were reported in 1860. For 1870, the "malarial fever" mortality rates are calculated from the total deaths for intermittent, remittent, and typho-malarial fevers; no other malaria-symptomatic fevers were reported in 1870. Beginning with 1880, the census included data on the number of deaths for malarial fever, and bilious, congestive, intermittent, and remittent fevers were identified as malarial fever (United States Bureau of the Census 1886, p. xxxv). Drake ([1850, 1854] 1964, p. 703) also lists bilious, congestive, intermittent, and remittent fevers, among other idiosyncratic names, as malarial fevers.

For 1850 to 1870, the census reported deaths for cholera. For 1850 to 1900, the census also reported deaths for cholera infantum, a common name for cholera symptoms among infants and children, which also was called the "summer complaint" and found primarily in the middle Atlantic and South during the summer months and hot weather. For 1850, 1880, and 1900, the census also reported deaths for cholera morbus, a common name for nonepidemic cholera as well as simple cholera, a disease with cholera symptoms most common in hot climates at the close of summer or early autumn. As a result, the cholera mortality rates are reported in two alternative ways: (1) For all six census years, cholera (all variants) mortality rates are calculated for a particular census from the total deaths from all the types of cholera that were reported in that census. (2) The mortality rates for cholera, cholera infantum, and cholera morbus are reported separately for each census year for which the data were reported.

The 1850 typhoid mortality rates are calculated from the total deaths reported as caused by "fever, typhoid" in Alabama, Connecticut, and South Carolina and from the total deaths reported (nearly certainly mistakenly) as caused by "fever, typhus" in all other states. For the 1860 to 1900 census, "fever, typhoid" was reported as a cause of death in all states. "Fever, typhus" was reported as a cause of death in all states (except Alabama, Connecticut, and South Carolina in 1850) in 1850, 1870, and 1880. The 1860 census (United States Bureau of the Census 1866, table 12, p. 215) presents a summary table of deaths in the United States for specific causes for 1850 and 1860 and lists "fever, typhoid" but not "fever, typhus." Moreover, the number of deaths listed for "fever, typhoid" for 1850 correspond to the total number of deaths reported in the 1850 census for "fever, typhus" and "fever, typhoid" combined. The 1870 Census (United States Bureau of the Census 1872, p. xvii) presents a summary table of deaths in the United States for specific causes for 1850 to 1870, indicating there were barely two thousand "typhus" deaths during 1850 to 1870. The summary table also indicates there were nearly 55,000 "typhoid" deaths in 1850 to 1870, which correspond exactly to the total number of deaths reported in 1850 as caused by "fever, typhus" and "fever, typhoid" and reported in 1860 and 1870 as "fever, typhoid." As a result, we surmise that the deaths reported as "fever, typhus" in 1850 were likely deaths caused by "fever, typhoid." (The 1860 census, United States Bureau of the Census 1866, p. 239, also indicates that the deaths reported as caused by "typhoid" in 1860 likely included some deaths that were actually reported as caused by "typhus.") Finally, the pneumonia mortality rates for 1850 are calculated from the total deaths reported for pneumonia and winter fever, a common name at the time for pneumonia. Deaths for winter fever were reported in 1850 only.

Several issues have been raised about the accuracy and reliability of the 1850 to 1900 mortality data reported in the federal censuses (see Condran and Crimmins 1979). (1) There is underenumeration of deaths in the 1850 to 1900 censuses, at least in part because retrospective questions about deaths were asked; respondents are unlikely to accurately recall the past concerning deaths during an entire year preceding the census enumeration (the period of the report). (2) The census mortality data are for one year only and the 1850 to 1900 responses were collected at a time when there was much year to year variation in the leading causes of death, epidemic and infectious diseases. (3) The recollection of age-specific deaths appears to be much worse for infants and the aged, which appear to be especially underenumerated. (4) There are variations in the completeness and quality of the enumeration of deaths and populations across states and over time. While the quality of the mortality censuses appears to have improved over time, scholars consider the 1870 mortality census to be the least complete (especially in the South) and the 1880 mortality census the most complete of the six censuses (Fisher 1899; Condran and Crimmins 1979). (5) By 1900, essentially all of the northeastern portion of the nation had death registration systems, which record more deaths than the retrospective censuses. Massachusetts had a registration system during all of 1850 to 1900 with other eastern states adopting such systems throughout the second half of the nineteenth century; only minor parts of southern and western states had any registrations of deaths by 1900. As a measure of the gap between the census enumeration and deaths recorded in registration systems, we can use an 1880 census comparison between the two different measures of deaths for Massachusetts (exclusive of Boston). In 1880, the census enumeration of deaths for all ages was 79 percent of the Massachusetts registration of deaths; the census enumeration of infant deaths was only 68.5 percent of the Massachusetts registration of infant deaths (United States Bureau of the Census, 1886, table 52, p. 650). (6) Many diseases had not been scientifically identified during the early part of the 1850 to 1900 period, leading to possible misidentification in earlier censuses but more accurate identification in later censuses. And (7) respondents might not have accurately identified any particular disease as a cause of death.

Condran and Crimmins (1979, p. 16) indicate that there is general agreement that overall mortality declined in the 1850 to 1900 period, as indicated in the census data. Yet they note that some suggest the decline began pre-1850 while others suggest that it began circa 1880. They recognize that the census mortality data show that overall infant deaths increased from 1850 to 1890 but suggest that the increase may not be real; it is likely due to the improving nature and greater completeness of the censuses later in the period. Condran and Crimmins

(1979, p. 16) also recognize, though, that infant deaths likely did increase in some areas (urban areas, for example). They further note that infant deaths reported in the 1850 to 1890 censuses are not strictly comparable to those reported in 1900 because the 1900 census did not include stillborn deaths in infant deaths as was the case in the 1850 to 1890 censuses.

Despite underreporting of deaths, especially for infants and the aged, the fact that diagnosis of diseases at the time was problematic, and other issues with the census mortality reports, what we are interested in is examining differences in death rates among various cohorts and across states (disease ecologies) for different diseases; we are not interested in the absolute level of mortality per se. We will have problems if there were systematic differences in the classification of diseases and the reporting of deaths across states in each census. We are not certain if there were such systematic differences, and even more troublesome, we do not believe the data would allow us to identify all such differences if they did exist. Is there evidence that different states reported, say malaria, or any specific infectious disease, differently or reported deaths differently in a given census? We are not sure if there is such evidence. Some scholars maintain that the relative level of mortality across states is reasonably accurate even if the absolute levels are not (Yasuba 1962); others, however, suggest there was large variation in the quality of the reports and completeness of enumeration from state to state (Condran and Crimmins 1979, pp. 10, 14).

While the absolute values of some of the death data reported in the 1850 to 1900 censuses are underenumerated, viewed cautiously, we believe the mortality estimates in this appendix can shed light on how widespread certain infectious diseases were and their trends in the second half of the nineteenth century. In particular, the mortality rates do well at indicating the relative prevalence of various groups of infectious diseases (warm-weather fevers, upper respiratory diseases, gastrointestinal tract diseases, and intestinal parasites/worms) in the second half of the nineteenth century across various regions of the United States (Northeast, East North Central, and the South), and among most age cohorts and ethnicities (race or ancestral heritages). Moreover, the US Census mortality data are the only data available on a (approximately) uniform basis for the 1850 to 1900 period for causes of deaths for specific diseases for all states.

The mortality and population data necessary to calculate the mortality rates are contained in United States Bureau of the Census (1854,

1855, 1864, 1866, 1872a, b, 1882, 1885, 1886, 1894, 1895, 1896, 1897, 1902a, b, c) and Historical Census Browser (University of Virginia Library). For 1850, the mortality data are from United States Bureau of the Census (1855, pt. 1, table 6; pt. 2, app., pp. 50–301). The 1850 population data are from United States Bureau of the Census (1854) and Historical Census Browser (University of Virginia Library). For 1860, the mortality data are from United States Bureau of the Census (1866, tables 1, 3, 4). The 1860 population data are from United States Bureau of the Census (1864, Recapitulation, pp. 592–97) and Historical Census Browser (University of Virginia Library). For 1870, the mortality data are from United States Bureau of the Census (1872b, tables 2, 5, 7, 9). The 1870 population data are from United States Bureau of the Census (1872a, table 1). For 1880, the mortality data are from United States Bureau of the Census (1885, app., tables 1, 2, 4; 1886, tables 13, 18, 57). The 1880 population data are from United States Bureau of the Census (1882, table 1). For 1890, the mortality data are from United States Bureau of the Census (1894, tables 1, 2, 5, 7; 1896, table 1). The 1890 population data are from United States Bureau of the Census (1895, table 9; 1897, table 2). For 1900, the mortality data are from United States Bureau of the Census (1902b, table 19; 1902c, tables 4, 8). The 1900 population data are from United States Bureau of the Census (1902a, table 2).

Table C.1
Cause-specific mortality rates per 10,000 for cholera (all variants) and consumption/tuberculosis by state, 1850 to 1900

	Cholera (all variants)						Consumption/tuberculosis					
State	1850	1860	1870	1880	1890	1900	1850	1860	1870	1880	1890	1900
Alabama	1.84	1.30	1.35	2.57	2.33	3.12	4.69	6.18	7.63	13.47	14.29	14.58
Arizona			3.11	0.74	0.68	3.09			1.04	4.45	12.92	12.36
Arkansas	13.39	1.17	0.83	3.33	1.99	3.44	6.29	7.56	8.90	11.85	10.72	14.40
California	43.74	0.74	4.05	2.14	1.80	2.17	0.97	13.79	22.24	20.74	24.00	23.43
Colorado			4.77	2.93	4.23	4.08			8.03	10.81	11.89	16.19
Connecticut	4.75	3.09	7.09	5.75	7.08	5.94	26.11	27.58	22.66	22.31	23.36	16.83
Dakota		4.13		1.55					9.17	8.58		
North Dakota					5.24	2.66					11.27	7.71
South Dakota					3.59	3.04					11.28	10.58
Delaware	12.13	3.39	6.96	8.12	9.08	5.58	12.89	17.91	23.68	24.35	28.25	20.68
District of Columbia	10.83	4.26	12.00	13.91	9.64	5.02	26.12	33.96	33.56	44.64	35.90	30.53
Florida	4.23	0.64	5.27	2.86	2.50	3.35	4.92	6.91	6.98	9.54	9.63	10.54
Georgia	1.52	1.31	2.96	4.12	3.04	3.40	3.08	4.64	7.39	11.07	11.73	11.96
Idaho			0.00	0.31	1.69	2.72			3.33	6.75	4.74	5.32
Illinois	25.20	2.25	7.48	6.61	4.80	4.30	10.17	11.38	14.34	15.09	14.89	14.07
Indiana	16.60	1.03	3.15	6.98	3.35	4.11	10.83	9.75	16.70	19.83	15.98	16.82
Indian Territory						6.02						8.80
Iowa	8.95	1.69	3.72	5.40	2.19	3.25	8.27	11.08	11.00	11.75	9.62	8.09
Kansas		2.43	5.49	8.32	2.77	5.60		10.91	11.33	11.16	9.59	9.62
Kentucky	22.78	1.60	2.73	3.71	1.65	2.73	13.11	15.07	18.92	22.58	19.04	18.24
Louisiana	57.48	2.01	4.36	2.32	2.87	3.72	12.38	11.91	19.38	16.09	13.55	14.60
Maine	6.53	1.15	2.94	2.97	5.02	7.07	29.19	34.52	31.76	28.12	22.34	16.49
Maryland	6.19	1.48	7.81	11.16	8.85	6.25	18.88	17.42	21.49	25.39	22.21	19.51
Massachusetts	15.48	7.14	11.59	8.23	9.27	7.40	34.45	39.36	35.39	29.20	26.71	18.62
Michigan	4.85	0.69	3.62	3.70	4.89	5.58	16.52	15.85	15.57	15.90	13.12	10.07

Table C.1
(continued)

	Cholera (all variants)						Consumption/tuberculosis					
State	1850	1860	1870	1880	1890	1900	1850	1860	1870	1880	1890	1900
Minnesota		2.91	2.50	4.73	4.49	3.36		8.78	10.44	10.72	12.01	10.53
Mississippi	12.05	1.86	1.81	1.76	1.50	1.83	5.47	7.00	8.39	11.13	11.11	13.72
Missouri	54.25	2.01	5.87	6.77	2.68	3.62	9.50	11.02	15.78	16.57	13.28	13.22
Montana			2.91	1.53	2.17	2.92			8.25	4.60	11.27	6.74
Nebraska		0.69	4.72	5.84	4.51	4.08		9.71	7.07	9.08	5.86	5.55
Nevada			3.77	3.69	1.06	3.31			7.06	9.48	7.87	13.23
New Hampshire	3.74	2.70	4.43	5.16	8.98	7.94	29.06	35.67	29.94	24.93	19.36	15.23
New Jersey	16.65	2.34	8.72	9.01	8.26	5.23	18.69	20.09	20.11	23.25	23.45	18.01
New Mexico		0.71	12.70	1.67	1.00	2.41		3.45	4.90	4.10	7.23	7.78
New York	20.88	2.21	8.26	6.30	7.90	4.61	21.60	21.27	26.42	25.29	24.77	19.41
North Carolina	1.65	1.01	3.37	4.73	2.88	2.97	6.47	7.67	11.54	15.07	13.67	12.41
Ohio	31.07	1.37	4.17	5.93	3.98	3.89	12.92	14.63	19.72	18.44	17.41	13.92
Oklahoma					1.66	4.92					4.20	7.23
Oregon		0.00	0.66	4.86	1.86	2.01		5.72	12.32	12.93	10.80	10.47
Pennsylvania	7.80	1.52	3.18	6.24	5.33	4.98	15.23	17.24	21.24	18.84	14.62	12.36
Rhode Island	15.45	4.24	9.06	6.62	11.95	10.94	31.85	32.47	25.40	24.92	26.66	19.53
South Carolina	2.32	1.65	3.61	3.10	2.90	3.24	3.99	5.50	9.31	15.47	18.35	15.91
Tennessee	9.94	1.32	2.32	4.01	2.32	3.08	8.77	12.98	18.89	24.37	20.58	22.03
Texas	14.44	0.89	1.42	3.79	2.26	3.81	5.27	6.95	8.31	10.06	9.21	9.68
Utah		0.99	11.41	2.71	2.47	3.94		4.47	7.26	4.79	3.27	5.17
Vermont	1.81	0.79	3.45	3.61	5.23	3.99	23.91	24.72	21.63	24.47	19.88	15.25
Virginia	6.94	1.32	4.73	5.84	3.45	3.64	11.37	13.21	17.10	20.00	18.42	17.38
Washington		0.00	2.92	3.46	2.63	2.49		6.90	14.61	13.31	8.99	10.87
West Virginia			2.47	4.07	2.86	3.22			16.02	15.67	14.98	13.28
Wisconsin	8.64	0.57	3.52	3.37	27.46	4.46	9.50	11.73	12.50	12.73	12.17	11.36
Wyoming			0.00	1.92	2.24	2.49			4.39	2.41	6.75	5.51

Table C.2
Cause-specific mortality rates per 10,000 for croup and diarrheal diseases by state, 1850 to 1900

	Croup						Diarrheal diseases					
State	1850	1860	1870	1880	1890	1900	1850	1860	1870	1880	1890	1900
Alabama	4.26	4.41	2.69	3.95	2.43	3.17	3.89	3.40	3.36	10.94	11.35	1.56
Arizona			0.00	0.00	1.68	0.81			5.18	0.00	6.04	0.89
Arkansas		8.66	3.78	4.81	3.16	4.28	2.24	2.07	3.57	13.66	8.44	1.27
California	7.05	1.92	2.52	1.40	1.65	0.64	10.80	1.03	2.34	6.09	4.50	0.55
Colorado	0.11		3.51	2.21	2.13	1.07			2.01	7.41	5.31	0.46
Connecticut	2.97	3.56	1.75	2.89	1.92	0.80	0.81	0.43	1.34	9.65	8.31	1.94
Dakota			2.82	3.03					3.53	4.22		
North Dakota				3.41	0.71	0.91					5.86	0.69
South Dakota				2.48	1.06	0.97					4.32	0.62
Delaware	3.06	5.26	3.36	1.60	4.75	1.79	2.51	2.50	2.48	11.73	7.77	0.27
District of Columbia	2.32	4.13	4.63	4.68	2.04	0.61	5.61	5.99	6.07	32.09	16.06	3.05
Florida	2.40	1.64	2.61	1.23	1.02	1.06	3.55	5.06	3.41	7.61	7.64	0.98
Georgia	3.80	4.00	3.01	4.45	2.18	3.10	2.10	3.47	3.78	12.44	9.76	1.05
Idaho				3.31	1.90	0.93				3.68	2.61	0.25
Illinois	5.60	6.76	3.49	3.80	2.50	1.17	3.39	3.55	5.06	14.58	8.19	0.52
Indiana	5.11	4.21	2.84	5.28	1.39	1.26	2.45	1.51	3.95	14.40	4.97	0.85
Indian Territory				4.66		4.11						1.20
Iowa	5.05	6.82	1.37	2.53	1.84	0.73	5.72	3.32	2.84	11.05	3.84	0.35
Kansas		7.56	2.77	2.23	1.81	1.59		3.82	4.69	17.26	3.87	0.82
Kentucky	6.24	6.81	4.17	3.22	3.07	3.58	2.10	1.64	2.70	11.29	7.34	0.91
Louisiana	2.74	2.42	1.73	3.20	1.74	1.46	5.72	6.62	7.00	12.87	10.12	2.27
Maine	3.00	1.89	0.94	2.66	1.24	0.94	2.69	1.61	1.64	7.41	4.39	1.08
Maryland	3.81	4.35	3.47	2.73	2.25	1.36	2.71	2.65	2.01	14.48	11.72	1.33
Massachusetts	3.41	4.88	3.43	3.31	2.19	0.73	2.38	1.19	2.79	14.56	7.39	1.13
Michigan	2.57	3.35	1.27	4.57	1.76	0.67	2.89	1.44	3.07	8.85	5.22	1.34
Minnesota		2.62	1.59	0.51	1.87	0.78		0.64	2.55	10.58	7.37	0.47

Table C.2
(continued)

	Croup						Diarrheal diseases					
State	1850	1860	1870	1880	1890	1900	1850	1860	1870	1880	1890	1900
Mississippi	5.59	5.41	3.39	5.42	1.75	2.64	3.99	3.32	3.93	8.23	7.79	1.38
Missouri	6.33	9.31	4.18	1.12	2.50	2.03	3.42	5.98	7.55	18.00	6.39	0.81
Montana			0.49	2.07	1.13	1.11			3.88	4.85	3.56	0.82
Nebraska		1.04	1.71	2.86	1.82	0.62		1.73	2.11	11.27	3.91	0.51
Nevada			1.88	1.09	1.31	1.18			1.18	7.07	3.06	0.71
New Hampshire	2.36	2.21	0.94	3.08	2.55	1.02	1.54	0.83	1.54	8.96	6.08	1.04
New Jersey	4.00	4.73	2.37	4.37	3.11	1.28	2.31	1.85	1.56	14.57	9.19	1.00
New Mexico		0.91	3.92	2.50	1.24	2.30		0.81	2.29	3.60	4.36	0.97
New York	3.43	4.63	2.59	0.97	2.61	0.85	3.46	2.03	5.10	14.15	11.01	1.46
North Carolina	3.73	4.30	2.66	10.82	2.15	2.66	1.69	4.67	3.90	13.70	12.79	1.36
Ohio	5.23	3.67	2.10	2.35	1.89	1.33	1.93	2.00	2.98	11.28	5.26	0.65
Oklahoma				2.68	0.49	1.66					4.69	0.93
Oregon		3.62	2.53	4.89	1.98	0.44		0.19	0.66	9.10	2.87	0.39
Pennsylvania	4.35	4.56	3.09	3.06	2.63	1.69	2.49	1.36	2.71	18.84	5.40	0.82
Rhode Island	3.05	3.89	1.79	4.93	2.32	1.26	3.05	2.35	1.24	11.32	8.71	2.01
South Carolina	3.02	3.58	1.53	1.81	1.48	1.60	1.93	3.68	3.94	11.68	11.08	1.17
Tennessee	6.50	8.15	5.18	14.63	3.38	4.74	2.66	1.93	3.54	10.33	9.80	1.54
Texas	4.23	4.93	3.35	1.86	2.07	2.13	2.26	3.38	4.14	17.74	8.63	1.07
Utah		5.71	1.38	4.48	3.85	0.76		2.48	5.30	8.40	5.15	0.61
Vermont	2.04	0.03	1.24	3.24	1.59	0.61	0.06	0.51	1.06	8.10	4.72	0.79
Virginia	3.05	3.87	2.38	2.41	1.77	1.95	2.28	2.31	4.03	20.00	9.81	1.30
Washington		5.18	2.50	3.95	1.75	0.87				7.06	3.01	0.39
West Virginia			3.12	0.00	2.57	3.40			2.90	8.63	5.95	0.69
Wisconsin			1.42	4.81	1.61	0.77	5.50	1.69	2.81	9.62	5.57	0.74
Wyoming	3.70	3.34	10.97	1.40	0.99	0.54				3.37	2.14	0.22

Table C.3
Cause-specific mortality rates per 10,000 for diphtheria and dysentery by state, 1850 to 1900

	Diphtheria						Dysentery					
State	1850	1860	1870	1880	1890	1900	1850	1860	1870	1880	1890	1900
Alabama		0.49	0.45	1.83	0.53	0.48	3.49	3.25	2.04	2.97		4.72
Arizona				0.00	2.68	1.22			5.18	0.49		1.79
Arkansas		0.23	0.68	1.62	0.57	0.82	2.76	4.09	0.81	6.08		4.13
California		1.53	4.57	4.27	2.81	1.53	5.94	1.84	1.62	0.79		0.91
Colorado			1.25	12.81	7.13	2.74			1.76	0.93		0.52
Connecticut		0.54	1.04	3.47	7.69	2.79	26.05	2.67	2.16	1.51		1.83
Dakota			0.71	22.27					2.12	0.74		
North Dakota					7.28	3.76						0.19
South Dakota					6.96	2.22						0.22
Delaware			2.88	4.91	4.93	6.01	7.43	4.19	1.60	2.11		1.30
District of Columbia		0.27	4.78	1.63	6.29	6.92	10.25	2.66	2.35	5.63		1.36
Florida		0.09	0.43	0.74	0.36	0.51	2.40	3.35	2.13	1.04		2.12
Georgia			0.52	3.81	0.83	0.60	1.41	3.73	2.76	3.52		3.52
Idaho		0.16	0.00	16.87	3.56	1.85			0.67	0.92		0.80
Illinois		0.24	2.37	7.81	6.81	3.12	5.30	4.94	2.61	2.27		0.74
Indiana		0.28	1.43	5.19	2.71	2.08	12.94	3.16	1.14	2.67		1.90
Indian Territory						0.61						4.36
Iowa		0.64	1.24	14.25	6.33	1.14	3.49	3.91	1.91	2.12		0.67
Kansas		0.09	1.26	10.94	2.70	1.65		4.01	1.62	2.77		1.48
Kentucky		0.70	1.10	2.32	2.93	1.03	9.11	1.98	1.60	3.69		2.05
Louisiana		1.23	0.91	1.88	1.67	0.65	4.36	6.09	4.62	3.71		2.79
Maine		0.02	1.28	13.71	3.12	1.48	8.73	2.18	0.80	0.72		1.79
Maryland		0.20	2.79	5.67	2.81	4.64	10.41	3.51	2.14	3.21		1.39
Massachusetts		0.22	1.92	9.03	7.69	3.82	24.50	4.61	2.93	2.36		0.95
Michigan			1.19	12.19	5.68	1.56	7.04	3.08	2.18	1.28		0.83
Minnesota		0.03	1.43	19.62	7.17	2.04		0.99	1.91	1.51		0.27

Table C.3
(continued)

State	Diphtheria 1850	1860	1870	1880	1890	1900	Dysentery 1850	1860	1870	1880	1890	1900
Mississippi		1.25	0.56	1.71	0.69	0.55	3.58	3.42	1.24	2.70		2.48
Missouri		0.58	2.07	4.03	2.64	1.59	3.49	3.75	2.92	4.22		1.26
Montana			0.49	6.38	3.25	0.99			0.49	0.51		0.16
Nebraska		1.04	0.98	22.90	5.81	1.52		4.16	0.98	1.08		0.68
Nevada			2.12	2.73	2.19	0.00			0.47	0.80		1.42
New Hampshire			1.60	9.91	6.11	1.58	18.18	2.61	2.23	1.38		0.70
New Jersey		0.24	1.95	4.51	7.38	3.60	12.05	2.07	1.98	1.97		0.91
New Mexico			3.05	0.50	50.33	2.87		2.54	3.16	0.50		0.10
New York		0.87	1.97	8.04	6.81	3.68	11.92	2.66	2.44	2.31		0.93
North Carolina		0.22	1.35	7.10	1.91	0.63	1.24	4.34	1.26	4.30		2.71
Ohio		0.23	1.78	6.57	4.98	1.68	12.94	2.22	1.73	1.44		0.96
Oklahoma					1.46	1.15						1.71
Oregon		0.19	3.74	10.59	3.09	0.70		0.57	0.66	1.37		0.41
Pennsylvania		0.84	0.82	1.99	5.66	4.45	11.61	2.48	1.94	1.10		0.72
Rhode Island		1.32	1.15	8.25	5.88	1.70	16.61	3.44	2.67	1.34		1.07
South Carolina			0.40	5.48	1.40	0.62	1.30	3.91	2.08	3.43		4.31
Tennessee		0.04	0.76	3.67	0.96	0.98	1.74	2.66	0.63	3.60		3.28
Texas		0.07	1.16	1.14	0.74	1.13	0.99	5.54	1.14	9.96		2.60
Utah			0.69	51.19	10.20	0.94		1.99	0.46	0.49		0.29
Vermont		0.19	1.85	8.91	6.74	1.31	9.55	1.52	3.12	1.47		0.96
Virginia		1.69	1.95	3.72	2.95	1.48	3.85	4.56	2.39	3.90		2.30
Washington			5.43	14.78	3.69	1.89		0.86	0.83	1.07		0.62
West Virginia			1.36	8.25	2.99	1.69			1.24	1.28		1.31
Wisconsin		0.03	1.76	14.58	5.63	1.70	4.26	3.12	2.51	1.78		0.56
Wyoming			1.10	8.66	4.45	2.49				0.00		0.43

Table C.4
Cause-specific mortality rates per 10,000 for fever not specified and malarial fever by state, 1850 to 1900

	Fever, not specified						Malarial fever					
State	1850	1860	1870	1880	1890	1900	1850	1860	1870	1880	1890	1900
Alabama	7.58			2.15	1.11	1.07	5.25	6.53	7.69	10.43	6.81	5.50
Arizona				3.46	1.68	2.36			4.14	1.48	5.37	1.38
Arkansas	13.29			1.16	1.05	0.62	9.39	22.80	9.06	13.99	13.54	13.19
California	8.75			0.65	0.20	0.22	0.11	4.92	2.48	1.84	1.27	0.80
Colorado				7.10	0.46	0.61			1.00	1.49	0.92	0.39
Connecticut	6.01			0.06	0.04	0.03	1.29	2.72	0.52	3.60	2.56	1.21
Dakota				0.30					0.71	1.18		
North Dakota					0.05	0.22					1.26	0.13
South Dakota					0.15	0.27					0.58	0.05
Delaware	1.42			0.14	0.06	0.11	8.08	1.87	1.84	2.39	1.66	1.03
District of Columbia	1.93			0.00	0.00	0.00	2.13	2.26	1.59	4.67	4.25	2.26
Florida	11.55			4.27	1.48	1.04	4.12	10.47	12.78	11.17	7.33	6.92
Georgia	7.65			1.82	1.23	1.34	2.04	5.37	6.22	6.87	5.10	4.56
Idaho				0.00	0.36	0.25			0.67	1.53	1.30	0.25
Illinois	7.22			0.25	0.22	0.07	5.61	6.69	3.56	3.62	1.91	1.03
Indiana	6.41			0.15	0.21	0.05	4.23	4.33	3.18	4.71	1.80	1.35
Indian Territory						1.35						9.03
Iowa	8.12			0.20	0.09	0.03	4.79	6.89	1.38	2.66	1.13	0.38
Kansas				0.39	0.17	0.28		24.35	6.94	7.25	2.80	1.77
Kentucky	9.64			0.62	0.96	0.63	2.13	6.69	2.54	4.48	2.77	1.60
Louisiana	14.45			2.29	1.96	1.32	5.60	11.67	11.65	9.25	10.76	7.46
Maine	6.22			0.63	0.24	0.01	0.58	2.90	0.64	0.42	0.48	0.23
Maryland	2.38			0.03	0.14	0.03	5.61	2.01	1.97	2.78	2.12	1.10
Massachusetts	4.92			0.07	0.04	0.02	0.76	2.15	0.45	0.43	0.51	0.25
Michigan	5.81			0.09	0.21	0.04	4.25	4.12	2.14	1.95	1.78	0.69

Table C.4
(continued)

State	Fever, not specified						Malarial fever					
	1850	1860	1870	1880	1890	1900	1850	1860	1870	1880	1890	1900
Minnesota				0.14	0.13	0.09		2.67	0.36	0.42	0.23	0.05
Mississippi	12.58			1.26	1.23	0.93	6.40	11.40	7.71	9.09	9.87	6.34
Missouri	8.81			0.30	0.25	0.20	5.60	11.89	6.19	7.88	3.78	3.11
Montana				0.00	0.08	0.08			1.46	2.04	0.76	0.21
Nebraska				0.27	0.17	0.12		16.64	1.30	2.23	0.91	0.30
Nevada				0.16	0.00	0.00			6.59	0.64	2.19	3.54
New Hampshire	8.24			0.20	0.58	0.00	0.50	3.10	0.66	0.49	0.53	0.44
New Jersey	3.33			0.04	0.07	0.02	2.10	2.31	0.86	2.87	1.90	0.58
New Mexico				26.26	12.04	9.93		20.40	4.68	12.13	4.69	4.56
New York	2.58			0.16	0.09	0.02	1.64	1.65	1.01	1.99	1.59	0.42
North Carolina	5.63			0.89	0.84	0.65	4.53	4.98	4.19	6.87	3.73	2.78
Ohio	7.47			0.16	0.10	0.04	2.11	2.56	1.40	1.70	1.29	0.38
Oklahoma					0.81	0.60					4.69	3.36
Oregon				0.06	0.19	0.17		1.91	1.54	1.77	1.05	0.56
Pennsylvania	4.39			0.01	0.10	0.03	2.16	2.02	0.73	0.95	0.62	0.22
Rhode Island	3.73			0.25	0.32	0.02	0.47	0.86	0.32	0.14	1.71	0.56
South Carolina	8.30			2.55	2.36	2.30	7.00	6.42	5.61	7.34	6.43	5.59
Tennessee	8.37			1.00	1.02	0.76	2.56	7.45	4.55	5.94	5.77	4.88
Texas	14.72			1.41	1.10	1.15	9.97	10.66	11.43	9.35	9.40	4.37
Utah				0.49	0.38	0.00		1.99	1.50	0.83	1.78	0.22
Vermont	6.18			0.00	0.48	0.03	0.70	1.36	0.45	0.90	0.42	0.26
Virginia	3.65			0.50	0.62	0.40	2.95	2.49	2.07	3.87	3.72	2.21
Washington				0.00	0.23	0.21			0.83	1.07	1.77	0.25
West Virginia				0.52	0.50	0.31			0.61	0.79	0.94	0.35
Wisconsin	4.03			0.18	0.11	0.09	2.29	2.86	0.56	1.02	0.45	0.18
Wyoming				0.96	0.82	0.11			4.39	2.89	0.16	0.00

Table C.5
Cause-specific mortality rates per 10,000 for measles and parasites/parasitic diseases by state, 1850 to 1900

	Measles						Parasites/parasitic diseases					
State	1850	1860	1870	1880	1890	1900	1850	1860	1870	1880	1890	1900
Alabama	0.52	0.64	4.04	2.83	3.28	2.34			0.86	0.00	0.35	0.24
Arizona				0.00	2.35	5.61				0.00	0.17	0.08
Arkansas	0.57	1.17	4.21	3.17	0.77	9.71			1.09	0.00	0.43	0.28
California	0.22	0.42	1.50	0.38	0.63	0.38			0.02	0.00	0.02	0.03
Colorado			0.25	3.55	1.60	1.09				0.00	0.00	0.02
Connecticut	0.86	1.85	0.56	0.74	0.58	1.77			0.11	0.00	0.03	0.02
Dakota				0.81						0.00		
North Dakota					1.04	0.50					0.00	0.09
South Dakota					1.73	0.97					0.00	0.02
Delaware	2.62	0.36	2.64	0.48	1.84	0.49				0.00	0.00	0.00
District of Columbia	0.19	0.27	1.59	0.34	0.26	1.36				0.00	0.13	0.04
Florida	0.57	0.07	1.23	0.48	1.74	0.95			1.17	0.00	0.64	0.28
Georgia	0.82	0.44	2.28	3.22	2.39	0.91			1.07	0.00	0.36	0.23
Idaho				0.61	0.59	0.62			1.33	0.00	0.00	0.06
Illinois	1.29	0.65	2.76	1.96	0.82	1.00			0.20	0.03	0.02	0.02
Indiana	1.65	1.06	1.20	2.58	1.17	0.43			0.14	0.03	0.02	0.03
Indian Territory						8.72						0.13
Iowa	2.65	0.65	2.24	1.06	0.98	0.20			0.06	0.01	0.03	0.02
Kansas		0.19	3.46	5.08	1.45	1.50			0.14	0.00	0.04	0.03
Kentucky	1.24	1.32	1.88	1.47	2.76	1.56			0.24	0.00	0.15	0.06
Louisiana	1.16	3.05	5.16	1.27	2.14	3.81			0.77	0.00	0.37	0.31
Maine	1.30	0.49	1.05	0.55	0.21	0.79			0.10	0.00	0.05	0.01
Maryland	1.01	1.75	2.27	0.75	2.61	0.86			0.14	0.01	0.08	0.03
Massachusetts	1.19	1.15	2.00	0.47	0.43	1.11			0.10	0.00	0.02	0.01
Michigan	1.23	0.71	1.12	1.49	1.35	1.54			0.08	0.00	0.05	0.02

Table C.5
(continued)

	Measles						Parasites/parasitic diseases					
State	1850	1860	1870	1880	1890	1900	1850	1860	1870	1880	1890	1900
Minnesota		0.17	2.21	1.19	1.21	0.45			0.14	0.00	0.08	0.01
Mississippi	0.76	2.27	3.29	1.14	3.49	6.12			0.93	0.00	0.49	0.30
Missouri	2.64	2.09	5.05	3.41	1.91	1.61			0.35	0.00	0.06	0.06
Montana				0.26	0.45	0.70			0.49	0.00	0.00	0.00
Nebraska		1.04	3.33	2.34	1.05	0.47			0.24	0.07	0.08	0.00
Nevada			0.71	0.00	0.44	1.18			0.24	0.00	0.00	0.00
New Hampshire	0.85	0.15	1.60	1.07	0.42	1.09			0.06	0.00	0.00	0.02
New Jersey	0.96	1.13	1.83	0.46	1.27	1.09			0.01	0.00	0.01	0.02
New Mexico				11.88	0.39	3.64				0.00	0.00	0.00
New York	1.63	1.92	2.45	1.29	1.26	1.62			0.11	0.00	0.02	0.01
North Carolina	1.29	1.27	0.81	2.50	0.98	1.18			0.68	0.01	0.39	0.22
Ohio	1.83	1.87	2.33	0.73	1.94	0.40			0.08	0.01	0.03	0.02
Oklahoma					0.16	1.21					0.00	0.03
Oregon		0.19	0.22	0.92	0.80	0.34			0.11	0.00	0.03	0.00
Pennsylvania	1.37	0.75	1.57	0.91	1.29	1.29			0.05	0.00	0.02	0.02
Rhode Island	0.54	0.17	1.47	0.04	3.44	4.76				0.00	0.03	0.02
South Carolina	1.03	0.69	3.87	2.32	1.26	0.76			0.57	0.00	0.51	0.37
Tennessee	0.33	1.09	2.66	0.69	1.73	3.93			0.32	0.05	0.29	0.15
Texas	0.38	2.23	5.17	1.64	2.09	4.63			0.60	0.00	0.11	0.06
Utah		0.25	6.45	1.67	0.10	0.54				0.00	0.05	0.00
Vermont	0.41	0.32	0.51	1.47	0.60	0.61			0.03	0.00	0.09	0.00
Virginia	1.56	0.88	3.32	2.50	2.08	1.60			0.76	0.00	0.37	0.19
Washington				1.46	1.35	0.21				0.00	0.06	0.00
West Virginia			1.11	1.71	1.43	2.38			0.34	0.00	0.13	0.14
Wisconsin	0.88	0.71	1.44	0.57	0.76	0.50			0.08	0.00	0.01	0.01
Wyoming				0.96	0.33	2.16				0.00	0.00	0.00

Table C.6
Cause-specific mortality rates per 10,000 for pneumonia and scarlet fever by state, 1850 to 1900

	Pneumonia						Scarlet fever					
State	1850	1860	1870	1880	1890	1900	1850	1860	1870	1880	1890	1900
Alabama	7.23	14.28	15.10	13.85	10.48	13.45	2.19	2.60	0.13	0.12	0.15	0.19
Arizona			43.49	7.42	14.42	8.54		10.04		0.00	1.85	1.46
Arkansas	10.81	35.02	24.58	24.32	14.10	20.50	4.67		0.33	3.21	0.22	0.45
California	0.43	3.08	9.98	11.87	12.67	11.60		11.61	8.55	0.82	0.46	0.50
Colorado			4.77	22.64	16.64	18.83			2.26	2.37	1.67	1.46
Connecticut	6.20	6.56	7.94	12.11	18.01	16.17	2.45	8.45	5.32	1.81	1.09	0.67
Dakota		0.00	5.64	8.14				0.00	1.41	1.18		
North Dakota					6.90	6.86					2.24	0.22
South Dakota					9.70	6.97					1.52	0.90
Delaware	0.98		10.08	9.62	15.91	16.46	2.08	6.59	4.64	2.25	1.07	0.15
District of Columbia	2.71	10.39	9.34	15.43	21.01	18.59	8.32	8.12	5.24	2.36	0.78	0.20
Florida	3.55	3.56	14.43	7.42	6.41	7.70		0.21	0.53	0.19	0.26	1.17
Georgia	7.21	13.53	11.51	10.93	9.46	11.72	2.23	2.05	0.10	0.20	0.04	1.33
Idaho		11.99	0.67	10.73	10.19	10.88				0.92	3.91	0.65
Illinois	8.91	7.93	11.35	14.22	12.84	14.40	2.47	9.92	8.51	4.45	1.16	0.66
Indiana	6.46	6.26	9.01	16.48	7.76	11.60	4.21	7.77	2.10	6.67	0.99	0.44
Indian Territory						15.61						0.46
Iowa	8.17	8.61	5.68	9.94	7.20	8.18	2.19	4.99	2.71	3.75	1.18	0.22
Kansas		13.53	16.44	15.53	6.64	9.77		5.69	9.71	5.14	0.74	0.70
Kentucky	4.75	8.82	10.33	11.62	10.35	11.30	2.25	13.02	0.61	2.29	0.58	0.32
Louisiana	5.18	17.27	17.77	15.21	10.84	14.08	1.51	5.75	0.94	0.24	0.23	0.33
Maine	4.68	4.66	7.90	9.92	14.49	16.40	5.66	5.52	6.73	4.41	0.54	1.37
Maryland	2.56	4.61	9.50	11.83	13.94	18.24	9.62	4.96	4.24	6.02	0.87	0.91
Massachusetts	5.52	8.13	11.64	14.22	17.71	18.78	5.74	6.57	6.25	4.56	0.87	0.53
Michigan	8.20	7.56	5.93	8.00	8.74	10.93	1.36	8.77	5.97	3.23	1.19	0.28
Minnesota		3.89	4.03	6.01	9.53	7.87		3.26	5.41	2.54	2.17	0.43

Table C.6
(continued)

	Pneumonia						Scarlet fever					
State	1850	1860	1870	1880	1890	1900	1850	1860	1870	1880	1890	1900
Mississippi	8.54	19.46	14.22	15.74	11.22	13.98	3.36	4.40	0.29	0.05	0.12	1.07
Missouri	5.54	11.89	16.26	20.75	12.32	14.30	1.33	7.58	6.09	1.37	1.06	0.78
Montana			1.46	8.17	13.47	16.73			0.49	6.13	4.16	0.47
Nebraska		11.44	7.15	9.22	6.22	7.72		3.47	7.32	8.64	1.34	0.70
Nevada			11.77	23.61	15.95	12.99			33.18	2.89	0.44	1.23
New Hampshire	3.62	6.87	11.44	11.90	16.57	21.21	6.45	5.18	3.02	3.98	0.53	2.25
New Jersey	2.64	4.15	7.73	11.77	18.51	19.47	2.47	10.33	8.62	5.01	1.43	1.12
New Mexico		0.20	6.86	13.38	13.09	11.88		0.20	3.92	9.87	2.73	0.13
New York	4.72	5.38	12.01	13.45	21.58	22.84	3.32	12.06	7.76	3.91	1.59	0.53
North Carolina	7.64	9.24	6.92	9.14	8.23	11.23	0.24	3.66	0.13	0.81	0.21	0.80
Ohio	4.79	5.49	7.49	8.49	9.87	11.08	6.57	14.30	2.07	4.17	1.11	0.28
Oklahoma					4.85	7.86					0.49	0.24
Oregon		3.62	3.30	5.09	7.27	7.38		7.62	1.76	2.69	0.64	1.42
Pennsylvania	2.10	3.85	7.87	10.06	12.43	15.56	8.54	10.86	16.03	3.88	1.48	0.82
Rhode Island	2.51	7.79	7.78	10.88	16.61	20.98	3.59	5.15	8.56	19.53	1.01	0.20
South Carolina	11.08	15.01	10.05	11.19	10.11	9.88	1.12	2.29	0.26	0.18	0.18	0.52
Tennessee	4.16	10.50	10.31	14.11	10.70	15.76	1.72	7.92	0.23	0.43	0.40	0.18
Texas	8.23	15.95	18.31	15.79	11.33	9.29	4.19	3.66	0.24	0.43	0.20	2.32
Utah		1.49	9.68	20.49	11.69	12.54		0.50	4.15	1.74	1.92	2.24
Vermont	2.96	5.08	6.81	14.96	16.91	18.36	1.56	7.74	1.63	1.96	0.63	0.41
Virginia	5.61	10.05	11.85	13.00	10.33	13.10	3.68	3.76	0.35	1.77	0.28	0.29
Washington		0.86	2.09	7.85	6.70	7.32		2.59	3.34	2.00	1.57	1.02
West Virginia			5.84	6.99	6.55	7.53			3.55	3.67	0.43	0.63
Wisconsin	6.35	5.54	4.62	8.06	9.20	9.77	3.18	11.56	9.63	3.52	1.28	0.97
Wyoming			2.19	8.18	7.41	11.78				17.80	2.64	1.08

Table C.7
Cause-specific mortality rates per 10,000 for smallpox and typhoid (enteric) fever by state, 1850 to 1900

	Smallpox						Typhoid (enteric) fever					
State	1850	1860	1870	1880	1890	1900	1850	1860	1870	1880	1890	1900
Alabama	0.05		0.20		0.00	1.22	4.19	8.67	4.10	6.15	5.78	9.39
Arizona			98.36		0.17	0.41			11.39	0.00	2.52	3.34
Arkansas	1.57	0.09	0.60		0.01	1.49	1.86	11.87	4.89	4.61	5.23	9.39
California		0.11	4.53	0.05	0.02	0.09	1.19	3.00	7.00	3.45	3.96	3.65
Colorado			0.25	0.10	0.07	1.00			2.76	4.01	10.14	4.11
Connecticut	0.46	0.28	0.19	0.18	0.16	0.00	4.07	4.69	8.26	3.15	4.44	2.74
Dakota				0.07					1.41	2.52		
North Dakota					0.00	0.13					4.43	4.87
South Dakota					0.00	0.02					4.20	8.07
Delaware	0.22	0.18		0.00	0.00	0.05	4.48	4.99	7.20	4.16	6.05	5.49
District of Columbia	6.00		0.23	1.07	0.00	0.18	1.93	5.73	4.71	4.62	8.68	7.15
Florida			0.05	0.00	0.00	0.30	1.03	6.27	5.70	3.75	4.16	2.29
Georgia		0.08	0.15	0.01	0.00	0.21	6.15	8.39	6.21	6.40	5.44	3.93
Idaho				13.80	0.00	0.37				3.68	5.45	5.94
Illinois	0.76	0.05	0.67	0.01	0.01	0.05	3.22	6.91	6.92	5.37	4.44	8.19
Indiana	1.42	0.04	0.36	0.02	0.00	0.08	3.89	5.20	6.12	7.37	4.90	2.46
Indian Territory						0.84						4.68
Iowa	1.87	0.07	0.20	0.01	0.02	0.08	1.56	6.12	4.36	4.43	1.91	7.77
Kansas		0.09	1.10	0.04	0.03	0.50		10.45	5.60	6.66	2.63	7.80
Kentucky	1.53	0.13	1.32	0.00	0.01	0.24	8.29	7.74	5.00	4.94	5.63	2.88
Louisiana	1.10	0.23	12.73	0.17	0.03	5.13	5.60	7.88	6.18	3.21	2.85	4.29
Maine	0.50	0.89	0.22	0.03	0.00	0.07	4.84	6.91	9.70	2.94	4.61	2.23
Maryland	2.47	0.10	0.08	0.09	0.01	0.01	6.17	3.71	5.56	3.91	4.96	2.81
Massachusetts	2.33	3.83	0.80	0.16	0.01	0.05	5.56	5.69	7.84	3.48	3.69	2.20
Michigan	0.65	0.11	0.22	0.04	0.00	0.03	1.38	2.15	5.62	3.34	3.28	8.83

Table C.7
(continued)

	Smallpox						Typhoid (enteric) fever					
Minnesota			0.82	0.01	0.00	0.13		4.37	5.37	4.07	3.76	5.76
Mississippi	0.20		0.65	0.04	0.02	5.04	4.24	10.21	4.02	2.93	4.04	1.73
Missouri	0.84	0.15	6.00	0.00	0.01	0.21	6.41	8.93	8.10	6.67	4.00	2.44
Montana			5.34	0.00	0.00	0.16			4.37	2.04	3.86	2.83
Nebraska		0.35	0.41	0.15	0.05	0.05		6.24	4.23	4.64	3.21	1.68
Nevada			6.82	0.00	0.00	0.00			3.29	2.73	1.75	2.11
New Hampshire	1.32	0.67	0.06	0.09	0.00	0.00	3.90	7.33	9.49	3.37	3.69	5.22
New Jersey	0.90	0.12	0.23	0.08	0.01	0.04	2.19	2.37	3.71	2.48	4.73	2.44
New Mexico		0.11	3.92	3.26	15.04	14.69		0.61	9.80	4.01	3.26	6.60
New York	0.89	0.78	1.33	0.13	0.03	0.02	3.35	2.63	4.63	2.48	2.86	2.04
North Carolina	0.37	0.01	0.03	0.01	0.00	0.27	3.85	10.16	8.05	6.88	5.69	4.32
Ohio	2.78	0.58	1.25	0.01	0.01	0.08	3.79	4.34	4.80	4.30	4.32	5.05
Oklahoma					0.00	0.60					1.62	2.56
Oregon			0.33	0.00	0.06	0.29		3.05	5.72	5.89	4.84	4.41
Pennsylvania	0.88	0.30	0.07	0.13	0.01	0.03	3.07	4.62	5.39	0.95	5.39	2.38
Rhode Island	0.68	0.46	0.51	0.00	0.00	0.05	3.32	3.78	4.05	3.04	4.34	7.24
South Carolina			0.04	0.01	0.00	0.63	6.13	9.38	7.30	5.81	4.79	1.82
Tennessee	0.61	0.09	0.75	0.01	0.01	0.47	6.28	8.27	5.46	4.41	6.13	8.46
Texas	1.03	0.02	1.53	3.25	0.41	0.48	3.10	11.62	5.67	5.60	4.59	6.61
Utah			0.23	0.00	0.10	0.11		1.99	2.77	3.82	4.57	2.64
Vermont	0.38	0.35	0.12	0.12	0.03	0.00	2.36	6.66	6.69	3.28	3.73	3.11
Virginia	0.32	0.15	1.66	0.03	0.00	1.42	5.25	6.62	5.51	4.48	4.57	4.93
Washington			0.00	0.00	0.03	0.33			5.43	2.00	6.64	3.30
West Virginia			0.05	0.02	0.00	0.04			3.78	3.75	5.62	6.11
Wisconsin		0.19	0.99	0.04	0.01	0.03	3.18	3.38	4.40	3.00	2.09	1.76
Wyoming	0.46			0.00	0.00	0.32			1.10	1.44	4.45	1.73

Table C.8
Cause-specific mortality rates per 10,000 for typhus fever and whooping cough by state, 1850 to 1900

	Typhus fever						Whooping cough					
State	1850	1860	1870	1880	1890	1900	1850	1860	1870	1880	1890	1900
Alabama			0.09	0.00			3.95	3.46	1.33	4.32	1.20	2.70
Arizona				0.00					0.00	2.47	0.17	1.79
Arkansas			0.14	0.05			2.62	4.29	4.52	5.56	1.03	2.41
California			0.91	0.09			0.00	0.61	2.39	1.56	0.97	1.02
Colorado			1.25	0.00					1.51	1.75	0.92	1.74
Connecticut			0.35	0.02			1.29	2.11	1.54	1.32	1.88	1.31
Dakota			1.41	0.37					0.71	0.52		
North Dakota											0.88	0.78
South Dakota											3.16	1.32
Delaware			0.08	0.00			3.71	1.51	3.36	2.32	0.59	0.81
District of Columbia			0.08	0.00			3.87	4.40	3.19	4.95	1.30	1.36
Florida			0.05	0.19			2.52	1.00	0.37	1.86	1.28	1.70
Georgia			0.24	0.03			4.25	3.16	0.78	4.21	0.48	1.00
Idaho			0.00	0.00						1.23	0.83	2.35
Illinois			0.52	0.07			2.24	2.23	2.52	1.59	0.94	1.03
Indiana			1.02	0.05			1.88	1.75	2.67	2.84	1.41	0.80
Indian Territory												2.88
Iowa			0.38	0.08			3.02	3.14	2.82	0.87	0.97	0.46
Kansas			0.55	0.09				3.64	3.40	2.17	1.45	1.65
Kentucky			0.26	0.02			1.96	3.77	2.47	3.24	2.90	1.30
Louisiana			0.69	0.01			3.40	4.52	5.78	1.74	1.14	1.30
Maine			0.51	0.09			2.19	1.15	1.13	0.86	1.45	1.40
Maryland			1.05	0.01			2.44	3.00	3.60	2.15	1.33	0.86
Massachusetts			0.23	0.07			2.41	2.86	2.48	1.63	1.63	1.34
Michigan			0.30	0.03			1.84	1.63	2.06	2.06	0.85	1.13
Minnesota			0.71	0.06				1.58	2.34	1.08	0.59	0.94

Table C.8
(continued)

	Typhus fever						Whooping cough					
State	1850	1860	1870	1880	1890	1900	1850	1860	1870	1880	1890	1900
Mississippi			0.07	0.00			3.99	4.65	1.92	2.92	2.13	1.13
Missouri			0.35	0.08			2.23	2.97	2.81	2.22	1.53	1.22
Montana			0.00	0.26						0.00	0.15	0.78
Nebraska			0.24	0.09				7.28	3.01	0.88	1.13	0.98
Nevada				0.16					1.41	1.77	0.22	1.65
New Hampshire			0.13	0.03			0.38	1.47	0.79	0.43	0.98	1.90
New Jersey			0.20	0.04			1.80	2.56	2.00	0.88	2.60	1.75
New Mexico			1.20	0.17				1.52	3.05	14.30	1.11	1.48
New York			0.84	0.01			2.10	1.82	1.97	1.47	1.80	1.36
North Carolina			0.19	0.09			2.61	4.03	2.76	4.66	0.86	1.43
Ohio			0.30	0.03			2.27	1.71	2.15	1.55	1.51	0.96
Oklahoma											0.49	1.26
Oregon			0.22	0.00				0.95	2.09	1.60	0.54	0.77
Pennsylvania			0.74	0.00			1.25	1.64	1.06	1.10	0.98	1.11
Rhode Island			0.09	0.00			0.88	3.44	3.22	1.01	2.95	2.59
South Carolina			0.58	0.04			4.02	4.77	0.52	4.61	0.83	1.31
Tennessee			0.29	0.06			2.23	2.62	2.87	3.03	1.38	2.10
Texas			0.20	0.10			2.30	2.55	2.53	3.67	1.16	1.89
Utah			0.35	0.07					0.23	1.18	0.67	2.20
Vermont			0.09	0.12			1.05	1.02	1.18	1.23	0.48	1.16
Virginia			0.02	0.01			1.52	5.77	2.32	2.76	1.81	1.57
Washington			0.83	0.13					0.83	1.07	0.63	0.66
West Virginia			0.05	0.00					2.44	2.02	3.12	1.59
Wisconsin			0.29	0.10			3.14	1.44	2.00	0.97	0.63	1.05
Wyoming				0.00						0.00	0.00	0.43

Table C.9
Cause-specific mortality rates per 10,000 for worms and yellow fever by state, 1850 to 1900

	Worms						Yellow fever					
State	1850	1860	1870	1880	1890	1900	1850	1860	1870	1880	1890	1900
Alabama	3.29	1.69		1.20			0.31	0.02	0.12	0.05		
Arizona				0.00						0.00		
Arkansas	6.24	3.05		0.87				0.05	0.02	0.44		
California	0.32	0.05		0.02					0.02	0.00		
Colorado				0.05						0.00		
Connecticut	0.08	0.28		0.05			0.11		0.07	0.00		
Dakota				0.15						0.37		
North Dakota										0.14		
South Dakota												
Delaware	0.44	0.80		0.07			0.11		0.08			
District of Columbia	0.00	0.13		0.00					0.15	0.00		
Florida	4.57	2.78		1.19			0.34	0.93	2.40	0.04		
Georgia	2.76	1.84		1.01				0.04	0.04	0.01		
Idaho				0.00						0.00		
Illinois	0.90	0.26		0.09			0.04	0.01	0.01	0.02		
Indiana	0.77	0.25		0.06			0.03		0.01	0.01		
Indian Territory												
Iowa	0.36	0.13		0.07					0.01	0.00		
Kansas				0.15						0.05		
Kentucky	1.16	0.60		0.39				0.06	0.01	0.05		
Louisiana	5.56	2.13		1.03			11.11	2.18	0.10	1.87		
Maine	0.26	0.19		0.06			0.03		0.27	0.18		
Maryland	1.03	0.35		0.11			0.10	0.29	0.27	0.00		
Massachusetts	0.17	0.12		0.04			0.09		0.08	0.01		
Michigan	0.55	0.29		0.10						0.01		

Table C.9
(continued)

State	Worms						Yellow fever					
	1850	1860	1870	1880	1890	1900	1850	1860	1870	1880	1890	1900
Minnesota		0.23		0.06						0.00		
Mississippi	4.91	1.63		0.77			0.03	0.08	0.06	0.46		
Missouri	1.29	0.63		0.20			0.06	0.06	0.03	0.05		
Montana				0.00						0.00		
Nebraska		0.35		0.09						0.00		
Nevada				0.00						0.00		
New Hampshire	0.16	0.15		0.00					0.06	0.03		
New Jersey	0.27	0.10		0.01			0.02		0.02	0.00		
New Mexico		0.10		0.08						0.25		
New York	0.48	0.21		0.04			0.05	0.01	0.02	0.01		
North Carolina	1.91	1.45		1.29			0.01	0.02	0.02	0.00		
Ohio	0.45	0.16		0.06			0.03	0.02	0.01	0.01		
Oklahoma												
Oregon		0.19		0.00						0.00		
Pennsylvania	0.21	0.13		0.04					0.01	0.01		
Rhode Island	0.14	0.29		0.04					0.05	0.00		
South Carolina	4.26	1.95		1.37			1.85	0.03	0.01	0.01		
Tennessee	1.65	0.87		0.65			0.01	0.01	0.02	4.31		
Texas	3.01	0.91		0.46				7.12	0.09	0.03		
Utah		0.25		0.07					0.12	0.00		
Vermont	0.22	0.13		0.03					0.03	0.00		
Virginia	1.32	1.03		0.69				0.01	0.01	0.01		
Washington		0.86		0.00						0.00		
West Virginia				0.21						0.02		
Wisconsin	0.33	0.24		0.11						0.00		
Wyoming				0.00						0.00		

Table C.10
Cause-specific mortality rates per 10,000 for cholera and cholera infantum by state, 1850 to 1900

	Cholera						Cholera infantum					
State	1850	1860	1870	1880	1890	1900	1850	1860	1870	1880	1890	1900
Alabama	0.89	0.26	0.05				0.54	1.04	1.30	2.30	2.33	2.34
Arizona									3.11	0.25	1.01	1.95
Arkansas	11.67	0.23	0.02				0.67	0.94	0.81	2.93	1.99	2.43
California	43.63	0.05					0.11	0.68	4.05	1.94	1.81	1.35
Colorado			0.25						4.52	2.83	4.25	2.83
Connecticut	1.73	0.41	0.04				2.29	2.67	7.05	5.48	7.08	5.52
Dakota		2.07						2.07		1.33		
North Dakota											5.47	1.57
South Dakota											3.80	1.44
Delaware	10.60	0.45					0.87	2.94	6.96	7.71	9.08	5.09
District of Columbia	5.22	0.27	0.61				4.84	4.00	11.39	13.34	9.64	4.66
Florida	2.97	0.21	0.11				1.14	0.43	5.17	2.34	2.50	2.33
Georgia	0.19	0.10	0.06				0.83	1.21	2.91	3.79	3.04	2.62
Idaho										0.31	1.78	1.36
Illinois	22.82	0.41	0.13				1.66	1.84	7.36	6.06	4.80	3.54
Indiana	14.35	0.19	0.03				1.58	1.16	3.12	6.65	3.35	3.03
Indian Territory												4.80
Iowa	6.97	0.22	0.03				1.46	1.47	3.69	4.92	2.19	2.11
Kansas		0.65	0.03					1.77	5.46	8.03	2.77	4.10
Kentucky	20.66	0.31	0.04				1.66	1.29	2.69	3.34	1.65	1.97
Louisiana	56.78	0.69	0.28				0.52	1.31	4.09	1.82	2.87	2.63
Maine	3.53	0.57	0.08				0.89	0.57	2.86	2.56	5.02	6.34
Maryland	2.85	0.31	0.08				2.85	1.18	7.73	10.71	8.85	5.85
Massachusetts	10.88	0.62	0.03				3.33	6.52	11.56	7.63	9.27	7.00
Michigan	3.52	0.27	0.03				0.33	0.43	3.59	3.37	4.89	4.60

Table C.10
(continued)

	Cholera						Cholera infantum					
State	1850	1860	1870	1880	1890	1900	1850	1860	1870	1880	1890	1900
Minnesota		0.23	0.05					2.67	2.46	4.11	4.52	2.15
Mississippi	9.68	0.30	0.08				1.88	1.55	1.73	1.48	1.50	1.10
Missouri	52.62	0.52	0.12				1.22	1.49	5.75	6.31	2.68	2.75
Montana									2.91	1.53	2.35	1.93
Nebraska		0.00						0.69	4.72	5.33	4.52	2.94
Nevada									3.77	3.21	1.09	0.94
New Hampshire	1.48	0.28	0.06				1.48	2.42	4.37	4.76	8.98	7.12
New Jersey	14.01	0.36	0.08				2.14	1.98	8.64	8.38	8.26	4.47
New Mexico		0.61						0.11	12.70	1.51	1.04	1.43
New York	18.80	0.42	0.10				1.44	1.79	8.16	5.86	7.91	4.15
North Carolina	0.41	0.14	0.01				0.85	0.87	3.36	4.25	2.88	2.32
Ohio	29.33	0.28	0.01				1.17	1.11	4.16	5.47	3.98	3.03
Oklahoma											2.10	3.64
Oregon									0.66	4.35	1.88	1.23
Pennsylvania	5.61	0.22	0.09				1.12	1.30	7.62	5.87	5.33	3.97
Rhode Island	10.78	0.29					3.80	3.95	9.06	6.22	11.95	10.45
South Carolina	1.03	0.24					0.96	1.42	3.61	2.78	2.90	2.59
Tennessee	8.51	0.21	0.09				0.96	1.12	2.23	3.59	2.32	2.24
Texas	13.26	0.18					0.56	0.71	1.42	3.46	2.26	2.63
Utah								0.99	11.41	2.36	2.50	2.31
Vermont	0.99	0.25	0.27				0.19	0.54	3.18	3.37	5.23	3.23
Virginia	5.59	0.28	0.05				1.06	1.04	4.68	5.30	3.45	3.07
Washington									2.92	3.20	2.69	1.62
West Virginia			0.05						2.42	3.61	2.86	2.65
Wisconsin	7.60	0.12	0.03				0.46	0.45	3.49	2.90	2.76	3.26
Wyoming								1.04		1.44	2.31	1.19

Table C.11
Cause-specific mortality rates per 10,000 for cholera morbus and miscellaneous other diseases by state, 1850 to 1900

	Cholera morbus						Dirt eating	Winter fever	Typho-malaria	Influenza
State	1850	1860	1870	1880	1890	1900	1850	1850	1870	1900
Alabama	0.40			0.26		0.78	0.19		0.13	42.54
Arizona				0.49		1.14				6.51
Arkansas	1.05			0.40		1.01		1.91		24.32
California				0.20		0.81			0.02	14.61
Colorado				0.10		1.24				7.41
Connecticut	0.73			0.27		0.43				70.89
Dakota				0.22						
North Dakota						1.10				7.83
South Dakota						1.59				6.47
Delaware	0.66			0.41		0.49				15.70
District of Columbia	0.77			0.56		0.36				41.26
Florida	0.11			0.52		1.02			1.38	50.14
Georgia	0.51			0.33		0.79	0.03	0.02	0.26	30.09
Idaho				0.00		1.36			0.67	6.80
Illinois	0.73			0.55		0.76		1.32	0.07	9.42
Indiana	0.68			0.32		1.08		0.38	0.07	18.12
Indian Territory						1.22				9.18
Iowa	0.52			0.49		1.14		0.57	0.03	9.23
Kansas				0.29		1.50			0.36	11.90
Kentucky	0.46			0.37		0.75	0.04	0.39	0.01	22.22
Louisiana	0.17			0.50		1.09	1.04		0.15	13.83
Maine	2.11			0.42		0.73			0.02	35.28
Maryland	0.50			0.45		0.40				18.60
Massachusetts	1.28			0.60		0.40			0.01	39.92
Michigan	1.01			0.33		0.98			0.03	17.31

Table C.11
(continued)

	Cholera morbus						Dirt eating	Winter fever	Typho-malaria	Influenza
State	1850	1860	1870	1880	1890	1900	1850	1850	1870	1900
Minnesota				0.61		1.21			0.02	8.68
Mississippi	0.49			0.28		0.73	0.05	0.15	0.06	37.84
Missouri	0.41			0.46		0.87	0.015		0.08	11.43
Montana				0.00		0.99			1.46	6.99
Nebraska				0.51		1.13				11.44
Nevada				0.48		2.36			2.82	23.62
New Hampshire	0.79			0.40		0.83				44.95
New Jersey	0.49			0.63		0.76			0.01	23.52
New Mexico				0.17		0.97				13.31
New York	0.64			0.44		0.46			0.02	19.99
North Carolina	0.38			0.48		0.65	0.01		0.04	42.19
Ohio	0.57			0.46		0.86		0.27	0.05	14.55
Oklahoma						1.28				5.77
Oregon				0.51		0.77				15.96
Pennsylvania	1.07			0.37		1.01			0.02	15.52
Rhode Island	0.88			0.40		0.49				75.60
South Carolina	0.33			0.32		0.65	0.12		0.41	36.71
Tennessee	0.48			0.43		0.84	0.02		0.02	51.91
Texas	0.61			0.33		1.18			0.16	13.02
Utah				0.35		1.63			0.35	12.65
Vermont	0.64			0.24		0.76			0.06	37.54
Virginia	0.30			0.55		0.57	0.02		0.02	40.66
Washington				0.27		0.87				10.23
West Virginia				0.47		0.57				19.40
Wisconsin	0.59			0.47		1.19			0.03	11.65
Wyoming	0.40			0.48		1.30			3.29	21.61

Table C.12
Population and adult mortality rates per 10,000 for all causes of death by state, 1850 to 1900

	Population mortality rate						Adult (20 years and older) mortality rate					
State	1850	1860	1870	1880	1890	1900	1850	1860	1870	1880	1890	1900
Alabama	117.82	132.34	108.03	142.01	138.12	140.53	100.89	114.25	107.37	131.46	149.88	153.26
Arizona			260.92	71.96	109.69	99.49			177.23	69.77	105.81	85.20
Arkansas	143.93	203.38	126.30	184.57	127.56	171.69	142.60	184.16	120.05	167.27	134.35	169.77
California	97.74	97.50	161.09	133.34	146.83	151.55	92.90	69.03	128.70	134.47	153.25	173.69
Colorado			94.07	131.07	132.73	137.63			64.29	92.64	106.08	137.87
Connecticut	155.91	133.41	126.45	147.41	193.90	169.77	159.42	131.89	129.33	151.52	190.04	175.20
Dakota		8.27	71.22	96.47				12.51	51.65	62.49		
North Dakota					101.08	71.66					78.07	65.50
South Dakota					104.86	76.90					83.26	75.20
Delaware	132.08	111.04	124.87	150.88	184.40	166.45	130.14	101.70	115.58	142.14	173.17	169.45
District of Columbia	163.68	171.15	153.00	236.00	258.47	228.33	140.18	138.88	116.54	187.80	210.71	207.18
Florida	106.47	125.98	120.59	117.22	105.90	122.64	89.97	120.21	118.93	112.77	114.17	124.43
Georgia	109.53	121.22	114.90	139.73	115.24	121.56	99.06	104.42	106.68	123.60	123.47	129.08
Idaho			33.34	99.05	86.63	76.77			28.46	80.36	67.98	75.41
Illinois	138.10	112.74	132.57	146.26	138.83	126.99	135.07	78.96	99.60	122.35	123.88	133.33
Indiana	128.57	113.49	105.09	157.78	110.29	133.47	124.33	92.20	100.90	199.60	112.02	145.17
Indian Territory						134.83						103.99
Iowa	106.34	107.55	79.62	119.27	91.74	87.72	91.67	80.01	69.98	101.83	94.03	102.78
Kansas		146.17	124.75	152.19	84.35	110.58		112.63	89.44	109.29	80.99	118.55
Kentucky	153.02	142.49	108.59	143.86	128.47	126.17	158.46	120.44	106.13	186.46	130.44	138.18
Louisiana	230.92	174.07	199.46	154.41	146.20	151.74	246.63	158.81	193.21	159.35	162.40	172.97
Maine	130.05	121.19	123.27	146.75	151.93	174.93	129.47	136.66	135.42	155.29	172.54	193.33
Maryland	165.02	107.33	124.73	180.87	172.68	171.90	146.57	98.28	111.34	149.54	161.91	178.43
Massachusetts	195.11	173.05	177.44	185.91	201.49	177.36	168.94	157.74	161.67	166.09	181.24	174.03
Michigan	113.54	98.80	94.43	120.61	119.47	138.67	106.87	382.50	83.13	102.64	114.06	151.18
Minnesota	47.67	64.47	80.19	115.74	119.83	97.09	23.48	12.23	66.46	86.71	102.90	107.44

Table C.12
(continued)

	Population mortality rate						Adult (20 years and older) mortality rate					
State	1850	1860	1870	1880	1890	1900	1850	1860	1870	1880	1890	1900
Mississippi	143.79	154.35	110.78	128.87	115.53	130.54	119.22	129.10	101.80	128.76	130.56	142.58
Missouri	180.22	149.36	162.56	168.86	121.06	122.59	195.18	116.38	131.66	151.86	116.31	129.26
Montana			89.83	85.80	99.35	89.92			80.91	67.31	84.04	84.02
Nebraska		132.10	81.31	131.08	81.00	77.50		81.21	50.55	78.69	66.68	83.63
Nevada			144.74	116.92	99.21	103.46			86.90	110.04	103.29	114.60
New Hampshire	133.06	137.06	134.81	160.93	187.87	179.79	133.52	149.20	194.09	169.07	190.58	181.52
New Jersey	132.06	111.97	116.83	163.33	210.00	173.78	129.88	93.77	96.32	127.06	179.96	179.87
New Mexico		139.55	128.44	203.74	180.54	136.91		138.35	102.99	148.41	115.82	106.42
New York	147.22	120.96	157.65	173.78	205.27	179.21	137.10	102.50	139.53	155.96	189.70	182.69
North Carolina	116.97	127.11	98.83	153.93	113.85	111.25	124.69	114.90	140.62	134.52	122.23	124.33
Ohio	146.22	105.69	110.94	133.24	135.73	128.35	144.15	87.25	108.87	127.20	136.63	145.33
Oklahoma					74.72	79.86					60.20	66.82
Oregon		57.18	68.41	106.66	85.64	82.12		36.71	67.50	91.81	85.47	93.34
Pennsylvania	123.50	104.06	149.46	149.15	139.84	143.12	111.90	93.72	127.95	135.78	134.58	144.50
Rhode Island	151.89	141.97	126.11	170.04	218.78	190.78	139.59	128.49	105.99	143.21	198.49	181.96
South Carolina	120.37	138.54	104.59	157.98	134.60	128.07	113.90	116.04	105.22	145.73	150.01	140.62
Tennessee	118.43	136.57	113.14	168.05	134.96	151.30	119.90	123.08	111.14	162.10	144.21	163.17
Texas	143.80	155.19	136.79	155.40	118.44	112.05	131.62	142.26	169.31	136.66	121.04	105.72
Utah		92.87	102.67	167.68	103.70	111.26		63.24	93.95	91.17	88.43	127.32
Vermont	99.61	106.47	107.25	151.20	163.20	169.62	114.25	122.61	126.53	160.01	177.96	197.02
Virginia	134.06	140.79	123.93	163.17	140.29	136.19	142.16	130.15	147.46	152.07	147.69	138.70
Washington		43.13	93.09	100.51	80.65	94.77		35.91	98.32	67.20	64.48	102.12
West Virginia			90.90	119.94	108.48	100.00			109.27	113.69	112.41	105.34
Wisconsin	95.06	92.04	94.44	121.71	111.16	120.48	72.81	71.04	101.84	108.64	116.97	137.92
Wyoming			81.16	90.91	80.72	82.89			67.91	54.61	59.80	69.45

Table C.13
Children/adolescent and young children mortality rates per 10,000 for all causes of death by state, 1850 to 1900

	Children/adolescent (5–19 years) mortality rate						Young children (1–4 years) mortality rate					
State	1850	1860	1870	1880	1890	1900	1850	1860	1870	1880	1890	1900
Alabama	54.00	47.64	45.74	50.91	43.81	46.80	185.96	217.88	152.11	202.91	179.39	174.26
Arizona			237.07	19.43	50.27	49.61			928.20	74.79	135.46	175.38
Arkansas	72.25	108.32	59.85	74.06	51.44	75.20	208.48	309.78	165.98	274.02	165.66	256.41
California	113.21	59.28	68.73	43.96	44.96	42.99	233.42	245.58	296.24	157.43	150.92	126.39
Colorado			33.12	91.14	64.79	49.55			137.95	302.16	194.53	164.49
Connecticut	57.04	52.49	45.54	45.67	56.79	38.98	275.85	220.78	174.76	198.83	245.05	161.21
Dakota		0.00	34.17	69.34				16.45	135.14	178.21		
North Dakota					45.76	33.38					140.79	84.47
South Dakota					60.11	34.43					154.62	94.17
Delaware	47.93	49.84	41.43	44.73	61.42	54.59	214.70	190.51	235.89	230.16	266.04	190.67
District of Columbia	73.33	67.53	55.13	58.06	74.31	71.97	342.67	296.09	339.31	417.21	380.78	450.91
Florida	51.35	53.28	64.78	50.13	37.38	41.76	202.89	208.01	183.56	168.60	133.36	158.95
Georgia	45.00	40.40	47.02	47.06	36.30	36.46	168.77	195.08	165.82	218.39	162.95	162.84
Idaho			10.16	65.77	50.24	36.52			58.55	167.22	144.20	86.95
Illinois	56.57	46.95	48.62	54.58	43.84	38.78	219.52	234.71	248.43	261.79	190.46	157.33
Indiana	54.85	50.26	37.71	46.22	38.74	41.74	216.52	219.18	168.26	184.45	135.50	146.68
Indian Territory						58.69						264.18
Iowa	41.09	41.66	28.31	56.52	37.41	25.17	185.17	202.30	131.62	204.90	83.04	74.53
Kansas		64.50	54.64	70.84	28.39	34.81		252.54	239.51	285.25	117.51	137.20
Kentucky	65.79	63.05	39.81	53.92	45.76	39.98	225.81	235.13	141.97	204.64	176.78	150.56
Louisiana	104.97	78.67	69.55	51.70	46.74	50.77	337.08	310.97	266.43	190.12	151.95	171.22
Maine	59.38	51.22	52.61	66.79	46.59	42.50	263.51	159.16	167.76	212.89	139.23	154.83
Maryland	68.06	37.79	43.34	56.20	41.78	48.93	299.44	194.82	236.86	302.81	238.65	190.42
Massachusetts	74.11	62.91	59.53	62.06	61.20	40.90	486.28	295.52	323.48	685.37	282.74	207.53
Michigan	44.46	205.76	36.54	56.99	42.72	36.25	199.21	583.29	153.68	187.46	150.13	135.98

Table C.13
(continued)

	Children/adolescent (5–19 years) mortality rate						Young children (1–4 years) mortality rate					
State	1850	1860	1870	1880	1890	1900	1850	1860	1870	1880	1890	1900
Minnesota	34.15	4.72	34.64	61.39	44.40	29.83	119.84	26.67	128.36	181.41	149.82	82.21
Mississippi	62.46	66.81	47.82	48.06	42.65	54.03	249.40	272.72	157.86	165.68	148.04	159.98
Missouri	75.14	60.93	60.71	57.16	37.50	40.31	268.02	286.66	292.75	264.15	162.78	168.73
Montana			46.32	61.83	67.09	40.32			172.84	156.56	175.83	96.49
Nebraska		61.33	37.12	77.96	32.02	24.04		205.99	169.99	260.75	124.73	90.32
Nevada			115.14	47.53	47.41	27.65			646.86	138.89	93.99	110.63
New Hampshire	56.28	50.82	47.46	67.78	50.10	40.74	280.87	169.11	186.00	203.01	221.49	197.79
New Jersey	47.29	45.30	38.23	54.51	55.66	42.71	242.21	218.27	235.07	252.62	300.06	219.68
New Mexico		51.23	49.26	84.13	135.34	61.25		198.03	208.57	462.87	384.06	261.06
New York	59.16	51.49	47.47	53.56	50.84	40.64	300.28	255.73	301.67	291.69	290.14	233.85
North Carolina	47.43	45.12	36.98	53.74	37.94	34.17	153.77	209.80	142.02	249.83	175.94	135.09
Ohio	62.09	46.96	34.12	46.81	42.67	34.57	263.29	212.55	172.31	188.12	182.40	132.54
Oklahoma					26.59	32.71					113.24	124.68
Oregon		35.91	29.21	56.60	42.39	33.41		94.21	107.37	167.59	99.99	75.90
Pennsylvania	47.60	42.69	50.13	56.15	41.81	40.80	240.55	187.97	275.13	241.26	189.62	185.25
Rhode Island	54.23	51.73	48.30	71.67	58.83	43.50	315.47	272.10	214.50	359.86	355.08	263.51
South Carolina	52.99	55.21	46.56	54.73	46.22	42.42	189.24	224.55	151.18	235.84	187.57	169.38
Tennessee	48.84	54.23	44.68	61.63	47.32	54.92	155.23	212.07	148.16	219.60	170.10	192.54
Texas	70.83	66.92	63.06	54.70	44.27	40.02	109.17	234.05	178.79	222.73	149.19	180.24
Utah		23.21	32.07	106.02	53.33	37.71		143.43	120.14	306.39	158.30	108.34
Vermont	39.93	42.96	38.02	60.63	55.49	39.25	153.92	137.19	71.44	176.72	148.07	117.25
Virginia	53.44	52.99	36.13	52.76	50.86	49.05	196.35	214.02	96.57	240.36	190.37	143.75
Washington		39.49	45.33	86.86	47.47	36.64		67.45	54.68	150.61	128.48	101.93
West Virginia			33.05	44.20	40.31	34.15			61.33	174.73	133.63	116.84
Wisconsin	39.51	38.42	36.91	53.90	34.59	30.37	190.73	163.54	92.49	179.83	120.37	99.31
Wyoming			63.81	49.47	44.38	48.50			99.60	285.56	96.15	106.95

Table C.14
Infant mortality rates per 10,000 for all causes of death by state, 1850 to 1900; and white and black infant and under 5 mortality rates per 10,000 for all causes of death by state, 1880

	Infant (under 1 year) mortality rate						White infant mortality rate	Black infant mortality rate	White under 5 mortality rate	Black under 5 mortality rate
State	1850	1860	1870	1880	1890	1900	1880	1880	1880	1880
Alabama	993.37	1110.40	728.35	1015.47	1052.40	945.20	811.32	1241.32	296.65	449.56
Arizona			1685.39	763.98	584.96	608.94				
Arkansas	793.44	1182.41	785.44	1099.32	763.08	1037.65	1069.32		465.91	
California	1318.68	645.23	1354.34	1166.70	1424.35	1000.12	1168.86		704.69	
Colorado			912.51	1114.71	1276.66	1010.88	1114.81		471.13	
Connecticut	912.90	800.18	929.17	1233.79	2039.53	1568.22	1233.71		410.86	
Dakota		0.00	543.74	650.35			651.41		280.85	
North Dakota					754.72	493.75				
South Dakota					688.15	517.95				
Delaware	963.19	699.64	955.28	1367.99	1875.33	1432.69	1295.87		442.01	
District of Columbia	1159.97	1345.44	1201.38	2774.65	4226.55	4027.14	1947.55	4066.31	611.35	1163.82
Florida	666.37	758.62	600.60	697.86	742.63	902.81	624.21	778.92	248.85	305.41
Georgia	901.12	1046.71	868.75	1040.50	847.30	872.34	873.94	1221.21	323.53	451.71
Idaho			407.24	536.31	555.05	459.92	536.14		246.02	
Illinois	855.67	760.33	1161.60	1248.49	1425.35	976.38	1248.26		716.14	
Indiana	730.43	699.14	761.64	712.16	924.62	1026.15	1263.74		474.33	
Indian Territory						954.39				

Table C.14
(continued)

State	Infant (under 1 year) mortality rate						White infant mortality rate	Black infant mortality rate	White under 5 mortality rate	Black under 5 mortality rate
	1850	1860	1870	1880	1890	1900	1880	1880	1880	1880
Iowa	752.58	714.43	621.68	820.82	772.66	594.51	820.92		333.03	
Kansas		1033.62	869.73	1166.31	728.62	820.29	1166.58		474.44	
Kentucky	872.88	998.16	845.07	1107.73	937.42	818.74	1107.80		397.44	
Louisiana	1050.52	1189.73	1526.28	1048.92	1186.06	968.43	994.17	1099.00	345.90	383.55
Maine	631.65	622.35	697.64	820.32	1070.08	1441.16	820.05		334.10	
Maryland	1149.13	787.47	928.64	1820.94	2049.60	1488.49	1696.21		585.95	
Massachusetts	1215.07	1322.34	1573.35	1938.97	2509.58	1778.05	1938.95		647.54	
Michigan	794.64	2248.34	787.03	1019.84	1136.78	1213.05	1020.10		357.96	
Minnesota	1164.99	131.52	608.92	911.62	1184.77	758.46	911.74		336.51	
Mississippi	870.09	1365.27	753.60	834.52	727.54	781.78	728.99	931.86	276.02	324.23
Missouri	757.65	993.90	1302.89	1427.52	1121.68	936.43	1427.39		508.00	
Montana			629.92	616.11	542.02	543.61	616.12		255.50	
Nebraska		1235.06	642.75	919.25	736.04	590.80	919.14		403.87	
Nevada			1269.59	846.68	707.35	596.63	847.05		278.49	
New Hampshire	792.27	923.77	846.69	1091.03	2018.28	1719.68	1090.93		381.04	

New Jersey	870.61	749.11	995.34	1538.02	2751.27	1673.59	1537.82		521.32	
New Mexico		930.23	1235.74	1567.97	919.56	912.49	1567.70		709.09	
New York	787.58	772.29	1492.33	1770.78	2439.49	1598.03	1770.67		598.00	
North Carolina	778.78	1055.85	662.98	1089.72	737.11	697.38	952.49	1327.87	342.51	501.23
Ohio	782.52	655.19	868.00	1153.00	1238.68	986.92	1152.83		388.39	
Oklahoma					557.29	599.42				
Oregon		352.53	398.94	728.49	567.83	461.02	728.74		284.18	
Pennsylvania	1008.31	652.23	1235.43	1186.66	1319.39	1181.75	1186.62		439.49	
Rhode Island	899.31	956.72	1349.59	1477.50	2634.25	1978.02	1477.24		599.59	
South Carolina	868.30	1242.09	655.04	1077.60	883.52	808.57	786.46	1248.03	310.00	460.09
Tennessee	900.87	1040.10	823.23	1177.81	940.85	961.66	1056.09		379.30	
Texas	454.96	1021.99	1011.81	1089.89	883.31	732.53	1059.73		415.15	
Utah		629.65	792.67	1113.31	728.18	632.08	1113.54		481.64	
Vermont	883.28	509.62	743.55	1076.92	1388.41	1221.32	1077.09		355.26	
Virginia	597.66	1115.34	942.13	1260.83	1096.76	939.34	1017.04	1568.70	355.86	543.30
Washington		151.06	658.86	653.29	607.50	600.59	653.78		254.95	
West Virginia			636.06	831.48	801.21	649.70	831.49		314.92	
Wisconsin	357.14	644.31	714.47	951.42	921.76	992.54	951.52		339.88	
Wyoming			384.62	675.42	586.85	674.58	675.27		369.93	

Table C.15
Black and white mortality rates per 10,000 for all causes of death by state, 1850 to 1900

	Black mortality rate						White mortality rate					
State	1850	1860	1870	1880	1890	1900	1850	1860	1870	1880	1890	1900
Alabama	137.90		126.90	159.97	155.91	154.21	101.57		90.85	125.78	123.63	129.22
Arizona			769.23	64.52	74.26	43.29			257.80	79.92	97.70	101.88
Arkansas	181.11		129.17	165.95	117.22	167.42	132.99		125.37	191.14	131.47	173.33
California	135.14		156.84	254.24	132.80	240.83	97.34		168.73	136.37	147.72	150.29
Colorado			87.72	94.46	111.25	208.87			94.34	131.90	132.69	136.28
Connecticut	158.67		125.16	212.18	241.03	241.04	155.85		126.43	146.18	193.08	168.62
Dakota			106.38	49.88					62.08	93.81		
North Dakota					67.11	244.76					94.00	65.64
South Dakota					72.46	64.52					82.31	64.30
Delaware	129.28		133.81	179.77	244.49	190.57	132.92		122.87	144.56	172.20	161.71
District of Columbia	192.78		189.15	352.71	382.18	311.53	152.77		135.25	177.12	197.94	191.09
Florida	111.69		120.30	113.74	108.49	133.23	102.11		120.87	120.47	103.98	114.62
Georgia	138.99		132.77	156.51	127.72	133.75	87.81		99.67	124.80	104.29	110.84
Idaho			166.67	377.36	143.64	102.39			39.56	105.47	82.54	69.58
Illinois	134.36		114.04	179.00	178.13	186.68	138.13		132.78	145.77	138.23	125.91
Indiana	80.97		135.18	251.10	188.75	220.33	129.12		104.60	155.83	108.62	131.40
Indian Territory						115.59						130.04
Iowa	510.51		185.70	167.09	149.86	147.33	105.64		79.84	119.03	91.31	87.27
Kansas			181.79	237.78	138.69	195.57			121.37	148.09	82.21	107.38
Kentucky	198.76		136.54	198.19	167.02	177.59	139.75		102.95	133.16	121.96	118.32
Louisiana	230.66		189.40	154.22	137.74	164.03	231.20		209.71	154.70	154.69	140.49
Maine	258.11		261.52	220.54	186.51	189.54	129.75		123.01	146.40	151.84	174.97

Maryland	170.27	130.79	216.76	204.77	216.11	162.94	122.97	170.58	164.30	161.07
Massachusetts	165.13	263.86	224.63	267.29	206.42	195.39	176.61	185.51	200.79	177.13
Michigan	143.41	134.19	149.01	196.14	156.17	113.35	93.46	119.71	118.69	138.44
Minnesota		39.53	159.85	176.46	125.03	48.03	148.31	115.33	118.72	96.81
Mississippi	173.24	122.80	131.26	114.94	140.44	113.32	96.95	125.62	116.34	116.09
Missouri	157.64	146.01	203.78	185.37	193.32	183.66	163.78	166.35	117.23	118.71
Montana		109.29	115.61	53.19	111.62		89.59	83.93	77.47	85.29
Nebraska		50.70	138.36	75.69	175.47		81.56	130.63	79.80	75.86
Nevada		28.01	184.43	29.95	447.76		151.95	126.97	105.93	98.57
New Hampshire	115.38	155.17	204.38	246.38	181.27	133.09	134.75	160.88	187.77	179.85
New Jersey	124.44	145.80	202.82	277.96	237.96	132.46	115.82	161.95	207.65	171.43
New Mexico		232.56	226.60	26.67	192.55		128.11	220.47	174.68	133.07
New York	164.36	263.63	246.99	257.51	273.46	146.95	156.36	172.84	204.62	177.92
North Carolina	143.27	113.60	175.88	128.59	125.11	101.97	89.72	140.30	105.99	104.60
Ohio	162.71	169.43	206.63	228.66	193.70	146.01	109.51	131.36	133.46	126.79
Oklahoma				66.49	85.50				56.44	73.57
Oregon		260.12	143.74	31.64	99.55		69.02	109.89	84.07	80.49
Pennsylvania	151.60	255.15	246.68	217.12	224.36	122.84	147.47	147.17	138.20	141.09
Rhode Island	177.21	164.66	275.89	292.93	259.57	151.24	125.25	167.56	217.10	189.45
South Carolina	133.84	118.68	174.31	151.61	145.17	102.31	84.41	132.80	109.24	104.12
Tennessee	151.58	138.40	213.37	175.76	198.63	107.66	104.45	152.02	121.81	136.54
Texas	150.68	119.78	145.23	106.01	127.88	141.20	144.48	158.68	121.93	108.03
Utah		254.24	215.52	54.84	163.69		102.74	168.72	102.33	109.08
Vermont	83.68	86.58	151.37	129.48	302.66	99.65	107.31	151.20	163.30	169.33
Virginia	173.93	149.17	195.29	170.15	169.12	110.61	105.77	140.15	121.68	117.95
Washington		193.24	153.85	73.22	167.06		89.66	104.61	77.24	92.56
West Virginia		135.71	167.66	158.63	117.93		89.00	117.87	106.24	99.14
Wisconsin	377.95	198.77	111.03	157.64	228.17	94.47	94.30	121.62	110.45	120.25
Wyoming		109.29	67.11	48.95	74.47		82.51	94.15	68.66	73.10

Table C.16
Native-born and foreign-born mortality rates per 10,000 for all causes of death by state, 1850 to 1900

	Native-born mortality rate						Foreign-born mortality rate					
State	1850	1860	1870	1880	1890	1900	1850	1860	1870	1880	1890	1900
Alabama	208.09		107.33		113.75	124.72	320.95		171.65		212.96	237.83
Arizona			415.69		78.97	96.58			158.37		96.78	97.79
Arkansas	182.45		126.33		125.85	169.86	135.96		105.45		194.28	197.38
California	108.33		177.22		129.63	126.01	53.21		131.73		180.07	217.18
Colorado			93.19		121.75	110.72			46.98		111.63	136.28
Connecticut	164.59		136.59		195.05	164.88	84.12		86.33		173.73	166.01
Dakota			77.94						58.15			
North Dakota					151.86	64.83					72.90	63.50
South Dakota					79.05	57.18					80.69	85.02
Delaware	135.99		126.51		162.72	152.16	123.74		103.98		229.81	171.90
District of Columbia	182.88		155.92		184.46	173.77	101.67		121.82		281.90	315.57
Florida	192.04		117.85		101.95	105.83	171.97		215.42		96.82	197.85
Georgia	187.88		114.33		96.81	108.08	275.89		344.27		226.20	213.79
Idaho			39.36		78.43	64.10			19.77		67.51	86.34
Illinois	137.00		138.86		179.99	112.84	142.17		106.91		138.53	166.40
Indiana	127.75		106.09		102.49	122.19	147.20		91.68		149.65	228.89
Indian Territory						129.68						77.31
Iowa	108.41		82.59		84.86	73.65	84.70		68.30		99.43	138.66
Kansas			130.98		78.06	87.90			80.80		89.48	135.89
Kentucky	194.97		109.28		113.94	110.07	177.91		94.32		198.68	243.55
Louisiana	449.86		183.22		136.45	124.90	385.74		331.89		287.47	322.06
Maine	132.12		125.22		147.96	175.16	84.52		99.63		147.21	160.00
Maryland	203.96		126.63		153.94	141.71	121.07		103.46		214.52	243.62

Massachusetts	201.91	185.52	209.67	181.13	163.51	150.18	173.33	162.42
Michigan	117.52	102.65	118.31	129.51	89.03	65.37	106.09	162.02
Minnesota	58.58	90.61	125.30	83.74	25.29	61.86	102.24	124.47
Mississippi	289.38	110.37	108.61	112.38	196.32	123.31	229.16	196.72
Missouri	183.52	161.72	106.79	107.67	363.61	164.85	170.95	221.11
Montana		94.32	71.89	65.22		63.92	67.44	85.61
Nebraska		90.85	77.32	68.71		50.08	71.30	98.07
Nevada		171.38	116.97	74.93		109.57	152.18	159.66
New Hampshire	135.10	139.80	232.41	181.15	89.03	84.77	117.60	122.44
New Jersey	137.55	126.05	208.00	165.16	89.91	81.08	191.17	184.05
New Mexico		131.82	169.42	133.46		71.17	153.78	87.47
New York	147.88	159.35	196.39	167.98	141.14	151.12	211.71	198.49
North Carolina	174.52	98.62	103.21	101.69	242.21	171.67	188.42	143.38
Ohio	140.21	110.27	123.13	111.65	189.69	112.59	166.84	204.32
Oklahoma			53.82	72.83			55.37	72.42
Oregon		70.22	77.15	70.79		54.31	70.26	117.34
Pennsylvania	125.44	149.57	131.02	130.31	107.51	142.62	149.30	166.45
Rhode Island	161.45	142.14	230.38	195.28	101.67	79.07	191.08	171.56
South Carolina	283.59	103.67	103.76	101.46	283.68	183.30	289.76	268.11
Tennessee	155.33	113.10	115.66	133.04	229.01	108.20	215.09	290.57
Texas	199.53	135.84	113.49	104.60	115.88	142.44	121.54	120.28
Utah		132.66	96.77	88.04		47.55	110.10	186.16
Vermont	106.98	115.39	158.53	163.88	37.08	57.05	140.16	188.84
Virginia	203.78	124.08	115.78	114.77	79.62	106.15	219.91	230.23
Washington		91.91	69.17	77.76		95.54	59.40	118.58
West Virginia		91.12	101.57	96.89		84.25	173.99	151.03
Wisconsin	114.89	103.19	99.56	99.20	58.38	77.50	125.09	174.01
Wyoming		87.42	57.53	65.41		48.39	65.84	82.62

Notes

Chapter 1

1. The case fatality rate of a disease is the number of fatal cases divided by total number of cases of the disease.

2. For medical and social historians who have emphasized the role of diseases in the history of the Americas, see Blanton (1930, 1957); Crosby (1991); Curtin (1968); Earle (1979); Kiple and Kiple (1980). Recently, economic historians also have examined the influence of diseases on the history of the American economy. See Cain and Rotella (2001, 2010); Coelho and McGuire (1997, 1999, 2000, 2006); Costa (2000, 2002, 2005); Costa and Steckel (1997); Fogel (1986, 1989); Haines (1995, 1999); Steckel (1986a, b, c, 1992, 2000, 2009); Steckel and Jensen (1986); Troesken (2001, 2002, 2004).

3. There is a voluminous literature on the role of institutions in explaining development and economic growth. See Acemoglu and Johnson (2004); Acemoglu, Johnson and Robinson (2001, 2002, 2005); Davis and North (1971); Djankov, La Porta, Lopez-de-Silanes, and Shleifer (2002, 2003); Easterly (2001, 2006); Glaeser, La Porta, Lopez-De-Silanes, and Shleifer (2004); Greif (1993, 1994, 2006); Jones (1981, 2000); La Porta, Lopez-de-Silanes, and Shleifer (2008); La Porta, Lopez-de-Silanes, Shleifer, and Vishny (1997, 1998); Moyo (2009); North (1981, 1990, 2005); North and Thomas (1973); North, Wallis, and Weingast (2009). In contrast, others have emphasized geography's role in economic growth and development. See Crosby (1986); Diamond (1997, 2005); Engerman and Sokoloff (1997, 2002); McNeill (1976); Sachs (2005, 2008).

Chapter 2

1. We use the term "family" rather than the more usual per person as a metric because this avoids the anomalous situation of living standards rising as dependent (nonworking) people die. We also use the metric of per capita (person) income, but we explicitly recognize that rising welfare is only unambiguously associated with an increase in income (the numerator in per capita income) and not with a decline in population (the denominator). For more on the difficulties of using per capita income as a measure of welfare, see Bauer (1991); Lebergott (1976, pp. 33–43).

2. Of course, this does not mean that a civilized person supports maiming, torturing, or unjustifiably killing animals.

3. The iron law of wages is the belief that over time real wages tend toward a subsistence level. The term "Dismal Science" was first used by Thomas Carlyle in his 1849 work

Occasional Discourses on the Negro Question. Carlyle advocated black slavery in the West Indies denigrating economists' reliance on markets to allocate labor and invented the term "Dismal Science" as an opprobrium for economics.

4. For other studies in the Malthusian tradition, see Blaugh (1997); Clark (1977); Cohen (1977); Easterlin (1980); Meadows, Meadows, Randers, and Behrens III (1972); Tudge (1999).

5. For studies advocating human overkill as the extinction mechanism, see Martin (1984); Martin and Steadman (1999); Solow, Roberts, and Robbirt (2006). For studies maintaining that the evidence cannot rule out deleterious human impacts on the megafauna, see Barnosky, Koch, Feranec, et al. (2004); Burney and Flannery (2005); Faitha and Surovell (2009); Steadman, Martin, MacPhee, et al. (2005).

6. For studies advocating climate change as the extinction mechanism, see Guthrie (1984, 2003, 2006); Graham and Lundelius (1984); Grayson and Meltzer (2003). For studies arguing that the evidence appears inconsistent with human overkill, see Guthrie (2004); Jones, Porcasi, Erlandson, et al. (2008).

7. The 2 percent figure comes from noting that early Paleolithic technologies would most likely have supported a human population that was less than 1 inhabitant per square kilometer. Given that the world's land area is about 149 million square kilometers (which includes Polar regions and deserts), and the human population in 2010 is about 6.8 billion, 2 percent of 6.8 billion is 136 million, which gives us a little less than 1 inhabitant per square kilometer (136 million people divided by 149 million square kilometers). The land mass and population figures can be found at https://www.cia.gov/library/publications/the-world-factbook/geos/XX.html.

8. We concentrate on agriculture rather than pastoral (herding animals) because societies are physically more permanent in agriculture. Permanent settlements allow the acquisition of societal capital that is not easily transported; capital such as forges, tools, pottery wheels, and looms that are implements of the beginnings of civilization.

9. These data and an analysis of the effects of parasitic diseases on contemporary populations come from Eppig, Fincher, and Thornhill (2010). Among their findings is that: "From an energetic standpoint, a developing human will have difficulty building a brain and fighting off infectious diseases at the same time, as both are very metabolically costly tasks" (p. 1).

10. Innate immunities are created by random genetic mutations. Possessing a genetic variation in an environment that does not give humans an evolutionary advantage will result in the variation having a low level of frequency in the population. In an environment where the occurrence of mortal diseases gives the possession of particular genetic allele an evolutionary advantage, the frequency of the allele will increase in the (absolutely smaller) population.

11. Other regions (Indus River Valley and China) also might have emerged at that time or even earlier, but neither primacy nor the exact chronology is important for our purposes; what are important are the cycles and the human adaptation to permanent settlement.

12. We emphasize Paleolithic peoples here. Historic and current-day hunter-gatherer societies almost certainly had cultural and genetic interactions with peoples who had descended from ancestors that were agriculturalists. There is no historic line of humanity that is descended solely from a long line of hunter-gatherers.

13. Mathematical purists may object that no positive rate of growth may be maintained forever because you eventually run into ridiculous situations—an infinite number of people per square meter, or the human population expanding so rapidly the increase in human numbers exceeds the speed of light are among our favorites—but the planet itself is not going to last forever. If the rate of population growth is 0.00001 percent per year, then population doubles once every 6.9 million years or so. But why object? Since planning for 100,000 years in the future is absurd; planning for millions of years in the future is surreal.

Chapter 3

1. We begin with an exchange economy rather than a less-developed subsistence economy because we can (1) put in observable economic phenomena (wages, prices, capital, and markets) and (2) our explanation of growth depends on specialization and trade.

2. While our book was in production, a book by Matt Ridley (2010) came out. In it Ridley argues that exchange led to specialization and influenced the physical and cultural evolution of humanity. His work and its emphasis on the benefits of increased population on specialization and enhanced productivity echo our analysis. Ridley's book, *The Rational Optimist,* may be somewhat too optimistic and not rational enough because it slights the impact of the increasing biomass on the transmission of diseases. Regardless, Ridley's book is a singular contribution.

3. There is a basic economic principle here too—there are always alternatives. Or put more idiomatically, "there is more than one way to skin a cat."

4. A "closed economy" simply means that we only deal with one economy; this is for simplification alone. The assumption does not affect the analysis.

5. Empirically, increased market size and increased productivity are found in the research of Boserup (1965, 1981); Coelho and Diagle (1982); Mak and Walton (1972); North (1968); Stigler (1951). This list is not exhaustive; for a more general treatment, see Barnett and Morse (1963); Simon (1989).

6. For discussion of the listed zoonotic infections, see, respectively, Brachman (1976) and Finch (1984); Geist (1978), Ledger (1976), and Finch (1984); Borts and Hendricks; (1976) and Ganguly (1984); Waldman (1984b) and Schwebach (1980); Benenson (1976b), Kluge (1984), and Schwebach (1980); Ellinghausen and Top (1976); Hattwick (1976); Overturf and Mathies (1976); Spaeth (1976); Mathies and MacDonald (1976); Feldman (1976). For discussion of the listed non-zoonotic infections, see, respectively, Brunell (1976a); Benenson (1976a); Wilson and Hayes (1973); MacDonald (1976); Mogabgab (1976); Contacos and Coatney (1976) and Khakoo (1984); Kim-Farley (1993); Brunell (1976b); Waldman (1984a); Top, Johnson, and Wehrle (1976); Top (1976); Waldman (1984c).

7. The outbreak of AIDS (acquired immune deficiency syndrome) in the 1980s and of the ebola virus in Zaire in 1995 are relevant and tragic examples of "new" diseases (Alessandri 1984).

8. In developing a more complete model for morbidity or for mortality, we envision a relationship where morbidity or mortality depends on (1) human density per square mile, (2) various environmental and biological variables, (3) various cultural variables, and (4) various economic variables. In this more complete model, an increase in density,

all other factors constant, yields an increase in morbidity or in mortality. For a general history of bacteriology, see Miles (1983).

9. Steinmann (1984) also has a model of economic growth and demographic change that, although it does not incorporate morbidity, does offer a number of interesting insights, particularly in simulations and modeling.

10. There are some major exceptions to this generalization, with the smallpox virus probably being the historically most important. This virus can be infectious for weeks on textiles and decaying bodies.

11. For implicit critiques of Fogel, see Livi-Bacci (1991); Meeker (1972, 1974, 1976).

12. For a sampling of the literature on the decline in heights of these birth cohorts, see Komlos (1987, 1992, 1996), Komlos and Coclanis (1997); Margo and Steckel (1983); Murray (1997); Steckel and Haurin (1994).

13. Explicit empirical support for this argument is problematic because explicit evidence on the spread of diseases during the first half of the nineteenth century does not exist; scientific evidence of the existence of most infectious parasitic diseases did not begin to appear until the last couple decades of the nineteenth century. As a result, direct evidence on the incidence and prevalence of these diseases is not available for the period of the Antebellum Puzzle; only implicit and indirect evidence is available to support our argument.

Chapter 4

1. For an example of model building applied to historical choices, see Gemery and Hogendorn (1974) who develop a model to explain the slave trade to the New World.

2. In the long run, the competitive mechanism forces firms to produce at the least cost, and these same competitive mechanisms, operating in the markets for agricultural output, force the price down so that over time the result of a lower cost production method is passed on to the consumer. This is the reason why economists presumptively favor competition and competitive markets.

3. We emphasize that the comparisons and choices do not have to be made consciously by picking the most profitable source of labor. Choices could be made for entirely non-economic reasons, but in a world of scarcity, those firms that choose least-cost techniques (for whatever reasons) will be the most likely to survive. Surviving firms are the ones most likely to be emulated. For an extended discussion on nonconscious profit-seeking behavior, see Alchian (1950).

4. The interest rate also can be seen as a measure of the premium placed on the present; interest rates indicate how much "more" borrowers are willing to pay so they can acquire an asset now and how much "more" lenders require to forgo the use of their capital in the present. The interest rate is the amount by which the future is discounted.

5. The financial calculations are expressed in the formula:

$$PV = \sum_{1}^{n} \left(\frac{Y_n}{(1+i)^n} \right),$$

where PV is the (discounted) present value, Y equals the net revenues the asset generates per year over each of the n years, and i is the market rate of interest. These calculations are common in the financial and economics literature. Galenson (1981a, pp. 152, 266) uses a variation of this formula to estimate the present values of slaves and servants in colonial America.

6. In this example, the servant is unprofitable. An investment in a servant returns £9.48 per £10 invested, or 94.8 percent of the initial investment in the servant, while an investment in a slave yields 106.4 percent of the initial investment in the slave (£21.28/£20.0 × 100 percent). Remember, these calculations all involve market payments to the capital invested in labor are discounted by 10 percent; the return to slave capital (in this example) is greater than the hypothesized market rate of 10 percent, while an investment in an indentured servant yields a return less than the market rate of 10 percent.

7. Bean (1975, pp. 74–78; 161–212) has an extensive discussion of how he constructed these data. The data are adjusted for sale in Jamaica; the price of slaves in what became the United States was £1.42 higher than the Jamaica price (Bean 1975, p. 179). Bean did not have extensive information on the age and sex ratios of the slave cargo; consequently, he only adjusted slave prices for males (males sold at a higher price than females) where information was available on the sex ratios of the slaves (Bean 1975, p. 132). Note that the last time period reported by Bean and shown in table 4.1 and figure 4.1 contains only three years (1773 to 1775).

8. Galenson (1981a, b, 1984, 1989, 1991, 1996) and Grubb (1985, 1988, 1992a, b, 1994, 2000, 2001) have written extensively on the economics and institutions of the trade in indentured servants. Also see Grubb and Stitt (1994). This paragraph is based on these studies.

9. Grubb (2000, p. 98) calculates that the costs of transporting servants (or paying passengers, or convicts) were the same and about £8.5 per person for most of the eighteenth century. Galenson (1981a, pp. 97–106) argues that the market for shipping servants was competitive and that the price per passenger was between £5 and £10. Both Grubb's and Galenson's estimates include normal returns to capital and adjust for losses during voyages.

10. We thank Farley Grubb for providing us with this information.

11. We thank John Komlos for suggesting to us that our servant price should take into account "freedom dues." Omission of freedom dues would have made servants more attractive relative to slaves; consequently, omitting freedom dues would bias the case against slavery. There is little explicit evidence on the value of freedom dues. The £1 amount was suggested to us by Komlos.

12. In table 4.1, which reproduces Bean's (1975) price data, the weighted average of the slave prices post-1752 is £37. But since, under an assumption of equal productivity of servants and slaves, we ultimately conclude that slaves would have been uneconomic and not employed in colonial America, we chose not to use the £37 price because at higher slave prices slaves are always less profitable. Likewise using a higher servant price of £12 would skew the choice of labor away from servants because at a higher servant price servants will become less profitable.

13. The symbol E_0 represents the expected working life of either type of labor. All servants have an expected working life of five years ($E_0 = 5$); this means that a servant is presumed to survive his indentureship (five years).

14. The impact of morbidity on labor may or may not be correlated with mortality (see Riley 1987, 1993). One group of people can have a higher mortality rate than another

group and still be healthier and potentially more productive (but for a shorter life) in a particular region or during a particular season.

15. The changed environment was irreversible at the time given the state of science and medicine in the sixteenth through nineteenth centuries. For more on path dependency, see David (1985).

16. For examples of this argument in the literature, see Beckles and Downes (1987); Galenson (1991); Grubb (1992a, b).

17. Location is a proxy for the ecological compatibility between the disease-causing organisms (microparasites) and the resources available to them at a specific site. For example, an organism that requires a mosquito to survive will not survive in arctic or desert regions.

Chapter 5

1. This chapter is a significantly revised version of Coelho and McGuire (1997), and is reprinted with permission.

2. While writing this book, we discovered that Stanley Engerman long ago remarked on the idea that biological and epidemiological differences might explain the different regional labor outcomes (at least for the Caribbean) in colonial America. As Engerman (1976b, p. 263) remarked, "That the mortality experience of blacks and whites apparently differed in these [Caribbean] areas suggests the existence of a different set of immunities to diseases in tropical areas—itself a reasonable explanation for differences in racial patterns of settlement which have been analysed in more blatantly racial terms" in Curtin (1968) and in a similar discussion in Wood (1974). Engerman (1976b), however, did not examine the issue any further.

3. Recent scientific evidence indicates that the first Americans migrated from Siberia in a single wave and likely traveled along the near-shore coastal waters south of the Land Bridge, migrating inland along their way south. See Goebel, Waters, and O'Rourke (2008); Wang, Lewis, Jakobsson, et al. (2007).

4. Endemic diseases are frequently termed childhood diseases because unexposed potions of the populations are the ones most affected by them. The modifier "childhood" when referring to diseases that are endemic in the adult population, but not in children, creates intellectual dissonance. Venereal diseases and alcoholism may be endemic to a population, but they typically do not affect children because children do not engage in behaviors that facilitate their transmission. So always equating endemic diseases and childhood diseases may lead to difficulties.

5. For a sampling of the literature on exposure to Old World diseases in the New World tropics, see Crosby (1972, 1986, 1993a, b), Dobyns (1983); Guerra (1988); Kiple (1984, 1993); McNeill (1976); Stannard (1989, 1993).

6. For an introduction to the historiography of the deates over the pre-Columbian population, see Mann (2002, 2005). For some informative estimates of the population of Amazonia before Contact, see Heckenberger, Russell, Fausto, et al. (2008); Neves, Petersen, Bartone, and Da Silva (2004).

7. For a sampling of the "virgin soil" literature, see Cook (1998); Crosby (1972); Dobyns (1983); McNeill (1976); Stannard (1989).

8. For studies of Native American slavery, see Childs (1940); Gallay (2002); Lauber (1913).

9. See Axtell (1981, especially ch. 7). For a comprehensive view of the change from hunting-gathering to agriculture, see Boserup (1966).

10. An account of a smallpox epidemic that in 1795 afflicted a small village in Japan, which may have been a virgin population, produced a morbidity rate of 85.7 percent and a case mortality rate of 38.3 percent; the crude death rate for this episode would be 328 per thousand (Fenner, Henderson, Arita, et al. 1988, p. 227).

11. Chapter 6 contains more detailed discussion of yellow fever that documents its spread in the American South and the disparate impact it had on individuals with different ancestral heritages.

12. At the end of five years, out of an initial cohort of 100,000, only 40,960 will be left alive if the death rate is 200 per thousand per year. The British sent 20,000 troops—1/5 of 100,000—and after five years 8,000—1/5 of 40,000—had not died from malaria or yellow fever, implying a death rate of about 200 per thousand per year from the diseases.

13. There is other biological evidence that supports the innate immunity hypothesis. Engelhard (1994, p. 60) reports that Adrian Hill "has found evidence that in humans susceptibility to malaria varies with the expression of certain Class I MHC molecules. Those forms of Class I MHC molecules that seem to confer the greatest resistance are especially common among people living where malaria is widespread, as natural selection would indicate."

14. For more complete discussion of the susceptibility of Europeans and Africans to these diseases in the Americas, see Cooper and Kiple (1993); Kiple (1984, 1993); Kiple and Higgins (1992); Kiple and King (1981).

15. The calculation of these values is detailed in chapter 4. The specific value for servants is reported in table A.5, fourth row, in appendix A. The calculations are fairly robust to modest variations in the parameters (contract lengths, interest rates, and prices), as indicated by a comparison of the various estimates contained in tables A.1 through A.5 in appendix A.

16. Chapter 6 contains more detailed discussion of malaria that examines (1) how malaria spread in the American South, (2) the relative resistance of individuals of different ancestral heritages to it, (3) the disparate impact it had on people of different ancestral heritages, and (4) the debilitating health effects of malaria.

17. Curtin's (1989) data are spread over a series of tables (tables A11–A16, pp. 174–80). The tables list the causes of morbidity and mortality for different spans of years for specific locations in the British West Indies and in the British West Indies in general. For example, table A11 is for the years 1859 to 1867; table A16 is for the years 1909 to 1916. The diagnosis for malaria was, at best, imperfect before the 1880s, when Alphonse Laveran first identified the plasmodia in the blood stream of an infected human. Consequently, the data for the years prior to 1900 (when the discoveries of Laveran had been fully disseminated) might be less than accurate concerning the incidence of malaria. To get the approximation for the malarial case mortality rate, we divided the mortality rate by the morbidity rate for each observation for malaria reported in tables A11 through A16. (Table A15 has two data points for the years 1895 to 1904, one for Jamaica and one for Barbados.) For the years in which the malaria category does not exist, we combined the categories "Other continued fevers" and "Paroxysmal fevers" and calculated a case mortality rate from these data. The simple mean of these calculations is 1.58 percent.

18. Chapter 6 contains more detailed discussion of hookworm that examines (1) how hookworm spread in the American South, (2) the relative resistance of individuals of different ancestral heritages to it, (3) the disparate impact it had on people of different ancestral heritages, and (4) the debilitating health effects of hookworm.

Chapter 6

1. This chapter is a greatly expanded and revised version of Coelho and McGuire (1999), and is reprinted with permission. Some findings reported in the chapter are also contained in Coelho and McGuire (2000, 2006).

2. A biography of James Augustine Healy, the first African-American to be ordained a Roman Catholic priest and the first to be ordained a Catholic Bishop, can be found at BlackPast.org and is available at http://www.blackpast.org/?q=aah/healy-bishop-james-augustine-1830-1900.

3. The discussion of diseases and antebellum slavery has implications for understanding American economic growth during the nineteenth century as well, a topic examined empirically in chapter 7.

4. For the initial studies among economic historians promoting the use of heights as a proxy for net nutrition, see Engerman (1976a); Fogel and Engerman (1979); Steckel (1979); Trussell and Steckel (1978).

5. See the findings on the time profile of slave heights in Margo and Steckel (1982, pp. 521–22, 526–27); Steckel (1979, p. 377; 1995b, p. 5 and figs. 1–5). Especially compare the two sets of time profile findings in Margo and Steckel (1982, pp. 521–22, 526–27) to each other.

6. The demand for slave imports was at its all time high after the Revolutionary War because (1) the war had depleted slave stocks as the British left the United States with American slaves who had either been confiscated or emancipated, (2) the increase in cotton production provided another crop that could be profitably grown with slaves, and (3) virgin lands in the West allowed for expansion of the slave economy provided slaves could be acquired.

7. Most slaves imported into the United States (or what became the United States) in the post–Revolutionary War period prior to the 1808 ban were African born and bred. Creole slaves from the British West Indies (those born there) were too valuable to send to the United States because of their skills in sugar and other tropical agriculture, and because they had had a lifetime of exposure to the pathogens abundant in the tropics of the New World (unlike any Africans that would have replaced them). Consequently, there were no "seasoning" costs (high rates of morbidity and mortality) to contend with when Creole slaves were kept in their birth places. There were transshipments of African-born slaves who were landed in the Caribbean and then shipped to the North American mainland. For a discussion of the origins of slaves imported into the North America mainland in 1783 to 1810, see McMillin (2004, ch. 3). For a discussion of the transshipment of African slaves through the Caribbean to the North American mainland, see O'Malley (2009).

8. The negative influence of the importation of African-born slaves on mean American slave heights during this period is explicitly recognized in parts of the anthropometric literature. See Margo and Steckel (1982, p. 534, fn. 3); Steckel (1979, p. 378; 1995b, p. 6; 1995c, pp. 1930–31).

9. The hypothesis that diseases differentially affected the southern states is not original to us; it has a long and illustrious pedigree. For a good review of the historical literature up to the date of its publication, see Breeden (1988). Krieger (2005) has a fairly comprehensive bibliography on the use of "race" in scientific and medical research.

10. While yellow fever also had disparate effects on people of different ancestral heritages, it was not endemic in the plantation South. And because it was an urban disease in the South, yellow fever had little impact on the southern *plantation* economy.

11. Corn soaked in an alkaline solution makes the niacin in it available to humans who consume it. The "nixtamalization" of corn (the treatment of corn in limewater or another alkaline solution to release niacin) is the reason that aboriginal Mesoamericans did not suffer from pellagra; this process was not used in the American South in the nineteenth century.

12. When the International Health Board, (re)surveyed southern counties for hookworm infection in the early 1920s, it examined several hundred individuals in each of sixty counties for hookworm and, secondarily, for other parasites. Of the surviving individual-level records for three counties (Leslie county, Kentucky; Marion county, South Carolina; and Whitley county, Kentucky) that we examined, there were usable records for 2,088 individuals, 43.6 percent of who tested positive for hookworm, 21.3 percent tested positive for *Ascaris*, and 6.03 percent tested positive for *Trichuris* ("Resurveys, Southern States" 1920–23). *Hymenolepis nana* (dwarf tapeworm) and *Strongyloides stercoralis* (threadworm) also were likely present in the antebellum South. But dwarf tapeworm is generally inconsequential in humans and threadworm most likely had a very low prevalence rate in the antebellum South.

13. Information on *Ascaris* is available at http://emedicine.medscape.com/article/788398-overview; http://www.nlm.nih.gov/medlineplus/ency/article/000628.htm; http://www.merck.com/mmhe/sec17/ch196/ch196d.html. Information on *Trichuris* is available at http://emedicine.medscape.com/article/788570-overview; http://www.nlm.nih.gov/medlineplus/ency/article/001364.htm; http://www.merck.com/mmhe/sec17/ch196/ch196t.html.

14. There is a considerable debate about slave living standards. For starters, see Fogel and Engerman (1974a, b), and in opposition to them, David, Gutman, Sutch, et al. (1976).

15. While there are nonhuman forms of hookworm and malaria—for example, there is canine hookworm and avian malaria—and humans can be infected with them, such infections are very rare compared to the human forms of these diseases. This is as expected; an organism (pathogen) that has evolved and is adapted to a specific environment will rarely thrive in another. However, when pathogens do successfully jump species, they can spread rapidly and become epidemic.

16. In addition, autoreinfection of hookworm can occur under circumstances of poor hygiene (Revista de la Sociedad Argentina de Biología 1925, p. 1263).

17. See Adams, Stephenson, Latham, and Kinoti (1994); Latham, Stephenson, Hall, et al. (1983); Latham, Stephenson, Kurz, and Kinoti (1990); Stephenson, Latham, Adams, et al. (1992, 1993a, b); Stephenson, Latham, Kinoti, et al. (1990); Stephenson, Latham, Kurz, et al. (1985a, b, 1986, 1989); Stephenson, Latham, Kurz, and Kinoti (1989); Stoltzfus, Albonico, and Tielsch (1997); Stoltzfus, Chwaya, and Tielsch (1997).

18. See Adams, Stephenson, Latham, and Kinoti (1994); Latham, Stephenson, Kurz, and Kinoti (1990); Stephenson, Latham, Adams, et al. (1992, 1993a, b); Stephenson, Latham, Kinoti, et al. (1990); Stephenson, Latham, Kurz, et al. (1985a, b, 1986, 1989); Stephenson, Latham, Kurz, and Kinoti (1989).

19. For studies of the relationship between hookworm and cognitive development, see Bleakley (2003, 2007, 2009); Hotez and Pritchard (1995); Kelley (1917); Myers (1920); Sakti, Nokes, Hertanto, et al. (1999); Smillie and Spencer (1926); Stephenson (2001); Stiles (1915); Strong (1916); Waite and Nielson (1919). For studies of the relationship between cognitive development and other helminthic infections (*Ascaris* or *Trichuris*) in contemporary populations, see Boivin and Giordani (1993); Nokes, Cooper, Robinson, and Bundy (1991); Nokes, Grantham-McGregor, Sawyer, et al. (1992); Simeon, Grantham-McGregor, Callender, and Wong (1995). The objective of these latter studies is to measure the influence of various anthelminthic treatments on improving the cognitive functions (and physical development) of infected children; the effectiveness of such treatments on improving cognition has been debated. See Dickson, Awasthi, Williamson, et al. (2000) and the critical comments on their study in Bhargava (2000); Bundy and Peto (2000); Cooper (2000); Michael (2000); Savioli, Neira, Albonico et al. (2000). See also the reply in Garner, Dickson, Demellweek, et al. (2000), and see Miguel and Kremer (2004). Eppig, Fincher, and Thornhill (2010) examine the effects of parasitization, in general, finding a significant correlation between increased parasitic stress and decreased measures of intelligence across a large number of contemporary populations.

20. The prevailing view today among specialists in obstetrical and gynecological research is that the evidence of any relationship between physical activity and work, and the incidence of preterm birth and low birth weight is inconclusive (see Berkowitz and Papiernik 1993, pp. 429–30, 433–34; Simpson 1993).

21. For studies indicating the deleterious consequences of hookworm infections among Africans, see Kilama (1990); Lwambo, Bundy, and Medley (1992); Ratard, Kouemeni, Ekanibessala, and Ndamkou (1992); Stephenson, Latham, Adams, et al. (1993a, b).

22. For historical studies indicating nontrivial hookworm stunting, see Dock and Bass (1910); Smillie and Augustine (1926); Strong (1916). For contemporary studies that suggest nontrivial hookworm stunting, see Adams, Stephenson, Latham, and Kinoti (1994); Latham, Stephenson, Hall, et al. (1983); Latham, Stephenson, Kurz, and Kinoti (1990); Stephenson, Latham, Adams, et al. (1992, 1993b); Stephenson, Latham, Kinoti, et al. (1990); Stephenson, Latham, Kurz, et al. (1985b, 1989); Stephenson, Latham, Kurz, and Kinoti (1989).

23. Steckel (2000) cites a personal telephone conversation with the lead author of the hookworm treatment study (Stoltzfus, Albonico, Tielsch, et al. 1997) to corroborate that hookworm infection causes only about 0.3 centimeter of stunting. Be that as it may, we are aware of no hookworm study that comes to such a conclusion nor do we know of any reputable hookworm authority who claims such a small amount of stunting if children faced an infancy and childhood of hookworm exposure and infection. Moreover, in our own personal correspondence with the same author on February 14, 2011, Rebecca J. Stoltzfus stated: "I very much agree with your interpretation. The effect that we measured can only be interpreted as the short-term effect of an intervention, delivered well after the majority of stunting takes place. To infer that it equals the cumulative effect of hookworm infection throughout childhood is a serious misinterpretation."

24. For the relationship of age to infection, see Keymer and Pagel (1990, pp. 187–91). For information on immunology, see Behnke (1991). For the empirical and theoretical evidence on acquired immunities, see Anderson and May (1991, pp. 451–65).

25. In chapter 7, we provide detailed empirical evidence on the nineteenth-century transport improvements that played a critical role in economic growth and the spread of diseases.

26. Steckel (1992) argues that these phenomena were the results of slaveowners systematically providing poor diets to pregnant slaves, infants, and young children; as we argued above, for this to make economic sense all of a number of stringent assumptions has to be met. Common sense and Occam's razor argue in favor of our explanation.

27. Also see Carrion (1994) who indicates that a region known to harbor malaria in nineteenth-century Spain was likely to have shorter people.

28. For a discussion of slavery in insect societies, see Wilson (1975, pp. 368–73).

Chapter 7

1. United States Census Bureau website (Mean Center of Population for the United States: 1790 to 2000). Aboriginal Americans were not considered part of the United States and not represented in much of the demographic data cited herein. In 1924, all Native Americans were granted American citizenship; before that individual state laws determined their legal status.

2. Carter, Gartner, Haines, et al. (2006, vol. 1, series Aa3843, pp. 1–254; series Aa4045, pp. 1–264; series Aa5195, pp. 1–318; series Aa5406, pp. 1–327; series Aa6100, pp. 1–359).

3. These travel times are from Paullin (1932, plates 138A, B, C), as cited in Atack and Passell (1994, figs. 6.1, 6.4, 6.8, pp. 145, 152, 161, respectively).

4. The inclusion of a particular disease into one of the four groups in certain cases involved judgments based on the primary characteristics, mode of transmission, and primary symptoms of the disease. As a result, typhus was classified as a warm-weather fever while typhoid (enteric) fever was classified as a gastrointestinal tract disease. Likewise, dirt eating was classified as an intestinal parasite/worm disease, since it has been identified as a possible symptom of iron-deficiency anemia secondary to hookworm disease.

5. All infant mortality rates for 1850 should be viewed with caution. As noted in appendix C, the census mortality schedules severely underenumerated infant deaths especially in the earliest of the census years during 1850 to 1900. Consequently, more accurate would be to use 1860 as the beginning date for examining any trends in infant mortality.

6. The black mortality rates are calculated from "negro" deaths reported in each census, except for the 1890 rates, which are calculated from "colored" deaths, and include negroes, Chinese, Japanese, and civilized Indians. The 1890 census reported only "colored" deaths. See appendix C for more details.

7. Determining the regional mortality rates for the population and the eight different cohorts for all causes and the four categories of diseases for 1850 to 1900 consisted of the calculation of forty-five series of mortality rates. Only a third of the forty-five are shown in the figures in this chapter. We will provide readers of this book the results and figures for the other regional mortality series on request.

8. The data in table 7.6 are not standardized for ethnic background (white/black), nativity of parents (native/foreign born), or urban/rural location (except Baltimore). For other treatments of infant mortality in the nineteenth century, see Haines (1977); Haines and Anderson (1988); Haines and Preston (1984); Preston and Haines (1991).

9. It is true that because the infant mortality data in table 7.6 are not completely standardized, it is conceivable that some more standardization could show falling mortality rates. But note that table C.14 in appendix C also presents white and black infant (and young children) mortality rates for 1880, which when combined with the infant mortality rates for all infants for 1850 to 1900 still suggest rising trends through circa 1890 (see table C.14 in appendix C).

Chapter 8

1. In the biological literature, there is the 50 generation rule; in a freely mating society it takes 50 generations or so for a mutant genetic allele that provides a significant probability of breeding success to embed itself in more than a majority of the population (Lumsden and Wilson 1981). Before the nineteenth century, a human generation was approximately 20 years, thus the thousand-year rule of thumb.

2. For a more complete description and analyses of the pre-historic disease environment and an introduction to the co-evolution of diseases and humanity, see the works of Cohen (1977, 1989); Diamond (1997, 2005); Mann (2002, 2005); McNeill (1976).

3. In *The Birth of the Modern*, Paul Johnson (1991) narrows the period when the concept of progress manifested itself to the decade and a half from 1815 to 1830. He believes that technological changes were instrumental in the origins of modernity. His arguments for focusing on that fifteen-year period are somewhat convincing, our reservations are that he identifies technology as the causal agent; we think it was the accelerating rate of growth of economic output. It may be a fine point, but as we have emphasized elsewhere in this book technological change is neither necessary nor sufficient to ensure economic growth.

4. The sickle cell trait is a random mutation that is estimated to occur spontaneously once in every 100,000 births. In some tropical West African populations, the sickle cell trait occurs in more than 30 percent of the people.

5. Influenza is the major exception. Its reservoirs are in animal populations as indicated by the names swine flu and avian flu.

6. The first paper published identifying hookworm disease in the Alpine tunnel workers was published in 1880.

7. Societies whose birth rates do not exceed their death rates will diminish and eventually vanish or, as discussed in chapter 2, revert to more primitive and less densely settled societies. Either way they will cease being societies with large urban components (civilizations). A more accurate statement would be that societies whose birth rates do not exceed their death rates will not long endure.

References

Acemoglu, Daron, and Simon Johnson. 2004. Unbundling institutions. *Journal of Political Economy* 113: 949–95.

Acemoglu, Daron, Simon Johnson, and James A. Robinson. 2001. The Colonial origins of comparative development: An empirical investigation. *American Economic Review* 91: 1369–1401.

Acemoglu, Daron, Simon Johnson, and James A. Robinson. 2002. Reversal of fortune: Geography and institutions in the making of the modern world income distribution. *Quarterly Journal of Economics* 117: 1231–94.

Acemoglu, Daron, Simon Johnson, and James A. Robinson. 2005. The rise of Europe: Atlantic trade, institutional change and economic growth. *American Economic Review* 95: 546–79.

Adams, Elizabeth J., Lani S. Stephenson, Michael C. Latham, and Stephen N. Kinoti. 1994. Physical activity and growth of Kenyan school children with hookworm, *Trichuris trichiura* and *Ascaris lumbricoides* infections are improved after treatment with Albendazole. *Journal of Nutrition* 124: 1199–1206.

Alchian, Armen A. 1950. Uncertainty, evolution, and economic theory. *Journal of Political Economy* 58 (3): 211–21.

Allison, A. C. 1961. Genetic factors in resistance to malaria. *Annals of the New York Academy of Sciences* 91: 710–29.

Anderson, Roy M., and M. May Robert. 1991. *Infectious Diseases of Humans: Dynamics and Control*. Oxford: Oxford University Press.

Atack, Jeremy, and Peter Passell. 1994. *A New Economic View of American History*, 2nd ed. New York: Norton.

Axtell, James. 1981. *The European and the Indian: Essays in the Ethnohistory of Colonial North America*. New York: Oxford University Press.

Barnett, Harold I., and Chandler Morse. 1963. *Scarcity and Growth*. Baltimore: Johns Hopkins University Press.

Barnosky, Anthony D., Paul L. Koch, Robert S. Feranec, Scott L. Wing, and Alan B. Shabel. 2004. Assessing the causes of late Pleistocene extinctions on the continents. *Science* 306 (70): 70–75.

Bauer, Peter. 1991. *The Development Frontier: Essays in Applied Economics*. Cambridge: Harvard University Press.

Bean, Richard Nelson. 1975. *The British Trans-Atlantic Slave Trade, 1650–1775*. New York: Arno Press.

Beckles, Hilary McD., and Andrew Downes. 1987. The economics of transition to the black labor system in Barbados, 1630–1680. *Journal of Interdisciplinary History* 18 (2): 225–47.

Behnke, J. M. 1991. Immunology. In H. M. Gilles and P. A. J. Ball, eds., *Human Parasitic Diseases*. Vol. 4: *Hookworm Infections*. Amsterdam: Elsevier: 93–155.

Benenson, Abram S. 1976a. Cholera. In Franklin H. Top Sr. and Paul F. Wehrle, eds., *Communicable and Infectious Diseases*, 8th ed. St. Louis: Mosby, 174–83.

Benenson, Abram S. 1976b. Plague. In Franklin H. Top Sr. and Paul F. Wehrle, eds., *Communicable and Infectious Diseases*, 8th ed. St. Louis: Mosby, 502–507.

Berkowitz, Gertrud S., and Emile Papiernik. 1993. Epidemiology of preterm birth. *Epidemiologic Reviews* 15: 414–43.

Bhargava, Alok. 2000. Letters—Treatment for intestinal helminth infection. Conclusions should have been based on broader considerations. *British Medical Journal* 321 (7270) (November 11): 1225.

Bishop, Jerry E. 1993. Strands of time. *Wall Street Journal*, September 10: A1, A8.

Black, Francis L. 1992. Why did they die. *Science* 258 (11): 1739–40.

Black, Francis L. 2004. Disease susceptibility among New World peoples. In Francisco M. Salzano and A. Magdalena Hurtado, eds., *Lost Paradises and the Ethics of Research and Publication*. New York: Oxford University Press, 146–63.

Blanton, Wyndham B. 1930. Epidemic diseases. In Wyndham B. Blanton, ed., *Medicine in Virginia in the Seventeenth Century*. Richmond, VA: William Byrd Press, 32–77.

Blanton, Wyndham B. 1957. Epidemics, real and imaginary, and other factors influencing seventeenth century Virginia's population. *Bulletin of the History of Medicine* 31: 454–62.

Blaugh, Mark. 1997. *Economic Theory in Retrospect*, 5th ed. New York: Cambridge University Press.

Bleakley, Hoyt. 2003. Disease and development. *Journal of the European Economic Association* 1 (2–3): 376–86.

Bleakley, Hoyt. 2007. Disease and development: Evidence from hookworm eradication in the American South. *Quarterly Journal of Economics* 122 (1): 73–117.

Bleakley, Hoyt. 2009. Economic effects of childhood exposure to tropical disease. *American Economic Review: Papers and Proceedings* 99 (2): 218–23.

Bodenhorn, Howard. 1997. A most wretched class: Height, health and nutrition of free blacks in Antebellum Virginia. Unpublished manuscript. Lafayette College.

Boivin, Michael J., and Bruno Giordani. 1993. Improvements in cognitive performance for schoolchildren in Zaire, Africa, following an iron supplement and treatment for intestinal parasites. *Journal of Pediatric Psychology* 18 (2): 249–64.

Borah, Woodrow Wilson, and Sherburne F. Cook. 1971–79. *Essays in Population History: Mexico and the Caribbean*. 3 vols. Berkeley: University of California Press.

Borts, Irving H., and Stanley L. Hendricks. 1976. Brucellosis. In Franklin H. Top Sr. and Paul F. Wehrle, eds., *Communicable and Infectious Diseases*, 8th ed. St. Louis: Mosby, 143–53.

Boserup, Ester. 1966. *The Conditions of Agricultural Growth: The Economics of Agrarian Change under Population Pressure*. Chicago: Aldine.

Boserup, Ester. 1981. *Population and Technological Change*. Chicago: University of Chicago Press.

Brabin, B. J. 1983. An analysis of malaria in pregnancy in Africa. *Bulletin of the World Health Organization* 61: 1005–16.

Brabin, B. J. 1991. *The Risks and Severity of Malaria in Pregnant Women*. Special Programme for Research and Training in Tropical Diseases/Applied Field Research in Malaria. Report No. 1. Geneva: World Health Organization.

Brachman, Philip S. 1976. Anthrax. In Franklin H. Top Sr. and Paul F. Wehrle, eds., *Communicable and Infectious Diseases*, 8th ed. St. Louis: Mosby, 137–42.

Breeden, James O. 1988. Disease as a factor in southern distinctiveness. In Todd L. Savitt and James Harvey Young, eds., *Disease and Distinctiveness in the American South*. Knoxville: University of Tennessee Press, 1–28.

Brinkley, Garland L. 1995. The economic impact of disease in the American South, 1860–1840. *Journal of Economic History* 55 (2): 371–73.

Brinkley, Garland L. 1997. The decline in southern agricultural output, 1860–1880. *Journal of Economic History* 57 (1): 116–38.

Brinkley, Garland Lee. 1994. *The Economic Impact of Disease in the American South, 1860–1840*. PhD dissertation. University of California, Davis.

Brooker, Simon, Peter J. Hotez, and Donald A. P. Bundy. 2008. Hookworm-related anaemia among pregnant women: A systematic review. *PLoS Neglected Tropical Diseases* 2 (9): e291. doi:10.1371/journal.pntd.0000291: 1–9. http://www.plosntds.org/article/info%3Adoi%2F10.1371%2Fjournal.pntd.0000291.

Brooks, Frances J. 1993. Revising the conquest of Mexico: Smallpox, sources, and populations. *Journal of Interdisciplinary History* 24 (1): 1–29.

Bruce-Chwatt, Leonard Jan. 1980. *Essential Malariology*. London: Heinemann Medical.

Bruce-Chwatt, Leonard Jan., and Julian de Zulueta. 1980. *The Rise and Fall of Malaria in Europe: A Historico-Epidemiological Study*. London: Oxford University Press.

Brunell, Philip A. 1976a. Chicken pox. In Franklin H. Top Sr. and Paul F. Wehrle, eds., *Communicable and Infectious Diseases*, 8th ed. St. Louis: Mosby, 165–73.

Brunell, Philip A. 1976b. Mumps. In Franklin H. Top Sr. and Paul F. Wehrle, eds., *Communicable and Infectious Diseases*, 8th ed. St. Louis: Mosby, 461–66.

Buikstra, Jane E. 1993. Diseases of the pre-Columbian Americans. In Kenneth F. Kiple, ed., *The Cambridge World History of Human Disease*. New York: Cambridge University Press, 305–16.

Bundy, Donald, Michel Kremer, Hoyt Bleakley, Matthew Jukes, and Edward Miguel. 2009. Deworming and development: Asking the right questions, asking the questions right. *PLoS Neglected Tropical Diseases* 3 (1):e362. doi:10.1371/journal.pntd.0000362: 1–3. http://www.plosntds.org/article/info%3Adoi%2F10.1371%2Fjournal.pntd.0000362.

Bundy, Donald, and Richard Peto. 2000. Letters—Treatment for intestinal helminth infection. Studies of short term treatment cannot assess long term benefits of regular treatment. *British Medical Journal* 321 (7270) (November 11): 1225.

Burney, David A., and Timothy F. Flannery. 2005. Fifty millennia of catastrophic extinctions after human contact. *Trends in Ecology & Evolution* 20 (7): 395–401.

Cain, Louis P., and Elyce J. Rotella. 2001. Death and spending: Urban mortality and municipal expenditure on sanitation. *Annales de Demographie Historique* 1 (1): 139–54.

Cain, Louis P., and Elyce J. Rotella. 2010. Urbanization, sanitation, and mortality in the Progressive Era, 1899–1929. Unpublished manuscript. Loyola University of Chicago and Northwestern University.

Cann, Rebecca L., Mark Stoneking, and Allan C. Wilson. 1987. Mitochondrial DNA and human evolution. *Nature* 325 (6099): 31–36.

Carrion, J. M. M. 1994. Stature, welfare, and economic growth in nineteenth-century Spain: The case of Murcia. In John Komlos, ed., *Stature, Living Standards, and Economic Development: Essays in Anthropometric History*. Chicago: University of Chicago Press, 76–92.

Carter, Susan B., Scott Sigmund Gartner, Michael R. Haines, Alan L. Olmstead, Richard Sutch, and Gavin Wright, eds. 2006. *Historical Statistics of the United States: Earliest Times to the Present, Millennial Edition*. 5 vols. New York: Cambridge University Press.

Cates, Gerald L. 1980. "The seasoning": Disease and death among the first colonists of Georgia. *Georgia Historical Quarterly* 64 (2): 146–58.

Chandler, Asa C. 1929. *Hookworm Disease: Its Distribution, Biology, Epidemiology, Pathology, Diagnosis, Treatment and Control*. New York: Macmillan.

Chernow, Ron. 2004. *Titan: The Life of John D. Rockefeller, Sr.* 2nd ed. New York: Vintage Books.

Childs, St. Julien Ravenel. 1940. *Malaria and Colonization in the Carolina Low Country, 1526–1696*. Baltimore: Johns Hopkins University Press.

Clark, Colin. 1977. *Population Growth and Land Use*. New York: St. Martin's Press.

Clark, Gregory. 2007. *A Farewell to Alms: A Brief Economic History of the World*. Princeton: Princeton University Press.

Cliff, Andrew, Peter Haggett, and Mathew Smallman-Raynor. 1998. Detecting space-time patterns in geocoded disease data: Cholera in London, 1854 and measles in the United States, 1962–65. In Lothar Gierl and Rainer Schmidt, eds., *GEOMED '97: Proceedings of the International Workshop on Geomedical Systems*. Stuttgart: Teubner Verlag, 13–42.

Cockburn, Aidan. 1980. Diseases. In Aidan Cockburn and Eve Cockburn, eds., *Mummies, Disease, and Ancient Cultures*. New York: Cambridge University Press, 157–74.

Coclanis, Peter, and John Komlos. 1995. Nutrition and economic development in post-Reconstruction South Carolina: An anthropometric approach. *Social Science History* 19: 91–115.

Coelho, Philip R. P., and Katherine H. Diagle. 1982. The effects of developments in transportation on the inland empire. *Agricultural History* 56 (1): 22–36.

Coelho, Philip R. P., and Robert A. McGuire. 1997. African and European bound labor in the British New World: The biological consequences of economic choices. *Journal of Economic History* 57 (1): 83–115.

Coelho, Philip R. P., and Robert A. McGuire. 1999. Biology, diseases, and economics: An epidemiological history of slavery in the American South. *Journal of Bioeconomics* 1 (2): 151–90.

Coelho, Philip R. P., and Robert A. McGuire. 2000. Diets versus diseases: The anthropometrics of slave children. *Journal of Economic History* 60 (1): 232–46.

Coelho, Philip R. P., and Robert A. McGuire. 2006. Racial differences in disease susceptibilities: Intestinal worm infections in the early twentieth-century American South. *Social History of Medicine* 19: 461–82.

Coelho, Philip R. P., and James F. Shepherd. 1979. The impact of regional differences in prices and wages on economic growth: The United States in 1890. *Journal of Economic History* 39 (1): 69–85.

Cohen, Mark Nathan. 1977. *The Food Crisis in Prehistory: Overpopulation and the Origins of Agriculture*. New Haven: Yale University Press.

Cohen, Mark Nathan. 1989. *Health and the Rise of Civilization*. New Haven: Yale University Press.

Condran, Gretchen A., and Eileen Crimmins. 1979. A description and evaluation of mortality data in the federal census: 1850–1900. *Historical Methods* 12 (1): 1–23.

Contacos, Peter G., and G. Robert Coatney. 1976. Malaria. In Franklin H. Top Sr. and Paul F. Wehrle, eds., *Communicable and Infectious Diseases*. 8th. St. Louis: Mosby, 419–24.

Cooper, Donald B., and Kenneth F. Kiple. 1993. Yellow fever. In Kenneth F. Kiple, ed., *The Cambridge World History of Human Disease*. New York: Cambridge University Press, 1100–1107.

Cooper, Ed. 2000. Letters—Treatment for intestinal helminth infection. Message does not follow from systematic review's findings. *British Medical Journal* 321 (7270) (November 11): 1225–26.

Costa, Dora L., and Richard H. Steckel. 1997. Long-term trends in health, welfare, and economic growth in the United States. In Richard H. Steckel and Roderick Floud, eds., *Health and Welfare during Industrialization*. Chicago: University of Chicago Press, 47–90.

Costa, Dora L. 2000. Understanding the twentieth century decline in chronic conditions among older men. *Demography* 37 (1): 53–72.

Costa, Dora L. 2002. Changing chronic disease rates and long-term declines in functional limitation among older men. *Demography* 39 (1): 119–38.

Costa, Dora L. 2005. Causes of improving health and longevity at older ages: A review of the explanations. *Genus* 61 (1): 21–38.

Crompton, D. W. T., and Lani. S. Stephenson. 1990. Hookworm infection, nutritional status and productivity. In G. A. Schad and K. S. Warren, eds., *Hookworm Disease: Current Status and New Directions*. London: Taylor and Francis, 231–64.

Cronin, Helena. 1991. *The Ant and the Peacock*. New York: Cambridge University Press.

Crosby, Alfred W. 1986. *Ecological Imperialism: The Biological Expansion of Europe, 900–1900*. New York: Cambridge University Press.

Crosby, Alfred W. 1993a. Influenza. In Kenneth F. Kiple, ed., *The Cambridge World History of Human Disease*. New York: Cambridge University Press, 807–11.

Crosby, Alfred W. 1993b. Smallpox. In Kenneth F. Kiple, ed., *The Cambridge World History of Human Disease*. New York: Cambridge University Press, 1008–13.

Crosby, Alfred W., Jr. 1972. *The Columbian Exchange: Biological and Cultural Consequences of 1492*. Westport, CT: Greenwood.

Crosby, Alfred W., Jr. 1991. The biological consequences of 1492. *NACLA Report on the Americas* 25 (2): 6–14.

Cross, David F. 2003. What killed the Yankees at Andersonville? *North and South Magazine* (6): 23–32. (An extended version, "Why Did the Vermonters die at Andersonville? The deadly hookworm," can be found at http://www.weldonrailroad.com/hookworm.html.)

Crutcher, James M., and Stephen L. Hoffman. 1996. Malaria. In Samuel Baron, ed., *Medical Microbiology*, 4th ed. Galveston: University of Texas Medical Branch, ch. 83. http://www.ncbi.nlm.nih.gov/bookshelf/br.fcgi?book=mmed&part=A4419.

Cullimore, D. Roy. 2008. *Practical Manual of Groundwater Microbiology*, 2nd ed. Boca Raton, FL: CRC Press.

Curtin, Philip D. 1968. Epidemiology and the slave trade. *Political Science Quarterly* 83 (2): 190–216.

Curtin, Philip D. 1989. *Death by Migration: Europe's Encounter with the Tropical World in the Nineteenth Century*. New York: Cambridge University Press.

Das, J. P., and Emma Pivato. 1976. Malnutrition and cognitive functioning. *International Review of Research in Mental Retardation* 8: 195–223.

Das, J. P., and Priyani Soysa. 1978. Late effects of malnutrition on cognitive competence. *International Journal of Psychology* 13: 295–303.

David, Paul A. 1985. Clio and the economics of QWERTY. *American Economic Review* 75 (2): 332–37.

David, Paul A., Herbert G. Gutman, Richard Sutch, Peter Temin, and Gavin Wright. 1976. *Reckoning with Slavery: A Critical Study in the Quantitative History of American Negro Slavery*. New York: Oxford University Press.

Davies, Kenneth G. 1975. The living and the dead: White mortality in West Africa, 1684–1732. In Stanley L. Engerman and Eugene D. Genovese, eds., *Race and Slavery in the Western Hemisphere: Quantitative Studies*. Princeton: Princeton University Press, 83–98.

Davis, Lance E., and Douglass C. North. 1971. *Institutional Change and American Economic Growth*. New York: Cambridge University Press.

Diamond, Jared. 1997. *Guns, Germs, and Steel: The Fates of Human Societies*. New York: Norton.

Diamond, Jared. 2005. *Collapse: How Societies Choose to Fail or Succeed*. New York: Viking.

Dickson, Rumona, Shally Awasthi, Paula Williamson, Colin Demellweek, and Paul Garner. 2000. Effects of treatment for intestinal helminth infection on growth and cognitive performance in children: Systematic review of randomized trials. *British Medical Journal* 320 (7251) (June 24): 1697–1701.

Djankov, Simeon, Rafael La Porta, Florencio Lopez-de-Silanes, and Andrei Shleifer. 2002. The regulation of entry. *Quarterly Journal of Economics* 117: 1–37.

Djankov, Simeon, Rafael La Porta, Florencio Lopez-de-Silanes, and Andrei Shleifer. 2003. Courts. *Quarterly Journal of Economics* 118: 453–517.

Dobyns, Henry F. 1983. *Their Number Become Thinned*. Knoxville: University of Tennessee Press.

Dock, George, and Charles C. Bass. 1910. *Hookworm Disease: Etiology, Pathology, Diagnosis, Prognosis, Prophylaxis, and Treatment*. St. Louis: Mosby.

Dollar, Clyde D. 1977. The high plains smallpox epidemic of 1837–38. *Western Historical Quarterly* 8 (1): 15–38.

Drake, Daniel. [1850, 1854] 1964. *Malaria in the Interior Valley of North America—A Selection by Norman D. Levine from "A Systematic Treatise, Historical, Etiological, and Practical, on the Principal Diseases of the Interior Valley of North America, as They Appear in the Caucasian, African, Indian, and Esquimaux Varieties of its Population" by Daniel Drake*. Urbana: University of Illinois Press.

Duffy, John. 1988. The impact of malaria on the South. In Todd L. Savitt and James Harvey Young, eds., *Disease and Distinctiveness in the American South*. Knoxville: University of Tennessee Press, 29–54.

Dunn, Frederick L. 1993. Malaria. In Kenneth F. Kiple, ed., *The Cambridge World History of Human Disease*. New York: Cambridge University Press, 855–62.

Dunn, Richard S. 1972. *Sugar and Slaves: The Rise of the Planter Class in the English West Indies, 1624–1713*. Chapel Hill: University of North Carolina Press.

DuPont, Herbert L. 1993. Diarrheal diseases (acute). In Kenneth F. Kiple, ed., *The Cambridge World History of Human Disease*. New York: Cambridge University Press, 676–80.

Earle, Carville V. 1979. Environment, disease, and mortality in early Virginia. In Thad W. Tate and David L. Ammerman, eds., *The Chesapeake in the Seventeenth Century: Essays on Anglo-American Society*. Chapel Hill: University of North Carolina Press, 96–125.

Easterlin, Richard A. 1961. Regional income trends, 1840–1950. In Seymour E. Harris, ed., *American Economic History*. New York: McGraw-Hill, 525–47.

Easterly, William. 2001. *The Elusive Quest for Growth: Economists' Adventures and Misadventures in the Tropics*. Cambridge: MIT Press.

Easterly, William. 2006. *The White Man's Burden: Why the West's Efforts to Aid the Rest Have Done So Much Ill and So Little Good*. New York: Penguin Press.

Ekirch, A. Roger. 1987. *Bound for America: The Transportation of British Convicts to the Colonies, 1718–1775*. Oxford: Clarendon Press.

Ellinghausen, Herman C., Jr., and Franklin H. Top Sr. 1976. Leptospirosis. In Franklin H. Top Sr. and Paul F. Wehrle, eds., *Communicable and Infectious Diseases*, 8th ed. St. Louis: Mosby, 395–409.

Eltis, David, and David Richardson. 2004. Prices of African slaves newly arrived in the Americas, 1673–1865: New evidence on long-run trends and regional differentials. In David Eltis, Frank D. Lewis, and Kenneth L. Sokoloff, eds., *Slavery in the Development of the Americas*. New York: Cambridge University Press, 181–218.

Eltis, David, Frank D. Lewis, and David Richardson. 2005. Slave prices, the African slave trade, and productivity in the Caribbean, 1674–1807. *Economic History Review* 58 (4): 673–700.

Engelhard, Victor H. 1994. How cells process antigens. *Scientific American* 271 (2): 54–61.

Engerman, Stanley L. 1976a. The height of U.S. slaves. *Local Population Studies* 16: 45–50.

Engerman, Stanley L. 1976b. Some economic and demographic comparisons of slavery in the United States and the British West Indies. *Economic History Review* 29 (2): 258–75.

Engerman, Stanley L., and Kenneth L. Sokoloff. 1997. Factor endowments, Institutions, and differential paths of growth among New World economies: A view from economic historians of the United States. In Stephen Harber, ed., *How Latin America Fell Behind*. Stanford: Stanford University Press, 260–304.

Engerman, Stanley L., and Kenneth L. Sokoloff. 2002. Factor endowments, inequality, and paths of development among New World economies. Working paper 9259. National Bureau of Economic Research, Cambridge, MA.

Eppig, Christopher, Corey L. Fincher, and Randy Thornhill. 2010. Parasite prevalence and the worldwide distribution of cognitive ability. *Proceedings. Biological Sciences* 277 (1710): 3801–808.

Ettling, John. 1981. *The Germ of Laziness: Rockefeller Philanthropy and Public Health in the New South*. Cambridge: Harvard University Press.

Ettling, John. 1993. Hookworm disease. In Kenneth F. Kiple, ed., *The Cambridge World History of Human Disease*. New York: Cambridge University Press, 784–88.

Ewald, Paul W. 1994. *Evolution of Infectious Disease*. New York: Oxford University Press.

Ewald, Paul W. 2000. *Plague Time: How Stealth Infections Cause Cancer, Heart Disease, and Other Deadly Ailments*. New York: Free Press.

Faitha, J. Tyler, and Todd A. Surovell. 2009. Synchronous extinction of North America's Pleistocene mammals. *PNAS: Proceedings of the National Academy of Sciences* 106 (49): 20641–45.

Feldman, Harry A. 1976. Toxoplasmosis. In Franklin H. Top Sr. and Paul F. Wehrle, eds., *Communicable and Infectious Diseases*, 8th ed. St. Louis: Mosby, 702–708.

Fenner, F., D. A. Henderson, I. Arita, Z. Ježek, and I. D. Ladnyi. 1988. *Smallpox and Its Eradication*. Geneva: World Health Organization.

Finch, Roger G. 1984a. Anthrax. In Robert H. Waldman and Ronica M. Kluge, eds., *Infectious Diseases*. Hyde Park, NY: Medical Examination Publishing, 771–75.

Finch, Roger G. 1984b. Clostridia. In Robert H. Waldman and Ronica M. Kluge, eds., *Infectious Diseases*. Hyde Park, NY: Medical Examination Publishing, 756–70.

Findlay, G. M. 1941. The first recognized epidemic of yellow fever. *Transactions of the Royal Society of Tropical Medicine and Hygiene* 35 (3): 143–54.

Fisher, Irving. 1899. Mortality statistics of the United States Census. In American Economic Association, *The Federal Census: Critical Essays by Members of the American Economic Association*. New York: Macmillan, 121–69.

Fleming, Alan. F. 1989. Tropical obstetrics and gynaecology. 1. Anaemia in pregnancy in tropical Africa. *Transactions of the Royal Society of Tropical Medicine and Hygiene* 83: 441–48.

Fogel, Robert W. 1991. The conquest of high mortality and hunger in Europe and America: Timing and mechanisms. In Patrice Higonnet, David S. Landes, and Henry Rosovsky, eds., *Favorites of Fortune: Technology, Growth, and Economic Development since the Industrial Revolution*. Cambridge: Harvard University Press, 33–71.

Fogel, Robert William. 1986. Nutrition and the decline in mortality since 1700: Some preliminary findings. In Stanley L. Engerman and Robert E. Gallman, eds., *Long-term Factors in American Economic Growth*. Chicago: University of Chicago Press, 439–555.

Fogel, Robert William. 1989. *Without Consent or Contract: The Rise and Fall of American Slavery*. New York: Norton.

Fogel, Robert William. 1992. Second thoughts on the European escape from hunger: Famines, chronic malnutrition, and mortality rates. In S. R. Osmani, ed., *Nutrition and Poverty*. Oxford: Clarendon Press, 243–86.

Fogel, Robert William. 1995. The contribution of improved nutrition to the decline in mortality rates in Europe and America. In Julian L. Simon, ed., *The State of Humanity*. Cambridge: Blackwell, 61–71.

Fogel, Robert William, and Stanley L. Engerman. 1971. The relative efficiency of slavery: A comparison of northern and southern agriculture in 1860. *Explorations in Economic History* 8 (3): 353–67.

Fogel, Robert William, and Stanley L. Engerman. 1974a. *Time on the Cross: The Economics of American Negro Slavery*. Boston: Little Brown.

Fogel, Robert William, and Stanley L. Engerman. 1974b. *Time on the Cross II: Evidence and Methods*. Boston: Little, Brown.

Fogel, Robert William, and Stanley L. Engerman. 1977. Explaining the relative efficiency of slave agriculture in the Antebellum South. *American Economic Review* 67 (3): 275–96.

Fogel, Robert William, and Stanley L. Engerman. 1979. Recent findings in the study of slave demography and family structure. *Sociology and Social Research* 63: 566–89.

Fogel, Robert William, and Stanley L. Engerman. 1980. Explaining the relative efficiency of slave agriculture in the Antebellum South: Reply. *American Economic Review* 70 (4): 672–90.

Foo, Li Chien. 1990. Hookworm infection and protein-energy malnutrition: Transverse evidence from two Malaysian ecological groups. *Tropical and Geographical Medicine* 42: 8–12.

Fox, John P., Carrie E. Hall, and Lila R. Elveback. 1970. *Epidemiology: Man and Disease*. New York: Macmillan.

Frick, Donald J. 1919. Examination and treatment of soldiers infected with hookworm, at Camp Beauregard, La., March 1 to Sept. 1, 1918. *American Journal of the Medical Sciences* 157 (2): 189–97.

Galenson, David W. 1981a. *White Servitude in Colonial America: An Economic Analysis*. Cambridge: Cambridge University Press.

Galenson, David W. 1981b. The market evaluation of human capital: The case of indentured servitude. *Journal of Political Economy* 89 (3): 446–67.

Galenson, David W. 1984. The rise and fall of indentured servitude in the Americas: An economic analysis. *Journal of Economic History* 44 (1): 1–26.

Galenson, David W. 1989. Labor market behavior in colonial America: Servitude, slavery, and free labor. In David W. Galenson, *Markets in History: Economic Studies of the Past*. New York: Cambridge University Press, 52–96.

Galenson, David W. 1991. Economic aspects of the growth of slavery in the seventeenth-century Chesapeake. In Barbara L. Solow, ed., *Slavery and the Rise of the Atlantic System*. New York: Cambridge University Press, 265–92.

Galenson, David W. 1996. The settlement and growth of the colonies: Population, labor, and economic development. In Stanley L. Engerman and Robert E. Gallman, eds., *The Cambridge Economic History of the United States. Vol. 1: The Colonial Era*. New York: Cambridge University Press, 135–207.

Gallay, Alan C. 2002. *The Indian Slave Trade: The Rise of the English Empire in the American South, 1670–1717*. New Haven: Yale University Press.

Ganguly, Rama. 1984. Brucella: Brucellosis. In Robert H. Waldman and Ronica M. Kluge, eds., *Infectious Diseases*. Hyde Park, NY: Medical Examination Publishing, 807–11.

Garner, Paul, Rumona Dickson, Colin Demellweek, Paula Williamson, and Shally Awasthi. 2000. Letters—Treatment for intestinal helminth infection. Authors' reply. *British Medical Journal* 321 (7270) (November 11): 1226–27.

Geist, Valerius. 1978. *Life Strategies, Human Evolution, Environmental Design*. New York: Springer.

Gemery, Henry A., and Jan S. Hogendorn. 1974. The Atlantic slave trade: A tentative model. *Journal of African History* 15 (2): 223–46.

Gilles, H. M., J. B. Lawson, M. Sibelas, A. Voller, and N. Allan. 1969. Malaria, anemia and pregnancy. *Annals of Tropical Medicine and Parasitology* 63: 245–63.

Glaeser, Edward L., Rafael La Porta, Florencio Lopez-De-Silanes, and Andrei Shleifer. 2004. Do institutions cause growth? *Journal of Economic Growth* 9: 271–303.

Goebel, Ted, Michael R. Waters, and Dennis H. O'Rourke. 2008. The late Pleistocene dispersal of modern humans in the Americas. *Science* 319 (5869): 1497–1502.

Graham, Russell W., and Ernest L. Lundelius Jr. 1984. Coevolutionary disequilibrium and Pleistocene extinctions. In Paul S. Martin and Richard G. Klein, eds. *Quaternary Extinctions: A Prehistoric Revolution*. Tucson: University of Arizona Press, 223–49.

Gray, Lewis Cecil. [1933] 1958. *History of Agriculture in the Southern United States to 1860.* Gloucester, MA: Peter Smith.

Grayson, Donald K., and David J. Meltzer. 2003. A requiem for North American overkill. *Journal of Archaeological Science* 30: 585–93.

Greif, Avner. 1993. Contract enforceability and economic institutions in early trade: The Maghribi traders' coalition. *American Economic Review* 83: 525–48.

Greif, Avner. 1994. Cultural beliefs and the organization of society: A historical and theoretical reflection on collectivist and individualist societies. *Journal of Political Economy* 102: 912–50.

Greif, Avner. 2006. *Institutions and the Path to the Modern Economy: Lessons from Medieval Trade.* New York: Cambridge University Press.

Grubb, Farley. 1985. The incidence of servitude in trans-Atlantic migration, 1771–1804. *Explorations in Economic History* 22 (3): 316–39.

Grubb, Farley. 1988. The auction of redemptioner servants, Philadelphia, 1771–1804. *Journal of Economic History* 48 (3): 583–603.

Grubb, Farley. 1992a. Fatherless and friendless: Factors influencing the flow of English emigrant servants. *Journal of Economic History* 52 (1): 85–108.

Grubb, Farley. 1992b. The long-run trend in the value of European immigrant servants, 1654–1831: New measurements and interpretations. *Research in Economic History* 14: 167–240.

Grubb, Farley. 1994. The end of European immigrant servitude in the United States: An economic analysis of market collapse, 1772–1835. *Journal of Economic History* 54 (4): 794–824.

Grubb, Farley. 2000. The trans-Atlantic market for British convict labor. *Journal of Economic History* 60 (1): 94–122.

Grubb, Farley. 2001. The market evaluation of criminality: Evidence from the auction of British convict labor, 1767–1775. *American Economic Review* 91 (1): 295–305.

Grubb, Farley, and Tony Stitt. 1994. The Liverpool emigrant servant trade and the transition to slave labor in the Chesapeake, 1697–1707: Market adjustments to war. *Explorations in Economic History* 31 (3): 376–405.

Guerra, Francisco. 1988. The earliest American epidemic: The influenza of 1493. *Social Science History* 12 (3): 305–25.

Guthrie, R. Dale. 1984. Mosaics, allelochemics, and nutrients: An ecological theory of late Pleistocene megafaunal extinctions. In Paul S. Martin and Richard G. Klein, eds. *Quaternary Extinctions: A Prehistoric Revolution.* Tucson: University of Arizona Press, 259–98.

Guthrie, R. Dale. 2003. Rapid body size decline in Alaskan Pleistocene horses before extinction. *Nature* 426 (6963): 169–71.

Guthrie, R. Dale. 2004. Radiocarbon evidence of mid-Holocene mammoths stranded on an Alaskan Bering Sea island. *Nature* 429 (6993): 746–49.

Guthrie, R. Dale. 2006. New carbon dates link climatic change with human colonization and Pleistocene extinctions. *Nature* 441 (7090): 207–209.

Haines, Michael R. 1977. Mortality in nineteenth century America: Estimates from New York and Pennsylvania census data, 1865 and 1900. *Demography* 14: 311–31.

Haines, Michael R. 1995. Disease and health through the ages. In Julian Simon, ed., *The State of Humanity*. Oxford: Basil Blackwell, 51–60.

Haines, Michael R. 1999. The great modern mortality transition. Presidential address to the Annual Meetings of the Social Science History Association, Fort Worth, TX, November 13, 1999 (revised: November, 2002).

Haines, Michael R., and Barbara A. Anderson. 1988. New demographic history of the late nineteenth-century United States. *Explorations in Economic History* 25 (4): 341–65.

Haines, Michael R., and Samuel H. Preston. 1984. New estimates of child mortality in the United States at the turn of the century. *Journal of the American Statistical Association* 79 (386): 272–81.

Haites, Erik F., James Mak, and Gary M. Walton. 1975. *Western River Transportation: The Era of Early Internal Development, 1810–1860*. Baltimore: Johns Hopkins University Press.

Hanes, Christopher. 1996. Turnover cost and the distribution of slave labor in Anglo-America. *Journal of Economic History* 56 (2): 307–29.

Harper, Kristin N., Paolo S. Ocampo, Bret M. Steiner, Robert W. George, Michael S. Silverman, Shelly Bolotin, Allan Pillay, Nigel J. Saunders, and George J. Armelagos. 2008. On the origin of the Treponematoses: A phylogenetic approach. *PLoS Neglected Tropical Diseases* 2 (1): e148. doi:10.1371/journal.pntd.0000148: 1–13. http://www.plosntds.org/article/info%3Adoi%2F10.1371%2Fjournal.pntd.0000148.

Harris, Jason B., Michael J. Podolsky, Taufiqur R. Bhuiyan, Fahima Chowdhury, and Ashraful I. Khan. Regina C. LaRocquel, Tanya Logvinenko, Jennifer Kendall, Abu S. G. Faruque, Cathryn R. Nagler, Edward T. Ryan, Firdausi Qadri, and Stephen B. Calderwood. 2009. Immunologic responses to *Vibrio cholerae* in patients co-infected with intestinal parasites in Bangladesh. *PLoS: Neglected Tropical Diseases* 3(3): e403. doi:10.1371/journal.pntd.0000403: 1–8. http://www.plosntds.org/article/comments/info:doi%2F10.1371%2Fjournal.pntd.0000403;jsessionid=5A7E5A182113A28282D454D2CC1CFD22.

Harris, Marvin. 1978. *Cows, Pigs, Wars, and Witches: The Riddles of Culture*. New York: Vintage Books.

Harris, Marvin. 1985. *Good to Eat: Riddles of Food and Culture*. New York: Simon and Schuster.

Hattwick, Michael A. 1976. Rabies. In Franklin H. Top Sr. and Paul F. Wehrle, eds., *Communicable and Infectious Diseases*, 8th ed. St. Louis: Mosby, 555–66.

Heckenberger, Michael J., J. Christian Russell, Carlos Fausto, Joshua R. Toney, Morgan J. Schmidt, Edithe Pereira, Bruna Franchetto, and Afukaka Kuikuro. 2008. Pre-Columbian urbanism, anthropogenic landscapes, and the future of the Amazon. *Science* 321 (5893): 1214–17.

Heinsohn, Gunnar. (2006) *Söhne und Weltmacht*. Zurich: Orell Fuessli Verlag.

Historical Census Browser, University of Virginia Library. http://mapserver.lib.virginia.edu

Homer, Sidney, and Richard Sylla. 1991. *A History of Interest Rates*. 3rd ed. New Brunswick, NJ: Rutgers University Press.

Hotez, Peter J., and David I. Pritchard. 1995. Hookworm Infection. *Scientific American* 272 (6): 68–74.

Hotez, Peter J., and Patricia P. Wilkins. 2009. Toxocariasis: America's Most Common Neglected Infection of Poverty and a Helminthiasis of Global Importance? *PLoS Neglected Tropical Diseases* 3 (3):e400. doi:10.1371/journal.pntd.0000400: 1–4. http://www.plosntds.org/article/info:doi%2F10.1371%2Fjournal.pntd.0000400.

Howard, William Travis. 1924. *Public Health Administration and the Natural History of Disease in Baltimore, Maryland, 1797–1920*. Washington, DC: Carnegie Institution of Washington.

Huber, J. Richard. 1971. Effect on prices of Japan's entry into world commerce after 1858. *Journal of Political Economy* 79 (3): 614–28.

Hurtado, A. Magdelana, Inés Hurtado, and Kim Hill. 2004. Public health and adaptive immunity among the natives of South America. In Francisco M. Salzano and A. Magdalena Hurtado, eds., *Lost Paradises and the Ethics of Research and Publication*. New York: Oxford University Press, 164–92.

Hurtado, A. Magdalena, and Francisco M. Salzano. 2004. Conclusions. In Francisco M. Salzano and A. Magdalena Hurtado, eds., *Lost Paradises and the Ethics of Research and Publication*. New York: Oxford University Press, 211–28.

Johansson, Shelia Ryan. 1994. Food for thought: Rhetoric and reality in modern mortality history. *Historical Methods* 27: 101–25.

Johnson, Paul. 1991. *The Birth of the Modern: World Society, 1815–1830*. New York: HarperCollins.

Jones, E. L. 1981. *The European Miracle: Environments, Economies, and Geopolitics in the History of Europe and Asia*. New York: Cambridge University Press.

Jones, E. L. 2000. *Growth Recurring: Economic Change in World History*. Ann Arbor: University of Michigan Press.

Jones, T. L., J. F. Porcasi, J. M. Erlandson, H. Dallas Jr., T. A. Wake, and R. Schwaderer. 2008. The protracted Holocene extinction of California's flightless sea duck (Chendytes lawi) and its implications for the Pleistocene overkill hypothesis. *PNAS: Proceedings of the National Academy of Sciences* 105 (11): 4105–108.

Jordan, Winthrop D. 1968. *White over Black: The Development of American Attitudes toward the Negro, 1550–1812*. Chapel Hill: University of North Carolina Press.

Karasch, Mary C. 1993. Disease ecologies of South America. In Kenneth F. Kiple, ed., *The Cambridge World History of Human Disease*. New York: Cambridge University Press, 535–46.

Kelley, Truman L. 1917. The effect of malaria and hookworm upon physical and mental development of school children. *Elementary School Journal* 18 (1): 43–51.

Keymer, A., and M. Pagel. 1990. Predisposition to helminth infection. In G. A. Schad and K. S. Warren, eds., *Hookworm Disease: Current Status and New Direction*. London: Taylor and Francis, 177–209.

Khakoo, Rasjida A. 1984. Nontuberculous mycobacterial infections. In Robert H. Waldman and Ronica M. Kluge, eds., *Infectious Diseases*. Hyde Park, NY: Medical Examination Publishing, 902–13.

Kilama, W. L. 1990. Hookworm infection and disease in Africa and the Middle East. In G. A. Schad and K. S. Warren, eds., *Hookworm Disease: Current Status and New Directions*. London: Taylor and Francis, 17–32.

Kim-Farley, Robert J. 1993. Measles. In Kenneth F. Kiple, ed., *The Cambridge World History of Human Disease*. New York: Cambridge University Press, 871–75.

Kiple, Kenneth F. 1984. *The Caribbean Slave*. New York: Cambridge University Press.

Kiple, Kenneth F. 1993. Disease ecologies of the Caribbean. In Kenneth F. Kiple, ed., *The Cambridge World History of Human Disease*. New York: Cambridge University Press, 497–504.

Kiple, Kenneth F., and Brian T. Higgins. 1992. Yellow fever and the Africanization of the Caribbean. In John W. Verano and Douglas H. Ubelaker, eds., *Disease and Demography in the Americas*. Washington, DC: Smithsonian Institution Press, 237–48.

Kiple, Kenneth F., and Virginia Himmelsteib King. 1981. *Another Dimension to the Black Diaspora*. New York: Cambridge University Press.

Kiple, Kenneth F., and Virginia H. Kiple. 1977. Black yellow fever immunities, innate and acquired in the American South, as revealed in the American South. *Social Science History* 1 (4): 419–36.

Kiple, Kenneth F., and Virginia H. Kiple. 1980. Deficiency disease in the Caribbean. *Journal of Interdisciplinary History* 11 (2): 197–215.

Klepp, Susan E. 1994. Seasoning and society: Racial differences in mortality in eighteenth-century Philadelphia. *William and Mary Quarterly* 51 (3): 473–507.

Kluge, Ronica M. 1984. Enterobacteriaceaell. In Robert H. Waldman and Ronica M. Kluge, eds., *Infectious Diseases*. Hyde Park, NY: Medical Examination Publishing, 790–800.

Knowlton, R. H. 1919. Hookworm infection among troops: Treatment with oil of chenopodium. *Journal of the American Medical Association* 72: 701–703.

Kofoid, Charles A., and John P. Tucker. 1921. On the relationship of infection by hookworm to the incidence of morbidity and mortality in 22,842 men of the United States Army at Camp Bowie, Texas, from October 1917, to April 1918. *American Journal of Hygiene* 1: 79–117.

Komlos, John. 1987. The height and weight of West Point Cadets: Dietary change in Antebellum America. *Journal of Economic History* 47 (4): 897–927.

Komlos, John. 1992. Toward an anthropometric history of African-Americans: The case of the free blacks in Antebellum Maryland. In Claudia Goldin and Hugh Rockoff, eds., *Strategic Factors in Nineteenth Century America Economic History*. Chicago: University of Chicago Press, 297–329.

Komlos, John. 1996. On anomalies in economic history: Reflections on the Antebellum Puzzle. *Journal of Economic History* 56 (1): 202–14.

Komlos, John, and Peter Coclanis. 1997. On the puzzling cycle in the biological standard of living: The case of Antebellum Georgia. *Explorations in Economic History* 34 (4): 433–59.

Krieger, Nancy. 2005. Stormy weather: Race, gene expression, and the science of health disparities. *American Journal of Public Health* 25: 2155–60.

Kunitz, Stephen J. 1988. Hookworm and pellagra: Exemplary diseases in the new South. *Journal of Health and Social Behavior* 29 (2): 139–48.

La Porta, Rafael, Florencio Lopez-de-Silanes, and Andrei Shleifer. 2008. The economic consequences of legal origins. *Journal of Economic Literature* 46: 285–332.

La Porta, Rafael, Florencio Lopez-de-Silanes, Andrei Shleifer, and Robert Vishny. 1997. Legal determinants of external finance. *Journal of Finance* 52: 1131–50.

La Porta, Rafael, Florencio Lopez-de-Silanes, Andrei Shleifer, and Robert Vishny. 1998. Law and finance. *Journal of Political Economy* 106: 1113–55.

Larsen, Clark Spencer, Alfred W. Crosby, Mark C. Griffin, Dale L. Hutchinson, Christopher B. Ruff, Katherine F. Russell, Margaret J. Schoeninger, et al. 2002. A biohistory of health and behavior in the Georgia bight: The agricultural transition and the impact of European contact. In Richard H. Steckel and Jerome C. Rose, eds., *The Backbone of History: Health and Nutrition in the Western Hemisphere*. Cambridge: Cambridge University Press, 406–39.

Latham, M. C., L. S. Stephenson, Andrew Hall, J. C. Wogelmuth, T. C. Elliot, and D. W. T. Crompton. 1983. Parasitic infections, anemia and nutritional status: A study of their interrelationships and the effect of prophylaxis and treatment on workers in Kwale District, Kenya. *Transactions of the Royal Society of Tropical Medicine and Hygiene* 77 (1): 41–48.

Latham, Michael C., Lani S. Stephenson, Kathleen M. Kurz, and Stephen N. Kinoti. 1990. Metrifonate or praziquantel treatment improves physical fitness and appetite of Kenyan school boys with *Schistosoma haematobium* and hookworm infections. *American Journal of Tropical Medicine and Hygiene* 43: 170–79.

Lauber, Almond W. 1913. *Indian Slavery in Colonial Times within the Present Limit of the United States*. New York: AMS Press.

Lebergott, Stanley. 1984. *The Americans: An Economic Record*. New York: Norton.

Ledger, William J. 1976. Anaerobic infections. In Franklin H. Top Sr. and Paul F. Wehrle, eds., *Communicable and Infectious Diseases*, 8th ed. St. Louis: Mosby, 125–36.

Lee, Ronald H. 1987. Population growth of humans and other animals. *Demography* 24 (4): 443–65.

LeRiche, W. Harding, and Jean Milner. 1971. *Epidemiology as Medical Ecology*. Edinburgh: Churchill Livingstone.

Livi-Bacci, Massimo. 1991. *Population and Nutrition: An Essay on European Demographic History*, translated by Tania Croft-Murray with the assistance of Carl Ipsen. Cambridge: Cambridge University Press.

Livi-Bacci, Massimo. 1992. *A Concise History of World Population*, translated by Carl Ipsen. Oxford and Malden, MA: Blackwell.

Livi-Bacci, Massimo. 2000. *The Population of Europe: A History*, translated by Cynthia De Nardi Ipsen and Carl Ipsen. Oxford: Blackwell.

Lovejoy, Paul E. 1983. *Transformations in Slavery: A History of Slavery in Africa*. Cambridge: Cambridge University Press.

Lucke, Baldwin. 1919. Statistical study of the prevalence of intestinal worms in 35,000 white and colored troops at Camp Zachary Taylor, Kentucky. *Military Surgeon* 44: 620–29.

Lumsden, Charles J., and Edward O. Wilson. 1981. *Genes, Mind, and Culture: The Coevolutionary Process*. Hackensack, NJ: World Scientific.

Lwambo, N. J. S., D. A. P. Bundy, and G. H. Medley. 1992. A new approach to morbidity risk assessment in hookworm endemic communities. *Epidemiology and Infection* 108: 469–81.

MacDonald, Kenneth. 1976. Hookworm. In Franklin H. Top Sr. and Paul F. Wehrle, eds., *Communicable and Infectious Diseases*, 8th ed. St. Louis: Mosby, 359–61.

MacPhee, Ross D. E., and Preston A. Marx. 1997. The 40,000 year plague: Humans, hyperdisease, and first-contact extinctions. In Steven M. Goodman and Bruce D. Patterson, eds., *Natural Change and Human Impact in Madagascar*. Washington, DC: Smithsonian Institution Press, 169–217.

Mak, James, and Gary M. Walton. 1972. Steamboats and the great productivity surge in river transportation. *Journal of Economic History* 32 (3): 619–40.

Mann, Charles C. 2002. 1491. *Atlantic Monthly* 289 (3): 41–53.

Mann, Charles C. 2005. *Ancient Americans* (first published under the title *1491: New Revelations of the Americas before Columbus)*. London: Granta.

Marcus, Alan I. 1988. The South's native foreigners: Hookworm as a factor in southern distinctiveness. In Todd L. Savitt and James Harvey Young, eds., *Disease and Distinctiveness in the American South*. Knoxville: University of Tennessee Press, 79–99.

Margo, Robert A., and Richard H. Steckel. 1982. The heights of American slaves: New evidence on slave nutrition and health. *Social Science History* 6: 516–38.

Margo, Robert A., and Steckel, Richard H. 1992. The nutrition and health of slaves and Antebellum southern whites. In Robert W. Fogel and Stanley L. Engerman, eds., *Without Consent or Contract: Technical Papers*, vol. 2. New York: Norton, 508–21.

Marks, Paul A., and Ruth T. Gross. 1959. Erythrocyte glucose-6-phosphate-dehydrogenase deficiency: Evidence of differences between negroes and caucasians. *Journal of Clinical Investigation* 38: 2253–62.

Martin, Larry K. 1972. Hookworm in Georgia: Survey of intestinal helminth infections and anemia in rural school children. *American Journal of Tropical Medicine and Hygiene* 21 (6): 919–29.

Martin, Mike G., and Margaret E. Humphreys. 2006. Social consequence of disease in the American South, 1900–World War II. *Southern Medical Journal* 99 (8): 862–64.

Martin, Paul S. 1984. Prehistoric overkill: The global model. In Paul S. Martin and Richard G. Klein, eds. *Quaternary Extinctions: A Prehistoric Revolution*. Tucson: University of Arizona Press, 354–404.

Martin, Paul S., and David W. Steadman. 1999. Prehistoric extinctions on islands and continents. In Ross D. E. MacPhee, ed., *Extinctions in Near Time; Causes, Contexts and Consequences*. New York: Kluwer Academic/Plenum, 17–55.

Mathies, Allen W., Jr., and Kenneth MacDonald. 1976. Trichinosis. In Franklin H. Top Sr., and Paul F. Wehrle, eds., *Communicable and Infectious Diseases*. 8th ed. St. Louis: Mosby, 719–23.

McCaa, Robert. 1995. Spanish and Nahuatl views on smallpox and demographic catastrophe in Mexico. *Journal of Interdisciplinary History* 25 (3): 397–431.

McCusker, John J., and Russell R. Menard. 1985. *The Economy of British America, 1607–1789*. Chapel Hill: University of North Carolina Press.

McDaniel, Antonio. 1994. Patterns of mortality by age and cause of death among nineteenth century immigrants to Liberia. *Population Studies* 48: 99–115.

McDaniel, Antonio. 1995. *Swing Low, Sweet Chariot: The Mortality Cost of Colonizing Liberia in the Nineteenth Century*. Chicago: University of Chicago Press.

McDougall, Ian, Francis H. Brown, and John G. Fleagle. 2005. Stratigraphic placement and age of modern humans from Kibish, Ethiopia. *Nature* 433 (7027): 733–36.

McMillin James A. 2004. *The Final Victims: Foreign Slave Trade to North America, 1783–1810*. Columbia: University of South Carolina Press.

McNeill, John. 2007. Social, economic, and political forces in environmental change: Decadal scale (1900 to 2000). In Robert Costanza, Lisa Graumlich, and Will Steffen, eds., *Sustainability or Collapse? An Integrated History of People on Earth*. Cambridge: MIT Press, 301–30.

McNeill, William H. 1976. *Plagues and Peoples*. Garden City, NY: Anchor Books.

Meadows, Donella H., Dennis L. Meadows, Jorgen Randers, and William W. Behrens III. 1972. *Limits to Growth*. New York: Potomac Associates.

Meeker, Edward. 1972. The improving health of the United States. *Explorations in Economic History* 9 (4): 353–74.

Meeker, Edward. 1974. The social rate of return on investment in public health. *Journal of Economic History* 34 (2): 392–419.

Meeker, Edward. 1976. Mortality trends of southern blacks, 1850–1910. *Explorations in Economic History* 13 (1): 13–42.

Meuris, Sylvain, Bokumu Bosango Piko, Peter Eerens, Anne-Marie Vanbellinghen, Michele Dramaix, and Philippe Henmart. 1993. Gestational malaria: Assessment of its consequences on fetal growth. *American Journal of Tropical Medicine and Hygiene* 48: 603–609.

Michael, E. 2000. Letters—Treatment for helminth infection. Contrary to authors' comments, meta-analysis supports global helminth control initiatives. *British Medical Journal* 321 (7270) (November 11): 1224–25.

Migasena, S., and H. M. Gilles. 1991. Clinical features and diagnosis. In H. M. Gilles and P. A. J. Ball, eds., *Hookworm infections*. Amsterdam: Elsevier, 179–93.

Miguel, Edward, and Michael Kremer. 2004. Worms: Identifying impacts on education and health in the presence of treatment externalities. *Econometrica* 72 (1): 159–217.

Miles, Sir Ashley. 1983. History. In Sir Graham Wilson, Sir Ashley Miles, and M. T. Parker, eds., *Topley and Wilson's Principles of Bacteriology, Virology and Immunity. Volume 1. General Microbiology and Immunity*. Sir Graham Wilson and Heather M. Dick, eds. 7th ed. London: Edward Arnold, 1–15.

Miller, Joseph C. 1988. *Way of Death*. Madison: University of Wisconsin Press.

Mogabgab, William J. 1976. Influenza. In Franklin H. Top Sr. and Paul F. Wehrle, eds., *Communicable and Infectious Diseases*, 8th ed. St. Louis: Mosby, 369–78.

Molleson, Theya. 1994. The eloquent bones of Abu Hureyra. *Scientific American* 271 (2): 70.

Moyo, Dambisa. 2009. *Dead Aid: Why Aid Is Not Working and How There Is a Better Way for Africa*. New York: Farrar, Straus and Giroux.

Murray, John E. 1997. Standards of the present for people of the past: Height, weight, and mortality among men of Amherst College, 1834–1949. *Journal of Economic History* 57 (3): 585–606.

Myers, Gary C. 1920. Intelligence of troops infected with hookworm vs. those not infected. *Pedagogical Seminary* 27 (3): 211–42.

National Library of Medicine. 1998. http://text.nlm.nih.gov/ahcpr/sickle/www/scdcat.html.

Nelson, G. S. 1990. Hookworms in perspective. In G. A. Schad and K. S. Warren, eds., *Hookworm Disease: Current Status and New Directions*. London: Taylor and Francis, 417–30.

Neves, Eduardo G., James B. Petersen, Robert N. Bartone, and Carlos Augusto Da Silva. 2004. Historical and socio-cultural origins of Amazonian dark earths. In Johannes Lehmann, Dirse C. Kern, Bruno Glaser, and William I. Woods, eds., *Amazonian Dark Earths: Origin, Properties, Management*. Norwell, MA: Kluwer Academic, 29–50.

Nokes, C., E. S. Cooper, B. A. Robinson, and D. A. P. Bundy. 1991. Geohelminth infection and academic assessment in Jamaican children. *Transactions of the Royal Society of Tropical Medicine and Hygiene* 85 (2): 272–73.

Nokes, C., S. M. Grantham-McGregor, A. W. Sawyer, E. S. Cooper, and D. A. P. Bundy. 1992. Parasitic helminth infection and cognitive function in school children. *Proceedings: Biological Sciences* 247 (1319): 77–81.

North, Douglass C. 1968. Sources of productivity change in ocean shipping, 1600–1850. *Journal of Political Economy* 76 (5): 953–70.

North, Douglass C. 1981. *Structure and Change in Economic History*. New York: Norton.

North, Douglass C. 1990. *Institutions, Institutional Change, and Economic Performance*. New York: Cambridge University Press.

North, Douglass C. 2005. *Understanding the Process of Economic Change*. Princeton: Princeton University Press.

North, Douglass C., and Robert Paul Thomas. 1973. *The Rise of the Western World: A New Economic History*. New York: Cambridge University Press.

North, Douglass C., and Robert Paul Thomas. 1977. The First Economic Revolution. *Economic History Review* 30: 229–41.

North, Douglass C., John Joseph Wallis, and Barry R. Weingast. 2009. *Violence and Social Orders: A Conceptual Framework for Interpreting Recorded Human History*. New York: Cambridge University Press.

Oaks, Stanley C., Jr., Violaine S. Mitchell, Greg W. Pearson, and Charles C. J. Carpenter, eds. 1991. *Malaria: Obstacles and Opportunities*. Washington, DC: National Academy Press.

O'Malley, Gregory E. 2009. Beyond the middle passage: Slave migration from the Caribbean to North America, 1619–1807. *William and Mary Quarterly* 66: 125–72.

Overturf, Gary D., and Allen W. Mathies Jr. 1976. Salmonellosis. In Franklin H. Top Sr. and Paul F. Wehrle, eds., *Communicable and Infectious Diseases*, 8th ed. St. Louis: Mosby, 598–611.

Perkins, Edwin J. 1980. *The Economy of Colonial America*. New York: Columbia University Press.

Pierson, Scott Alan. 2008. The effect of geography and vitamin D on the African-American status in the nineteenth century: Evidence from prison records. *Journal of Economic History* 68 (3): 812–31.

Powell, Adam, Stephen Shennan, and Mark G. Thomas. 2009. Late Pleistocene demography and the appearance of modern human behavior. *Science* 324 (5932): 1298–1301.

Preston, Samuel H., and Michael R. Haines. 1991. *Fatal Years: Child Mortality in Late Nineteenth-Century America*. Princeton: Princeton University Press.

Pritchett, Jonathan B., and Insan Tunali. 1995. Strangers' disease: Determinants of yellow fever mortality during the New Orleans epidemic of 1853. *Explorations in Economic History* 32 (4): 517–39.

Pyne, Stephen. J. 1991. *Burning Bush: A Fire History of Australia*. New York: Holt.

Ramenofsky, Ann. 1993. Diseases of the Americans, 1492–1700. In Kenneth F. Kiple, ed., *The Cambridge World History of Human Disease*. New York: Cambridge University Press, 317–27.

Ratard, R. C., L. E. Kouemeni, M. K. Ekanibessala, and C. N. Ndamkou. 1992. Distribution of hookworm infection in Cameroon. *Annals of Tropical Medicine and Parasitology* 86: 413–18.

Rees, Ray, John Komlos, Ngo Van Long, and Ulrich Woitek. 2003. Optimal food allocation in a slave economy. *Journal of Population Economics* 16 (1): 21–36.

Resurveys, Southern States. 1920–23. Folder 43, Box 5, Record Group 5, Series 3, International Health Board. Rockefeller Foundation Archives, Sleepy Hollow, NY.

Revista de la Sociedad Argentina de Biología. 1925. Auto reinfection of hookworm. *Journal of the American Medical Association* 85: 1263.

Riley, James C. 1987. Disease without death: A new source for a history of sickness. *Journal of Interdisciplinary History* 17 (3): 537–63.

Riley, James C. 1993. Measuring morbidity and mortality. In Kenneth F. Kiple, ed., *The Cambridge World History of Human Disease*. New York: Cambridge University Press, 230–38.

Roberts, Charles A. 1979. Inter regional per capita income differentials and convergence: 1880–1950. *Journal of Economic History* 39 (1): 101–12.

Rogoziński, Jan. 1992. *A Brief History of the Caribbean: From the Arawak and the Carib to the Present*. New York: Facts on File.

Rosenberg, Nathan. 1982. *Inside the Black Box: Technology and Economics*. New York: Cambridge University Press.

Rutman, Darrett B., and Anita H. Rutman. 1976. Of agues and fevers: Malaria in the early Chesapeake. *William and Mary Quarterly* 33 (1): 31–60.

Sachs, Jeffrey D. 2005. *The End of Poverty: Economic Possibilities for Our Time*. New York: Penguin Press.

Sachs, Jeffrey D. 2008. *Common Wealth: Economics for a Crowded Planet*. New York: Penguin Press.

Sakti, Hastaning, Catherine Nokes, W. Subagio Hertanto, Sri Hendratno, Andrew Hall, Donald A. P. Bundy and Satoto. 1999. Evidence for an association between hookworm infection and cognitive function in Indonesian school children. *Tropical Medicine and International Health* 4 (5): 322–34.

Sambasivan, G. 1979. Malaria. In W. Hobson, ed., *The Theory and Practice of Public Health*, 5th ed. Oxford: Oxford University Press, 278–94.

Savioli, Lorenzo, Maria Neira, Marco Albonico, Michael J. Beach, Hababu Mohammed Chwaya, David W. T. Crompton, John Dunne, John P. Ehrenberg, Theresa Gyorkos, Jane Kvalsvig, Martin G. Taylor, Carlo Urbani, and Feng Zheng. 2000. Letters—Treatment for intestinal helminth infection. Review needed to take account of all relevant evidence, not only effects on growth and cognitive performance. *British Medical Journal* 321 (7270) (November 11): 1226.

Savitt, Todd L. 1989. Black health on the plantation: Masters, slaves and physicians. In Ronald L. Numbers and Todd L. Savitt, eds., *Science and Medicine in the Old South*. Baton Rouge: Louisiana State University Press, 327–55.

Savitt, Todd L., and James Harvey Young, eds. 1988. *Disease and Distinctiveness in the American South*. Knoxville: University of Tennessee Press.

Schad, G. A. 1991. The parasite. In H. M. Gilles and P. A. J. Ball, eds., *Hookworm Infections*. Amsterdam: Elsevier, 15–49.

Schwebach, Gerhard H. 1980. *A Practical Guide to Microbial and Parasitic Diseases*. Springfield, IL: Charles C. Thomas.

Shiff, C., W. Checkley, P. Winch, Z. Premji, J. Minjas, and P. Lubega. 1996. Changes in weight gain and anemia attributable to malaria in Tanzanian children living under holoendemic conditions. *Transactions of the Royal Society of Tropical Medicine and Hygiene* 90: 266–69.

Siler, J. F., and C. L. Cole. 1917. Prevalence of hookworm disease in the Fourth Texas Infantry, First Mississippi Infantry, and First Alabama Cavalry Regiments. *Military Surgeon* 41: 77–99.

Simeon, Donald T., Sally M. Grantham-McGregor, Joy E. Callender, and Michael S. Wong. 1995. Treatment of Trichuris trichiura infections improves growth, spelling scores and school attendance in some children. *Journal of Nutrition* 125 (7): 1875–83.

Simon, Julian L. 1977. *The Economics of Population Growth*. Princeton: Princeton University Press.

Simon, Julian L. 1989. On aggregate empirical studies relating population variables to economic development. *Population and Development Review* 15 (2): 323–32.

Simon, Julian L. 1996. *The Ultimate Resource*. Princeton: Princeton University Press.

Simon, Julian L., ed. 1998. *The Economics of Population: Classic Writings*. New Brunswick, NJ: Transaction.

Simpson, Joe Leigh. 1993. Are physical activity and employment related to preterm birth and low birth weight? *American Journal of Obstetrics and Gynecology* 168: 1231–38.

Smillie, W. G., and D. L. Augustine. 1925. Intensity of hookworm infestation in Alabama: Its relationship to residence, occupation, age, sex and race. *Journal of the American Medical Association* 85 (25): 1958–63.

Smillie, W. G., and D. L. Augustine. 1926. Hookworm infestation: The effect of varying intensities on the physical condition of school children. *American Journal of Diseases of Children* 31 (2): 151–68.

Smillie, W. G., and Cassie R. Spencer. 1926. Mental retardation in school children infested with hookworms. *Journal of Educational Psychology* 17 (5): 314–21.

Smith, Abbott E. 1947. *Colonists in Bondage: White Servitude and Convict Labor in America, 1607–1776*. Chapel Hill: University of North Carolina Press.

Smith, Adam. [1776] 1937. *The Wealth of Nations*. New York: Modern Library.

Smith, G. 1990. The ecology of the free-living stages: A reappraisal. In G. A. Schad and K. S. Warren, eds., *Hookworm Disease: Current Status and New Directions*. London: Taylor and Francis, 89–104.

Solow, Andrew R., David L. Roberts, and Karen M. Robbirt. 2006. On the Pleistocene extinctions of Alaskan mammoths and horses. *PNAS: Proceedings of the National Academy of Sciences* 103 (19): 7351–53.

Spaeth, Ralph. 1976. Tetanus. In Franklin H. Top Sr. and Paul F. Wehrle, eds., *Communicable and Infectious Diseases*, 8th ed. St. Louis: Mosby, 688–701.

Stampp, Kenneth M. 1956. *The Peculiar Institution: Slavery in the Antebellum South*. New York: Knopf.

Stannard, David E. 1989. *Before the Horror: The Population of Hawaii on the Eve of Western Contact*. Honolulu: Social Science Research Institute, University of Hawaii Press.

Stannard, David E. 1993. Disease, human migration, and history. In Kenneth F. Kiple, ed., *The Cambridge World History of Human Disease*. New York: Cambridge University Press, 35–40.

Steadman, David W., Paul S. Martin, Ross D. E. MacPhee, A. J. T. Jull, H. Gregory McDonald, Charles A. Woods, Manuel Iturralde-Vinent, and Gregory W. L. Hodgins. 2005. Asynchronous extinction of late Quaternary sloths on continents and islands. *PNAS: Proceedings of the National Academy of Sciences* 102 (33): 11763–68.

Steckel, Richard H. 1979. Slave height profiles from coastwise manifests. *Explorations in Economic History* 16 (4): 363–80.

Steckel, Richard H. 1986a. Birth weights and infant mortality among American slaves. *Explorations in Economic History* 23 (2): 173–98.

Steckel, Richard H. 1986b. A peculiar population: The nutrition, health, and mortality of American slaves from childhood to maturity. *Journal of Economic History* 46 (3): 721–42.

Steckel, Richard H. 1986c. A dreadful childhood: The excess mortality of American slaves. *Social Science History* 10: 427–65.

Steckel, Richard H. 1992. Work, disease, and diet in the health and mortality of American slaves. In Robert W. Fogel and Stanley L. Engerman, eds., *Without Consent or Contract: Technical Papers*, vol. 2. New York: Norton, 489–507.

Steckel, Richard H. 1995a. Percentiles of modern height standards for use in historical research. Historical working paper 75. Paper Series on Historical Factors in Long-Run Growth. National Bureau of Economic Research, Cambridge, MA.

Steckel, Richard H. 1995b. The health of American slaves: New evidence and analysis. Paper presented at the Social Science History Association meeting, Chicago, Nov. 16–19.

Steckel, Richard H. 1995c. Stature and the standard of living. *Journal of Economic Literature* 33: 1903–40.

Steckel, Richard H. 1999. Nutritional status in the colonial American economy. *William and Mary Quarterly*, third series, 56 (1): 31–52.

Steckel, Richard H. 2000. Diets versus diseases in the anthropometrics of slave children: A reply. *Journal of Economic History* 60 (1): 247–59.

Steckel, Richard H. 2009. Heights and human welfare: Recent developments and new directions. *Explorations in Economic History* 46 (1): 1–23.

Steckel, Richard H., and Donald R. Haurin. 1994. Health and nutrition in the American Midwest: Evidence from the height of Ohio National Guardsmen, 1850–1910. In John Komlos, ed., *Stature, Living Standards, and Economic Development*. Chicago: University of Chicago Press, 117–28.

Steckel, Richard H., and Richard A. Jensen. 1986. New evidence on the causes of slave and crew mortality in the Atlantic slave trade. *Journal of Economic History* 46 (1): 57–77.

Steinmann, Gunter. 1984. A model of the history of demographic-economic growth. In Gunter Steinmann, ed., *Economic Consequences of Population Change in Industrialized Countries: Proceedings of a Conference on Population Economics Held at the University of Paderborn, June 1983. Studies in Contemporary Economics* 8. Berlin: Springer-Verlag, 29–49.

Steketee, Richard W., Jack J. Wirima, Allen W. Hightower, Laurence Slutsker, David L. Heymann, and Joel G. Breman. 1996. The effect of malaria and malaria prevention in pregnancy on offspring birthweight, prematurity, and intrauterine growth retardation in rural Malawi. *American Journal of Tropical Medicine and Hygiene* 55 (1 Supplement): 33–41.

Stephenson, Lani S. 2001. Optimising the benefits of anthelminthic treatment in children. *Paediatric Drugs* 3 (7): 495–508.

Stephenson, Lani S., Michael C. Latham, Elizabeth J. Adams, Stephen N. Kinoti, and Anne Pertet. 1992. Treatment with one or two doses of albendazole improves growth of Kenyan school children with hookworm, *T. trichiura* and *A. lumbricoides* infections. *FASEB Journal* 6: A1650 [abs.].

Stephenson, Lani S., Michael C. Latham, Elizabeth J. Adams, Stephen N Kinoti, and Anne Pertet. 1993a. Weight gain of Kenyan school children infected with hookworm, *Trichuris trichiura* and *Ascaris lumbricoides* is improved following once- or twice-yearly treatment with albendazole. *Journal of Nutrition* 123: 656–65.

Stephenson, Lani S., Michael C. Latham, Elizabeth J. Adams, Stephen N Kinoti, and Anne Pertet. 1993b. Physical fitness, growth and appetite of Kenyan schoolboys with hookworm, *Trichuris trichiura* and *Ascaris lumbricoides* infections are improved four months after a single dose of albendazole. *Journal of Nutrition* 123: 1036–46.

Stephenson, Lani S., Michael C. Latham, Stephen N. Kinoti, Kathleen M. Kurz, and Heather Brigham. 1990. Improvements in physical fitness of Kenyan school boys with hookworm, *Trichuris trichiura* and *Ascaris lumbricoides* infections following a single dose of albendazole. *Transactions of the Royal Society of Tropical Medicine and Hygiene* 84: 277–82.

Stephenson, Lani S., Michael C. Latham, Kathleen M. Kurz, and Stephen N. Kinoti. 1989a. Single dose of metrifonate or praziquantel treatment in Kenyan children. II: Effects on growth in relation to *Schistosoma haematobium* and hookworm egg counts. *American Journal of Tropical Medicine and Hygiene* 41: 45–53.

Stephenson, Lani S., Michael C. Latham, Kathleen M. Kurz, Stephen N. Kinoti, and Heather Brigham. 1989b. Treatment with a single dose of albendazole improves growth of Kenyan schoolchildren with hookworm, *Trichuris trichiura* and *Acaris lumbricoides* infections. *American Journal of Tropical Medicine and Hygiene* 41: 78–87.

Stephenson, Lani S., Michael C. Latham, Kathleen M. Kurz, Stephen N. Kinoti, Martin L. Oduori, and D. W. T. Crompton. 1985a. Relationships of *Schistosoma haematobium*, hookworm and malarial infections and metrifonate treatment to hemoglobin level in Kenyan school children. *American Journal of Tropical Medicine and Hygiene* 34: 519–28.

Stephenson, Lani S., Michael C. Latham, Kathleen M. Kurz, Stephen N. Kinoti, Martin L. Oduori, and D. W. T. Crompton. 1985b. Relationships of *Schistosoma haematobium*, hookworm and malarial infections and metrifonate treatment to growth of Kenyan school children. *American Journal of Tropical Medicine and Hygiene* 34: 1109–18.

Stephenson, Lani S., Michael C. Latham, Kathleen M. Kurz, Dennis Miller, Stephen N. Kinoti, and Martin L. Oduori. 1986. Relationships of Schistosoma haematobium, hookworm, and malarial infections and metrifonate treatment to nutritional status of Kenyan coastal schoolchildren: A 16-month follow-up. In Lani S. Stephenson, ed., *Schistosomiasis and Malnutrition*. Cornell International Nutrition Monograph Series 16. Ithaca, NY: Cornell University International Nutrition Program, 26–68.

Stigler, George. 1951. The division of labor is limited by the extent of the market. *Journal of Political Economy* 59 (3): 185–93.

Stiles, C. W. 1915. Intestinal infections: The school grades attained by 2,166 white school children (1,062 boys, 1,104 girls) in the city of x, classified by age, sanitation, and intestinal parasites. *Public Health Reports* 30 (28) (July 9). Washington, DC: Government Printing Office, 2060–67.

Stiles, Charles Wardell. 1909. *Hookworm Disease and Its Relation to the Negro*. Washington, DC: Government Printing Office.

Stoltzfus, Rebecca J., Marco Albonico, James M. Tielsch, Hababu M. Chwaya, and Lortenzo Savioli. 1997. School-based deworming program yields small improvement in growth of Zanzibari school children after one year. *Journal of Nutrition* 127 (11): 2187–93.

Stoltzfus, Rebecca J., Hababu M. Chwaya, James M. Tielsch, Kerry J. Schulze, Marco Albonico, and Lorenzo Savioli. 1997. Epidemiology of iron deficiency anemia in Zanzibari schoolchildren: The importance of hookworms. *American Journal of Clinical Nutrition* 65: 153–59.

Strickland, G. Thomas, and Kenneth W. Hunter Jr., eds. 1982. *Immunoparasitology: Principles and Methods in Malaria and Schistosomiasis Research*. New York: Praeger.

Strong, Edward K., Jr. 1916. *Effects of Hookworm Disease on the Mental and Physical Development of Children, International Health Commission, Publication No. 3*. New York: Rockefeller Foundation.

Sunder, Marco. 2004. The Height of Tennessee Convicts: Another Piece of the 'Antebellum Puzzle,'. *Economics and Human Biology* 2: 75–86.

Thornton, John. 1992. *Africa and Africans in the Making of the Atlantic World*. New York: Cambridge University Press.

Top, Franklin H., Jr. 1976. Rubella. In Franklin H. Top Sr. and Paul F. Wehrle, eds., *Communicable and Infectious Diseases*, 8th ed. St. Louis: Mosby, 589–97.

Top, Franklin H., Sr., Karl M. Johnson, and Paul F. Wehrle. 1976. Enteroviruses: Poliomyelitis. In Franklin H. Top Sr. and Paul F. Wehrle, eds., *Communicable and Infectious Diseases*, 8th ed. St. Louis: Mosby, 260–78.

Troesken, Werner. 2001. Race, disease, and the provision of water in American cities, 1889–1921. *Journal of Economic History* 61 (3): 750–77.

Troesken, Werner. 2002. The limits of Jim Crow: Race and the provision of water and sewerage in American cities, 1880–1925. *Journal of Economic History* 62 (3): 734–73.

Troesken, Werner. 2004. *Water, Race, and Disease*. Cambridge: MIT Press.

Trussell, James, and Richard H. Steckel. 1978. The age of slaves at Menarche and their first birth. *Journal of Interdisciplinary History* 8: 477–505.

Tsoulouhas, Theofanis C. 1992. A new look at demographic and technological changes: England, 1550 to 1839. *Explorations in Economic History* 29 (2): 169–203.

Tudge, Colin. 1999. *Neanderthals, Bandits and Farmers: How Agriculture Really Began*. New Haven: Yale University Press.

United States Bureau of the Census. 1854. *Statistical View of the United States: Compendium of the Seventh Census. Part II: Population*. Washington, DC: Beverley Tucker, Senate Printer.

United States Bureau of the Census. 1855. *Mortality Statistics of the Seventh Census of the United States, 1850*. Washington, DC: A.O.P. Nicholson.

United States Bureau of the Census. 1960. *Historical Statistics of the United States: Colonial Times to 1957*. Washington, DC: Government Printing Office.

United States Bureau of the Census. 1864. *Population of the United States in 1860; Compiled from the Original Returns of the Eighth Census: Classified Population of States and Territories by Counties*. Washington, DC: Government Printing Office.

United States Bureau of the Census. 1866. *Statistics of the United States (including Mortality, Property, &C.) in 1860; Complied from the Original Returns and Being the Final Exhibit of the Eighth Census*. Washington, DC: Government Printing Office.

United States Bureau of the Census. 1872a. *The Statistics of the Population of the United States, from the Original Returns of the Ninth Census (June 1, 1870)*, vol. 1. Ninth Census. Washington, DC: Government Printing Office.

United States Bureau of the Census. 1872b. *The Vital Statistics of the United States, from the Original Returns of the Ninth Census (June 1, 1870)*, vol. 2. Ninth Census. Washington, DC: Government Printing Office.

United States Bureau of the Census. 1882. *Statistics of the Population of the United States at the Tenth Census (June 1, 1880)*, vol. 1. Washington, DC: Government Printing Office.

United States Bureau of the Census. 1885. *Report on the Mortality and Vital Statistics of the United States as Returned at the Tenth Census (June 1, 1880). Part I.* Washington, DC: Government Printing Office.

United States Bureau of the Census. 1886. *Report on the Mortality and Vital Statistics of the United States as Returned at the Tenth Census (June 1, 1880). Part II.* Washington, DC: Government Printing Office.

United States Bureau of the Census. 1894. *Report on Vital and Social Statistics in the United States at the Eleventh Census: 1890. Part III. Statistics of Deaths.* Washington, DC: Government Printing Office.

United States Bureau of the Census. 1895. *Report on Population of the United States at the Eleventh Census:1890. Part I.* Washington, DC: Government Printing Office.

United States Bureau of the Census. 1896. *Report on Vital and Social Statistics of the United States at the Eleventh Census: 1890. Part I: Analysis and Rate Tables.* Washington, DC: Government Printing Office.

United States Bureau of the Census. 1897. *Report on Population of the United States at the Eleventh Census:1890. Part II.* Washington, DC: Government Printing Office.

United States Bureau of the Census. 1902a. *Twelfth Census of the United States, Taken in the Year 1900: Population. Part II*, vol. 2. Census Reports. Washington, DC: United States Census Office.

United States Bureau of the Census. 1902b. *Twelfth Census of the United States Taken in the Year 1900: Vital Statistics. Part I: Analysis and Ratio Tables*, vol. 3. Census Reports. Washington, DC: United States Census Office.

United States Bureau of the Census. 1902c. *Twelfth Census of the United States, Taken in the Year 1900: Vital Statistics. Part II: Statistics of Deaths*, vol. 4. Census Reports. Washington, DC: United States Census Office.

United States Census Bureau website. Mean Center of Population for the United States: 1790 to 2000. http://www.census.gov/geo/www/cenpop/meanctr.pdf.

Varley, G. C., G. R. Gradwell, and M. P. Hassell. 1973. *Insect Population Ecology: An Analytical Approach.* Berkeley: University of California Press.

Vlach, John Michael. 1993. *Back of the Big House.* Chapel Hill: University of North Carolina Press.

Wahl, Jenny B. 1996. The common law of American slavery: An economic history approach. Unpublished manuscript. St. Olaf College, Northfield, MN.

Waite, J. H., and I. L. Nielson. 1919. Effects of hookworm disease on mental development of North Queensland schoolchildren. *Journal of the American Medical Association* 73 (25): 1877–79.

Waldman, Robert H. 1984a. Nematodes. In Robert H. Waldman and Ronica M. Kluge, eds., *Textbook of Infectious Diseases*. Hyde Park, NY: Medical Examination Publishing, 1083–1103.

Waldman, Robert H. 1984b. Togaviruses (arboviruses). In Robert H. Waldman and Ronica M. Kluge, eds., *Textbook of Infectious Diseases*. Hyde Park, NY: Medical Examination Publishing, 544–55.

Waldman, Robert H. 1984c. Trematodes. In Robert H. Waldman and Ronica M. Kluge, eds., *Textbook of Infectious Diseases*. Hyde Park, NY: Medical Examination Publishing, 1111–18.

Walsh, Lorena S., and Russell R. Menard. 1974. Death in the Chesapeake: Two life tables for men in early colonial Maryland. *Maryland Historical Magazine* 69 (2): 211–27.

Walton, Gary M. 1967. Sources of productivity change in American colonial shipping, 1675–1775. *Economic History Review* 20: 67–78.

Walton, Gary M., and Hugh Rockoff. 2010. *History of the American Economy*, 11th ed. Mason, OH: South-Western, Cengage Learning.

Wang, Sijia, Cecil M. Lewis Jr., Mattias Jakobsson, Sohini Ramachandran, Nicolas Ray, Gabriel Bedoya, Winston Rojas, Maria V. Parra, Julio A. Molina, Carla Gallo, Guido Mazzotti, Giovanni Poletti, Kim Hill, Ana M. Hurtado, Damian Labuda, William Klitz, Ramiro Barrantes, Maria Cátira Bortolini, Francisco M. Salzano, Maria Luiza Petzl-Erler, Luiza T. Tsuneto, Elena Llop, Francisco Rothhammer, Laurent Excoffier, Marcus W. Feldman, Noah A. Rosenberg, and Andrés Ruiz-Linares. 2007. Genetic variation and population structure in native Americans. *PLoS Genetics* 3 (11): e185. doi:10.1371/journal.pgen.0030185:2049–067. http://www.plosgenetics.org/article/info:doi/10.1371/journal.pgen.0030185.

Warren, Christian. 1997. Northern chills, southern fevers: Race-specific mortality in American cities, 1730–1900. *Journal of Southern History* 63: 23–57.

Weisbrod, Burton A., Ralph L. Andreano, Robert E. Baldwin, Erwin H. Epstein, Allen C. Kelly, and Thomas W. Helminiak. 1973. *Disease and Economic Development: The Impact of Parasitic Diseases in St. Lucia*. Madison: University of Wisconsin Press.

Wesenberg-Lund, Carl. 1920–21. *Contributions to the Biology of the Danish Culicidae*. Copenhagen: Andr. Fred. Host and Son.

White, Tim D. 2001. Once were cannibals. *Scientific American* (August): 59–65.

Wilson, Sir Graham, Sir Ashley Miles, and M. T. Parker, eds. 1984. *Topley and Wilson's Principles of Bacteriology, Virology and Immunity*. Vol. 3: *Bacterial Diseases*. G. R. Smith, ed. 7th ed. London: Edward Arnold.

Williams-Blangero, S., J. Blangero, and M. Bradley. 1997. Quantitative genetic analysis of susceptibility to hookworm infection in a population from rural Zimbabwe. *Human Biology* 69: 201–08.

Wills, Christopher. 1996. *Yellow Fever, Black Goddess*. Reading, MA: Addison-Wesley.

Wilson, Benjamin J., and A. Wallace Hayes. 1973. Microbial toxins. In F. M. Strong, ed., *Toxicants Occurring Naturally in Foods*. Washington, DC: National Academy of Science–National Research Council, 372–423.

Wilson, Edward O. 1975. *Sociobiology: The New Synthesis*. Cambridge, MA: Belknap Press.

Wood, Peter H. 1975. *Black Majority: Negroes in Colonial South Carolina from 1670 through the Stono Rebellion*. New York: Norton.

Woodward, C. Vann. 1974. The jolly institution. *New York Review of Books* 21 (7) (May 2): 3–6.

Wrigley, E. A. 1986. Malthus's model of a pre-industrial economy. In Michael Turner, ed., *Malthus and His Time*. New York: St. Martin's Press: 3–18

Wrigley, E. A., and R. S. Scholfield. 1981. *The Population History of England*. Cambridge: Harvard University Press.

Yasuba, Yasukichi. 1962. *Birth Rates of the White Population in the United States, 1800–1860: An Economic Study*. Baltimore: Johns Hopkins University Press.

Zeltner, Esther, and Helen Hirt. 2003. Effect of artificial structuring on the use of laying hen runs in a free-range system. *British Poultry Science* 44 (September): 533–37.

Index

Numbers followed by a "t" or an "f" refer to pages with tables or figures.